Democracy in a Communist Party
Poland's Experience Since 1980

DEMOCRACY
IN A
COMMUNIST PARTY

Poland's Experience Since 1980

WERNER G. HAHN

COLUMBIA UNIVERSITY PRESS
New York, 1987

943.8
H14d

Library of Congress Cataloging-in-Publication Data

Hahn, Werner G.
    Democracy in a communist party.

    Bibliography: p.
    Includes index.
    1. Polska Zjednoczona Partia Robotnicza.
    2. Poland—Politics and government—1980–
    I. Title.
JN6769.A52H34   1987   943.8′056   87-6639
ISBN 0-231-06540-X

Columbia University Press
New York   Guildford, Surrey
Copyright © 1987 Columbia University Press
All rights reserved
Printed in the United States of America

To Marina

Contents

Introduction

Can a communist party be democratic, i.e., operate with such features of internal democracy as uncontrolled secret elections with a choice of candidates and open debate? Past experience of virtually all communist parties has indicated that this would be a contradiction in terms, that the very nature of a communist party as a disciplined instrument carrying out orders from a small group of leaders precludes openness and decisions by majority vote of rank and file members. Yet the Polish United Workers Party (PZPR) during the "renewal" from August 1980 to December 1981 developed features which were unmistakably democratic and which in fact worked for much of a year—before martial law suspended normal communist party operations. The PZPR appeared to have done the impossible, in effect, inventing a square wheel and, somehow, making it roll.

Communist parties have operated on the basis of the top deciding and the bottom obeying—the principle called "democratic centralism," which normally consists of much centralism and precious little democracy. The first duty of party members and local party organizations has been to carry out the decisions of the party leadership, even if they disagree with those decisions. Criticism of decisions on policy or personnel risks censure as violation of party discipline or even factionalism, violations punishable by expulsion from the party. Party organizations are obliged to elect as their leaders officials selected from above—officials whose first loyalty is normally to those who selected them, their patrons higher up, rather than to the organizations they lead. The nomination of candidates from below or the possibility of choice between two or more candidates would threaten the whole system, since the higher organs, and ultimately the central Politburo, would no longer be assured of control. The central leadership itself, immune from challenge from below and in control of its own reelection, holds power permanently, and changes in its composition can only occur when new members approved by most incumbent Politburo members are added.

During late 1980 and early 1981, however, a number of basic changes occurred in the way the Polish communist party operated. Free, meaningful elections were held in the party from bottom to top, conducted with secret balloting and a choice of candidates, many of whom were nominated by rank and file party members rather than from above. With their posts now dependent on those below them who elected them, many party officials became more responsive to their "constituents" than to higher officials. Higher organs realized that they could no longer dictate decisions on policy or personnel to lower bodies and switched to "consultations" with lower organs—sending draft decisions on policy or personnel to lower organs for debate and comment—so that decisions could be reached by consensus. Censorship and central control over the media also broke down, and many party papers began operating independently and publicizing internal party disputes.

The result of these changes was truly revolutionary: a communist party turned on its head, where the rank and file could sometimes dictate to the leaders, where power frequently flowed from the bottom, not the top. By establishing its right to vote leaders out of office, the rank and file of the PZPR could force leaders up and down the line to be responsive to demands for reform. The unprecedented publicity for internal party activities and exposures of leadership mistakes and corruption amplified the power of reformers and weakened conservatives. Centralism largely dropped out of democratic centralism, as various groups and factions pressed their views on the leadership, and the leadership could not enforce discipline.

In establishing control over leaders, reformers even developed a remedy for one of communist parties' most serious flaws: the lack of any system for peaceful transfer of power. Leaders who control their own reelection and do not need to be responsive to their subordinates or electors normally can be removed only by secret plotting by other officials in key positions or when they have led their party or party organization into such a disastrous situation that virtually everyone comes to a consensus that they must be removed. In either case, such a change of leadership— at the national or local level—is a severe shock, disrupting party activity and often doing irreparable damage to the economy and to party morale. Polish party reformers set the goal of establishing a system whereby leaders would serve for only two or three terms and even in midterm could be voted out of office in a routine manner. Party officials began referring to such rotation of offices as a "principle," and some of these practices were written into the party rules.

One of the most startling features of the Polish developments was that a communist leadership elite more or less voluntarily gave up power, allowed itself to be voted out of its positions of power and privilege. One of the greatest hindrances to reform in communist parties is the insistence of party officials on hanging on to power at any cost (something perhaps understandable in view of the privileges that power confers in these systems and the lack of meaningful and rewarding positions outside the party and government—in sectors not dependent on politics, such as private industry in capitalist countries). In the PZPR, party leaders, willingly or unwillingly, consented to abide by the results of uncontrolled elections, and most of them were turned out of office. They began to accept the view of office holding as a temporary privilege rather than as a permanent right and that the party would not collapse if others took over the reins.

That many of the features adopted by the PZPR in 1980–81 are democratic is clear; the question is whether a communist party with such features is still a communist party or whether it has in fact become a social democratic party. By allowing uncontrolled contests for party posts and open debates over policies, the Polish communist party became openly pluralistic and began to reflect much of the same ideas and interests as the rest of Polish society. It no longer was a disciplined army ruling over society and trying to change society in accordance with its will. But even though the PZPR seriously infringed on such key communist principles as democratic centralism and appeared on its way to becoming de facto a social democratic party, the Soviet leaders and most Polish conservatives reluctantly stretched their normal standards and avoided claiming that the PZPR had crossed the line and had ceased to be a Marxist-Leninist party. Moreover, even the Jaruzelski regime, while using martial law to suspend most of the reforms in practice, has continued to maintain that the democratic election procedures adopted in 1980–81 remain valid and correct for a communist party.

Democratization in the party was stopped after martial law was imposed in December 1981, and power now clearly flows from the top again. This was done not by the Politburo, which had lost its control over the party, but by Jaruzelski calling on force from outside—the army and police—to reimpose democratic centralism and discipline on the party as well as the rest of society. Party members were prevented from using their democratic rights through intimidation. The most activist reformers were expelled from the party or quit in disgust, while other reform-minded party members have become disheartened or cynical and lapsed into silence.

However, the system did not completely revert to Soviet-style communist orthodoxy, despite its heavy-handed repression of any manifestations of opposition. The Jaruzelski regime not only did not directly repeal the 1981 reforms, it repeatedly has proclaimed its commitment to them—even though it upholds them only in form, rather than spirit. Those elected to the CC and other bodies under the democratized 1981 procedures were only slowly and partially removed during the succeeding years. The regime, through martial law, mainly changed the atmosphere in the party, smothering the rank and file activism of 1981. The democratic structures themselves still exist and some reform-minded party members remain in party posts, so that if control weakens—for example, through a leadership split or power vacuum—an activated party rank and file could again take advantage of the democratic rules to influence the party's direction.

The failure to revert to complete orthodoxy reflects both the practical difficulties of reimposing strict regimentation on a party and nation no longer accustomed to it and the recognition by the regime, or at least important parts of it, that some degree of democratization is necessary, both for the party and for society—that a somewhat more democratized model of communism is the only feasible path for Poland, since over the long term the regime has to win some measure of cooperation from the public to make the system viable. The regime hopes that the less hostile citizens may eventually be willing to settle for a less dictatorial, even if still undemocratic, regime—as in Kadar's Hungary. Hence, the Jaruzelski regime operates with a curious combination of democratic laws (party and state), some new, some left over from 1981, and undemocratic practices which nullify those laws and ensure control. For example, party rules still call for more than one candidate in party elections, but in practice this has usually not been permitted, at least for important offices. In another example, this time outside the party, the state election laws adopted for the June 1984 province government council elections and the October 1985 Sejm (parliament) elections for the first time made it mandatory to have two candidates for every seat, but manipulation of the nomination process, of placing of names on the ballot, and of election-day procedures ensured that the candidate preferred by the authorities won in every case.

Even with the reestablishment of control from above, Poland's system, in the communist party and outside, remains more liberalized and pluralistic than that of other countries in the Soviet bloc. The subject of democratization in the party and in society and the possibility of pluralism and of a unique, more democratic Polish model of socialism were still discussed openly in the official press during 1982 and 1983—a fact which stirred repeated expressions of displeasure in Soviet media. Unorthodox ideas have become less and less frequent in the press in 1985 and 1986, but there still is more openness in the media than in the USSR. Limited choice still occurs in many party elections, and party members still express dissent by casting negative votes in secret balloting or by direct statements recorded in the press. And with clearly differing opinions in the regime itself over the direction to follow, the system is still evolving.

Why did it happen? Why did this democratization arise and take hold in the Polish communist party? Most reasons are purely Polish and relate to the fact that the communist party never had very complete control over society and that democratic concepts were well implanted despite years of communist rule. Farmers were not collectivized, the Church remained strong and independent, and public hostility to the communist system imposed by Moscow never was eradicated. Moreover, Poles long had tended to look to the West and to Western ideas of pluralism and democracy, and Polish workers had taken to the streets repeatedly in the past when angered by government actions.

The Polish communist party itself was more receptive to democratization than most communist parties because it had long been less disciplined, had been openly riven with factionalism, and had repeatedly debated reforms in the past. Many ideas for democratization of the party had been raised when Gierek replaced Gomulka as party leader after the December 1970 riots: "renewal" within the party, "guarantees" against misuse of power, and the need for consultations were all discussed. While these ideas were soon dropped by the Gierek leadership, they were not forgotten by reformers and came under discussion again in the late 1970s. The base of support for change was increased by the great expansion of party membership during the late 1970s which brought in many new members who were poorly indoctrinated and shared the public's increasing desire for basic reform.

More immediately, the demands for democratic reforms were set off by the onset of political and economic crises which discredited the increasingly autocratic leadership. The Gierek regime had gotten the country into a serious economic situation and had largely alienated the public by its economic policies and its unrealistic propaganda. The disastrous use of force in the 1970 crisis persuaded many leaders that force was not a reasonable alternative to deal with crises and that the only feasible way to get the country out of the situation was by winning the confidence and cooperation of the public via reform of the party: cleaning out the old leadership and trying to persuade the public—starting with the rank and file of the party itself—that the party could change and change drastically. The extremely skeptical Polish public—alienated for so many years—was largely unconvinced by wide-ranging reforms and even by the replacement of almost all party leaders. In this sense, the "renewal" failed to achieve its objective of winning the trust of the overwhelming majority of Poles.

The democratization in the party began to a large extent outside the party, as part of a democratic spirit in society which invaded the party and eventually swept it along. The crystallizing element in that democratization was Solidarity. In fact, one may question whether the reform process in the party could have ever really taken hold without the prodding from Solidarity. (At the same time, however, the formation of Solidarity itself and its continued existence at least partly depended on the liberal and tolerant attitudes which had gradually developed within the party.)

Solidarity forced democratization on the party in a variety of ways, direct and indirect. The mere existence of Solidarity impelled the party toward democracy, since it was forced to compete with Solidarity for influence in society and hence had to become more forthcoming. The example of democratic practices in Solidarity prompted party leaders to recognize the need for free elections within the party also.

Moreover, the party even had to compete for the allegiance of its own members. Hundreds of thousands of party members immediately joined Solidarity in 1980, and many soon attached greater value to their membership in Solidarity than to their party membership. If workers found that they were not allowed to speak their mind at party meetings, they could simply abandon the party and join Solidarity, where they *could* speak their mind. As *Gazeta Krakowska*, April 29, 1981, quoted Torun party reformer Ryszard Kapuscinski:

> Solidarity from the beginning advanced the motto of a democratic style of trade union life. It exists in all workplaces in the whole country, just as the factory party organizations exist everywhere. Party members at those enterprises know that two organizations with such a different style of internal life cannot exist beside each other. The fact of Solidarity's existence will always objectively put on pressure for democratizing life in the party. Simply put, if a worker cannot express himself in his party organization, he will find that chance in Solidarity. The comrades in workplaces understand this situation well. They know that the only path for maintaining the party's authority in the workplaces—and on a nationwide scale for maintaining the party's authority in society—is its democratization.

The party's difficulty in holding its own members was evident in the wave of resignations by party members after August 1980—almost 200,000 by mid-1981. Many remaining party members argued that meaningful reform was the only way to stem the tide and prevent the party from disintegrating.

Solidarity also forced democratization in the party in a number of others ways as well. During the initial period in mid- and late 1980, some local Solidarity units directly accused various local party officials of corruption and misuse of power. The popular pressure they helped generate soon forced the leadership in Warsaw to ask for the resignations of many local first secretaries and to send emissaries down to preside over the election of new local leaders who hopefully could win more local acceptance.

Solidarity also had great impact on the evolution of democratization in the party because of the challenge it posed to party control and the policy decisions it forced on the leadership. The factions which developed in the party to a considerable extent grouped around contrasting ideas about how to deal with Solidarity. Liberals argued that the party could work with good people in Solidarity to resolve the country's problems and win voluntary cooperation of the workers in improving the economy; moderates recognized that Solidarity was a fact of life that had to be accepted and dealt with; while conservatives maintained that Solidarity was threatening the party's very existence and had to be crushed or at least brought under control. The reaction within the party against the aggressive stands taken at Solidarity's September 1981 congress appeared to be the main factor in the pressure which prompted CC First Secretary Kania to resign at the mid-October 1981 CC plenum. And finally, martial law was adopted in December 1981 mainly as a means of dealing with Solidarity's increasing challenge to the regime. Thus, Solidarity's existence played a key role not only in initiating democratization in the party but also in ending it.

The competition factor also played a major role in opening up the party press and reducing censorship. With the distrust of the press built up over many years and the more convincing information being put out by Solidarity, it was clear that only basic changes in the press could enable it to influence a skeptical public. Liberal editors and writers insisted that they had to publish franker, more detailed information to compete with information Solidarity put out, that this was the only way to save the party press and give the party a chance to get its message across.

The aim of this book is to throw light on possible future directions for communist parties by examining reform and change in one communist party, a rather unusual, pluralistic party. It presents a detailed history of the evolution of the PZPR and the struggle within its ranks from August 1980 through the martial law regime imposed in December 1981 into the post–martial law system of 1986. It also aims to aid the comparative study of communist parties by presenting much of the unprecedented detailed information on intraparty procedures which appeared in the Polish press during renewal.

This is not a comprehensive record of Polish developments during the period; it does not seek to explore economic developments or the role of the Church. It only deals with Solidarity to the extent needed to work in its influence on political developments in the party. This study focuses on the internal political dynamics in the PZPR; hence, it is only part of the story.

The book is basically a study of material in the Polish press. The two sources that presented the most extensive and invaluable information were the Polish provincial newspapers and the apparently full texts of speeches at Central Committee plenums as published in the CC journal *Nowe Drogi*. Provincial papers provided remarkable information on normally unpublicized party activities, for example, by sending their own reporters to the party congress to talk to delegates and develop independent, little-censored reports on what was really occurring at the congress—reports sometimes reminiscent of U.S. reporters describing and analyzing politicking at a U.S. political convention. The many hundreds of pages of *Nowe Drogi* versions of CC plenum speeches provided a wealth of unique material on leadership politics and policies in the PZPR.

The amount of detail on the inner workings of a communist party which appeared in the Polish press during 1980–81 provides an unprecedented opportunity to observe a communist system in action. While communist politics usually must be pieced together from relatively subtle hints and incomplete scraps of information, the Polish press during this period provided a rich and full picture of politicking. Instead of one heavily censored official version of events such as individual CC plenums, numerous and varied reports and even interpretations of events in the Polish press made it possible to write descriptions and analyses similar to those of political developments in Western democracies, where a variety of sources are available and information is rather open. There have been other invaluable revelations about communist politics—for example, in the USSR during Khrushchev's de-Stalinization campaign from 1956 to 1964 and again later in Khrushchev's memoirs, and in China during the cultural revolution—but never has so much information about a relatively short period appeared.

Even though the PZPR in 1980–81 did not operate exactly as the

CPSU and other communist parties normally operate, the details of its activities provided in the press are nonetheless very useful for understanding the functioning of other communist parties. For example, very little has ever been revealed about how communist party congresses are organized and conducted. Even Khrushchev in his voluminous recollections in retirement said little about this. The detailed press reporting on the July 1981 PZPR congress provides the only available look at the inner workings of a communist party congress and hence invaluable material for study of other communist parties. The conduct of party elections up and down the line, as reported in the Polish press, throws light on procedures used in other communist parties also.

The material which surfaced in the press also gives us valuable insight into attitudes within the Polish communist party—and, to some extent, other communist parties. The hostility among the rank and file toward higher authorities and the party apparat so sharply expressed in the PZPR surely exists elsewhere, even if in less extreme form. The differing ideas among party members over policies, over the nature of the party, and even over the nature of party unity, discipline, and obligations demonstrate how unmonolithic and nonideological communist parties in practice may be—even given the fact that the PZPR has probably always been more divisive than most other communist parties. The desire for reform and the clear recognition of some of the basic defects in the traditional communist party system which so quickly came to the surface in the PZPR in 1980 suggest that some members in various other communist parties also do not really believe much of the oft-repeated official propaganda and rationales. The ability of reformers in the Polish communist party to quickly focus on the need to establish a system of control over leaders and to end absolutism provides evidence of pressure from within to eventually change communist parties from traditionally secretive, conspiratorial organizations to parties which recognize the need to reflect the pluralism of ideas and interests in society and openly debate and decide policies.

The layout of the book is roughly chronological. The first five chapters describe the step-by-step loss of control over the party by its leadership: Chapter 1 examines the beginning of pressure for reform with the

August 1980 strikes and the spread of proposals for reform to the party. It traces two of the key trends which helped bring about democratization: the increasing replacement of officials by rank and file party members on leadership bodies, and the rejection of higher organs' control over lower organs, especially as epitomized in the so-called "horizontal ties" movement.

Chapter 2 describes the rewriting of the party election rules and the development of democratic election procedures. It traces the process as it started with provincial government councils and local party committees in the fall of 1980 and gradually worked its way up through province party committees and finally to the CC itself. It also details the spring 1981 campaign for election of regional party leaders and delegates to the party congress using the new election rules, the mass ouster of established leaders by the rank and file wielding its uncontrolled ballots, and the struggle by the Politburo members just to get elected delegates to the party congress.

Chapter 3 traces the developing split among party leaders over how to respond to Solidarity and the demands for reform, the open emergence of liberal, moderate, and conservative factions in early 1981, their fierce struggles, and finally the unsuccessful conservative attempt at the June 1981 plenum to oust First Secretary Kania and adopt a tougher stand.

Chapter 4 describes the July 1981 party congress—a congress not thoroughly controlled this time by the leadership—the open political competition and debate over candidates and ideas, and the stunning defeat of most leaders during the election of a new party leadership.

Chapter 5 presents the culmination of the takeover from below—the resignation of the first secretary himself in the face of growing criticism by the rank and file, as reflected by their representatives in the CC. It describes Jaruzelski's election as party leader and his eventual resort to martial law to reimpose control over the party as well as the country.

Chapter 6 deals with how martial law was used to reestablish control over the media and the party in 1982 and how Jaruzelski dealt with party reformers and then with hard-liners.

Chapter 7 describes the situation since the suspension of martial law at the end of 1982, the conduct of elections, the debate over democratization, and finally the next party congress in 1986. This chapter attempts to assess the success or failure of the 1981 reforms and the prospects for resumption of democratization.

The appendixes include an essay comparing the 1981 Polish system with other communist parties and discussing the bases for reform in communist parties, a chart of leadership changes, and a rough guide to pronunciation of Polish names. The bibliography includes a list identifying Polish newspapers and journals referred to in the text.

I wish to thank Paul Goble, John Haskell, Andrew Urbanik, Marc Zlotnik, Bernice Lewandowski, Robert Nash, Sophia Sluzar, Matthew Gallagher, Fred Tibbetts, Myron Hedlin, Ildiko Foldvary, and Heinz Timmermann for editorial and substantive suggestions and help with source material.

Poland's Provinces

Chronology of Key Events, 1980–1986

July 2, 1980	Strikes begin after July 1 raising of meat prices.
August 24, 1980	4th CC Plenum addressed by Kania, takes conciliatory approach.
August 31, 1980	Agreements signed at Gdansk and Szczecin ending strikes.
September 5–6, 1980	6th CC Plenum accepts Gierek resignation, elects Kania as leader.
October 4–6, 1980	Continuation of 6th Plenum hears flood of demands for reform.
December 1–2, 1980	7th CC Plenum supports limited reforms, adopts new party election rules, creates Congress Commission.
February 9, 1981	8th CC Plenum hears diverging views of reformers and hard-liners.
March 19, 1981	Police use force against rural Solidarity members in Bydgoszcz.
March 29–30, 1981	9th CC Plenum compromises to avert ouster of hard-liners.
April 15, 1981	National convention of horizontal units opens in Torun.
April 29–30, 1981	10th CC Plenum calls for start of party elections and holding of party congress in mid-July.

May 15, 1981	Katowice Party Forum meets, starts attack on Kania.
June 5, 1981	Soviet letter warns Polish leadership to crack down.
June 9–10, 1981	11th CC Plenum rebuffs hard-liners' attack on Kania.
July 14–20, 1981	9th Party Congress shakes up leadership, reelects Kania.
September 5–10, 1981	First part of Solidarity congress issues provocative appeal.
September 26–October 2, 1981	Second part of Solidarity congress reflects radical influence.
October 16–18, 1981	4th CC Plenum accepts Kania's resignation, elects Jaruzelski.
December 13, 1981	Jaruzelski imposes martial law.
February 24–25, 1982	First CC Plenum under martial law held.
July 15–16, 1982	9th CC Plenum demotes Olszowski.
October 8, 1982	Sejm adopts new trade union law dissolving Solidarity.
November 14, 1982	Walesa released from detention.
December 18, 1982	Sejm orders "suspension" of martial law on December 31.
January–February 1983	Nationwide province party conferences held, but without elections.
June 16–23, 1983	Pope visits Poland.
July 21, 1983	Sejm lifts martial law.
October 1983–January 1984	Nationwide regional party conferences hold first party elections since imposition of martial law.
March 16–18, 1984	Delegates to 1981 congress reassemble for "National Conference of Delegates."
June 17, 1984	Province people's councils elected.

October 19, 1984   Father Jerzy Popieluszko
                                murdered.
December 27, 1984   Secret policemen put on trial for
                                Popieluszko murder.
October 13, 1985   Sejm election held.
November 6–12, 1985   Barcikowski, Rakowski,
                                Olszowski dropped in
                                leadership shake-up.
June 29–July 4, 1986   10th PZPR Congress held.

Democracy in a Communist Party
Poland's Experience Since 1980

CHAPTER 1

THE DRIVE FOR REFORM

THE 1980–81 reforms in the Polish United Workers Party (PZPR) were an outgrowth of the mid-1980 strikes which led to the formation of Solidarity. But they quickly took hold within the party because of growing reform sentiment among party members and weakness and division in the party leadership. The PZPR leadership, realizing that it lacked the power to put down the strikers by force and that it lacked firm support even within the party, chose a course of offering concessions to the strikers and promising internal reform to its own dissatisfied rank and file.

The upheaval which struck Poland in mid-1980 began with massive strikes arising from worsening economic conditions and worker discontent. Workers, fed up with the regime, demanded not only immediate concessions on pay and working conditions but also creation of their own, "free" trade unions to defend their interests against the government on an ongoing basis. To accommodate the surging demands for change, Polish party chief Edward Gierek promised reforms and free, uncontrolled elections in Poland's existing trade unions. Workers viewed the existing trade unions as organs of the government, however, and the regime soon had to agree to strikers forming their own trade unions and electing their leaders by secret, uncontrolled elections. Thus was born "Solidarnosc," which quickly became the symbol of a new democracy and attracted the support of the vast majority of workers.

The PZPR leadership responded to the demands for reform with a policy of concessions, rather than of repression. This was determined partly by the weakness of the Gierek regime. Not only was discontent so widespread among workers that force would be difficult to use, but Gierek did not have a united party and government apparatus behind him. Criticism of his leadership had been increasing, both among rank and file members and in the Central Committee. And the Soviets, who had refused to use force to keep Gomulka in power during the 1970 crisis, would clearly not do so for Gierek either.

But weakness was not the only reason—or even the most important reason—for this response. Under Gierek the regime was already the most liberal in the Soviet bloc and contained influential elements which had long been agitating for reform. Gierek himself had come to power in 1970 offering reforms and concessions instead of repression to deal with strikes. Moreover, the bloodshed resulting from use of force against strikes and demonstrations in the past—especially in 1970—had been a national trauma and had made use of force almost unmentionable for most politicians.

The 1970 disaster had an especially great effect on the PZPR secretary in charge of internal security, Stanislaw Kania, who had been closely involved in the 1970 tragedy. Kania was in charge of studying the 1980 strike situation and presenting recommendations on how to handle it. The interpretation of events he presented to the August 1980 Central Committee plenum virtually ruled out use of force. He presented workers' grievances as largely legitimate, cast most of the blame on the regime, and proposed concessions as the only answer. Kania himself soon replaced Gierek as party leader, and he came into office pledging to use only peaceful means to settle social conflicts.

The strikers' demands for political reforms such as more democratization and less censorship quickly found widespread support elsewhere and led to demands for reform in other institutions, including the communist party—a process which began to be called "renewal" (*odnowa*). Reformers insisted that the PZPR's control over society had to be reduced and that other institutions—such as trade unions and government bodies—had to become more independent and more responsive to public desires. Genuinely free elections had to be held in these institutions so that citizens could select the leaders they wished, free from manipulation and control by the party leaders. These pluralistic ideas also were applied to the party, where reformers wanted various political viewpoints to coexist and compete, rank and file members to freely elect leaders without control from above, and party organizations to be responsive to their own members' wishes and relatively autonomous from central organs.

The demands for democratization found fertile ground in the communist party because many rank and file members were dissatisfied with corruption and unresponsiveness on the part of entrenched and privileged party officials. Many party members immediately joined Solidarity after its formation, and some even participated in the August strikes. Moreover, even some party officials at various levels had been advocating reforms, and influenced by the attitudes of the rank and file and outraged at corruption and incompetence in the leadership, increasing numbers of party leaders began swinging to reform. In addition, most leaders, including CC Secretary Kania and Defense Minister Wojciech Jaruzelski, who were in charge of the police and armed forces, were unwilling to use force against the strikers and preferred to offer limited reforms instead. Reform sentiment was significant in the party already before August 1980, but the August events provided the motor force to overcome inertia and opposition and finally prompt the party to begin adopting the proposals of reformers.

The demands for reform in the PZPR basically came from below and boiled down to establishing control by party members over their leaders, so that they would never again be able to abuse their power and ignore the wishes of the rank and file. Past efforts to correct abuses of power had centered on replacing the dictatorial leaders with new men committed to reforms (Gomulka in 1956 and Gierek in 1970), but, as reformers remarked, the new leaders had gradually abandoned ideas of reform and reverted to the absolutist methods of rule characteristic of the system. Hence, reformers this time focused on changing the system as well as the leaders, writing "guarantees" of intraparty democracy into party statutes and election rules.

The changes centered on guaranteeing party members the right to replace leaders—the ultimate sanction to keep leaders responsive and prevent reestablishment of a self-appointed oligarchy. Reformers argued that the goal must be a system wherein leaders could be removed whenever they had lost the support of the majority of party members. To this end, the new rules allowed for a choice of candidates for elective party posts up and down the line, nomination of candidates from below rather than just from above, secret balloting, and strict limits on the number of terms a leader can hold an office.

In addition to pressing for changes in the rules, party reformers pushed for other changes which would increase the political power of the rank and file and provide physical guarantees that the legal guarantees would be respected. The first of these was to demand the addition of rank and file workers and farmers to leadership bodies at all levels. This was quickly embraced by the Kania leadership as an ideologically proper increase in the proportion of real workers in the leading organs of the "workers'" party. However, it turned out to have much more impact than was probably expected. No longer willing to act as symbolic "tokens" and obedient stooges in the leadership, workers in the CC and local party committees began speaking out as representatives of local party organizations and their fellow workers and conveyed the fury boiling in the local organizations which had elected them. Playing a bigger and bigger role, workers began to dominate CC plenums, pushing the formerly dominant party and government officials to the sidelines. These workers in the CC eventually played a key role in ousting First Secretary Kania himself.

A second way reformers moved to force change on the party was to organize local party organs for joint action, without authorization from above and often in direct opposition to higher organs. This came to be called the "horizontal ties" movement, since it linked party organs horizontally or territorially to counter the normal vertical chain of command in which a party organ had to obey its higher organ. These horizontal organs lobbied for reforms in the party statute and rules, and for holding a new party congress and for changing leaders. This movement was much more controversial than just adding workers to the leadership, since it directly challenged party leaders' authority. Conflicts quickly erupted between horizontal units and regular party units, and hostile party officials even expelled some horizontal ties leaders from the party. Party leaders at the top were badly split on whether to fight this movement or try to work with it, and Kania himself long avoided taking a clear stand. Eventually, however, the aggressive activities of horizontal units alienated most leaders, and the movement gradually waned in the face of determined official resistance.

The new Kania regime responded to the thrust from below by promising reforms but moving slowly to work them out. This reflected Kania's dilemma of having to not only please insistent domestic reformers, but also to appease alarmed Soviet leaders. As Polish party leaders were forced to accept more and more reforms strengthening Solidarity and democratizing the party, Poland's neighbors watched with growing concern and soon began applying pressure from the other side, to slow change and preserve the traditional policies and organs of authority. By late November, Soviet and other bloc troops were on the move around Poland's borders, and Western governments were alarmed at the prospect of invasion. The crisis finally eased after an emergency meeting of bloc leaders on December 5, during which Kania apparently was able to calm Soviet, Czechoslovak, and East German leaders.

Regime harassment of Solidarity and foot-dragging on reform reassured the Soviets and conservatives, but persuaded many reformers that the regime was basically against any reform. At the same time, Kania repeatedly gave way in confrontations with Solidarity or party reformers and accepted more reform than he intended, making the Soviets view him as weak and unreliable. This gave the Kania regime a very unclear image, unsatisfactory to either side. Nevertheless, with all the vacillations, Kania did manage to successfully follow a very important principle throughout this rather impossible situation: resolving conflicts by political negotiation and gradual reform rather than by use of force, hence avoiding repetition of bloodshed.

STRIKES AND THE REGIME RESPONSE

From the onset of the mid-1980 crisis, the Polish regime took a conciliatory approach to the demands of striking workers, acknowledging mistakes and promising reforms. Party leader Edward Gierek humbly confessed making errors and offered limited concessions. Other leaders—even Stefan Olszowski and Andrzej Zabinski, who later became leaders of the conservative wing—blamed the situation on the Gierek regime rather than the strikers. Stanislaw Kania, who was most directly in charge of handling the response, proposed a policy of concessions, and he was soon chosen to replace Gierek as party leader.

The caving in to strikers' demands all happened within just a matter of days—between mid-August when strikes became massive and more political and early September when Gierek resigned. The system had apparently been ripe for collapse, since officials in the official trade union organizations, the parliament, and the party leadership itself showed themselves quite aware of the regime's defects and joined in the strikers' criticisms. While some may have just been going along with the tide of public sentiment, others appeared to really see the regime policies as bankrupt and leadership as dictatorial. With no one willing to defend the system—especially if force was needed—events moved rapidly, and the drive for "renewal" began encompassing one institution after another.

The strikes started in early July, in response to government attempts to raise meat prices. Though dozens of factories were on strike by late July, it was only with the beginning of widespread strikes along the Baltic coast, especially in Gdansk, in mid-August that strikers began getting organized into effective strike committees and began presenting detailed political as well as economic demands. The Gdansk Interfactory Strike Committee demanded both economic concessions (on wages, prices, working conditions) and also political steps by the government: guarantee of the right to strike, reduction of press censorship, release of political prisoners, and more rights for the Church.[1]

Party First Secretary Gierek attempted to deal with the strikes by promising concessions rather than attempting to use force. In an August 18 television speech he admitted "errors" by the regime, conceded that workers had legitimate grievances, but pleaded that "strikes won't change anything for the better." He spoke of resolving the problem by "compromises" and "dialogue" and acknowledged the "urgent need for deepening democratization" at workplaces.[2]

As the strikes spread to Szczecin and elsewhere, a plenum of the CC was held on August 24 to decide tactics on dealing with the situation. This plenum approved the approach of making concessions instead of using force—an approach which was to be the basic line until imposition of martial law in December 1981. The chief spokesman for this line at the plenum was CC Secretary Stanislaw Kania, who two weeks later replaced Gierek as first secretary.

Kania probably largely determined the outcome of the August 24 plenum by the tenor of his speech which opened the plenum. Delivering a report on the situation on behalf of the leadership, he presented a remarkably frank and objective picture. After he presented the strikers as basically responsible people protesting legitimate grievances, including gross mismanagement by the regime, it was probably difficult for hard-line CC members to argue that the strikers were hostile, antisocialist forces which had to be suppressed by force. Kania apparently delivered the report (simply entitled "Information"—indicating it was not a formal Politburo report to the CC) in his capacity as secretary in charge of internal security. His remarks were apparently sensitive enough that no account of his speech was published until later.[3]

Kania opened by stressing the seriousness of the situation, declaring that there was a "real threat" of a "national catastrophe." He stated that in less than two months 640,000 workers in forty-nine provinces had gone on strike, making this the "most massive and longest wave of strikes" since communist rule had begun in Poland. He reported that the strikers were presenting not only economic demands but also political demands and that "the acceptance of some of these demands would mean a turn in the direction of weakening the socialist character of our state." "Antisocialist" forces were seeking to turn the strikes against the socialist system, and hostile demands were circulating, he said.

Nevertheless, Kania presented the strikes in a relatively favorable light. He argued that "it would be a mistake, a serious mistake, if we judged the strikes by what was being shouted at meetings and written in various leaflets by our political foes." He noted that the strikes had been peaceful and orderly and, unlike the December 1970 and June 1976 strikes, had not involved demonstrations and street disturbances. He even acknowledged that in many plants party members were participating in the strikes and that in Szczecin many members of the strike committees were actually party members. He characterized the strikes as a "workers' protest, a protest against errors in the state's policy, against bad methods of ruling and administering the country."

Instead of attacking the strikers, he placed the blame for the strikes mainly on the party leadership, the government, trade unions, and other institutions. He criticized the government's decision to change meat prices as having been poorly handled and as serving as the "detonator" for the strikes. He reported that even at party meetings it was being said that the "main reasons" for the present difficulties lay in the Politburo and government. Noting workers' demands for new, "so-called free trade unions," he criticized the existing unions and acknowledged that strikers had "real bases for dissatisfaction with the work of trade unions."

Addressing the question of how to deal with the strikes, Kania came out flatly for negotiations and concessions and against use of force. "From the first day" our "basic method" of dealing with the strikes had been "dialogue" with the strikers, "studying the reasons for the dissatisfaction and ameliorating them as much as possible." Our "aim, the guiding idea in all these actions," has been to win over the strikers and prevent them from falling under the influence of hostile forces. He rejected the arguments of hard-liners: "Here and there in talks we encounter various suggestions that we should deal with strikers more resolutely and show them that we are strong." "This is a very mistaken idea," he added, because there are "no bases for using force against the striking workers and there never will be such bases." Kania declared that the "decisive" factor in past social conflicts had been the public's trust in the authorities, but this is precisely "what we lack the most today."

Kania's report was followed by a short speech by Gierek, who also acknowledged that the workers' dissatisfaction was well founded and that negotiations with the strikers was the "only correct course." Admitting errors by the leadership, he declared that the "initial condition" for winning back public confidence was "far-reaching changes" in the Politburo and government. He announced that all members of the Politburo and Secretariat had turned in their resignations ("postawili do dyspozycji swoje mandaty") in order to enable him to propose leadership changes to the CC. He stated that "after consultations with a number of comrades," he was presenting a new list of Politburo and Secretariat members. Dropped from Politburo membership were his protégé Edward Babiuch (who was also replaced as premier), CC Ideology Secretary Jerzy Lukaszewicz, trade union chief Jan Szydlak, and Deputy Premier in charge of planning Tadeusz Wrzaszczyk, while Deputy Premier Tadeusz Pyka (who had been unsuccessful in dealing with the Gdansk strikers) and CC Secretary Zdzislaw Zandarowski were dropped as Politburo candidate members.

Perhaps the most humiliating step taken by Gierek at the plenum was to admit that he had been wrong in ousting two leaders who had directly criticized his economic policies a few months earlier and to consent to restore them to leadership posts. Stefan Olszowski, who had been ousted from the Politburo and Secretariat in early 1980 and exiled abroad as ambassador to East Germany, was elected a Politburo member and CC secretary.[4] Tadeusz Grabski, ousted as Konin province first secretary and demoted to director of a plant in 1979, was co-opted to CC membership and nominated to become deputy premier. Gierek in his initial speech at the plenum stated that "we also recall the signals from comrades here present which were not taken into consideration." At the end of the plenum, in his concluding speech, Gierek said that "we have raised to responsible positions those comrades who earlier pointed out growing mistakes and tried to counter them but whose voices we did not heed in time."[5] Ironically, both Olszowski and Grabski, while calling for reforms under Gierek, later emerged as hard-liners, rather than liberal reformers.

The remaining speakers, judging by the *Nowe Drogi* versions of their speeches, virtually all echoed the view that the strikers had legitimate grievances and should be dealt with by negotiations and that the regime had made errors—although few were as sharp in their comments as Kania was. The lineup of speakers was, moreover, overwhelmingly weighted in favor of those who had been dealing with the strikers and who were optimistic about reaching agreement with them. Gierek announced at the start that "we must primarily listen to those CC members who have come from the coast," and of the twelve speakers, half came from the coastal provinces hit by strikes (including Gdansk province First Secretary Tadeusz Fiszbach, First Secretary Stanislaw Miskiewicz of the Warski shipyard in Szczecin, and First Secretary Jan Labecki of the Lenin shipyard in Gdansk). Other speakers included First Secretary Wladyslaw Kruk of Lublin (one of the other main strike centers) and longtime reform spokesman Mieczyslaw Rakowski, editor of *Polityka*.

No one—not even Stefan Olszowski, later a sharp critic of Solidarity and reformers—really criticized the strikers (judging by the *Nowe Drogi* versions of the speeches). Olszowski focused on criticizing his old foe Gierek. While not attacking him by name, he reminded everyone that some people (he himself) had told the "truth about the situation" at earlier plenums, and if their views had been heeded the present crisis could have been checked. Instead, he stated, the "unnecessary arrogance of the authorities which characterized the government team after the 8th congress [February 1980] deepened the difficulties," and so "there was nothing surprising" about the fact that the policies "led to a wave of strikes." He laid down reform proposals of his own on economic and social policy, urging more intraparty democracy and more independence and powers for the Sejm (parliament) and trade unions. He declared that the Sejm should be able to conduct real debates over paths of development and government activity and that trade unions should concentrate on defending workers' rights, even to the point of employing warning strikes.

At the end of the plenum Gierek delivered a concluding speech which was published in the press. Noting the "sharp" but "just" criticism voiced by speakers, he declared that only "elimination of the causes of the social dissatisfaction" would end the conflict and that "we are making a fundamental change in the policy of the party and state" to do this. Responding to strikers' criticisms of the official trade unions, he called on the Central Council of Trade Unions (CRZZ—Centralna Rada Zwiazkow Zawodowych) to immediately hold new elections wherever workers desired this and to use secret balloting "with an unlimited number of candidates." He invited leaders of strike committees to participate and try to win positions in the trade union leadership.

Gierek's conciliatory reaction to the strikes was not surprising. He had won election as first secretary in December 1970 in the reaction against Gomulka's misguided use of force against strikers, and hence was implicitly associated with peaceful settlement of such problems. Moreover, he also had little choice, since sentiment in the party was turning against him and he was being blamed for causing the strikes by his erroneous policies and one-man rule. In his plenum speech Gierek mentioned proposals flowing in from local party meetings and also the local meetings' complaints that the leadership had ignored their opinions. Some speeches at the plenum itself—by Olszowski, Rakowski, and Poznan First Secretary Jerzy Zasada—also criticized the leadership, sometimes implicitly attacking Gierek's personal rule. For example, Zasada criticized the "departure from the practice of consultation on important social and economic decisions" and adoption of such decisions "single-handedly or within a very narrow group."[6]

Within a week—on August 30—another plenum was convened, this time to consider the terms for agreement with the strikers proposed by the negotiating teams under Deputy Premiers Mieczyslaw Jagielski and Kazimierz Barcikowski.[7] Rumors circulated that hard-liners objected to the terms and that there was hot debate, both at the plenum and at the August 29 Politburo session which preceded it. Reporter Neal Ascherson writes that in the August 29 Politburo debate Olszowski favored using force against the strikers, but that Gierek—as well as Kania and Defense Minister Jaruzelski, who were in charge of the police and armed forces—opposed using force.[8] There is no public evidence to confirm this story of the Politburo session, however. Ascherson also reports that Kania, when asked what would happen if 90 percent of the workers joined new independent unions, declared: "Better a step to the right than a step over the precipice."[9]

The official accounts give no details of the August 30 plenum, however. The reports on the plenum—in both the September 1, 1980 *Trybuna Ludu* and the September *Nowe Drogi*—only relate that Kania again delivered an "information" report and that Jagielski and Barcikowski reported on their negotiations. There is not even any mention of a debate or of other speakers. But the CC plenum did approve the terms, and on the next day Jagielski and Barcikowski returned to Gdansk and Szczecin to sign the agreements.

In these agreements the regime caved in and went along with most of the strikers' demands, both economic (gradual wage rises, revocation of price rises, better housing and working conditions, etc.) and political. The accords signed by the government team under Jagielski on August 31 in Gdansk provided for creation of "new, independent trade unions which would be the authentic representative of the working class" and which would be separate from the existing Central Council of Trade Unions. In the accords, the regime also promised to guarantee the right to strike, to introduce a new law reducing censorship, to speed economic reform, to "release all political prisoners," and to allow the press, radio, and television to express a "variety of thought, views, and opinions" and have wider access to government documents.[10] The shorter accord signed the same day in Szczecin by a team under Barcikowski also committed the regime to permit "independent trade unions" based on the existing committees of strikers, which would elect leaders by "secret elections," and additionally granted new rights to the Church (in particular, access to the media).[11] Neither agreement made any demand for election reform, although they called for independent trade unions which would use uncontrolled elections.

The demands for reform raised by the strikers quickly brought a radical shake-up in the official unions. The Central Council of Trade Unions (CRZZ), whose job it supposedly was to represent workers' interests and satisfy their needs, had become simply a compliant arm of the government and party headed by a member of the party Politburo, Jan Szydlak, and was dismissed as irrelevant by the strikers. Prompted by Gierek's August 24 demand for reform in the official unions, many union officials immediately sided with the strikers' demands and castigated their union leadership for failing to represent workers' desires. At an August 26 plenum of the CRZZ Szydlak resigned as council chairman and Romuald Jankowski, head of the metal workers union, was elected chairman. Speakers at the plenum assailed the unions for not opposing government decisions which hurt workers' interests and for letting government organs ride roughshod over union rights.

The shake-up in the CRZZ occurred quickly and was accompanied by talk virtually unheard of in a trade union in a communist state: that the trade unions should have the right to call a strike against the "workers' government" in order to defend the workers against the government. Speakers at the August 26 plenum demanded that the unions have a veto over all government decisions affecting wages and prices, and demanded union independence from the government and more internal union democracy. Responding to demands by some local unions for new union elections, the plenum recommended setting up procedures to carry out such elections, "with unlimited number of candidates" and secret balloting. The plenum ordered drafting of a new trade union constitution (*ustawa*) guaranteeing union independence. The August 27 *Trybuna Ludu* account of the plenum indicated that opinion favored a constitution obligating the unions to object to government actions "violating the interest" of workers and allowing the unions to call a strike "in case of exhausting all other possibilities of influencing a change of these decisions."

Only two days after his election, new CRZZ chairman Jankowski went on national television to try to catch up with public opinion by promising radical changes in the official unions. Conceding that strikers' criticisms of the unions were correct, that they had not been effectively defending workers' interests, Jankowski called for "renewal" (*odnowa*) in the unions and for a new union constitution with "guarantees" that unions would be consulted in any government decisions on wages and social policy and would have the right to strike if other methods of pressure failed. He declared that the "hugh majority" of strikers' demands were acceptable and agreed that if some member unions wanted to elect new leaders, they could elect whomever they wished.[12]

A union group was appointed to write a new constitution and quickly met on August 30. According to the September 1 *Trybuna Ludu*, it discussed drafting a new constitution providing for elections with secret balloting and unlimited number of candidates, the right to object to any government decision "in conflict with the law or social interest," and the option of calling a strike if all else failed.

But all these efforts failed to capture public support. The Central Council of Trade Unions was soon bypassed as workers joined Solidarity and whole unions quit the council to become independent.

The movement to reform the country's discredited institutions soon spread to Poland's parliament, which had been totally submissive to party control and had lost the respect of the public. When the normally tame Sejm met on September 5, deputies suddenly began asserting independence, criticizing a wide range of regime shortcomings and expressing sympathy for the strikers and their demands. The deputies' speeches, which appeared in *Trybuna Ludu* from September 6 to 9, 1980, criticized censorship of the press, overcentralization of authority, and lack of responsiveness on the part of leaders of the trade unions and government. Several deputies (primarily non-PZPR members) complained that the Sejm was considered simply a "rubber stamp" for regime decisions and demanded that the Sejm should play the role assigned it by the Constitution: of "supreme organ of state authority."

Ironically, the new assertiveness was led by one of the communist party's CC secretaries, Andrzej Zabinski, who was speaking on behalf of PZPR members in the Sejm. Delivering the first speech at the session, he set an extremely critical tone, stressing the unprecedented scale and force of the "wave of strikes" and declaring that the workers were "reminding us sharply and angrily" that we have neglected many of the people's concerns and have "listened too little to their voices and opinions." He praised the accords reached with the striking workers and said that they involve "consistent democratization of intraparty life and proper functioning of representative institutions and all public organizations." Zabinski was fresh from signing the accords with the strikers in Szczecin and was still enthusiastic about reform.

Zabinski took an especially critical approach to the regime and even

Gierek personally—although Gierek was still first secretary at this point. He criticized the "erroneous information policy" and "excessively detailed regulation of information" and the "excessively centralized system of leadership and administration." He spoke of "errors" and asked why the program "designed under the leadership of comrade Edward Gierek" was subject to "distortion and deformation" in its implementation. He asked for determination of people's accountability for work and warned that "the higher the position the greater the responsibility."

The mounting criticism of regime policy both inside and outside the party reflected a growing consensus that Gierek, the one most responsible for the crisis, had to be replaced. The party had conceded that strikers had legitimate grievances and that regime policies had sometimes been wrong, and Gierek was the author of those policies. No amount of promises by him to change his policies and his autocratic style of ruling could persuade the public that the regime was serious about changing. Only days after the CC plenum had approved the course of peaceful negotiation and concession Gierek was dropped as party leader and Kania was installed in his place.

At a late night CC plenum on September 5 President Henryk Jablonski announced that Gierek had had a heart attack earlier in the day and could no longer lead. According to the version of Jablonski's speech published in the September 1980 *Nowe Drogi*, he explained that the Politburo had called the plenum to elect a new first secretary. "After weighing various possibilities" and consulting province first secretaries, he said, the Politburo "decided unanimously" to propose a person "enjoying universal confidence"—Stanislaw Kania. He explained that in recent weeks Kania had headed a commission coordinating actions in the areas hit by strikes and disorders, and the comrades from these areas well knew "how much good judgment" he had demonstrated. Kania was then "unanimously" elected first secretary—with no sign that conservatives even put up a fight.

The plenum made other leadership changes also, promoting some of Gierek's sharpest critics. CC Secretary Zabinski, who had so strongly criticized the regime at the Sejm session earlier that day, and Deputy Premier Barcikowski, who had signed the accord with strikers in Szczecin, were added to the Politburo, while old Gierek foe Tadeusz Grabski, CC Organizational Department chief Zdzislaw Kurowski, and CC Agriculture Department chief Jerzy Wojtecki were elected CC secretaries. There was no indication of any discussion or debate in the extremely brief announcement in the September 6–7, 1980 *Trybuna Ludu* and September *Nowe Drogi*. After making the personnel changes, the 6th plenum took the unusual step of adjourning, to resume its work—still as the 6th plenum—a few weeks later.

Kania's speech to the plenum was published in the next day's (September 8) *Trybuna Ludu*. Responding to the resentment at Gierek's high-handed rule, Kania modestly declared that although some speakers had called upon him to be "leader" (*przywodca*) of the party, he did not think the party needed a "leader" (in the sense of a boss), and so he would attempt to lead on the basis of the "collective wisdom" of party leaders. He acknowledged that the strikes had been caused by serious policy errors and reflected legitimate dissatisfaction and hence must be resolved by dialogue, by political means (rather than force). He declared "our most important task" to be winning back public confidence in the authorities and urged more rights for the Sejm and local people's councils and "a genuine renewal" of unions so that they would effectively defend workers' interests. Addressing the party, he endorsed proposals in some letters to the CC urging the calling of a new party congress on grounds that the situation had changed so radically since the last congress in February 1980.

In view of Jablonski's remarks in nominating Kania, it appears that Kania's commitment to peaceful settlement with the strikers and to political reform were key elements in the Politburo's selecting him to replace Gierek. Later, Jagielski, in speaking to the Gdansk party aktiv on September 8, stated that from the very beginning of the strikes the authorities had "sought a solution exclusively by political methods," and he "stressed Stanislaw Kania's personal participation in formulating such a line of action."[13] Kania, as CC secretary in charge of police and internal security, had demonstrated this commitment to peaceful settlement by resisting any idea of using the forces under him against the strikers. He apparently gave private commitments that he would never use force. Liberal CC media chief Jozef Klasa said later that on the eve of becoming first secretary Kania "told me very clearly that as long as he held this post he would not allow workers to be fired on."[14] Upon becoming first secretary, Kania immediately chose controversial reformer Klasa to be his media supervisor (chief of the CC Department for Press, Radio, and Television; see chapter 3 for more on Klasa) and controversial liberal *Gazeta Krakowska* editor Zbigniew Regucki as his main personal assistant (head of the CC's Chancery).[15]

Was it surprising that the party should turn to Kania and a soft line? It had similarly turned to Gomulka in 1956 and Gierek in 1970 for reform in similar crises. Moreover, reformers were clearly renewing their efforts toward the end of the 1970s, probably in a tide running deeper throughout the party than during earlier crises. At the top level, the well-known editor of the magazine *Polityka*, Mieczyslaw Rakowski, called for a shift to decentralization of decision making in a November 5, 1977 *Polityka* article entitled "The Limits of Centralization." This was promptly labeled revisionism and a blow to democratic centralism in a November 8, 1977 *Zycie Warszawy* article, but Rakowski persisted. In a July 5, 1980 *Polityka* article he directly criticized the government for slowness in taking measures to improve the worsening economic situation and, citing increasing shortages of meat and other goods, defended the public's impatience with its low living standard.

At a middle level, a group of party members and others in November 1978 formed the "Experience and the Future" (Doswiadczenie i Przyszlosc) group to discuss the problems facing Poland and to present ideas for improvement to the authorities. The leadership initially gave some support, apparently to demonstrate its openness to ideas for change. The ideas expressed at the first meeting of the group apparently shocked the authorities, and they quickly canceled any sponsorship. During 1979 and early 1980 the group published a collection of opinions calling for reduced censorship, economic decentralization, limitation of the party's role, revitalization of representative organs, and a new relationship between rulers and ruled.[16] The views were not intended to challenge the regime but to help it reform and better deal with problems. Stefan Bratkowski, who later became the chairman of the Union of Polish Journalists and stirred much controversy with his reformist views and actions, was one of the members of the group, while CC Secretary and Gierek rival Stefan Olszowski was linked to the group also.[17]

The party rank and file was especially receptive to unorthodox ideas because Gierek had just drastically expanded party membership, drawing in hundreds of thousands of new members who were not ideologically indoctrinated or committed to traditional party ways. Advancing the slogan "A party of 3,000,000 by the 8th congress," Gierek increased membership by 650,000 between the 7th party congress in 1975 and the 8th in early 1980. Membership stood at 3,080,000 on January 1, 1980,[18] and another 106,000 were admitted during the first half of 1980 as well.[19] The Central Party Control Commission's report at the July 1981 congress stated that "the real reason for lowering ideological demands on party members was the adoption of the course of rapid expansion of party ranks. The slogan of a party of 3,000,000 by the 8th congress led to the fact that the statistical data on numerical expansion of party ranks became the chief criterion for evaluating the work of party organizations and bodies. Rapid numerical growth was considered a sign of support for the party's policy, regardless of the method of carrying out the task set."[20] The new members formed the bulk of those who rebelled and quit the party in 1980–81. Kazimierz Cypryniak, head of the CC's Organizational Department, told *Trybuna Ludu* (July 16–17, 1983) that 51.7 percent of those who left the party after 1980 were those joining the party between 1975 and 1980.

This undisciplined rank and file began expressing its desire for change during the late 1979 local party election conferences before the February 1980 party congress. Some party meetings became unruly, as members protested the food situation, corruption, lack of worker representation in factory management, and misleading official propaganda.[21] Gierek in his speech at the congress recognized some of the problems, but little was done, so some party members started discussing changes in the party's structure and practices, such as free elections and rotation of posts.[22] Dissidents like Jacek Kuron recognized the discontent in the party and fashioned programs to appeal to dissatisfied party members.[23]

In at least one case, reform-minded rank and file members organized and took effective action. At the Elmor plant in Gdansk, Bogdan Lis and several other party members decided to run for election to the party committee at their plant, and their "democratic opposition" slate swept twenty-seven of the twenty-nine seats and took over leadership of the party organization. When this plant decided to join other Gdansk strikers on August 15, 1980, the party organization chairman Lis led the strike.[24]

PROPOSALS FOR REFORM IN THE PARTY

The 6th plenum, after replacing Gierek, adjourned on September 6 with the stated intention of reconvening shortly to take up substantive matters. However, during September tension between Solidarity and the government grew as Solidarity organizations formed and began accusing the authorities of not living up to various provisions of the August accords. Local strikes broke out around the country. Leaders apparently had difficulty agreeing over how to deal with the situation, and the resumption of the plenum was delayed. When it finally reopened on October 4, it was in the immediate wake of a one-hour national strike on October 3 called by Solidarity to force wage increases by the government.

The October plenum was the first plenum to discuss in detail ideas about the direction of reform in the party. Kania cautiously raised some ideas, but other speakers loosed a flood of proposals for democratization. These proposals ranged from institutional guarantees in the party statute and election rules to practical steps such as packing leadership bodies with rank and file representatives to keep close watch on leaders. They basically focused on how to keep control over the top party leaders, and, if necessary, to strip them of office if they abused their power.

This focus—on controlling the top party leaders—was clearly a reaction to the increasingly arbitrary and unpopular rule of First Secretary Gierek in the late 1970s. Gierek's image as an autocratic ruler was ironic, since he himself had become first secretary ten years earlier during a similar reaction against the autocratic rule of First Secretary Wladyslaw Gomulka. During the December 1970 strikes in Gdansk and elsewhere, Gierek, then first secretary of Katowice province, had opposed Gomulka's decision to raise food prices. When Gomulka's misguided use of force against strikers brought bloodshed, the divided Politburo turned to Gierek to replace him. Gierek began his reign by urging "renewal" within the party and "guarantees" against misuse of power.[25]

Gierek's apparent good intentions on reform gradually fell by the wayside as popular agitation for change eased and other problems—especially economic—built up. By the late 1970s he had concentrated power in his own hands and those of a small number of cronies and had become increasingly intolerant of alternate views. When Konin First Secretary Tadeusz Grabski and CC Secretary Stefan Olszowski criticized the leadership's economic policy in 1979 and 1980, Gierek reacted angrily: Grabski was demoted to a plant director and dropped from the CC at the February 1980 congress, while Olszowski lost his leadership posts at the congress and was sent abroad as an ambassador. Angered by the negative reports prepared by the CC's Planning and Economic Analysis Department, Gierek simply forbade their circulation and finally in early 1980 abolished the department itself.[26]

When the first post-Gierek plenum opened on October 4, 1980, new First Secretary Kania in his opening report pointed out the excessive concentration of power in the former first secretary's hands and called for guarantees against recurrence of such "deformations." He urged more precise definition of the duties of the first secretary, Politburo, and Secretariat in the party statute and measures to ensure more "constant and effective" CC control over the leadership. He noted that local party organizations were making proposals for secret balloting, unlimited nomination of candidates, and limits on terms of office to prevent leadership abuses, but he did not specifically endorse these himself. He cautioned that "no formal formulation itself will guarantee democracy" and that "institutional changes are important, but no less important is thorough change of internal relationships in the party."

Other speakers more boldly raised the issue of how to control the leader, noting the absence of any mechanism for changing leadership before severe crises developed. CC Secretary Andrzej Werblan complained that socialism "still has not created sufficiently precise mechanisms for changing leadership teams," and each time the first secretary has had to be changed it has required "dramatic wrenching and conflicts."[27] *Chlopska Droga* chief editor Mieczyslaw Rog-Swiostek noted that the socialist system lacked the opposition groups that provided a check on leaders in Western states and added that while "I'm far from advocating freedom for opposition parties or for factional opposition inside our party . . . I think a mechanism to signal irregularities can and should be established within the organizational system of our party."

Speakers advanced an impressive list of changes aimed at "guaranteeing" that leaders would not abuse power. As Wloclawek First Secretary

Edward Szymanski said, "Changes in leading posts will not suffice"; workers "expect us to introduce mechanisms and establish guarantees, often statutory." Urging "institutional guarantees," Werblan stated that "we cannot anymore count only on fortunate choice of people; that is too accidental." Rog-Swiostek called for "statutory insurance against excessive concentration of power in the hands of one person."

One of the first proposals was to bring more rank and file workers and farmers into leadership bodies. Elaborating most extensively on this idea, mining academy rector Roman Ney complained that the party leadership had failed to listen to the rank and file, and so he proposed that at least half of the Politburo members be local party workers outside the "central party and government apparat," or ordinary workers and farmers. This would guarantee that the Politburo would have "better contact with what is happening locally." As a corollary to expanding the representation of rank and file in the CC, Wloclawek leader Szymanski argued that the number of central government officials in the CC should be reduced.

Many speakers urged that party officials be allowed to hold offices for no more than two terms and that the principle of "rotation" of leadership posts be firmly established. In particular, Szymanski complained that "we do not have a good mechanism for giving up posts. . . . Departure too often becomes political death. . . . Removal of those holding power at all levels must be something natural and not a desperate act." He proposed that CC members be limited to two terms and members of regional committees to three terms (because their terms are shorter, only two-year terms), and that at least half of the CC members be replaced in each rotation. Ambassador to Switzerland Jozef Tejchma stated that "departure from leadership should become an institutionally normal thing," and we should "dedramatize" personnel changes.

Various proposals were made which would subordinate the Politburo and Secretariat to the CC and make the CC the real center of power in the party. Minister for Materials Eugeniusz Szyr insisted that the "CC should elect Politburo members in secret voting, after learning their views, especially on the methods and directions of work of that body," and membership in the Politburo should be rotated. Moreover, the CC should evaluate the work of the Politburo and be consulted by the Politburo before decisions are adopted, he added. Deputy Chairman of the Central

Auditing Commission Eugeniusz Stawinski proposed that the party statute should provide for the CC to vote in secret on Politburo members and that Politburo members must receive the votes of at least three-fourths of the CC. He also called for an end of the practice of Politburo members presenting a facade of unity to the CC "despite differences existing between them." In fact, he said, the statute should include a rule that "each Politburo member have the right and party obligation to demand that the CC debate questions which he feels require this because they were not properly resolved in the Politburo." Moreover, a group of ten or more CC members should have the right to require debate on a subject at a plenum. Roman Ney insisted that members of the Politburo must not work "anonymously," that "we must know the persons who lead our party and also their views and their conduct."

In addition to the talk of checks on the top leaders, there were proposals for democratization throughout the party. The party congress held in February 1980 was regarded as undemocratic and as having been manipulated by the discredited Gierek regime, and so there was a flood of demands to call an "extraordinary" party congress which would elect a new leadership and adopt a new party program reflecting the party's "renewal." To ensure a more democratic congress, some, such as Warsaw workers Zygmunt Wronski and Zygmunt Gajewski, insisted that delegates to the congress be elected directly at big party organizations, where elections would be less subject to manipulation than in the normal regional step-by-step process (election of delegates to district conferences, then city conferences, then province conferences). Gdansk shipyard worker Jan Labecki called for changes in the party election system so that elected officials "will consider the opinions of the rank and file which elected them and not look only at those higher up" who gave them their jobs. Other speakers demanded reduction of the power of higher organs (especially of the party apparat) over lower, elective organs—a demand striking at the very basis of democratic centralism. Warsaw worker Wronski and Minister for Materials Szyr called for "higher organs" to stop foisting their choices for leadership on lower organs.

The plenum thus not only reacted against Gierek's misrule but openly addressed basic problems in the functioning of a communist party and in a more concrete manner than in the past. After the plenum, Mieczyslaw Rakowski, chief editor of the magazine *Polityka*, in an October 9 television commentary on the plenum stressed that this plenum differed from the plenum after the December 1970 Gdansk demonstrations in that it focused on proposals for specific institutional guarantees: limiting the number of terms of office, defining powers of the first secretary and Politburo, and separating party and government posts.[28] He said that these were being discussed at meetings throughout the country.

The October plenum raised an agenda of reforms, but before the next plenum was held, on December 1–2, a number of pressures and counterpressures developed (in addition to the foot-dragging by entrenched party officials), complicating progress on reform. The new labor organization Solidarity pressed the regime to live up to the August accords and give it its legal rights, while the regime, pressed by Soviet leaders and Polish conservatives to prevent Solidarity's development, harassed the new movement. During October Solidarity and the authorities had a sharp confrontation over officially recognizing the new union (by the legal registration of its statute), which ended with a government concession to avert a general strike. At the end of October Kania and Premier Pinkowski flew to Moscow to try to calm the agitation among Soviet and other bloc leaders over Poland's internal situation and concessions to Solidarity. Another crisis arose over the November 19 police raid on Solidarity's Warsaw office in search of a confidential document from the prosecutor's office and the subsequent arrest of Jan Narozniak and Piotr Sapielo for taking and circulating the document. Outraged local Solidarity leaders called for a general strike in protest. Meanwhile, the Soviet government newspaper *Izvestiya* warned against any strike that would cut Soviet rail lines to East Germany—something that would affect Soviet military security. Narozniak and Sapielo were finally released, easing government-Solidarity tension. But pressure from Moscow intensified, and the December plenum met amid military maneuvers by Soviet and other bloc forces—maneuvers which only ended after an emergency December 5 summit meeting between Kania and other bloc leaders.

Pressure also built up within the party during this period, and the leadership worked frantically to persuade the restive rank and file that they were being responsive to the proposals for change. When the December plenum opened, Kania moved to accept more of the reformers' demands than he had before and came up with a new, democratized set of party election rules—the first real document of party reform. Kania's opening report praised the increasing ousters of local leaders by rebellious party organizations and endorsed some of the specific demands for radical change. He stated that many local party organizations were demanding new elections and that some local leaders were asking their organizations for "votes of confidence," and he approved these local initiatives, although stating his opposition to immediate elections for the party as a whole. "One of the important tasks is creation of a proper climate around cadre changes and opposing persecution and accusations. By the effort of the whole party we must form an atmosphere in which giving up party and government leadership functions becomes a normal thing; likewise with demotion from a higher to a lower function or from mainly political activity to work as a specialist."[29] While reasserting that democratic centralism "was and will remain the basic principle of intraparty life," he also stated that "democracy in the party is the key to democracy in society, in all units of sociopolitical life."

Kania spoke of proposals for change in the party statute and procedures coming to the CC from all over the country, and he endorsed several of them, including limits on the number of terms of office and use of secret balloting. "In accord with the position of many organizations, we propose that where half of the members of a body are in favor, election of the first secretaries, Executive Committees, and Secretariats be by secret ballot." Responding to the resolutions by many organizations calling for changes in the party's election rules, he announced that a draft of new rules incorporating many of these proposed changes was being submitted to the present plenum. He even spoke favorably of the developing horizontal ties movement, praising the development of joint work and exchange of views between local party organizations, and asked local authorities to aid this initiative. At the same time, he cautioned against one important aspect of the movement: the "creation of extrastatutory organizational structures," which he said involved factionalism. (For more on the horizontal ties movement—the banding together of local party organizations outside the control of regular party channels—see the section on "Rebellion Against Higher Organs" later in this chapter.)

Other speakers at the December plenum made relatively few new proposals for change, but pressed for action on reforms already proposed, especially on calling an extraordinary party congress. Many stressed the growing impatience by the rank and file.[30] Rakowski voiced the problem of the growing gap between the rank and file and the leadership most eloquently. He stated that thousands of letters and resolutions of local party organizations were coming to the CC and to publications such as his own *Polityka* expressing popular distrust of the leadership and criticizing its slowness in pressing reform. "Many party members feel that at the top inertia and inability to change the old style of work reign," and "often one sees the opinion that the party leaders, meaning the CC, Politburo, CC Secretariat, and CC departments, simply don't respond to proposals, for example, for calling an extraordinary party congress or on questions of [calling leaders to] responsibility because they think first of all about themselves, to put it brutally, about their own jobs." The present crisis, he said, will not end until the causes for the "misunderstanding and tension between the party base and its organs"—the CC, Politburo, and provincial party committees—are cleared up.[31] Lodz worker Janina Zalewska declared that workers she had spoken to in her hometown unanimously assailed the "lack of real action" by the leadership to carry out the decisions of the October plenum, and she declared, "I present the opinion . . . of all Lodz" that the extraordinary congress "absolutely cannot be delayed."[32]

ADDITION OF WORKERS TO THE LEADERSHIP

One of the first reform proposals to be accepted by the leadership and put into effect was that calling for addition of workers and farmers and other nonofficials to leadership bodies, both locally and nationally. Whether or not all leaders realized it, this was to be a very far-reaching change and became a key element of democratization, since it helped to make party bodies more responsive to those below than to those above and hence helped to reverse democratic centralism.

The weight of rank and file workers and farmers increased dramatically even in the CC in late 1980, and when the new CC was elected in July 1981, workers and farmers became the absolute majority, while most officials, local and central, were excluded from the CC. The workers and farmers, reflecting the views and demands of their local party organizations and rank and file colleagues, spoke out vigorously, were no longer dependent on party bosses for their jobs, and largely ignored leadership opinions. The worker-farmer element soon began openly assailing the Politburo and eventually helped force First Secretary Kania himself to resign. The leadership found this kind of CC impossible to control and difficult even to manipulate.

The Polish CC had had a substantial worker element even under Gierek—much more than the proportion in the Soviet CC. The CC elected at the party congress in February 1980 had included about 30 workers among its 143 full members—about 21 percent. However, the workers on the Polish CC were not very outspoken before August 1980. When the Polish rank and file began attacking the lack of responsiveness by party leaders, one of its strongest complaints was over the low representation of workers in leadership bodies. Many party members did not trust their leaders, whom they viewed as privileged—even corrupt— bureaucratic bosses who had lost touch with the people. The addition of hardworking, unspoiled workers to leadership would introduce a healthier element and would ensure that leading organs could not ignore the daily problems of ordinary party members. Outspoken worker Albin Siwak at the December 1980 plenum complained that many province executive committees included only one, two, or three workers or, in some cases, none at all.[33] Seamstress Jadwiga Nowakowska, in a *Trybuna Ludu* interview (February 2, 1981), expressed her resentment at the way officials dominated CC plenums and urged that more workers instead of party secretaries belong to the CC: "When, for example, I became a CC member, already at the first plenum I was amazed by the large number of ministers, directors, chairmen, and province committee first secretaries and secretaries. I understand that province committee first secretaries should participate in plenums of the CC, but probably not all should be members of it. Let them make space in it for social activists: workers, farmers, and creative intelligentsia." There are so "few of us" workers, she said, that we feel uncomfortable at plenums; "we feel nervous and timid; we are overwhelmed by the speeches of state figures."

Many complaints about this low representation of workers came to the leadership already in September and were voiced at the first post-Gierek plenum, the 6th plenum on October 4–6. The plenum took concrete steps to respond, adding 15 new full members to the CC and 8 new candidate members, many of whom were workers. As a result, at the end of the plenum about 35 of the 151 CC members were workers (plus 2 farmers), as against about 30 central government officials (exclusive of military) and 27 provincial and city party secretaries. Further expulsions and resignations from the CC over the coming months extended this trend.

In addition to adding workers to the CC, the October plenum gave recognition to the need to raise the role of workers in other ways. It created a 15-member commission on motions, in which workers were the largest element (5 workers plus a farmer, as against 4 CC secretaries, 3 regional party secretaries, and 1 deputy premier). And it promoted mining academy rector Roman Ney, who at the plenum had urged that at least half of the Politburo be workers and local representatives, to candidate member of the Politburo. Later, at the April 1981 plenum, two rank and file workers, Gerard Gabrys and Zygmunt Wronski, were elected full members of the Politburo—an unprecedented move.[34] Moreover, these two workers did not become officials; they continued to work at their factory jobs between Politburo sessions.

Nonofficials, especially workers, not only increased in numbers but also played an increasing role at plenums. At the October plenum, the 70-some speakers included 13 workers (including shipyard party secretary Miskiewicz) and 1 farmer, as compared with 14 regional secretaries, 12 Politburo and Secretariat members, and 5 demoted officials. At the December plenum, however, workers formed a much larger proportion: 14 (including Miskiewicz) out of the 48 speakers. Politburo members and central officials kept a much lower profile (only 1 Politburo member and 4 government officials spoke), leaving the floor to the 14 workers and 14 regional party secretaries. In a 218-member commission appointed at the December plenum to prepare for the upcoming congress, workers and farmers formed the biggest group. It included 59 workers and 12 farmers, as well as 14 local party secretaries (mainly factory-level secretaries, who probably were relatively close to rank and file workers in their sympathies or attitudes). Among other major groupings, the commission included 48 province and city party secretaries, 20 central government officials (including 3 military men), and 19 members of the Politburo and Secretariat.[35] At the February 9, 1981 plenum, workers comprised almost half the speakers: 10 out of 25 (exclusive of those who delivered main reports). Likewise, at the March 29 plenum, the 43 speakers included 20 workers (as against 5 province secretaries, 5 ministers, and 4 Politburo and Secretariat members).

The workers became more outspoken as well. Whereas at the October plenum most of the proposals for change were voiced by central and regional party officials and editors apparently responding to the ferment in the party, at later plenums workers themselves increasingly dominated the discussion by their sharp criticisms of the leadership and prodding for reform.

The process of adding workers to leadership bodies also proceeded at the local level. A November 19 Rzeszow province plenum added 6 new members (including 4 workers and farmers) to the province committee's Executive Committee, 5 new members (including 3 workers) to the province committee itself, and 11 members (including 6 workers) to the province control commission.[36] A November 17 Czestochowa plenum added 15 farmers and workers as province committee members and 9 as candidate members, as well as adding 4 to its Executive Committee.[37] Workers were also added to province committees or Executive Committees at October plenums in Katowice, Olsztyn, Elblag, Tarnow, Bialystok, Tarnobrzeg, and Biala Podlaska, at November plenums in Gdansk, Nowy Sacz, and Slupsk, and at December plenums in Krosno, Poznan, Zamosc, Kielce, and Lublin.

REBELLION AGAINST HIGHER ORGANS

The main driving force for reform in the party came from below, from the rank and file which had become alienated from the party leadership. Party members and local organizations had come to regard higher authorities in general as corrupt and interested only in protecting their power and privileges. It was the party base that kept up constant pressure for change, forcing Kania and other leaders to accept more meaningful reform than they wished to. Party members no longer obediently accepted orders from above; they spoke out and used the rights existing in the party statute and, when necessary, went beyond these rights. The atmosphere in the party changed dramatically, and central authorities lost effective control over many local party organizations at this juncture—even before any changes in the statute and election rules.

The most extreme expression of the rebelliousness in party ranks was the so-called horizontal ties movement. Convinced that existing party organs and their undemocratically elected leaders would not really reform anything, some local party organizations began joining together to form new coordinating organs independent of the existing party structure. Since these ties were between primary party organizations or factory party organizations at the lowest level, they became known as "horizontal"—as opposed to the normal "vertical" structures, where higher bodies sent down orders to lower, subordinate bodies (the CC to province committees, province committees to city committees, etc.). By banding together, local party organizations could pressure the entrenched officials in the regular party structure to go along with reforms. The movement represented a basic violation of democratic centralism and a challenge to the whole system.

The party leadership was not as negative to this movement as one might have expected. Some party leaders welcomed this activism in the party base as a healthy reinvigoration of party life. Others, however, fought the movement, accusing it of undermining party discipline and unity, of factionalism, and of trying to subvert the whole party.

The movement spread rapidly, and by April 1981 held a national convention of horizontal units—the "Torun Forum." The radical denunciations of the party leadership and the existing system at the conference and the worldwide publicity for this movement frightened the party leadership into firmly opposing the movement. The efforts to form an alternative system of party organs subsequently faded in the face of roadblocks by a more determined leadership, and the horizontal ties organizers turned their energies more to winning control of regular party organs in the spring 1981 party election conferences.

The horizontal ties movement was one of the most original and controversial aspects of the 1980–81 changes. It would have institutionalized methods for dissatisfied party members to exert pressure on party leadership outside the normal channels controlled by the apparat—in effect, an alternative party within the party. Although the horizontal ties movement failed in its efforts to set up new institutions controlled from below, it played a big role in reformers' successful efforts to win control of many regular party organizations during the spring 1981 elections.

The drive for reform was closely linked with the anger and resentment against higher authorities—the gap between the "doly" (those below, or the lower ranks) and "gora" (those up there, or the higher ranks). The widespread attacks on party officials and especially on the apparat prompted Kania in his opening report to the December plenum to warn against "the widespread tendency" of blaming "the whole leadership cadre" for past abuses.[38] The party apparat became a special object of attack, since it typified the nonelected officials picked from above who dictated to local organizations. Bialystok First Secretary Stefan Zawodzinski complained in an April 3–5, 1981 *Gazeta Wspolczesna* interview that "a CC instructor feels more important than a province committee secretary, even though the first is only an employee while the second was elected by tens or even hundreds of thousands of members." Worker Jan Buras at the December CC plenum declared that party activists did not want apparat workers to be over any party organs and insisted that CC decisions on the congress or election campaign should be "announced by the Secretariat or Politburo and not by the CC Organizational Department." "One must uphold the principle that only a higher organ or the party statute, and not the will and opinion of one of the CC departments, can be over the party in a region," he said.[39] Reformers pressed for establishment of commissions and other bodies made up of rank and file or elected officials to take over as much of the apparat's functions as possible. The 1981 revised party statute subordinated the apparat to elected organs, defining its role as a "serving function" for party organs.[40]

Party organizations began asserting their independence from higher organs and proposed revisions in the party statute and election rules to reduce control from above. Some actually rejected orders from above (see chapter 2 for examples), and occasionally expressions of opposition to control by higher organs were quite direct. A February 1981 article in the CC organizational journal *Zycie Partii* reported an official Gdansk party unit as laying down the principle that "mistakes in cadre policy begin precisely at the moment one departs from the principle of elective democracy and applies a system of recommendations by higher organs," since officials then are responsible to higher organs and not to their electors.[41]

The system of controlling party appointments from above—the "nomenklatura" or list of posts whose occupants must be approved by higher organs—also came under attack and was weakened. For example, the Bialystok Executive Committee cut its province nomenklatura in half (from 984 to 472 names) and promised further reduction.[42] There was emotional debate over the system at the July 1981 congress, with most speakers supporting the system but insisting it be opened to people "regardless of party affiliation and worldview" and that appointments be made openly.[43] Even after the martial law regime halted reform, the size of the nomenklatura stayed below its previous level.[44]

The anger against the authorities and distrust of party officials led some party members and local organizations to get together informally to coordinate actions and soon to form coordinating committees of local party organizations in order to stimulate reforms which existing party organizations were unenthusiastic about. Many incumbent party officials saw this as a threat to their authority and took action against this so-called horizontal ties movement. In fact, according to an article in the Krakow paper *Gazeta Krakowska* (May 19, 1981), in most areas relations between horizontal units and regular party organs were poor and got worse as regular organs sought to abolish their new competitors.

The movement began in the city of Torun, at the Towimor plant, which was the first plant in Torun to go on strike in August 1980 in response to the Gdansk strikes. Party members at the plant became rebellious and called for a new election in their party committee "without waiting for instructions from above."[45] On September 14 they elected a new plant committee, the first such new election in Poland.[46] The thirty-two-year-old economic secretary of the old plant party committee, Zbigniew Iwanow, a member of the strike committee, was elected first secretary. According to a *Polityka* account, Iwanow said: "I announced to my comrades that I am a believer and practice [my religion]," but "they accepted me" anyway. All the other incumbent secretaries were defeated, and the whole plant party committee joined the new Solidarity union.[47]

The Towimor committee under Iwanow and the party organization of the Social Sciences Institute of Mikolaj Kopernik University in Torun joined with seven other big plant party organizations in Torun to coordinate activities and at the end of October created a "Consultative Commission of Party Organizations" (Komisja Porozumiewawcza Organizacji Partyjnych) to work out "from below" a party program for the upcoming congress which would be "binding" on Torun's delegates to the congress.[48] The organizers declared that creation of the commission was a "result of the passiveness and lack of proposals" on the part of the Torun city and province party committees, according to *Polityka*.

The organs which appeared in Torun began to be labeled "horizontal" (*poziomy*) because they linked local party organizations horizontally, as against the normal "vertical" (*pionowy*) chain of command. These units did not usually call themselves "horizontal"; in various provinces they were called "party debate clubs" (*dyskusyjny klub partyjny*), "political thought forums" (*forum mysli politycznej*), etc. Their basic characteristic was that they were formed of representatives from local organizations rather than appointees from above. Thus, for example, even Gdansk's officially established "Precongress Commission" (Przedzjazdowa Komisja) was considered a horizontal unit because its members were elected from below.[49] Legnica's "Province Congress Commission" (Wojewodzka Komisja Zjazdowa)—whose members had been picked by the province party committee—was transformed into a horizontal unit in May 1981; renamed a "Province Congress Forum" (Wojewodzkie Forum Zjazdowe), its members were thereafter "designated by individual party organizations" from below.[50]

The movement spread rapidly from Torun. Correspondent Bernard Margueritte reported in *Le Figaro*, December 1, 1980, that such consultative commissions had already been established in several other cities, including Warsaw, where seventy party cells had joined. He wrote that these organizations were demanding a party congress and had threatened to organize their own congress and even suggested forming a new party. Correspondent Bernard Guetta in the December 2 *Le Monde* reported the mid-November emergence of horizontal coordination between cells which by early December had spread to seventeen provinces.

Local meetings of these horizontal structures pressed for reform and challenged democratic centralism. For example, a December 17 meeting of an "Interunit Party Forum" (Miedzysrodowiskowy Forum Partyjny) attended by representatives of many party organizations held a long, controversy-filled debate in Krakow on the functioning of democratic centralism.[51] A "lively debate" occurred over a proposition that a higher party body "have the right to set aside a resolution of a subordinate organization if it conflicts with a resolution of the higher body and have the right to remove the Executive Committee of a lower level or some of its members in case of failure to carry out the party program or resolutions of the higher body."

The new horizontal organs attempted to carefully abide by the party statute, but foes in the apparat soon asserted that they were creating a "second party" and causing a split in the PZPR.[52] Foes labeled it the "Torun infection."[53] Torun authorities initiated action against the movement's leader, Iwanow, and on November 24 the Torun party control commission and later (March 3) the Central Party Control Commission in Warsaw voted to expel him from the party for factional action, violating democratic centralism, and expressing views incompatible with the party line.[54] Iwanow aggravated matters with controversial statements, for example, telling a Szczecin Debate Forum on May 14, 1981 that "I never was a communist, I always was a social democrat."[55] The Towimor party organization defied the higher authorities by reelecting him its first secretary.[56]

Although much of the party apparat in Torun and elsewhere was openly hostile to the horizontal ties movement, more liberal party organizations found it possible to coexist and even work with these new organs. A spokesman for the movement later said in *Gazeta Krakowska*, April 29, 1981, that "many" province committees worked well with the horizontal structures. He attributed many of the attacks on the movement to "misunderstanding of intentions" and argued that after the initial conflicts "a considerable part of the apparat" had evolved in "the direction not only of understanding the movement but of correctly appreciating it" as a "chance to rejuvenate the party." At the March 1981 plenum, liberal Krakow First Secretary Krystyn Dabrowa cautioned against condemning horizontal ties "too easily and in a simplified manner," since they represented an opportunity to rebuild ties between the party's top and bottom.[57]

Moreover, there was some sympathy for the movement even in the CC apparat itself. At the end of November the CC's Organizational Department studied the movement and sent the Politburo and province committees a rather objective analysis of it, portraying it as a natural outgrowth of the failures of existing party organizations and the distrust of authorities and indicating it was making a contribution to enlivening and democratizing the party and producing proposals for reform.[58] The report did note some negative features, such as "instigators from outside" and "tendencies to set primary party organizations against the party leadership." Asked about horizontal structures at an early April Bialystok meeting, Kurowski, the CC secretary in charge of organizational work, called them "valuable initiatives, drawing in the most involved people" and said they "must be developed because they bring much that is new into precongress discussion."[59] At the December plenum Kania himself gave some praise to local party organizations for showing initiative in coordinating work and exchanging views, although he warned that "factionalism and splitting activities cannot be tolerated in the party."[60]

Meanwhile, conservatives were attacking the horizontal ties movement and some of its defenders in the party establishment. At the March 29–30 plenum CC Secretary Tadeusz Grabski assailed former Politburo member Andrzej Werblan, who had been especially outspoken in defense of the movement and even of expelled horizontal ties leader Iwanow. Grabski jibed that Werblan, who he said did "so little for the cause of expanding intraparty democracy" during his "many years" as a member of the Politburo and Secretariat, was now going overboard in propounding forms of intraparty democracy, even forms in violation of the party statute.[61] Werblan defended himself at the plenum against Grabski's "sharp" criticism of "my views on the matters of democracy and so-called horizontal structures" and concretely about "the expulsion of Comrade Zbigniew Iwanow from the party." Werblan defended horizontal structures and, on the Iwanow case, declared that it should involve "debate, polemics, and criticism but not organizational sanctions."[62] Grabski stepped up his attack on the movement after the plenum, at an April 11 local election conference in Krakow. He denounced efforts to promote horizontal structures and refusal of these units to recognize the legitimate authority of higher party committees as "factionalism."[63]

Despite the conservative attacks on the horizontal ties movement, the party leadership decided to cooperate with it and try to demonstrate the party's receptivity to reform. Horizontal ties leaders for some time were attempting to organize a national convention of horizontal units, but until March or early April the party leadership would "not agree to holding it, asserting that it would have a factional character."[64] But in early April CC Secretary Kurowski expressed support for such a convention,[65] and representatives of the Torun horizontal ties unit were informed that CC officials themselves would attend the gathering.[66] The *Polityka* article, April 25, 1981, which reported the latter fact interpreted it as amounting to official "recognition." The Organizational Department not only sent representatives but even helped with funding. As *Polityka*'s writers Marta Wesolowska and Piotr Moszynski wrote, "The newborn child with amazement ascertained that it had more parents than expected."

The conference was called the "Precongress Party Consultative Forum" (Przedzjazdowe Forum Porozumienia Partyjnego) and was held on April 15 in Torun, with one thousand representatives from over a dozen provinces. It was attended by deputy chief of the Organizational Department Lukasiewicz and even by Torun First Secretary Zygmunt Najdowski—something *Polityka* characterized as a "pleasant surprise" for participants. This suggested a surprising turnabout on the part of Najdowski. His party organization had fought the movement aggressively and only weeks earlier was reported as having denounced the Torun horizontal ties commission for fighting legal party bodies and for claiming "a monopoly on renewal."[67] Interviewers asked Najdowski during the forum whether holding the present forum meant a change in relations between the Torun province party committee and horizontal units.[68] The April 25 *Polityka* even carried a photo of Najdowski and Iwanow together, as if to signal Najdowski's softer attitude. However, when a reporter later asked him if the photo meant a reconciliation, he denied this and stated with irritation that it had been published "without my consent."[69]

Although the outspoken delegates at the forum voiced harsh criticisms of the party leadership and advanced radical proposals,[70] Lukasiewicz and former Politburo member Andrzej Werblan, now director of the Institute of Basic Problems of Marxism-Leninism, both addressed the forum. And at a press conference during the forum, reported by the local paper *Gazeta Pomorska*, April 17–20, 1981, Lukasiewicz said that the Organizational Department and CC Secretary Kurowski supported the forum. Najdowski also praised the forum, and he and Lukasiewicz both denied that their organizations had ever used the term "Torun infection," according to *Gazeta Pomorska*.

The mid-April Torun Forum, however, appears to have been the peak. The great publicity won by the movement at the forum proved its undoing. The numerous Western reporters and television crews and the extensive Western coverage of the events as a dramatic movement directed against the leadership not only provoked harsh reaction in other communist states but alarmed many party officials in Poland and helped sway even some moderates against the movement. Thereafter, the leadership's attitude hardened and it refused to permit any more such gatherings.

The shift and the reasons for it were most clearly conveyed in the lengthy comments on the movement by CC Organizational Department deputy chief Lukasiewicz at the April 29–30 CC plenum. Even though the forum was "organized with the knowledge of the CC and province committee," he complained, it "was used by certain forces in the West and also by some forces inside the country to set the horizontal movement against the party leadership," and "one must fully understand that even in spite of the intentions of its participants the movement can be pushed into factional positions and therefore be used to weaken, to negate achievements of, and even split the party. . . . Why do I say this? . . .The debate at the forum did not depart from what you hear now in the party and at various meetings, but the very fact that the forum met was presented in Western propaganda as the creation of a new center [*osrodek dyspozycyjny*] in the party and as a sign of the PZPR's departure from Leninism." Moreover, he indicated that press reaction in socialist countries was negative, while within Poland the publicity, the forum's appeals, and also its pressure on the CC plenum "show that some (I stress, some) participants in this movement are crossing the delicate line of debate and criticism and are undertaking organizational actions, and from there, as we know, it is not far to actions outside the statute."[71]

Lukasiewicz's supervisor, CC Organizational Secretary Barcikowski, also appeared to shift toward a more negative appraisal after the Torun Forum. In an April 27 discussion in Warsaw's Karl Marx Debate Club, he stated (in *Trybuna Ludu*'s paraphrasing) that the Torun meeting had "seriously weakened the faith of our friends in our party's ability to manage the crisis. The situation in our party is the subject of lively interest both in the East as well as in the West."[72] A *Gazeta Krakowska* article by Marian Szulc about the horizontal and vertical organizations (May 19, 1981) conceded that "from Western newspapers, whose correspondents—though not specially invited—were present in Torun, you could learn that the party was falling apart." "I have no doubt" that if one takes excerpts from the forum speeches criticizing the leadership and sets them against attacks on horizontal units by leaders, "one could see evidence of a 'state of war.' "

Disagreement over the horizontal structures became the hottest issue of debate at the April 29–30 CC plenum. The issue was aggravated by the fact that the horizontal units sent observers to the plenum and that the Politburo then decided to bar them from attendance. This decision was communicated to the observers at the last minute, on April 29, and produced protests. Radio broadcasts on April 29 reported that Torun's consultative commission had protested this exclusion and that the home party organization of Torun First Secretary Najdowski had sent him a telex message "instructing" him to formally propose to the plenum the admission of these observers.[73]

The debate on the movement at the plenum was heated but inconclusive. As before, First Secretary Kania took an ambiguous but moderate position. In his opening report, he praised the development of "various discussion commissions and groups" for "enlivening" the party, but cautioned that such activity must not undermine traditional party structures.[74] Several speakers still strongly defended the horizontal structures: Bialystok First Secretary Stefan Zawodzinski argued that they worked well with his province party organization in Bialystok and that "none of the informal leaders of the forum intends to create another center of political power or is calling for departure from the principles of Marxism-Leninism or democratic centralism." Deputy Premier and *Polityka* editor Mieczyslaw Rakowski, whose magazine *Polityka* had presented the Torun movement sympathetically, argued that the hostility between horizontal structures and party leadership organs was mainly a matter of "misunderstanding." Addressing claims that the movement was a threat, Gdansk shipyard worker Jan Labecki argued that "if we don't recognize it, channel it, and use it for the good of the party, it can indeed threaten us." Denying accusations that he was promoting the movement in hopes of using it to return to power, former Politburo member Andrzej Werblan declared that the "only sensible policy" is to debate with it and work with it to "hasten its political maturation," since fighting it will push it to "extremes." He complained that "the CC's positive step of recognizing the Torun Forum was quickly weakened by exaggerated and panicky information about threats which were outlined there."[75] Legnica worker Genowefa Maciejewska declared that "horizontal contacts in our party are created by the will of its members and were an answer to the absence of decisive action by the party leadership and were a result of the loss of confidence of the rank and file in the leadership." In cases where they have been fought by party organs, she said, "they have been pushed outside the borders of statutory action into factional forms."

Several speakers attacked the horizontal movement and especially the Torun Forum. Lodz worker Halina Zielinska called the horizontal structures "dangerous because they threaten to break the unity of the party by creating various centers [*osrodki dyspozycyjne*] outside the CC." Conservative writer and editor Jerzy Putrament assailed Werblan for delivering a speech at the Torun Forum, a body which he said pleased the West as an "anticommunist center."[76] Central Auditing Commission member Kazimierz Kakol criticized the "presence of prominent representatives of party bodies at a factional convention" and complained about all the American reporters "invited" to the forum. He also criticized the reelection of horizontal ties originator Iwanow, "who was expelled from the party, rightly or wrongly, but expelled," as first secretary of a Torun party organization.[77]

In his closing speech, Kania still avoided a clear stand, but appeared more negative. He noted that some speakers "asserted that we should do nothing to aggravate the situation and create tension in party organizations," and "we in the Central Committee also want this very much." Yet as a member of the leadership, he must "stress my fears—about the creation of permanent structures, the creation of centers of leadership," since the "most important thing" is the unity of the party and its ability to act.[78]

Some other leaders expressed their opposition after the plenum. At a May meeting in Opole, Katowice First Secretary Andrzej Zabinski flatly stated that "Comrade Andrzej Werblan headed and supported this movement" and jibed that Werblan had earlier been personal secretary to Poland's Stalinist leader Boleslaw Bierut, as well as adviser to Gomulka and Gierek, but now was changing his views. Zabinski also stated that in his province, representatives of horizontal structures had been "coopted into the province congress commission" and were not dangerous there.[79] At a mid-May question-and-answer session at Krakow's Jagiellonian University, Olszowski responded to a question about horizontal units: "I am not a supporter of horizontal structures, and probably no one would suspect me of that."[80]

By the time the next plenum was held, on June 9, the shift of attitude was striking. Although Kania's remarks were relatively mild and non-committal (his main complaint was that some horizontal units were trying to take over party organizations), many speakers assailed the horizontal structures and no one defended them.[81] For example, Gorzow First Secretary Ryszard Labus claimed that they were taking advantage of current party elections to circulate lists of candidates to strike off in order to ensure election of the candidates they favored. He insisted that "the destructive activity of some horizontal structures" should be "recognized as factional activity."[82] Warsaw worker Albin Siwak urged expelling Andrzej Werblan from the party for his activities in supporting such divisive movements.[83] Editor Mieczyslaw Rog-Swiostek asserted that horizontal units were already announcing that at the coming congress they would block election of the present Politburo members to the presidium of the congress and that they already had an alternative list of CC members.[84] The plenum's resolution declared that horizontal units "which do not abide by the principles of democratic centralism and create their own centers of leadership independent of the statutory party organs" will be regarded as conducting "factional activity" and must cease.[85] CC Secretary Olszowski did not speak at the June plenum but in a June 4 speech asserted that the Torun Forum demonstrated "the goal of changing the character of the party into a social democratic one."[86]

Plans had been started to hold a second forum, in Gdansk, but these came to nothing, apparently because the alarm in the leadership after the Torun Forum prompted the CC to stop its encouragement and sponsorship. At the conclusion of the Torun Forum, the Gdansk affiliate (called a "precongress commission") invited the delegates to a second forum, to be held in Gdansk in May.[87] On April 27, 1981, the Gdansk paper *Glos Wybrzeza* reported that the Gdansk commission was appealing to the CC to help organize the second forum in early June. At the April 29–30 plenum, Labecki discussed the effort to call a second forum, but indicated that the latest organizing session had decided to only hold it if the CC and Politburo or province committee gave its approval.[88] Another conference of Gdansk horizontal units on May 4 appealed to the Politburo to help organize a second forum in early June to discuss material for the congress.[89] Some began discussing the possibility of a forum in Silesia, on the basis that that area is the "biggest and therefore potentially most opinion-setting part of the party."[90] The Krakow party committee on May 21 "urgently" asked the Politburo to call a Krakow province conference of horizontal units.[91] However, it appears that the CC never did give its approval for a second forum, and as the May-July elections of new local leaders and delegates to the congress got under way, the horizontal movement seems to have focused its efforts on trying to influence the elections and organize elected delegates, rather than institutionalizing horizontal ties.[92]

The case of the expelled Torun horizontal ties leader Iwanow continued to drag on and kept the Torun party organization in turmoil. Iwanow, still head of his local party committee although technically no longer even a party member, stirred new controversy by running for delegate to the Torun city party conference. The May 28 Torun city party conference hotly debated whether to recognize Iwanow's credentials as a delegate from the Towimor party organization and voted 363 to 354 to seat him, despite the fact that the Central Party Control Commission had expelled him from the party. The rationale was that Iwanow was appealing the decision to the congress and so his expulsion was not final.[93] The losers were so angry that 180, including province First Secretary Najdowski, threw down their credentials as delegates and walked out. Some, including Najdowski, returned after a while, but Najdowski announced "that in this situation he would not run for election as a delegate to the province party conference."[94]

Iwanow later told an interviewer that during a break in the session Najdowski and CC Ideology Department head Walery Namiotkiewicz had tried to talk him into resigning as a delegate "in the name of party unity," but he had refused because he felt that the party needed alternatives, not unity.[95] Eventually, however, he did decide not to run for delegate to the province conference.[96]

After the walkout, the remaining delegates sent a letter to Kania asking him to attend the second stage of the city conference when it resumed on June 4 and asking him to condemn those who walked out. Those who walked out wrote Kania asking him to take their side against this "violation of principles of democratic centralism."[97] Kania replied with a letter calling Iwanow's election as a delegate illegitimate but also criticizing the other side for walking out. He urged reconciliation.[98]

When the city conference resumed on June 4, Najdowski appealed for a decision on whether Iwanow should participate in the second stage and urged readmission of the delegates who walked out. The conference voted 302 to 286 against readmitting the protesters.[99] Iwanow gave a speech calling the PZPR "unreformable" and based on "principles of feudal obedience and wrongly understood unity" and argued that the remedy was for the party to have alternative programs to choose from. Nevertheless, Iwanow was well received by the conference, which accepted his proposal to strip former province First Secretary Boleslaw Kapitan of his title of Sejm deputy. The conference elected a commission to study the materials the Central Party Control Commission had used to expel Iwanow, with the aim of making a Torun recommendation on the case to the congress.[100]

When the province conference opened on June 17, First Secretary Najdowski in his opening report denied that the party apparat was picking on "poor Iwanow" and cited Kania's letter calling the city conference's decision contrary to the party statute. Some delegates moved to allow Najdowski to run for reelection even though he was not a delegate to the province conference, but Najdowski continued to insist that he would not run.[101]

Hence, by early 1981, after only a few months of "renewal," substantial reforms—new election rules, more worker representation in the leadership, and even some reduction of democratic centralism—had been firmly implanted in the party. Democratization in the party may have been triggered or forced by Solidarity's direct and indirect pressure, but it quickly developed a momentum of its own within the party. Local party organizations demanded change, and "horizontal" units, even though not accepted and institutionalized, exerted organized pressure from below for more reform. Leaders at various levels recognized defects in the system, and First Secretary Kania himself went along with many of the proposals for reform. These reforms were to produce a drastic transformation of the communist party, altering the relationship between upper and lower organs and putting in question the party leadership's ability to lead the party. The most dramatic effects came via the new uncontrolled party election procedures, which began taking hold locally and gradually working up the structure, bringing widespread replacement of old leaders with new ones more sympathetic to reform (see chapter 2).

CHAPTER 2
REFORM IN ELECTION PROCEDURES

THE MOST IMPORTANT of the reforms clearly was democratization of party elections, since it opened the way for a peaceful revolution in the party. Party reformers focused on the need to bring an end to the traditional elections controlled from above and to establish elections where the rank and file could make their will felt. The rank and file, angry and resentful at years of domination by high-handed officials who felt no obligation to the members of their organizations, used the democratized election procedures to throw out the leaders they regarded as corrupt and unresponsive.

The process of election reform began spontaneously at the bottom. Already in September local party organizations began demanding changes in the party election rules, and some organizations began holding elections on their own, voting out incumbents or forcing Warsaw to encourage unpopular local leaders to resign. Some adopted their own more democratic election rules and presented their members with a choice of candidates to replace the ousted incumbents.

Party leaders reacted to this pressure by hastening to put forward revised election rules providing for secret balloting, the right to nominate opposition candidates, and guarantees against dictation from above. Continuing pressure forced the leadership to gradually liberalize the rules ever further. The Politburo also quickly began retreating from its practice of blatantly dictating the choice of leaders for local organizations. In choosing local first secretaries, Politburo representatives began consulting beforehand with local party officials and even ordinary members and presenting as candidates for leadership those local men suggested by local officials and who had the most support in the organizations concerned.

On some occasions when Warsaw tried to push changes on local organizations, their suggestions were resisted or even rejected.

At first, only the lowest-level party organizations offered their members a choice of candidates to replace ousted incumbent leaders. But during October and November local government bodies began using secret balloting with two or more candidates to elect their council chairmen. In January 1981 province party committee plenums began using secret balloting in choosing new first secretaries and occasionally nominating two candidates for the post. By spring even the CC began using secret balloting at its plenums and publicizing the voting results, instead of claiming unanimity and keeping splits secret.

The new democratized election procedures were first put into universal practice during the late spring nationwide party elections. In preparation for the July 1981 party congress, all party organizations had to hold conferences and elect leaders and also delegates to conferences at the next level. The process was capped by the June province conferences, which chose province party committees and first secretaries and delegates to the congress. Normally in the past these conferences were carefully stage-managed by the party apparat and simply elected candidates selected from above. But with the new democratized procedures and the strong demand for change, the rank and file, rather than incumbent officials or higher organs, were able to dominate most party conferences. Central officials avoided trying to select local leaders, and local party members nominated their own candidates to run against incumbent leaders. Delegates, for the first time able to really exercise choice, expressed their frustration at years of dictation from above by voting large numbers of incumbent officials out of office. These elections, thoroughly reported in local papers, provide the best examples of how intraparty democracy actually worked during this period.

The Polish leaders found it difficult to influence these conferences, many of which flatly refused to elect any national leaders to their delegations to the congress. Kania appealed to some conferences to elect at least some of the incumbent CC members as delegates in order to preserve a little continuity in leadership. Even the Politburo members themselves had difficulty winning election to the congress. Some—such as Barcikowski and Olszowski—were humbled by having to overcome stiff opposition to gain election as delegates. Four of the nineteen members of the Politburo were not even elected delegates and hence lost any chance to be reelected to the CC and its top bodies.

These uncontrolled elections elected a body of delegates to the congress which proved difficult for party leaders to manipulate, and at the congress almost all incumbent CC members (of those who managed to become delegates) were defeated for reelection to the CC. The result of the whole election was a massive purge—conducted from below—with the rank and file taking an unprecedented degree of control over the party, from primary party organizations to the CC.

REFORM OF ELECTION RULES

Central to party reform was the wave of demands to change the party election rules and statute. These proposals centered on establishing the universal practice of secret balloting, the right to have at least two candidates for each post and to nominate candidates from the floor, and the right of party organizations to pick their own leaders and representatives independent of higher organs. Moderates in the leadership promptly took up these proposals and tried to satisfy reform demands by quickly working out a new, considerably democratized set of election rules which were adopted already at the December 1980 plenum. Work on a revised party statute proceeded much more slowly, however, since it was conducted in a large, formal commission which included prominent conservatives who resisted many reforms. Nevertheless, most reform demands were eventually worked into both documents.

The leadership appeared to have no real choice but to reform. The rank and file anger against the leadership was so strong that some party organizations simply used their own rules to oust unwanted leaders. The reform of the election rules and statute to provide choice of candidates and secret balloting, combined with the rebelliousness of party organizations, virtually demolished democratic centralism and enabled the party rank and file to oust most incumbent leaders in local and national party organizations.

Demands for reform of the party statute and election rules erupted already during September at local party meetings, many of which sent proposals or outright demands for reform to the CC. At the October plenum, for example, Wroclaw worker Janina Kostrzewska stated that her factory party committee on September 23 had sent a list of proposed changes in the statute and election rules to the CC's Organizational Department.[1] Kania in his opening report to the October plenum mentioned the resolutions from various party organizations proposing secret balloting and other changes in election rules.

Moderates responded to this pressure by hurriedly preparing new election rules which went a long way toward satisfying reformers' demands. As a result, while the rank and file repeatedly assailed the leadership for slowness in working out economic reforms, in punishing former leaders, and in taking other actions during late 1980 and early 1981, rank and file spokesmen were caught by surprise by the speed with which the new election rules appeared and wound up voicing suspicion that the new rules were being pushed through before they could be properly discussed.

The speedy reform of election rules was possible because the CC Organizational Department, which received the local proposals for changes and which worked out the new rules during October and November, was controlled by officials sympathetic to reform, who recognized the defects under Gierek, and who after August 1980 openly and strongly advocated party reform. Upon Gierek's fall, Zdzislaw Kurowski was elected junior CC secretary for organizational affairs at the September 1980 plenum,[2] while Kazimierz Barcikowski was elected senior organizational secretary at the October plenum.[3] Kurowski and Barcikowski supervised the working out of the new rules and publicly promoted these rules for their democratic features. In a speech reported in the January 15, 1981 *Trybuna Ludu*, Barcikowski praised the provisions in the new rules allowing for 50 percent more candidates than positions and for the use of secret balloting. Kurowski in a November 29–30, 1980 *Trybuna Ludu* article promoted the new rules for "ensuring more influence" for local party organizations and reducing the apparat to a "serving role." In a February 3, 1981 *Trybuna Ludu* article on the renewal process, Kurowski wrote that "the most important effect" of the new rules "is the creation of real conditions for secrecy in elections, free nomination of candidates for leadership and as delegates, restoring the practice of consultations to its proper place, and ensuring authentic influence of party members in the election of leaders and in the content of programs of action. . . . We understand the application of the principle of democratic centralism as observing in practice the necessary balance between centralism and democracy."

The draft rules were sent out to CC members in late November and presented already at the early December plenum for adoption. They met general approval at the plenum. Only one member—Gdansk seaman Czeslaw Drozdowicz—complained that they fell short of party members' expectations.[4] Some members did complain that they had received the draft rules only on the eve of the plenum and the leadership was not giving local party organizations enough time to discuss them,[5] but the rules were approved anyway (as "provisional").[6]

The new rules were published in the February 1981 issue of the CC's organizational journal, *Zycie Partii*, along with explanation of how they differed from the old rules. The journal stated that the old rules had been subjected to "universal criticism in primary party organizations for limiting intraparty democracy." The new rules were a big step forward in democratization, although they also contained a few limiting provisions which became targets of reformers. The most important features of the new draft rules were:

- Party members were given more rights to nominate alternative candidates for party posts, opening the door for more choice and for challenging incumbents. In addition to the number of candidates nominated by the official election commission of the congress or conference—usually exactly equaling the number of positions to be filled—delegates at a congress or conference now could nominate up to 50 percent more candidates. The earlier rules had provided only a very small range of choice, allowing only 15 percent more candidates than positions. One provision clearly handicapped opposition groups, however; it specified that each delegate could nominate only one candidate from the floor. Hence, any attempts to nominate enough candidates to defeat the official slate would require organization of a large number of people to each nominate one candidate.
- Secret balloting was extended to virtually all party elections, although if a majority so wished, a meeting could use open voting for election of secretaries and Executive Committees. The list sys-

tem was to be used in voting for the CC and other party committees: delegates would receive a list of candidates and cross off the names of those they opposed. They had to reduce the list to no more than the number of positions available or the ballot would be considered invalid. Candidates would be ranked according to the number of votes they received and, to be elected, had to fall in ranking within the number of positions available and additionally get over 50 percent of the votes. In voting for secretaries and Executive Committees (or the Politburo), the CC members or regional committee members first had to elect a first secretary, who then would prepare a list of nominees for the Secretariat and Executive Committee (or Politburo), who were then voted on in secret. Nominations from the floor of up to 50 percent more candidates were also permitted in these elections.

- The powers of higher party organs over lower organs were reduced. Most important, the new rules limited the role of higher organs to simply confirming the "correctness" of the procedure followed by local organizations in electing their secretaries. The old rules specified that secretaries elected by lower organizations must be "confirmed by higher party organs." In this, the new rules actually ran counter to the existing party statute, which, as *Zycie Partii* pointed out, still specified that secretaries elected in lower organs were subject to confirmation by higher party organs.
- Concentration of power in the hands of local (or national) leaders was barred. The rules added a provision banning persons from holding several elective party posts at the same time or simultaneously holding party and state posts.
- The possibilities for manipulation to ensure election of high officials were severely hampered by several provisions. The rules indicated that candidates were to be chosen from among delegates at the conference in question and that outsiders could only become candidates at a conference if the conference specially voted to allow them this right. This provision became very important during the spring 1981 election of delegates to the July party congress, since many province conferences refused to allow outsiders to run for any offices, making it very hard for national leaders to find any conference that would elect them delegates to the congress. In addition, the new rules stipulated that persons who run at one

conference and are defeated are ineligible to run at any other conference during the same election campaign.

Many party members were dissatisfied even with the more democratic rules, however, and insisted on using even more liberalized rules. In early March Krakow Secretary Zdzislaw Les revealed that only 146 of 700 recent local party elections had used the new rules, while the rest used "rules spontaneously worked out in the organizations themselves."[7] He explained that party members were especially dissatisfied because they wanted to be able to put up a whole list of alternative candidates instead of being limited to only 50 percent and that they insisted that election commissions at conferences only "passively register candidates nominated during consultations before the conference" instead of choosing candidates and acting as a possible tool of higher organs. He noted that many wanted to elect their local first secretaries directly at their conferences instead of allowing their party committee to do so. (He raised objections to this procedure on grounds that it would make the first secretary responsible only to the whole party organization and hence too powerful; it would mean that only the next party election conference could replace him, instead of the party committee.)

Pressure for further democratization thus continued, and finally the leadership caved in and further liberalized the rules. The March 1981 plenum, "considering numerous remarks and proposals from party members and party organizations," amended the rules to remove the limit of only 50 percent more candidates than posts, throwing nominations open to an unlimited number of candidates.[8] The revisions also further restricted the use of open voting and the role of higher organs at election meetings (totally excluding representatives of higher organs from the work of vote-tallying commissions, for example).[9]

The election rules were not finally settled even at the July 1981 congress. The congress passed a resolution ordering the CC to continue work on the draft rules and present them for more discussion by party organizations. It stipulated that they were to be adopted at a national conference of congress delegates to be held in the near future.[10] They were finally adopted formally by a March 1984 national conference of delegates and published in the March 28, 1984 *Zycie Partii*.

The moderates did not dominate efforts to revise the basic party statute, however, and work on the statute proceeded slowly, bogged down in protracted debates between liberals and conservatives over how far to go in reforms. The December plenum selected a 218-member "Congress Commission" to begin revising the statute and preparing a new party program. The overall commission was chaired by Kania, and its working group for intraparty life was headed by a moderate, Kurowski,[11] but conservative CC Secretary Olszowski headed the commission's Secretariat[12] and soon emerged as an outspoken foe of many proposed reforms in the commission debates. At a February 2 meeting of the congress commission held to discuss a draft program prepared by the commission, Olszowski objected to many of the proposals from local party organizations, for example, those which sought to undermine democratic centralism and the subordination of lower organs to central organs or which he said sought to change the ideological orientation of the party.[13] The commission became the stage for bitter squabbles between liberals and conservatives. For example, hard-line worker Albin Siwak later told of his nasty exchanges with reformist Journalists Union chairman Stefan Bratkowski during commission sessions.[14]

Nevertheless, a new draft statute was eventually produced for presentation to the July 1981 congress, and although not published, it appeared to constitute a considerable liberalization, judging by the description given by deputy head of the Organizational Department Lukasiewicz in the May 1981 *Zycie Partii*. He stated that the draft statute provided for secret balloting and an unlimited number of candidates in elections for committees and for delegates, limited officials to two terms of office (with the possibility of one additional term, if approved by a two-thirds vote), limited the number of posts a person could hold at the same time, defined the "sphere of competence and obligations" of the CC, Politburo, Secretariat, and first secretary, expanded openness of party procedures, and increased information on party actions. To prevent the party apparat from replacing elective organs as in the past, according to Lukasiewicz a new provision was added specifying that "party committees are superior to the party apparat, which stands at their disposal" and that "workers of the party apparat cannot represent elective bodies in the party or act and issue decisions in their name without authorization." The draft statute set the principle of "intraparty democracy" on an equal basis with "democratic centralism," according to Lukasiewicz, and stressed the need to "balance" democracy and centralism and avoid the "bureaucratic centralism" existing until 1980. It specified that "intraparty democracy and freedom of debate cannot be restricted or limited." At the same time, however, it also warned against "actions of a fractional character leading to establishment of formalized groups in the party which spread a particular program, a political line, rules of activity, and create an autonomous center as against the statutory party bodies." And to strengthen democratic centralism, said Lukasiewicz, the draft insisted that party organizations and members had the obligation to carry out resolutions and decisions of higher bodies adopted democratically, even if their own positions on the subject differed.

The new draft statute was finally presented to the party congress near the close of its proceedings, on Sunday, July 19. Kurowski, chairman of the Statute Commission elected by the congress on its first day, answered questions on the draft during seven hours of debate. Finally, at 11:00 A.M. Monday morning the congress voted to accept the draft (with 38 voting against and 53 abstaining). According to the brief July 21–22, 1981 *Trybuna Ludu* account, there was much discussion of changes in the draft, including its sections on democratic centralism.

The amended statute as finally adopted by the congress, a document of some forty-two pages, included a significant number of the guarantees demanded by reformers.[15] It carried an extensive section on election principles incorporating the principles of secret balloting and unlimited number of candidates. It even insisted that party members had to be presented a choice, specifying that "the number of candidates must exceed the number of elective positions." It specified that elective officials be limited to two terms, although it allowed committees in exceptional cases to allow a leader to run for a third term—if approved by a two-thirds vote. It declared that mandates of delegates to the congress or to conferences last until the next election of delegates. Hence, delegates to the party congress could reconvene if necessary and vote changes in the leadership which they elected at the congress. (Normally, the job of a delegate is over once the congress has been held; reformers in 1980–81 argued that delegates should have a continuing role, as another check on party leaders.) The statute's section on party organizations even gave limited approval to the formation of the controversial "horizontal" party units: "party organizations with the knowledge of the appropriate party committees can arrange joint work to exchange experience and work out proposals, opinions, and concepts which serve to enrich party activity," although these units have no rights over the party organizations joining them. The statute did include a section reaffirming democratic centralism. It stated that resolutions of higher organs "must be carried out" by lower organs, and it permitted province committees to dissolve party organizations "whose activity conflicts with the ideological principles, political line, program, and statute of the party." It banned "actions of a fractional character," defined as "consisting of creating formalized groups in the party, which spread a separate program, political line, and organizational principles, and create an autonomous center as against statutory party leadership bodies."

ELECTION CONTESTS AND SECRET BALLOTING

Nomination of alternate candidates and use of secret balloting began at the bottom as part of the drive to replace unpopular leaders. The rank and file in many places accused incumbent leaders of corruption and abuse of power, and Solidarity groups sometimes made the ouster of certain local leaders one of the conditions for ending local strikes. Not wanting to simply repeat the undemocratic elections of the past and citing the spirit of "renewal," some low-level party organizations chose their new leaders by new, more democratic procedures.

Apart from these sporadic local outbursts, the first opportunity for widespread use of new election practices occurred in the local government bodies—the province people's councils. Caving in to pressure to reduce local monopolies on power, Warsaw in October decided that province PZPR first secretaries should no longer also head the local government organs, and so starting in early November, province first secretaries began resigning as chairmen. In the subsequent elections of new council chairmen, more than one candidate was nominated in many areas and the elections were often conducted with secret, rather than open, balloting.

At the province level there was also widespread change of party leaders in late 1980—almost half of the forty-nine province first secretaries— but there was no choice of candidates or use of secret balloting. The Politburo still presented only one candidate—although it was more careful to now consult local leaders beforehand and present candidates with extensive local support, rather than outsiders. After adoption of the new election rules in December, province-level party committees also began using secret balloting and sometimes presenting two candidates. Spirited contests developed with no preference expressed by the Politburo and with the outcome apparently not predetermined. In other cases, contests were avoided by widespread preelection consultations, which developed a consensus behind one candidate. In some other provinces contests did not develop because there was less pressure for reform and traditional practices continued.

Slowest to change was the top. It was apparently late April before a CC plenum used secret balloting, and there were still no opposition candidates put up against the official nominees for promotion to the Politburo and Secretariat. Nevertheless, the voting results were for the first time publicly announced, revealing how many CC members had voted against the official candidates.

Many party organizations, eager to replace unpopular leaders, began clamoring for new elections as soon as Gierek fell, but new party-wide elections were only sanctioned by a decision of the late March 1981 CC plenum. By that time, however, 12 percent of party organizations had already gone ahead and held elections.[16] Some party meetings presented a choice of candidates and voted out incumbent leaders. For example, at a mine in Wodzislaw (Katowice province), fifty-one candidates were nominated for the twenty-nine seats on the mine's party committee, and among those defeated for membership in the committee was one of its top leaders—its representative in the ruling body for the whole province (the province committee's Executive Committee).[17] Province First Secretary Andrzej Zabinski, who was present, was so surprised that he questioned the results, and a revote was held, confirming the defeat.

Some local party organizations even adopted new, democratized election rules to make it easier to change leaders. Conservative Warsaw Secretary Henryk Szablak complained at the December CC plenum that "more and more organizations insist on beginning the election campaign relying on their own election rules,"[18] and reporter Izabella Wajszczuk wrote in the February 9, 1981 *Trybuna Ludu* that "many party organizations have conducted elections according to new instructions" which they themselves worked out. For example, an election conference of the Krakow Polytechnic party organization condemned the old election rules as "deviating from the spirit of the present time" and adopted new rules "formulated by itself" which stipulated secret voting, unlimited number of candidates, and a two-term limit on the first secretary and members of the Executive Committee.[19] Two candidates ran for first secretary of the school committee, and the voting was done by all delegates at the conference—an "innovation," according to the press account. Traditionally, first secretaries of party committees were elected by the party committees, but giving all delegates—not just the committee members— the right to participate in the election was judged more democratic.[20] This practice eventually spread to the national level, and the July 1981 party congress—rather than the CC elected by the congress—elected the party's first secretary.

The opportunity for wider introduction of more democratic election procedures came first on the local government side, rather than in the party. Growing pressure to break up concentrations of power in the hands of individual leaders prompted the October CC plenum to adopt a new "principle" of separation of government and party posts, whereby province party first secretaries had to surrender their posts as local government heads. The vacating of all these posts brought new elections for chairmen of the province people's councils (WRN—Wojewodzka Rada Narodowa) starting in late October, and many of these elections used secret balloting and presented a choice of candidates. Of forty-seven province people's council elections from the October plenum until the end of January, twenty-five reportedly used secret balloting, while seventeen used open balloting.[21] In nineteen cases it was indicated that there was more than one candidate, and in only fourteen was there reportedly only one candidate.[22] It appears that in most cases the new chairman was elected in a split vote—either because there was an opposing candidate, or, in cases where there was only one candidate, because some council members voted against the candidate or abstained. Of the twenty-nine cases where the press accounts gave details on the voting results, only seven were characterized as "unanimous" votes, the rest as split or including abstentions. Some votes were close. The victor in the Wroclaw council vote won by 75 to 52, the new Radom chairman was elected with 69 of the 117 valid votes, and the winner in Lodz received 81 votes to his opponent's 68.[23]

On the other hand, the contests were not completely uncontrolled. In most cases, it was indicated that all candidates had been nominated by prearrangement of local authorities, i.e., the leaders of the PZPR and other parties represented in the local council met ahead of time and agreed on the candidates who would run. The only cases where nominations from the floor were mentioned were at the December 18 Rzeszow session and December 22 Jelenia Gora meetings.[24] Nor was there evidence of rejection of officially selected candidates.

As part of the liberalization, the PZPR decided to share the top leadership posts with the other parties. Whereas earlier all province people's council chairmen had been PZPR members (the province communist party first secretaries), now in many cases members of other parties or "nonparty" persons were nominated for the post of chairman by the PZPR deputies to local councils in conjunction with deputies from other parties. About half of the chairmen elected during the period were non-PZPR members. An official report on 1980–81 events prepared for the July party congress stated that after the October plenum's decision against "automatic combination" of the posts of party first secretary and council chairman, forty-six provinces elected new council chairmen, and of these twenty-five (54.3 percent) were PZPR members, nine (19.6 percent) were ZSL (United Peasant Party) members, three (6.5 percent) were SD (Democratic Party) members, and nine (19.6 percent) were nonparty.[25]

It is unclear whether these elections provided any direct contests between PZPR and non-PZPR candidates (candidates from the ZSL or SD or independents). In twelve of the nineteen cases where it is clear that there were two or more candidates, non-PZPR members were elected.[26] However, the party identification of the losing candidates was not reported, leaving it uncertain whether any non-PZPR candidates actually defeated a PZPR candidate. It is likely that in most or all of these cases two or more non-PZPR candidates were nominated for the post and no PZPR candidate was even put up. Nevertheless, there were still contests between individuals, if not between parties.

While there were contests with two or more candidates already in November in province government elections, there were no contested elections at the province level in the party until well after the December plenum adopted the new election rules. There were twenty-two new province first secretaries elected from September to the end of December, but judging by the available local and national press accounts, there was always only one candidate and open balloting was used to elect him.[27]

The first contested election of a province committee first secretary occurred on January 23 at an Olsztyn province plenum and had the central leadership's sanction.[28] Politburo representative Kurowski nominated two candidates for the post of first secretary and stated that the Politburo had no favorite. He stated that in "advance consultations with the province party aktiv about the province committee first secretary, the candidates proposed most often were Zbigniew Bialecki and Wlodzimierz Mokrzyszczak." He announced that the "CC Politburo and Secretariat had adopted no decision on who should be first secretary in Olsztyn and had just approved the candidates." A lively debate over the candidates quickly developed, but one candidate withdrew before the vote, averting a showdown vote.[29]

A few days later, in February, a similar contest in Bielsko-Biala province actually came down to a vote, becoming the first province committee election where secret balloting was specifically used to select a new first secretary from among two candidates. The local paper reported that Politburo representative Kurowski, "after consultations with the party aktiv," proposed two candidates: province Secretary Andrzej Gdula and local factory director Tadeusz Paleczny. "In a secret vote," Gdula received 61 votes and Paleczny 18.[30]

Another contest occurred in Radom on March 16, with two candidates and secret balloting. The local paper reported that Politburo representative Grabski, after widespread consultations with local party members, presented two candidates: province committee agriculture secretary Bogdan Prus and director of a sales bureau Zdzislaw Kwiecinski. Grabski also stressed that other candidates could be nominated from the floor— although none were. The secret vote resulted in 52 for Kwiecinski and 38 for Prus. A secret vote was taken also on accepting outgoing First Secretary Janusz Prokopiak's resignation, 74 voting in favor, 15 against.[31]

Thus, at the province level there were three contested elections for first secretary and several cases of using secret balloting—all starting in early 1981.[32] At the same time, uncontested elections also continued in some places, some using secret balloting.[33] In all, the big turnover of province first secretaries from September 1980 to May 1981—twenty-eight of the forty-nine—was accomplished largely without open contests and secret balloting. Nevertheless, contested elections began catching on so that in some places they came to be regarded as a requirement. For example, an election to fill the vacant post of Olsztyn province economic secretary had to be temporarily postponed when a second candidate could not be found. Prevote consultations had produced the names of seven candidates, but six refused to run, and the four additional candidates nominated from the floor at a March 28 plenum also declined. "As a result," said the local paper, "there was no other solution but to postpone the election."[34]

The big turnover of first secretaries in late 1980 was a result of intensive pressure from the rank and file, who accused local bosses of an "autocratic method of rule"[35] or corruption,[36] and from Solidarity, which demanded removal of some first secretaries as a condition for ending strikes.[37] Sensitive to the local agitation, the Politburo quickly altered its method of dealing with local party organizations to avoid the appearance of dictating the choice of new leaders. Customarily, the Politburo sent a representative to a province party committee plenum to announce the nominee for first secretary "in the name of the Politburo," but already in October and November the Politburo's representative sometimes used new terminology, nominating a candidate "proposed by the province committee Executive Committee and approved by the Politburo"[38] or in the name of both the Politburo and the province Executive Committee.[39] As time passed, the local Executive Committee was increasingly cited as the initiator of the nomination, and the Politburo was presented as just approving this choice.[40]

Starting in January there was more and more stress on advance consultation with local party members and on winning consensus for a candidate (or sometimes two candidates). CC Secretary Kurowski proposed candidates for first secretary at the January 23 Olsztyn plenum and February 12 Bielsko-Biala plenum "after consultation with the party aktiv" and "in the name of the province committee"—with no reference at all to the Politburo.[41] At the March 16 Radom plenum, CC Secretary Grabski presented two candidates for first secretary and stressed that since March 12, consultations with 162 party members, including 67 members and 20 candidate members of the province committee and 69 local party secretaries, had been conducted and that the consultations had resulted in the Politburo nominating these two candidates.[42] At the May 12 Szczecin plenum, outgoing First Secretary Kazimierz Cypryniak nominated his successor, stressing that he had "personally conducted consultations" on the choice with twenty local party organizations.[43] Sometimes when a consensus could not be developed, the election was postponed. The October 30, 1980 *Gazeta Poludniowa*, reporting on an October 29 Tarnow plenum, said that advance "consultations had not produced a clear answer regarding the position of secretary for propaganda," so the election was put off.

The Politburo also began avoiding attempts to send in outsiders as candidates for first secretary. Whereas in September and October eight of the twelve new province first secretaries were outsiders (government ministers, directors of CC departments, diplomats),[44] during November and December only one of the ten new first secretaries was not from the local party organization (and this was Warsaw First Secretary Stanislaw Kociolek, who was brought back from diplomatic exile). From January through May, three of the seven new first secretaries were outsiders, and in one of these cases opposition arose precisely on the grounds that he was an outsider. At the January 23 Olsztyn plenum, some committee members opposed the candidacy of Suwalki First Secretary Bialecki on grounds that he was an outsider.[45] As *Chlopska Droga* editor Mieczyslaw Rog-Swiostek complained at the April 1981 plenum, some people were insisting that "the CC and Politburo should not even have the right to recommend anyone, for example, for the position of province committee first secretary."[46]

There were at least some cases of defiance of Politburo wishes by a province committee plenum. At the December 10, 1980 Koszalin plenum Politburo representative Grabski proposed the removal of three province committee secretaries, and even though this had been "consulted" in advance with over fifty province committee members, it did not go smoothly. The removal of two of the secretaries was approved by a "majority," but some speakers urged keeping the third, Barbara Polak, and a "lively debate" developed. Grabski spoke again and stated that while the province committee "has the full right to adopt its own decision," it would have to also accept "full political responsibility for such a decision." Despite this, a majority decided to keep Polak as secretary, turning back thc Politburo proposal.[47] At a February 12, 1981 Bielsko-Biala plenum, Kurowski called for changes in local leadership and urged adoption of recommendations by a local investigation commission that five local leaders be fired for mishandling strikes. A majority of the province committee rejected the commission's proposals and dissolved the commission. Kurowski then criticized local leaders again for failing to "clean up their party ranks" and slowness to react to criticism made at the February 1981 CC plenum.[48]

Finally, in the early spring of 1981 democratic procedures began making some impact on the level of the CC itself, as the CC began using secret balloting and announcing voting results—results that often were not unanimous. The normal practice at CC plenums, both in electing officials and in adopting decrees, had been to use open voting, which strongly encouraged unanimity. Secret balloting had been used briefly at CC plenums after the election of Gomulka at the October 1956 plenum but later faded out again as reform pressure declined.[49] An unsigned article about the March CC plenum in the April 2, 1981 *Trybuna Ludu* stated that past plenums had normally operated "under conditions of artificial unanimity. The isolated persons expressing their own opinion caused sensations and in general suffered high costs for their civic courage."

The pattern of unanimous, open voting at plenums began breaking down at the March 29–30, 1981 CC plenum, and soon the leadership began revealing that voting results sometimes were split. At the March plenum the vote on a controversial compromise resolution to withdraw the resignations of Politburo members Olszowski and Grabski and give the Politburo a vote of confidence was not characterized as "unanimous,"[50] and following the plenum details on the vote leaked out during frank and heated discussions between plenum participants and curious local party organizations and reporters. First secretary of the Gdansk shipyard party organization Jan Labecki told a Gdansk paper that he had voted against the resolution and that many others had abstained. The vote had apparently been open, by show of hands.[51] Another Gdansk paper revealed that there had also been one abstention on the plenum decision to ask the party control commission to take up the case of Stefan Bratkowski, who had circulated a letter asserting that there was a faction in the Politburo fighting Kania and reform.[52]

At the next plenum—on April 29–30, 1981—more democratic procedure was used and attempts at maintaining the facade of unanimity were dropped. This time the plenum account announced that secret balloting was used (reports on previous plenums had not specified open or secret balloting) and that a special commission had been named to count the votes. Moreover, the voting results were published in *Trybuna Ludu's* April 30, 1981 account of the plenum. Four new members of the Politburo and Secretariat were elected: With 123 valid votes cast, Katowice miner Gerard Gabrys and Warsaw worker Zygmunt Wronski were elected to the Politburo with 111 and 110 votes respectively, Opole First Secretary Jozef Masny was elected a Politburo candidate member with 107 votes, and Szczecin First Secretary Kazimierz Cypryniak was elected a CC secretary with 87 votes. There was no choice of candidates and all those elected had been nominated by First Secretary Kania, but the reporting of split votes was itself an innovation. Moreover, the results of other votes were also reported. *Trybuna Ludu* reported that Jozef Pinkowski's resignation from the Politburo was accepted with 5 abstentions, that of Emil Wojtaszek as Politburo candidate member was accepted with 1 vote against and 6 abstentions, that of Zbigniew Zielinski as Secretariat member was accepted with 1 abstention, while Jerzy Wojtecki's as CC secretary was accepted "unanimously." Results of voting on resolutions were also announced: The resolution calling for holding the party congress and election of delegates to the congress was adopted unanimously, a resolution on precongress debate was adopted with 1 abstention, and a resolution on electing a party control commission during the election campaign was adopted with 1 vote against.

THE SPRING 1981 ELECTION CONFERENCES

The full effect of the new democratized rules was felt when nationwide party elections were called in preparation for the July 1981 congress. In contrast to late 1980 and early 1981 when party organizations here and there sporadically held elections for a variety of reasons and in varying circumstances, this time all party organizations had to hold elections for all posts and under the new rules. The result was a massive replacement of incumbent leaders at all levels and the takeover of many party organizations by reformers and members of Solidarity.

The operation of the new procedures can be best observed in the elections at the province conferences—the highest level below the CC and Politburo. The local press usually reported extensive detail on these conferences—including the number of candidates running, details about the candidates, political debates and politicking, and the outcome of the voting. Many province leaders were clearly under fire from below and retired rather than face a tough battle for reelection, and the Politburo usually avoided going to bat for the incumbents. Some incumbents who did run for reelection were defeated in open combat. Most conferences had contests for first secretary and for other leadership posts, and the voting results were sometimes close and the winners a surprise. Some new province leaders were highly unorthodox, active reformers, or even Solidarity members. It was usually clear that the conferences were not manipulated or controlled and that the province leaders could only win election by appealing to the delegates at their conferences. The conferences offered a convincing display of pluralism in action within a communist party.

The election campaign leading up to the congress began with conferences of primary party organizations in April and moved up through factory, city, and district conferences, reaching the province level in late May. At the lower levels, some conferences not only followed the requirement of nominating two or more candidates for each post and using secret balloting but even added other innovations to promote competition between candidates, fostering debate on issues and candidates—something normally abhorred by communist party organizations. Some required candidates to spell out their views on various subjects by answering detailed questions or presenting personal platforms. The newly elected Torun city committee required each of the four candidates for first secretary to give "short speeches presenting their concepts of the city committee activities" and to answer questions.[53] The party conference in Krakow's Lenin Steel Works (the biggest factory party organization in the country) required each of the eight candidates for the five positions as delegates to the congress to present his views and answer questions from the hall on "how he personally views the need for changes in the party" and how he would represent the party organization at the congress.[54]

Some organizations held two-stage conferences, which gave more opportunity to compare the candidates. Candidates were nominated at the first stage, and the interval between the stages was used to discuss qualifications and policy positions of the candidates before the election at the second stage. For example, the newly elected first secretary of the Wroclaw Polytechnic party committee described how he won in a contest with six other candidates, each of whom had "had to present his election program and tell what he wants to do and will do" before the election at the second stage.[55] This two-stage procedure was occasionally used at higher levels also. The Olsztyn city conference met in two stages with the interval used for discussion of candidates in local organizations.[56] Also meeting in two stages were the Bydgoszcz city conference and province conferences in Torun, Lodz, and Wroclaw.[57]

As the results of the lower-level conferences—primary party organizations, factory party organizations, and city and district party organizations—began appearing in May, the massive turnover of officials was soon apparent. A May 27, 1981 *Trybuna Ludu* article stated that "more or less half" of the newly elected first secretaries and committee members of primary party organizations were "persons who were not in the leadership before." Final figures given in a report for the party congress specified that 50 percent of the 100,000 first secretaries of primary party organizations and of the 600,000 members of executive committees of these organizations were new, while 52 percent of the 2,359 factory party first secretaries and 60 percent of the 45,000 factory party committee members were new.[58] Of course, the turnover in May–June was all the more impressive when one considers that many officials had already been replaced during the "renewal" starting in August 1980.

Not only was the turnover virtually unprecedented, but so was the fact that these changes were carried out at the conferences themselves, rather than behind the scenes. Commentator Henryk Galus wrote in the Gdansk paper *Glos Wybrzeza*, May 20, 1981, that in past election campaigns changes in membership of party committees and their executive organs had been below 30–40 percent and that there were "practically no cases of change of leadership of party committees at conferences" themselves, since "such changes were done on the initiative of higher organs before the conferences or sometimes even after the conferences."

In some places the turnover was much heavier than indicated above.[59] In Lodz, 75 percent of the first secretaries at 300 local party organizations were replaced.[60] In Slupsk province only 91 of 218 local party secretaries were reelected, and in Walbrzych province only 100 of 280 local first secretaries were returned to office.[61] In Bydgoszcz city, 322 of the 393 primary party organization first secretaries were replaced, and 81 percent of the members of executive committees of primary party organizations.[62] In 75 Lodz factory party organization elections, 49 (65 percent) elected new first secretaries.[63] In the biggest province, Katowice, 67 percent of the factory party committee first secretaries were new, and 40 of 72 local town first secretaries.[64] In one striking "negative assessment" of incumbent leaders, a local factory party organization in Podgorze failed to reelect any of its three incumbent secretaries even to its factory party committee. According to the local paper, the vote counting had lasted four hours because the election commission members could not believe the "stunning" results and kept recounting in order to see "if there were not some kind of error in their counting."[65]

City and province officials were often not reelected members of their city or province committee or even delegates to their city or province conference, virtually forcing their retirement. At the Piotrkow city conference, none of the incumbent city secretaries were elected to the new city committee, and some province committee leaders—including province First Secretary Skladowski—were not even elected delegates to the province conference.[66] At the Piotrkow province conference, the new ninety-five member province committee included not one of the previous province committee leaders.[67] The whole leadership of Bielsko-Biala city was not elected delegates to the city and province conferences.[68]

The influx of new leaders led to a takeover of some organizations by Solidarity or other reformist or radical elements. In Elblag province, half of the delegates elected to the province conference were members of Solidarity, as were 70 percent of the leaders of primary party organizations. According to the local paper, "there are also cases where all members of the leadership and the first secretaries" belonged to Solidarity.[69] According to the June 6 *Polityka*, 138 of the 414 delegates to the Gdansk conference were Solidarity members (as opposed to 182 members of the traditional branch trade unions). In Olsztyn, a young railroad dispatcher was elected first secretary of the large Olsztyn railroad party organization in a secret vote after he assailed the party in harsh terms. Mieczyslaw Pabian angrily asserted that "the party never has had the confidence of society," since it has "hidden" its history and failed to publish information about such things as "right nationalist deviations, the terror of the period of Stalinism," and past Polish plenums.[70]

The best measure for the extent of democratization was the series of province conferences during June, since detailed accounts are available in provincial papers for virtually all conferences. Most conferences had significant choices, both in electing their new province party committees and in electing their new first secretaries. Of eighteen conferences where the number of candidates for province committees was reported, fourteen offered over 30 percent more candidates than seats. In Lodz, for example, there were 196 candidates for 121 seats on the province committee—62 percent more candidates than posts. In electing province first secretaries, thirty-seven of the forty-nine province conferences had at least 2 candidates for first secretary.[71] Secret balloting was used in virtually all cases,[72] and in all cases except Olsztyn it was the conference itself that elected the first secretary, rather than allowing the newly elected province committee to choose the first secretary.

Many province contests were thrown wide open by the fact that the incumbent first secretaries were not candidates for reelection—either because they had dropped out or had been defeated at a lower level. Some clearly quit in anger or frustration or under fire. Beleaguered Nowy Sacz First Secretary Henryk Kostecki was described on one occasion as becoming "very upset" (*bardzo zdenerwowany*) at badgering by local questioners.[73] Opole First Secretary Jozef Masny complained of unjust allegations against him,[74] and according to the June 15 *Trybuna Ludu*, simply did not run for reelection. Torun First Secretary Zygmunt Najdowski announced that he would not run for reelection when the Torun city conference voted to seat his foe, horizontal ties leader Iwanow, as a delegate.[75] Tarnobrzeg First Secretary Tadeusz Haladaj, who had announced before the conference that he would not run, expressed discouragement at the "lack of results" of his work.[76]

A number of first secretaries had lost out in bids for election as delegates to the province conferences—or for some reason had simply not run for delegate—and hence became technically ineligible to run for reelection as first secretary, unless the conference voted to make a special exception for them. Poznan First Secretary Jerzy Kusiak was defeated for election as a delegate, and his chance at remaining first secretary was ended when the province conference refused to allow nondelegates to run for office.[77] Lomza First Secretary Waldemar Szpalinski was nominated for ree¹ection at the conference but declined to run, citing his failure to get elected a city conference delegate to the province conference. He told the conference: "There are moments when one needs to leave a post and join the rank and file. I see in this no personal tragedy."[78]

With incumbents under fire and a strong desire for change evident, the Politburo largely kept out of these province contests. A representative of the Politburo endorsed an incumbent first secretary in only four cases: Kania made strong pitch for Warsaw First Secretary Kociolek and Katowice First Secretary Zabinski (see below); Jagielski announced the Politburo's "warm support" for Lublin First Secretary Kruk at that province's conference;[79] and President Jablonski endorsed First Secretary Bednarski in Bydgoszcz.[80] All four won.

Some of those incumbent first secretaries who did attempt to run for reelection ran into open opposition at the conferences and changed their minds about running or were actually defeated in the voting. Piotrkow First Secretary Stanislaw Skladowski was attacked for praising the conservative Katowice Forum and criticizing Kania in his opening report and decided not to run for reelection.[81] Olsztyn First Secretary Zbigniew Bialecki's conference report was attacked as "one-sided," and he also bowed out.[82] Krosno First Secretary Wladyslaw Kandefer ran for reelection but lost 122 to 160 to plant director Wojtal on the second ballot at the Krosno conference.[83] Legnica First Secretary Ryszard Romaniewicz lost to Solidarity member Stanislaw Jasinski on the second ballot, 126 to 157, at the Legnica conference.[84] Katowice's Zabinski, although reelected, underwent questioning for over an hour at his conference,[85] and Warsaw's Kociolek was also questioned sharply.[86]

The contests for first secretary were sometimes very close: In fourteen cases the winner won by only 60 percent or less of the vote, and in seven cases the contest was settled only in a runoff second ballot. In two cases, a third ballot was needed.

Table 2.1 summarizes the contests for first secretaries at province con-

TABLE 2.1

Province	Number of Candidates	First Secretary Ran for Reelection yes/no	won/lost	Victor's Margin in Votes	New First Secretary's Prior Position
Biala Podlaska	2	no	—	202 to 59	Province organizational secretary
Bialystok	3	yes	won	170 of 281	(incumbent reelected)
Bielsko-Biala	2	yes	won	"majority"	(incumbent reelected)
Bydgoszcz	3	yes	won	301 of 372	(incumbent reelected)
Chelm	2	no	—	"majority"	Gmina (parish) first secretary
Ciechanow	2	yes	won	176 of 297	(incumbent reelected)
Czestochowa	1	yes	won	306 of 319	(incumbent reelected)
Elblag	1	yes	won	277 of 311	(incumbent reelected)
Gdansk	1	yes	won	360 to 38	(incumbent reelected)
Gorzow	3	no	—	191 of 291	Province ideology department head
Jelenia Gora	2	yes	won	158 to 98	(incumbent reelected)
Kalisz	4	yes	won	212 of 335	(incumbent reelected)
Katowice	3	yes	won	332 of 492	(incumbent reelected)
Kielce	4	no	—	207 of 385	Province propaganda secretary
Konin	1	yes	won	282 of 291	(incumbent reelected)
Koszalin	3	no	—	150 to 89 (on second ballot)	Town first secretary
Krakow	2	yes	won	280 of 389	(incumbent reelected)
Krosno	3	yes	lost	160 to 122 (on second ballot)	Plant director
Legnica	4	yes	lost	157 to 126 (on second ballot)	Deputy director of mine
Leszno	3	?		"majority"	Province control commission chairman
Lodz	1	yes	won	331 of 392	(incumbent reelected)
Lomza	5	no	—	136 to 106 (on third ballot)	Province secretary

City	No.	Secret ballot	Result	Vote	Position
Lublin	1	yes	won	225 of 299	(incumbent reelected)
Nowy Sacz	3	no	—	181 of 245	Province economic secretary
Olsztyn	3	no	—	100 to 12	Province cadres secretary
Opole	3	no	—	217 of 313	Province organizational department head
Ostroleka	1	yes	won	265 of 266	(incumbent reelected)
Pila	1	yes	won	283 to 2	(incumbent reelected)
Piotrkow	5	yes	lost	180 to 145 (on second ballot)	Head of flying school
Plock	4	yes	won	200 of 355	(incumbent reelected)
Poznan	3	no	—	260 of 485	Plant first secretary
Przemysl	4	no	—	151 to 117 (on third ballot)	Province cadres secretary
Radom	2	no	—	"majority"	Province agriculture secretary
Rzeszow	1	yes	won	237 of 255	(incumbent reelected)
Siedlce	2	no	—	199 to 45	Province governor (wojewoda)
Sieradz	7	yes	lost	203 of 338 (on second ballot)	Province agriculture department head
Skierniewice	1	yes	won	196 of 223	(incumbent reelected)
Slupsk	2	no	—	"majority"	Chairman of agricultural co-op
Suwalki	4	no	—	150 to 92 (on second ballot)	Director of agricultural co-op
Szczecin	2	yes	won	197 to 111	(incumbent reelected)
Tarnobrzeg	5	no	—	"majority"	Forester
Tarnow	1	yes	won	251 of 265	(incumbent reelected)
Torun	2	no	—	"majority"	Province secretary
Walbrzych	2	yes	won	198 of 276	(incumbent reelected)
Warsaw	2	yes	won	247 to 132	(incumbent reelected)
Wloclawek	3	no	—	"majority"	Town first secretary
Wroclaw	1	yes	won	288 of 340	(incumbent reelected)
Zamosc	6	no	—	146 to 131 (on second ballot)	City secretary
Zielona Gora	2	yes	won	271 to 65	(incumbent reelected)

ferences, based on local press reports. It gives the number of candidates competing, whether the incumbent ran for reelection and was reelected, the margin of victory, and the profession of the winner.

In some wide open contests very unusual candidates wound up as first secretary, outsiders who had not even held lower-level party jobs.[87] Thus, Piotrkow First Secretary Stanislaw Kolasa was director of a flying school, Tarnobrzeg First Secretary Janusz Basiak was a forester and director of an experimental forest project, Krosno First Secretary Henryk Wojtal was a factory director, and Suwalki First Secretary Waldemar Berdyga and Slupsk First Secretary Mieczyslaw Wojcik were officials of local agricultural organizations.[88]

Some of the new secretaries themselves expressed amazement at their election to top party leadership. New Krosno First Secretary Henryk Wojtal told a reporter he had agreed to run against the incumbent just to provide an alternate and had not expected to win.[89] Juliusz Kropnicki, who suddenly jumped from first secretary of the Wlodawa *gmina* (parish) to Chelm province first secretary, Mieczyslaw Wojcik, who rose from local agricultural official to Slupsk first secretary, and forester Janusz Basiak, who became Tarnobrzeg first secretary, also expressed surprise at their election.[90]

Two new first secretaries were clearly liberals. Stanislaw Jasinski, deputy director of a mine and a member of Solidarity, defeated incumbent Legnica First Secretary Ryszard Romaniewicz by 157 to 126.[91] Edward Skrzypczak, party secretary at Poznan's big Cegielski metal plant and an active member of the liberal Poznan Forum of Political Thought,[92] apparently helped defeat conservative Poznan First Secretary Jerzy Kusiak, who had attacked Kania at the June plenum (see next chapter). Kusiak had run for delegate to the Poznan conference at Skrzypczak's plant but was defeated and later complained of a campaign of "agitation" against him at the plant.[93] At the province conference, delegates refused to allow nondelegate Kusiak to run for reelection, and three candidates, including Skrzypczak, competed for his job as first secretary, "presenting their positions and intended programs of action" and answering questions. Skrzypczak won with 260 of the 485 votes. Immediately upon election, he told reporters that he intended to work with Solidarity and the Church and to return to his job at the factory after two years or two terms.[94] Asked where he stood politically, he later told a reporter that his views were close to those of Rakowski, Fiszbach, Dabrowa, and Hieronim Kubiak (all relatively liberal), that he was a "pragmatist," that he "unconditionally" favored political resolutions of conflicts, and "even would expand the line of accord to a line of joint work."[95]

In all, almost half (twenty-four) of the forty-nine conferences elected someone new as first secretary. Most (fifteen) of the twenty-four replaced were Gierek appointees. The June replacements, on top of those in late 1980 and early 1981, left only six Gierek holdovers among province first secretaries: Zdzislaw Lucinski (Ciechanow), Tadeusz Fiszbach (Gdansk), Krystyn Dabrowa (Krakow), Wladyslaw Kruk (Lublin), Michal Niedzwiedz (Pila), and Janusz Kubasiewicz (Skierniewice). Fiszbach and Dabrowa were clearly the two most liberal province first secretaries and probably owed their reelection to that fact. There was much less turnover among first secretaries elected in the late 1980—early 1981 period: nineteen of the twenty-eight who had taken office since renewal began in August 1980 were reelected.

While the turnover of first secretaries at the June province conferences was heavy, the changes among other province party leaders was even more drastic. Thus, one breakdown reported that 24 percent of the province first secretaries were not even elected delegates to their province conferences, but well over 50 percent of the other secretaries (propaganda, organizational work, etc.) and 63 percent of province party control commission chairmen failed to be elected. Only 147 of the 243 incumbent province committee secretaries actually ran for reelection to their province committees, and only 73 were reelected to the committee. Of these 73, only 43 were reelected secretaries. Hence, only about 17 percent of the incumbent province secretaries managed to get reelected as secretaries. In twelve provinces, all province secretaries were replaced and in thirteen all but one (usually the first secretary).[96]

ELECTION OF DELEGATES TO THE PARTY CONGRESS

The election of delegates to the congress at the June province conferences displayed both the wide choice offered in elections and the breakdown of central control as much as anything had before. Province conferences often were presented with twice as many candidates as there were delegate seats, and the voting sometimes took several ballots lasting for many hours. In this uncontrolled situation Warsaw officials had great difficulty winning election as delegates. The Politburo tried desperately to persuade various conferences to add some prominent central figures to their lists of delegates, since all central officials could hardly be delegates from Warsaw. But many conferences adopted the principle that only local people duly elected delegates to the province conference could run for delegate to the congress, and still others in practice voted down candidates from outside the province. Occasionally, this led to clashes between a province conference and the Politburo, but the Politburo could only rely on its powers of persuasion.

The new democratized rules and local independence did not even spare the top leaders, who also found it difficult to gain election as delegates—normally something taken for granted. Despite their exalted status, some Politburo members had to fight for election in the face of open hostility, and some leaders actually lost. Several leaders appeared to shop around for sympathetic party organizations which would elect them.

In most province conferences for which data is available there were roughly twice as many candidates as there were delegate seats available, although in Bialystok there were four times as many and in Olsztyn three times. In addition to candidates placed on the ballot by election commissions after consultations before the conference, many were nominated from the floor. In Olsztyn, 44 of the 97 candidates were nominated from the floor, 12 of the 38 in Elblag, 24 of the 46 in Konin, 12 of the 26 in Przemysl, and 32 of the 53 in Tarnobrzeg. Voting sometimes required as many as six, seven, or eight ballots before a complete slate was picked. (With such a large number of candidates, many failed to get the required 50 percent of the votes on the first ballot.)

Table 2.2, based on *Trybuna Ludu* and local newspaper accounts, demonstrates the range of choice in elections for delegates, the number of delegates elected at the province conferences, and the number elected beforehand at factory party organizations. It indicates which conferences adopted rules barring nondelegates from running and which in fact elected any outsiders (central candidates) as delegates to the congress.

As the table indicates, fourteen conferences actually adopted rules barring those who were not elected delegates to the conference from running for delegate to the congress.[97] What is more, some allowed outsiders to run but then voted them down, while others were not even asked by the Politburo to elect any outsiders. In sum, twenty of the forty-nine province conferences failed to elect any outsiders.

Local resistance to outsiders had been clearly demonstrated even below the province level. The CC Organizational Department had asked the Olsztyn city party conference to elect six central officials—including CC Secretariat member Stanislaw Gabrielski, Minister of Education Boleslaw Faron, and trade union chairman[98] Albin Szyszka—delegates to the province conference, which could then elect them to the congress. But on May 22 the city delegates refused, objecting to surrendering six of their conference seats to outsiders and insisting that everyone follow the same rules in winning election to the congress.[99]

This attitude led to some notable tests of will between local conferences and the Politburo, which could hardly let most provinces—especially the big ones—exclude all outsiders. The most tense confrontation between a province conference and the Politburo came in Poznan—the fourth biggest party organization—where the conference on its opening day adopted a rule to allow only delegates to run for office.[100] CC Secretary Grabski, representing the Politburo at the conference, delivered a harsh speech assailing "various kinds of manipulation, a symptom of the activity of horizontal structures," and declaring the vote contrary to the June plenum decisions, "a violation of democratic principles of party life and a blow at party unity."[101] Grabski threatened that if the conference did not reverse the vote he would walk out. Grabski's threat simply aggravated the delegates, who argued that the new election rules gave conferences the right to decide for themselves whether nondelegates would be allowed to run. Speakers also criticized Grabski's claim that horizontal units were manipulating the conference. Delegates refused to revote, so Grabski and some other guests walked out.[102]

A break was called and members of the conference presidium phoned Kania to ask his opinion and to urge him to personally come to Poznan. Kania indicated that he could not come but urged the conference to reconsider whether they would accept candidates for delegates recommended by the Politburo, saying that this would ease his problems as first secretary in preparing for the congress. On the second day, at Kania's

TABLE 2.2

	Candidates for Delegates	Delegates Elected at Conference	Number of Ballots	Delegates Elected Earlier at Plants	Total Delegates	Outsiders Elected
Biala Podlaska	16	12	?	1	13	1[a]
Bialystok	108	26	2	1	27	0[a]
Bielsko-Biala	?	33	?	8	41	1
Bydgoszcz	108	52	3	13	65	2[a]
Chelm	?	12	2	0	12	0[b]
Ciechanow	?	21	3	0	21	1
Czestochowa	?	32	5	6	38	0[a]
Elblag	38	20	4	1	21	1[a]
Gdansk	86	47	3	15	62	0
Gorzow	43	24	?	1	25	1
Jelenia Gora	53	22	2	1	23	0
Kalisz	68	35	3	4	39	1
Katowice	?	127	?	106	233	1
Kielce	?	45	?	12	57	1
Konin	46	22	2	1	23	1
Koszalin	57	26	7	1	27	2[b]
Krakow	105	44	6	14	58	5
Krosno	?	18	3	4	22	1
Legnica	?	20	?	5	25	1[a]
Leszno	?	21	?	0	21	1
Lodz	125	51	4	28	79	0
Lomza	?	15	?	0	15	1
Lublin	73	35	2	7	42	0

Nowy Sacz	?	19	2	4	23	0
Olsztyn	97	31	2	3	34	0[a]
Opole	?	46	2	9	55	0
Ostroleka	?	15	1	0	15	0[a]
Pila	?	24	3	1	25	1
Piotrkow	?	28	3	7	35	0[a]
Plock	?	24	?	2	26	2
Poznan	26	63	?	13	76	0
Przemysl	76	15	3	1	16	0[a]
Radom	?	26	2	4	30	1
Rzeszow	?	24	?	5	29	1[a]
Siedlce	?	24	1	0	24	1
Sieradz	?	19	2	2	21	1
Skierniewice	41	19	3	2	21	1
Slupsk	45	22	8	0	22	0[a]
Suwalki	?	17	?	0	17	0[b]
Szczecin	52	37	?	10	47	2
Tarnobrzeg	53	21	5	5	26	0[b]
Tarnow	40	21	?	3	24	2
Torun	66	28	4	6	34	0[a]
Walbrzych	61	29	4	7	36	1[b]
Warsaw	169	90	3	35	125	4
Wloclawek	42	22	?	2	24	0[a]
Wroclaw	?	46	?	12	58	1
Zamosc	40	19	2	0	19	1
Zielona Gora	73	29	2	3	32	1

[a] Adopted rule against allowing nondelegates to run for office.
[b] Adopted rule allowing nondelegates to run for delegate to the congress but not for province committee.

urging, Grabski returned to the hall and the delegates voted a second time, adopting a compromise that reaffirmed that only delegates could run but, "accepting the personal appeal of the CC first secretary," added four officials recommended by the Politburo to the list of candidates, as an "exception": Gen. Edward Lukasik (deputy commander of the air force), Leslaw Tokarski (new head of the CC's press department), Jerzy Wiatr (professor at Warsaw University and a frequent target of conservatives), and Gen. Stanislaw Zaczkowski (commander in chief of the national police). Grabski thanked the delegates for accepting these four. However, during the election itself only the two generals—Lukasik and Zaczkowski—were actually elected delegates. The whole process humiliated Grabski, who had to turn to Kania for help (after attacking Kania personally only two weeks earlier at the June plenum—see next chapter).

Central leaders could hardly let the largest province, Katowice, exclude all outsiders, since it had 233 seats—almost 12 percent of the total number of delegates. But the conference was difficult to control, partly because 430 of the 494 delegates to the conference had never been delegates before.[103] Both Kania and Jaruzelski went to the Katowice conference, and Kania argued the need to accept central candidates.[104] After debate, the conference finally agreed to accept 7 outsiders recommended by the Politburo—but only after they answered questions.[105] In the actual election of delegates, however, all were defeated. Krakow's *Gazeta Krakowska* on June 29 revealed the votes these 7 unsuccessful central candidates had won in secret balloting:

> Deputy Premier and Planning Commission chairman Zbigniew Madej—257;
> Deputy Minister of Internal Affairs Adam Krzysztoporski—244;
> Rector of the Higher School of Social Sciences Norbert Michta (an outspoken conservative)—192;
> Director of the CC Culture Department Mieczyslaw Wojtczak—179;
> Mining Minister Mieczyslaw Glanowski—161;
> "publicist" Kazimierz Kakol—138;
> and deputy chairman of the Supreme Control Chamber Tadeusz Bejm—117.

The especially low votes for the last two reflected special hostility voiced before the vote. Bejm had argued with some delegates about the course of investigation of former officials,[106] and hard-liner Kakol's role in suppressing students in 1968 was questioned.[107] Madej had also been proposed as a candidate at the June 17 Lodz conference, but had been rejected. (Lodz, the third biggest party organization, did not adopt a ban on outsiders, but there was much sentiment against letting in "people from outside."[108])

Kania and Rakowski were able to sway the conference in Bydgoszcz (the fifth biggest party organization) to accept some outsiders. The June 27 Bydgoszcz conference initially decided that only delegates could run as candidates, but a phone call from Kania asked the conference to add four outsiders:[109] Minister for Trade Unions Stanislaw Ciosek, deputy commander of the Pomeranian military district Gen. Henryk Kondas, Deputy Minister of Internal Affairs Wladyslaw Pozoga, and Central Auditing Commission member Eugeniusz Stawinski, a "veteran of the workers' movement." According to the June 29 *Trybuna Ludu* account, some speakers argued that the conference should accept these four as an "expression of confidence and support" for Kania. After urging by Rakowski, who represented the Politburo at the conference, the conference voted, 187 in favor and 149 against (22 abstentions), to add the four— but only if they answered questions, especially about their ties with Bydgoszcz and whether they had run anywhere else. Ciosek said he had not planned to run at all, but Kania and Rakowski had persuaded him to run, and he had chosen Bydgoszcz because of his involvement in the March Bydgoszcz events (see next chapter). Kondas said he had lived for years in Bydgoszcz and was a member of the present province committee. These two were elected, but Pozoga and Stawinski, who had been unable to make a strong case for their ties to Bydgoszcz, were defeated in the election of delegates. One delegate asked Rakowski why he and Kania risked all their hard-won authority by recommending such candidates from outside.

Less effort was made to get smaller conferences to accept central candidates. In fact, the Jelenia Gora conference debated whether to allow outsiders to run until Politburo representative Olszowski announced that the leadership had not even selected anyone to run in Jelenia Gora— whereupon the conference magnanimously agreed to adopt a rule letting outsiders run.[110] Barcikowski asked the Torun province conference to allow Ludwik Krasucki (deputy editor of the CC journal *Nowe Drogi*) to run by way of exception, but the discussion of this was so negative that the conference did not even bother to vote. It had already adopted the principle that only province delegates could run.[111] Moczar had success in getting the Suwalki conference to include CC Ideology Department head Walery Namiotkiewicz as a candidate,[112] and in persuading the Siedlce conference to accept chairman of the Polish Scout Union (ZHP) Andrzej Ornat, even though the conference had adopted a rule against nondelegates.[113] Ornat was elected but Namiotkiewicz was not.

The military had relatively good success in persuading conferences to accept generals as candidates, perhaps because of the military's high prestige. The Main Political Administration asked the Walbrzych conference to include Deputy Minister of National Defense Gen. Zbigniew Nowak[114] and the Zielona Gora conference to include Deputy Minister of National Defense Gen. Tadeusz Tuczapski.[115] Both were accepted and elected. The Gorzow conference in open voting agreed to add border troops commander Gen. Czeslaw Stopinski to its list of candidates and then elected him.[116] However, the Olsztyn conference refused to accept Brig. Gen. Zdzislaw Ostrowski, who was proposed by the Main Political Administration.[117]

Some conferences were quite receptive to outsiders. The liberal Krakow party conference in particular elected more Warsaw officials than any other province—CC First Secretary Kania, Deputy Premier Rakowski, CC Press Department head Jozef Klasa, and Socialist Polish Youth Union chairman Jerzy Jaskiernia[118]—and gave them big votes.[119] In addition, CC Secretary Roman Ney was elected at a local conference in Krakow. All of these were moderates, however, and most had ties with Krakow. In Gdansk, the subject of outsiders appears not to have been an issue, but no Warsaw candidates were elected.

With the strong resistance to outsiders at many province conferences, even many Politburo members had great difficulty in getting elected delegates to the congress. Kania in his closing speech to the June CC plenum stressed the need to elect Politburo and Secretariat members as delegates and stated that "we must oppose the creation of artificial barriers which make it impossible for activists of the central level to be nominated." Province conferences should assess leaders on their work as members of the Politburo, CC secretaries, or CC members "and not just as members of a particular party organization." "We should be interested in ensuring that present members of the Politburo and of the CC Secretariat take part in the congress as delegates. . . . Let the congress assess and verify them."[120] Toward this end, the June plenum adopted a resolution stating that "limitation of the passive right of election during the election of party leaders and delegates is contrary to the PZPR Statute and violates the democratic principles of intraparty life."[121] Zbigniew Glowacki put it bluntly in his plenum speech: Central leaders "cannot be petitioners running from conference to conference seeking someone kind enough to nominate them."[122]

Although almost all other delegates to the congress had to get elected starting at the bottom (getting their home primary party organization to elect them delegates to local city and then province conferences, which then elected them to the national congress), most top leaders chose an easier, surer way: having a province conference put them on its list of candidates for delegates. Only a few more liberal top leaders risked running in local party units where they might face harsh personal questioning and direct opposition.

Running in local party units worked well for CC Secretaries Ney and Cypryniak, Deputy Premier Rakowski, and Gdansk First Secretary Fiszbach, but almost ended in disaster for CC Secretary Barcikowski. Popular Gdansk leader Fiszbach started at the bottom as a delegate to the Gdynia city conference,[123] and was elected a congress delegate at the June 7 Gdansk province conference, winning the largest number of votes of any delegate elected.[124] Ney on June 6 was elected a delegate to the congress from the party unit at the Krakow Mining Academy,[125] where he had been director until promoted to the party leadership in late 1980. He was also elected a delegate to the Krakow province conference at a local conference.[126] Rakowski was elected a delegate to the Krakow province conference at a Nowa Huta district conference, where he received more votes than any of the other forty delegates elected,[127] and he was elected a congress delegate at the June 14 province conference.[128] Cypryniak, former first secretary of Szczecin, was elected a congress delegate at a local party conference in Swinoujscie in Szczecin province, receiving 85 of 97 votes in a contest with another candidate.[129]

Barcikowski, however, ran into repeated difficulties. First, he antagonized his home party organization by announcing in April that he would not run there but in Szczecin where he had signed the historic August 30, 1980 agreement ending the strike. Local party members in Krakow, who had already nominated him, questioned his decision at an April 29 local election conference, asking him why he was not following the widely accepted postulate of "running in one's own home organization."[130] Barcikowski answered: "I want to run in Szczecin precisely because I went through the most difficult period in Szczecin. And if there, in Szczecin, they decide that Barcikowski is not worthy to be a delegate to the congress, I will accept that evaluation—that will be for me a correct evaluation of my capability in the party."[131] His local party organization harassed him with sharp questions about people he had appointed while Krakow first secretary (1977–1980) who had since turned out to be corrupt, and they also complained about the conservative tone of his March plenum report. Liberal Gdansk shipyard party secretary Labecki was present at the Krakow meeting and gave Barcikowski his endorsement: "I value and respect him because he does not go for cheap applause and does not say what can easily win universal approval."[132] Barcikowski later told a Szczecin paper that although he had offers to be nominated in his Krakow organization and another organization, he felt an "emotional tie" to Szczecin because of the momentous events of August 1980 when "we jointly arrived at a platform of understanding at that difficult time."[133]

But Barcikowski also ran into difficulties in Szczecin. He persuaded the primary party organization in one of the divisions of Szczecin's shipyard to accept him as a member on May 22[134] and then to elect him a delegate to the Szczecin province party conference, but at the province conference some challenged this on grounds that he was an outsider. Foes cited the fact that the shipyard plant committee as a whole, after debate, had failed to give Barcikowski a recommendation on May 30. Eventually, a vote (secret vote) was taken, and by 214 of 307 valid votes the conference decided to include him on its list of candidates for delegate to the congress. He was elected delegate by 215 votes.[135]

Later statements claimed that the efforts against him had been organized and bitter. At the June plenum Janusz Brych, head of the CC's Socio-Professional Department, charged that some Szczecin Solidarity leaders had organized the campaign to bar Barcikowski from running at the province conference. He stated that the shipyard's radio spread anti-Barcikowski stories and that some even went from workshop to workshop "agitating against Barcikowski." He quoted an announcement by the Szczecin Solidarity plant committee that Barcikowski "cannot be a member of the shipyard party organization nor a delegate to the 9th extraordinary congress."[136] Szczecin worker Edward Pustelnik stated: "I admired Comrade Barcikowski and his coolness when he agreed to run, because I would not have been able to take . . . that enormous psychological pressure. Comrade Barcikowski withstood it and it turned out well that he withstood it. . . . I think his stance in this really difficult time gave . . . an example of a communist's position. . . . Despite opposition, despite agitation, he was elected."[137] Grabski in a June 13 Leszno speech also assailed Solidarity for trying to defeat Barcikowski.[138] Rakowski's liberal weekly *Polityka* on June 6 criticized the Szczecin Solidarity leaders for carrying on an "open campaign" against Barcikowski "which was a shock, since he was widely regarded as one of the defenders of democratic changes in the party."

Most other top leaders ran only at the province level, often choosing provinces other than where their home party organizations were located. Kania surprised most observers by choosing to run in Krakow, although he had closer ties to other areas. As he told a Gdansk shipyard audience on April 9, he was a Sejm deputy from Gdynia in Gdansk province, member of a primary party organization in Plock, and worked in Warsaw.[139] Moreover, he had been elected a delegate to the February 1980 congress from Gdansk. During an early May visit to Plock, Kania announced to his local party organization that he would not be running there, arguing that he felt central leaders should run at province conferences and let local plant conferences elect workers as their delegates.[140] Kania was elected a delegate to the congress at the June 14 Krakow province conference, where he received the "greatest number of votes" among the candidates, winning 365 of the 396 valid votes.[141] In addressing the conference, Kania stressed that Krakow was "the place of my birth" and that he had long lived there.[142] Krakow First Secretary Dabrowa lauded him as "defender" of the line of accord, and *Gazeta Krakowska* described the "stormy applause" for Kania and lack of any opposition, adding, "After all, a CC first secretary had never been a delegate at a Krakow conference."[143] Krakow, which elected the most liberal delegation of all provinces,[144] was favorable territory for Kania.

Deputy Premier Jagielski followed Barcikowski's example, running for election in the coastal area where he had helped negotiate the August 1980 Gdansk agreements. Delegates at the province conference in Elblag, which neighbors Gdansk, voted (with 12 against and 19 abstaining) to allow outsider Jagielski to run for delegate because of the "high authority" he had won during the August negotiations.[145] He was subsequently elected.

President Jablonski originally told the May 31 Olsztyn province conference that he would not even run for delegate: "I asked the CC Secretariat not to nominate me at any conference as a candidate for central bodies," even though, he said, he was honored that his longtime party organization at Warsaw's Warynski plant had unanimously elected him delegate to that conference.[146] But when he arrived in Tarnow and local delegates offered him nomination as delegate, he expressed surprise and then, saying that he was "moved," allowed them to nominate and elect him.[147]

Grabski ran in Konin, although he belonged to a Poznan party organization and said that he had received offers of nomination in Leszno and Kalisz. At the Konin conference a letter was read from Grabski's home party organization in Poznan recommending him as a candidate for delegate, and the conference delegates unanimously agreed to add him to their list of candidates. He was easily elected.[148] Grabski had been first secretary of Konin province until his run-in with Gierek, and as the April 28, 1981 *Gazeta Zachodnia* said, "people here know and value" him. Moczar was elected at the June 17 Kielce conference,[149] Jaruzelski at the June 15 Warsaw Military District conference,[150] and Kurowski at the June 16 Ciechanow province conference.[151]

Conservatives Zabinski and Olszowski were elected at province conferences but only with aid from Kania. Kania addressed the June 25 Katowice province conference, where Zabinski was running against two other candidates for reelection as first secretary. Declaring that "the Politburo is not in the habit of issuing its own opinions" on candidates, Kania nevertheless said that the Politburo is not "indifferent" about who is elected first secretary in the biggest province in the country. "It is no secret that I know Comrade Andrzej Zabinski well. Everyone knows that

I was the author of the proposal to entrust him with the function of first secretary of the Katowice party committee last year." Saying that Zabinski's role in the Szczecin and Jastrzebie settlements showed his attitude to change, Kania stated that if the conference elects Zabinski, "I and the PZPR CC Politburo will be very satisfied."[152] Zabinski won reelection as first secretary with 332 of the 491 valid votes, and subsequently was also elected a delegate to the congress.[153]

At the June 27 Warsaw conference Kania also spoke up for Olszowski, calling him a "consistent supporter" of renewal. Olszowski was allowed to run there by "overwhelming" majority vote and then elected delegate by 246 votes out of 440 voting.[154] Olszowski had been nominated at the Piotrkow conference but had declined, saying he was running in Warsaw. Explaining that "his activity had won him more enemies than supporters," he said that he wanted to run in Warsaw precisely because he expected "especially sharp criticism" there and this would test his "suitability for further party activity."[155] It was also possible, however, that Olszowski chose to run in Warsaw because that party organization had a conservative reputation. In fact, the Warsaw conference appeared to favor conservatives in electing delegates, defeating liberal Journalists Union head Stefan Bratkowski,[156] while electing conservatives such as Internal Affairs Minister Miroslaw Milewski, outspoken worker Albin Siwak, and Central Party Control Commission deputy chairman Jerzy Urbanski.

Four Politburo members lost out during the election of delegates. Politburo members Wronski and Gabrys were defeated in their local party organizations in Warsaw and Katowice,[157] and Politburo candidate member Waszczuk was defeated at the Chelm province conference.[158] Politburo candidate member and Opole First Secretary Jozef Masny did not run for reelection as first secretary and was not included in the list of delegates elected in Opole.[159] Ironically, those losing at this stage included three of the four added to the leadership at the April plenum: Wronski, Gabrys, and Masny. Wronski was apparently not popular among his fellow workers,[160] Gabrys was probably discredited by involvement with conservatives (see next chapter), and Masny had been accused of abuses.[161]

The result of these uncontrolled elections was a body of delegates which included remarkably few officials and apparatchiks and which proved largely uncontrollable when the congress convened. Only fifteen of the nineteen members of the Politburo and Secretariat and 5 CC department

TABLE 2.3
LEADERS' BIDS FOR ELECTION AS DELEGATES

Politburo Members	Elected in	CC Secretaries	Elected in
Kania	Krakow	Kania	Krakow
Jaruzelski	Warsaw Military District	Barcikowski	Szczecin
		Olszowski	Warsaw
Jablonski	Tarnow	Grabski	Konin
Jagielski	Elblag	Ney	Krakow
Barcikowski	Szczecin	Waszczuk	(defeated
Olszowski	Warsaw		in
Grabski	Konin		Chelm)
Moczar	Kielce	Kurowski	Ciechanow
Zabinski	Katowice	Cypryniak	Szczecin
Wronski	(defeated in Warsaw)	*Secretariat Member*	
Gabrys	(defeated in Katowice)	Gabrielski	Lomza
Politburo Candidate Members			
Ney	Krakow		
Fiszbach	Gdansk		
Kruk	Lublin		
Masny	(did not run in Opole)		
Waszczuk	(defeated in Chelm)		

heads were elected delegates, and even fewer central government leaders: the premier, president, 3 deputy premiers (Rakowski, Jagielski, Andrzej Jedynak), 7 ministers, and 1 state committee chairman. Of the province level leadership, only forty-three of the forty-nine province first secretaries gained seats at the congress.[162] Of 141 incumbent CC members, only 43 were elected delegates, and only 24 of the 94 candidate members (by my count).[163] The July 18 *Polityka* gave the current number of CC members as 142 and CC candidate members as 94, and said that 43 members and 28 candidate members were elected delegates.

According to statistics given in the July 2 *Trybuna Ludu* and on a July 1 English-language PAP broadcast,[164] there was a total of 1,964 delegates, 365 elected at local plant conferences,[165] and 1,599 at province conferences. The bulk of the delegates—61 percent—were "mental workers" (white-collar workers). Of these 1,202 workers, 276 were technicians and engineers, and 257 directors. The next largest category was party workers—524, including 202 first secretaries of factory committees, 140 first secretaries of city and town committees, as well as the 43 first secretaries of province committees, 11 other secretaries of province committees, 7 CC secretaries, and 5 CC department heads. Rank and file workers comprised 393 (only 20 percent) and farmers 190.[166] Thus, the delegates were mainly low-level party activists and relatively well-educated office workers. According to official count, 405 delegates (20.6 percent) belonged to Solidarity, plus 9 members of rural Solidarity, while 1,099 (56 percent) belonged to the traditional branch trade unions.[167]

Taking advantage of the election of so many delegates not beholden to the leadership, militants began to organize blocs to operate at the congress in opposition to the Politburo, both on policy matters and in election of leaders. Judging by statements in local papers, such efforts to coordinate emanated to a considerable degree from horizontal units. During May, as election of delegates moved into full swing, meetings of horizontal units, usually called "discussion forums," began calling on newly elected congress delegates to get together with fellow delegates from their province to work out common positions.

On May 21–22 the Poznan "Forum of Political Thought," with representatives from Bydgoszcz, Lodz, Olsztyn, Pila, Plock, Szczecin, Torun, and Wroclaw, met and criticized congress preparations and sent a letter to Kania urging holding of a national forum of delegates on June 10— which would also be attended by representatives of horizontal units— and then forums of delegates in each province to "prepare program and cadres proposals."[168] Another account of the Poznan meeting stated that the "basic theme of the forum was to set postulates and proposals advanced by the party masses against the documents worked out by the Central Congress Commission."[169] Among the criticisms was the failure of the draft party statute to recognize "the right to establish contacts between party organizations" (horizontal units) or "to establish continuing mandates for delegates" (so that congress delegates could be called back into session at any time before the next congress). Wojciech Lamentowicz, one of the most outspoken advocates of basic party reforms, urged efforts to coordinate the positions of the approximately three hundred delegates elected at factory party conferences (on the assumption that these would be more independent of control from above than delegates elected at province conferences).

A Lodz "Forum of Delegates" met on May 12 to exchange views and discuss "promoting the best and most suitable candidates for party leadership,"[170] and again on May 23 to enable delegates to "prediscuss their positions" on issues in preparation for debate at the congress.[171] On May 19 the "group for joint work of Lublin party organizations" proposed creating a "club" of Lublin delegates to develop "common views" and promote candidates.[172] The May 28 *Gazeta Krakowska* reported that the Krakow horizontal units, "which officially go by the name the 'Party Aktiv Forum,'" had called for publication of a list of candidates for leadership and for "all party horizontal coordination groups—in all regions of the country—to immediately exchange views on the theme of specific leaders and their suitability for leadership," on the "makeup of the new Central Committee."

Another horizontal group formed in Glogow,[173] in Legnica province, and held a meeting on May 15 with representatives from 175 party organizations in five lower Silesian provinces, encompassing 35,000 party members. In a fiery speech at the meeting, Jerzy Jankowski, a Wroclaw delegate to the congress, assailed the CC and announced that his local party organization had adopted a "vote of no confidence" in the CC. He declared that "horizontal structures are not our goal"; they are a "means to a goal," which is "to win the congress." Warning that "the congress may be manipulated," he called for forming "horizontal structures of our delegates at the congress" to work out the main lines of their speeches and "settle on candidates for the leadership."[174]

Over the course of just a few months in late 1980 and early 1981 the PZPR moved from the traditional tightly controlled and manipulated communist party elections to democratized forms unique among communist parties. Starting sporadically in the party base, new practices—secret balloting and choice of candidates—moved up through the party, became institutionalized in the party's election rules, and became the norm for all party organizations by mid-1981. Party organizations could now nominate a variety of candidates for leadership and choose freely between them and even debate issues. As a result, many reform-minded party members and Solidarity members were elected to positions of responsibility, as committee members, secretaries, and delegates to higher conferences. Politicians, even conservative politicians, had to recognize their dependence on those below them, rather than rely on their superiors. Power was beginning to flow from below, reversing traditional democratic centralism, and the breakdown of control from the top left the party pluralistic, as local organizations and members could ignore leadership decisions with little concern about enforcement of party discipline. The party no longer was a pliant tool of its leadership, and when martial law was imposed in December 1981, one of the main tasks facing Jaruzelski was how to make party organizations and members obedient to the leadership once again.

CHAPTER 3

FACTIONS' STRUGGLE FOR CONTROL

THE ELECTION REFORMS and breakdown of party discipline opened the door for pluralism in the party. No longer forced to echo one viewpoint, party members and leaders formed up into factions representing different views. Factions had always existed in the PZPR, but now with the lack of discipline, they could express their views openly and contest with each other. Moreover, the challenges facing the party—how to respond to Solidarity and how to reform the party and political system—raised extremely divisive issues and stimulated disagreement. The breakdown of censorship and control from above soon made it impossible to keep debates at the top a secret. With the activism of the rank and file and of "horizontal ties" units and the right to choose between party leaders by secret ballot, the party membership soon was able to join in the debate on such issues. This opening up of political debate to the whole party was devastating for the conservatives, since the rank and file was overwhelmingly for reform.

Party leaders divided into roughly three groups, largely defined by their attitudes to Solidarity and party reform:

- Liberals, reflecting the public mood outside the party, pressed for faster and more meaningful reforms and accused conservatives and often all party leaders of resisting change. They saw Solidarity as an ally or at least a positive force in forcing improvements on the system. This group ranged from those who wanted drastic reform (like Torun horizontal ties leader Zbigniew Iwanow and many Solidarity members) to more pragmatic, establishment types (like Gdansk shipyard party secretary Jan Labecki and *Polityka* editor Mieczyslaw Rakowski).

- Conservatives questioned most reforms and concessions by the party and government and insisted on getting tough with Solidarity, even to the point of using force against strikes. Although conservatives included many holdovers from the pre-August period, the most important hard-liners were those who came to power during renewal. Stefan Olszowski and Tadeusz Grabski, who had called for economic reform under Gierek, soon became the leading symbols of hard-line policies through their attacks on Solidarity and their maneuvers against most reforms. Andrzej Zabinski, who initially had a somewhat liberal image because of signing the August accords with the strikers in Szczecin and because of his sharp attacks on regime policies at the September Sejm session, soon became one of the most outspoken advocates of fighting Solidarity.
- Moderates were caught in the middle. They acknowledged the need for changes in the discredited system and the need to win back the support of the rank and file by "democratizing" the party, but worried about reform getting out of hand and accepted most changes grudgingly and slowly. Typified by First Secretary Kania, Organizational Secretary Barcikowski, and Defense Minister Jaruzelski, they saw bloodshed as the only alternative to making concessions to Solidarity and so resisted conservative calls to use force against strikes. Their most notable position was that conflicts had to be resolved exclusively by peaceful means—by political negotiations. Most political leaders appeared to fall into this category.

The divisions in the leadership began publicly emerging during January and February and were aggravated by a cycle of crises during the first half of 1981. Liberals pushed for an early congress, while conservatives dragged their feet. Debates in the Congress Commission over changes in the party program, statute, and election rules set CC secretaries Olszowski and Grabski against the liberals. Strikes and threats of strikes intensified leadership differences over how to deal with Solidarity, and the contrasting viewpoints were voiced openly and clearly at the February 9 CC plenum. There was a temporary lull after the plenum when General Jaruzelski was named premier and popular reformer Rakowski became deputy premier in charge of dealing with Solidarity and trade union problems. The great popular respect Jaruzelski enjoyed as head of the armed forces helped him to win partial acceptance for a temporary moratorium on strikes and improved the atmosphere.

The crisis situation returned in mid-March when police beat rural Solidarity organizers in Bydgoszcz—a probable provocation organized by hard-liners—and the Politburo, with some members absent, issued a hard-line statement siding with the police and condemning Solidarity. Outraged Solidarity leaders protested and called a general strike for March 31. The Soviet Union applied pressure from the other side in the form of prolonged Warsaw Pact military maneuvers. Tension intensified within the party when Journalists Union head Stefan Bratkowski circulated a letter alleging that hard-liners in the Politburo were obstructing reform and resisting the moderate leadership of Kania, Jaruzelski, and Barcikowski. Local party organizations began demanding the ouster of Olszowski and Grabski, and open conflict between reformers and conservatives broke out at the late March CC plenum. The party appeared on the verge of a showdown, but Kania and the moderates, fearing Soviet intervention to protect the more orthodox party leaders, managed to avert a showdown vote at the plenum, which would probably have ousted the leading hard-liners. To assuage liberal forces, which were disappointed at the lack of a leadership shake-up, Kania promised changes at the next plenum. He also managed to avert a general strike by making more concessions to Solidarity.

The balancing act continued during April. The mid-April Torun Forum of horizontal ties units increased pressure for faster reform, while Soviet leader Suslov made a sudden April 23 visit apparently to pressure Kania to stand firm and to bolster the position of the embattled Olszowski and Grabski. The next plenum, in late April, also avoided action against the conservatives, but appeased reformers by making limited leadership changes and finally setting a date for the party congress.

The compromise began unraveling again in May and June as local party elections leading up to the congress began widely defeating conservatives, and desperate hard-liners began forming groups to attack Kania and change the direction of the party. Soviet leaders, worried about the reformist victories in party elections, on June 5 sent Kania and Jaruzelski a sharply worded letter warning them to take action against the growing "antisocialist" threat. Emboldened by the letter, conservatives challenged Kania's leadership at the June 9 plenum. They were defeated, but Kania made no move to oust them and carefully kept the Soviet favorites in the leadership. He even managed to build an alliance with some conservatives (Olszowski and Zabinski) by helping them win re-election at local conferences and by agreeing to oust liberal media chief Jozef Klasa—a special target of hard-liners.

The jerry-built leadership balance broke down at the July congress when uncontrolled delegates elected a new CC which excluded some of the most prominent conservatives (Grabski and Zabinski) as well as liberals (Fiszbach). To maintain the balancing act, Kania carefully reconstructed a new Politburo at the end of the congress again balanced with conservatives (Olszowski, Miroslaw Milewski, Albin Siwak) and liberals (Labecki, Hieronim Kubiak).

THE EMERGENCE OF FACTIONS

The outlines of the factions developing within the party began publicly emerging in early 1981. At the October and December CC plenums virtually everyone had pressed for reforms, but at the February 9 plenum some—such as Politburo member Zabinski—began raising Solidarity as a threat and warning that reform might get out of hand. Others closer to the workers and party rank and file pressed for working with Solidarity and speeding party reforms. Delays in calling the new party congress and enacting reforms had created growing public suspicion that conservatives were obstructing reform, and two events in March dramatically confirmed for the public that there was indeed a hard-line faction fighting Solidarity and reform. The police beating of rural Solidarity organizers in Bydgoszcz appeared to be a provocation by hard-liners to force a general confrontation between the party and Solidarity. The event sharpened the identity of the factions, as conservatives Grabski and Olszowski defended the police action, liberals condemned it, and moderates—some of whom were initially confused—soon recognized it as a mistake. The second event was a letter sent to all party organizations by Journalists Union chairman Stefan Bratkowski asserting that there was a hard-line faction opposing reform and fighting the moderate leadership of Kania, Jaruzelski, and Barcikowski. The letter raised the issue of conservative opposition openly for party discussion, and many party organizations reacted strongly, demanding removal of Politburo members who were obstructing reform. By the time the next plenum opened on March 29, a grass-roots campaign had been whipped up against the conservatives, and the prospect of a drastic purge of reform foes in the leadership loomed.

Statements at the February plenum reflected the development of sharply contrasting views, especially on Solidarity. The viewpoints were clearest in the speeches of conservative Katowice First Secretary Andrzej Zabinski, reform-minded Gdansk shipyard party secretary Jan Labecki, and moderate Bialystok First Secretary Stefan Zawodzinski.

Zabinski's speech reflected strong hostility toward Solidarity and opposition to concessions and was filled with calls to fight "enemies." He declared that "the present situation is diametrically different from that at the end of August and beginning of September of last year," since "the foe has revealed his counterrevolutionary face. . . . Today the problem is whether to defend the power of the people and working class or to put it in the hands of our enemies." He accused many Solidarity leaders of "hostility" to the party and not really representing the working class. He called on party members belonging to Solidarity "to consistently oppose the influence of antisocialist and anarchist forces and oppose the strike movement." He assailed concessions to Solidarity, stating that accord "cannot mean further concessions in the face of escalation of demands which further and further depart from the spirit of the agreements [with Solidarity], political demands par excellence, aimed at the basic system of our socialist state." "All permissible barriers of concessions are being crossed," and "the party and people's government can retreat no further." If we slide over into "capitulationism," "we will lose the confidence of [our party] aktiv," and "every concession supposedly mollifies the foe but really, without any supposedly, weakens our aktiv." He added that "although I know it is very unpopular" to say this, he felt that because of the strikes conditions for holding a congress were worsening and the congress should be delayed.[1]

Zabinski in the months ahead became one of the most obvious conservatives. Someone secretly taped a speech he made to Katowice police on tactics to use in discrediting Solidarity. His remarks were taken abroad and carried in the April 6, 1981 *Der Spiegel*. The tape was circulated in "many regions of the country," according to the Opole province paper *Trybuna Opolska*, April 28, 1981, and its authenticity was later confirmed by Zabinski himself. Responding to questions about the tapes during a visit to Opole, Zabinski admitted that he had given a five-hour talk to police in late September 1980 but complained that the excerpts on the tapes were misleading.[2]

In contrast to Zabinski, openly reformist and pro-Solidarity views were expressed at the plenum by Gdansk shipyard worker and party secretary Jan Labecki, who denied that Solidarity ("to which most party members belong") was an enemy or "antisocialist force." He assailed those who pressed for "confrontation" with Solidarity, because, he said, it "would be political suicide for the party." To confront Solidarity, he argued, we must draw the majority of the public to our side, but this "first of all requires clean hands," which the party will not have until it removes and punishes all those guilty of past abuses. Labecki also pressed for calling the next party congress, since, he recalled, the October plenum had said that the date would be set at the next plenum, but the December plenum simply promised the same thing. "If today we repeat this same thing again, doubts will grow."[3]

The division between conservatives and liberals was openly confirmed by moderate Bialystok leader Zawodzinski. He stated that there were two basic views of the causes of the country's crisis being expressed at party meetings: that "renewal is being slowed down by conservative groups in the party and government and economic administration, especially at the central level," and that "extremist elements" of Solidarity are "keeping up tension" by threats of strikes. Reflecting the moderate viewpoint, he took a much more optimistic view of Solidarity than the hard-liners did, stressing that most of Solidarity's leaders—at least in his home province—sincerely "want authentic socialist renewal" and apply pressure on the government and make overly categorical demands simply because they do not know any better method. Hence, we must use "much understanding and patience" in dealing with them. If people follow Solidarity's calls to strike, it is not out of great eagerness to strike but often is "our fault" for not presenting the public with more convincing and complete information via the media. He declared that today renewal is equivalent to "full objective information," and "I am for giving more freedom of action to journalists" and for "objective evaluation of the trade union movement, both Solidarity and branch [traditional] trade unions."[4] Zawodzinski later classified himself specifically as a "centrist" in an interview in a local paper.[5]

Not long after the February plenum some conservatives organized a provocation apparently aimed at widening the split between the party and Solidarity and forcing the predominant moderate leadership to come down against Solidarity. At a March 19 meeting of the Bydgoszcz province people's council, a group pressing for recognition of a rural counterpart for Solidarity, a Solidarity union for farmers, was ejected by police when local authorities closed the session and protesters refused to leave. In the process, some Solidarity organizers, especially Jan Rulewski, were severely and unnecessarily beaten. The incident had overtones of deliberate provocation because of the abrupt handling of the meeting, the unnecessary roughness of the police, and the fact that police themselves later complained of central politicians misusing them in this case.[6]

This brutal police action provoked the predictable reaction by Solidarity and then produced a hard-line regime response against Solidarity. Outraged Solidarity units called for strikes to protest the action, first a warning strike on March 27 and then a general strike for March 31. Although versions of the Bydgoszcz events differed over whether the Solidarity people or the local authorities and police were more to blame, the Politburo on March 22 went ahead and issued a statement taking a hard-line stance, endorsing the tough action by local authorities, criticizing Solidarity, and calling on all party members to counteract the threatened strikes.

The Politburo statement appeared to be a coup by the hard-liners, since it was adopted hastily and apparently when some Politburo members— relatively moderate ones—were not present. Of the ten voting Politburo members, it was clear that CC secretaries Olszowski and Grabski had voted for the statement, since they both later endorsed and defended it, while Katowice First Secretary Zabinski, in view of his hard-line statements at the February CC plenum and elsewhere, probably backed it also. Moderates First Secretary Kania, Organizational Secretary Barcikowski, President Jablonski, and Deputy Premier Jagielski probably voted against, although some of them may also have been alarmed enough by the initial misleading reports to vote with the conservatives. Premier

Jaruzelski and Supreme Chamber of Control chairman Mieczyslaw Moczar were apparently absent, the first attending military exercises in Silesia and the latter in the hospital after a heart attack.[7] The question of which members were present and who voted for the statement was put to Barcikowski at an April Rzeszow meeting, but he refused to answer, declaring this an "internal matter of the Politburo" and that "I am not in the habit of tattling, so to say, on my colleagues." Members, he said, "must have assurance of a certain discretion in work," and "I would be disloyal as one of the Politburo members if I told who participated in the meeting and who did not, and who took which position, because that would have to lead to limiting freedom of expression of one's views in the Politburo."[8]

Moderate leaders soon began publicly criticizing the March 22 Politburo statement. Jablonski told a Krakow factory party meeting on April 8 that the "Politburo had not received correct data" when it adopted its statement, and it "was undoubtedly a mistake by the bureau."[9] Politburo candidate member Roman Ney at an April 5 Krakow meeting declared that the Politburo had not had "full knowledge of the events" when it adopted the decision "which aroused so much opposition. . . . For me personally this is a lesson, so that in the future we should examine in detail information of this type presented to Politburo members to determine if it is correct and reliable. I think the party has corrected the evaluation and evaluated it critically."[10]

The uproar over the Bydgoszcz beatings and the March 22 Politburo statement was compounded by a March 23 letter from Journalists Union chairman Stefan Bratkowski to all party organizations asserting that a group of conservatives in the leadership was fighting reforms. The letter, according to available versions,[11] declared that there are people in the leadership

> who do not seek agreement, even with their party grass roots. . . . They avoid the test of honest elections and use all the means available to postpone the extraordinary congress. . . . These are the men who try to set the forces of public order in conflict with their own community so as to preclude all other ways out except confrontation. . . . I have been observing their activities for months and I cannot discern even a single proposal which goes beyond the protection of their own positions, beyond the ambition to reach out for still higher ones. Virtually everything they do increases tension and

mutual mistrust. . . . I am not in the habit of getting involved in personal matters of power and, therefore, I am not mentioning any names. But, as is generally known, there are comrades among these men who occupy the highest positions in our party, supported by a group of comrades rallied around the Warsaw party echelon and also by various people from the apparatus of power.

He then went on to voice support for those he considered moderate leaders: "We have staked all on Comrade Kania, on Barcikowski. We also do not see any alternative to the government of General Jaruzelski. . . . It seems to me that we rank and file members of the primary party organizations, all primary party organizations, should loudly proclaim our choice, both to the Central Committee of our party and to the country."

While not naming his targets, Bratkowski clearly had Olszowski and Grabski in mind, and his perception of their position probably came from his arguments with Olszowski in the Congress Commission during January and February. Olszowski, who played a key role in the commission,[12] later recalled his disputes with Bratkowski at commission meetings. At an April 3 meeting at the Warsaw Steel Plant, Olszowski was asked about Bratkowski's letter and stated that "I have engaged in polemics with Comrade Bratkowski several times, directly, eye to eye, during sessions of the Congress Commission, concerning a number of views he holds," including "the question of democratic centralism" and "relations with our neighbors and allies. . . . I and Comrade Bratkowski used to engage repeatedly in polemics in the past. We have known each other for a long time now."[13] Bratkowski in the Congress Commission had made controversial proposals, for example, to elect the Politburo "directly in party organizations."[14] Grabski, who headed one of the Congress Commission's teams,[15] clearly considered himself a target of Bratkowski's letter. He later told a local plant audience that Bratkowski's letter, "read over Radio Free Europe," had listed him among the "so-called hardliners."[16]

These two led the attack on Bratkowski when the March plenum opened. Grabski attacked Bratkowski's " 'open letter' distributed by Solidarity" for sowing "confusion and disorganization among wide groups of party members" by asserting divisions in the leadership. He denied opposing compromise and dialogue and denied a division in the Politburo between "reformers" (*odnowicieli*) and "hard-liners" (*twardoglowy*). He stated that the wide distribution of the letter was "clear subversive activity" and that "to be classified by Bratkowski in a group of 'hard-liners' when it is a matter of defending socialism is an honor."[17] Olszowski assailed Bratkowski for accusing him in his letter and some other statements of manipulating the press and providing misinformation (Olszowski as CC secretary was in charge of the media), and he asserted that Bratkowski "as a member of the Congress Commission had taken the course of dividing the party and its leadership."[18]

The Bratkowski letter and the Bydgoszcz affair riled up party organizations to a greater degree than ever. Although never published in the central press, the Bratkowski letter was widely discussed in party organizations and provoked many demands that any such foes of reform be removed from the leadership. The Politburo statement on the Bydgoszcz situation turned out to be very unpopular and was repudiated by many party organizations. The Bydgoszcz provocation, rather than rallying the party against Solidarity, caused many party members and even organizations to side with Solidarity against the party leadership.

Deputy Premier Rakowski described the seriousness of the situation graphically in his March plenum speech. Stating that for several days resolutions from local party organizations and Solidarity demanding "full and objective" explanation of the Bydgoszcz events had been flowing in to the CC "without letup," he declared, "I think that this is the first time since September that such significant sections of the party have massively sided with Solidarity organizations. . . . I think the unusually sharp reaction of the public to the Bydgoszcz events arises from the fact that the whole people or a significant part of it believe that the law was broken in Bydgoszcz and not just by Solidarity. . . . Our foes can break the law, although they shouldn't, but we must never do this." Expressing his sympathy for the unenviable position of the local authorities and police in handling the situation, he stated that nevertheless, "I ask you comrades, why the events in Bydgoszcz have aroused such a great wave of dissatisfaction, why the country has been brought to the point of a political crisis? Is it only because the industrious propagandists of Solidarity knew how to play on people's feelings?" While this may have been a factor, he stated, "the main reason for the misfortune is that both the party base and significant sections of the public hold certain rather important doubts regarding the trustworthiness of our words and deeds" and "don't believe that we really sincerely want to carry out the renewal program."[19]

Bratkowski came under attack at the plenum for violating party discipline by publicly alleging divisions in the leadership. In addition to Grabski and Olszowski, Barcikowski's opening report at the plenum criticized Bratkowski for spreading his views outside the party and introducing divisions into the party and its leadership.[20] But moderates were not really interested in punishing Bratkowski, since he was supporting their position, and Barcikowski himself later indicated to his home party organization in Krakow that he had had to criticize the letter precisely because it had praised him: "I had to speak out so that people do not say I'm agreeing with Bratkowski's letter for private reasons, because it praised me."[21] CC Secretary Zdzislaw Kurowski later told a Bialystok audience that no one accused Bratkowski of "ill will" but that his letter was "simply incorrect" in dividing the leadership into "adherents and opponents of renewal," and "moreover, he had distributed his letter, dealing with internal party matters, by channels outside the party."[22]

The plenum wound up taking symbolic but weak action against Bratkowski. Although Gorzow worker Antoni Pierz attacked Bratkowski's letter for "weakening the party" and setting the rank and file against the leadership and urged that Bratkowski be removed from the Congress Commission,[23] the plenum just remanded his case to the Central Party Control Commission (CKKP) for "consideration."[24] Even this weak rebuke was undercut by statements defending him by liberals. CC Press Department chief Jozef Klasa told a Krakow audience that the plenum's action was correct, since the Politburo and CC should not decide this sort of thing hastily, and the control commission had little power to punish Bratkowski. He added that "I personally value Bratkowski for courageous thinking, for being involved."[25] In a later interview, Klasa stated that those who voted to send his case to the CKKP "not for a moment intended to have him expelled from the party."[26] Wloclawek First Secretary Edward Szymanski praised Bratkowski when asked about the plenum's decision at a March 30 meeting in his home province,[27] and a number of local organizations publicly voiced support for Bratkowski. Immediately upon the end of the plenum, a Gdansk student union sent a letter to Bratkowski expressing support for him.[28] The party organization of the newspaper *Zycie Warszawy* also adopted a resolution of support for Bratkowski.[29] Politburo candidate member Roman Ney told an April 5 Krakow audience that the decision on Bratkowski "had not found support among party members, as evidenced by numerous resolutions."[30]

In the end, the action taken against Bratkowski turned out to be virtually meaningless. When the Central Party Control Commission met with Bratkowski on April 8, it merely pointed out to him the "inappropriateness" of his actions and chided him for his letter, which was causing "speculation that does not serve party unity."[31]

SHOWDOWN AT THE MARCH PLENUM

The March 29–30 plenum opened in an atmosphere of anger stirred by the Bydgoszcz events and Bratkowski's letter and with a deluge of demands by local party organizations for action against conservatives. Speeches at the plenum delivered unprecedented attacks on the Politburo, badly shaking not only the conservatives but all leaders. In the end, moderates, worried by possible Soviet reaction to a sudden reformist takeover and citing the threat of a general strike on March 31, managed to avert a showdown and purge of hard-liners and paper over the factional split. Many local party organizations reacted angrily against the compromise, and the Politburo had to quickly schedule another plenum and promise changes. Kania managed to skillfully appease reformers by sacrificing several less important leaders and adding some workers to the Politburo without ousting the main hard-liners and upsetting the Soviets.

The 9th plenum opened on March 29 amid resolutions and messages from local party organizations and individuals expressing sharp stands on the issues dividing the party. During the plenum Kania reported that in the days just preceding the plenum 350 resolutions and messages had arrived, some containing criticism of the Politburo, calls for cadre changes, demands for fuller explanation of the Bydgoszcz events, and attacks on the Politburo statement on Bydgoszcz.[32] In a postplenum April 2 speech at Warsaw's Rawar radio factory, he stated that some of these resolutions criticized "specific comrades" and others alleged that the Politburo was "the arena of a tug of war in the form of factional struggles."[33] Messages continued to arrive during the plenum, and one, from the radical Gdansk shipyard party organization, assailed the opening report at the plenum and urged that the whole Politburo resign, that all Politburo members should "retire by placing themselves at the disposal of CC First Secretary Kania, who should be entrusted with proposing a new Politburo which would guarantee real implementation of renewal."[34]

The criticisms of the Politburo and of conservatives in local resolutions were repeated in many speeches delivered at the plenum itself. Speakers, especially rank and file workers on the CC, demanded a fuller, more convincing explanation of the Bydgoszcz events and punishment of those who broke the law—implicitly meaning the authorities also if they had done so. Wroclaw worker Janina Kostrzewska declared that her party organization "considered the Bydgoszcz events a clear violation of the constitutional freedoms and rights of citizens" and felt that the Politburo's statement on Bydgoszcz was "premature" and failed to consider the "will and opinions of party members." A worker from Bydgoszcz itself, Jozef Blajet, said that the Politburo statement was "in disagreement with the feelings of rank and file party members." Lodz worker Jadwiga Nowakowska in the name of Lodz party organizations demanded punishment for "that part of the present party leadership which knowingly misinformed the public and especially party members" about the events in Bydgoszcz and similar confrontations in Bielsko-Biala and Lodz. Ryszard Bryk, party first secretary in Siedlce, acknowledged that "the majority of party organizations did not support the Politburo's stand" on Bydgoszcz, and he stated that the party should deal with Solidarity "conscientiously" and not as it had in Bydgoszcz. Krystyn Dabrowa, first secretary in Krakow, "fully agreed" with all these statements by Bryk.[35]

Many party members clearly sided with Solidarity against the party leadership. Szczecin worker Edward Pustelnik stated at the plenum that his local party organization (of which 99 percent belonged to Solidarity) did not approve of the Politburo's call for party members not to participate in the threatened strike and that many party members were convinced that "the whole Bydgoszcz affair was provoked by our leaders, or to put it differently, that it was a move worked out in detail by conservative forces and those hostile to the unfolding process of renewal who place their own, often personal interest completely above the interest of the party and public." Wroclaw worker Janina Kostrzewska belligerently declared that her party organization had gone out on the March 27 warning strike "knowing that we were violating party discipline." Katowice worker Andrzej Bosowski stated that despite the Politburo order to party members, "most party members took part in the strike" and some organizations had voted unanimously to participate.

The Politburo statement and Bydgoszcz crackdown were defended by CC Secretaries Grabski and Olszowski and a few others. The characteristically blunt Grabski declared that "I would not be a communist and would not be me" if he did not declare his support for the March 22 Politburo stand on Bydgoszcz, "although this sounds unpopular everywhere today, even in this hall." Later, at an April 9 meeting in Belchatow, Grabski again defended the Politburo statement and added that he had been in Bydgoszcz just before the events and it had been evident then that Solidarity was carefully preparing for a confrontation at the council session.[36] Olszowski declared at the March plenum that "I wish to support what was contained in the March 22 Politburo communiqué" and that "all charges that the Bydgoszcz incident was a provocation are simply made up." Olszowski was in a particularly vulnerable position because he had gone on television before the Politburo decision to defend the Bydgoszcz crackdown and was criticized for this at the plenum by Plock worker Antoni Wrobel. Olszowski defended himself by saying that "of course, I was proceeding at that time on the basis of the state of information in the CC's possession," but he still "fully subscribe[s]" to the statements. He may have felt doubly threatened because of the charges that the media, which he supervised, had misrepresented the Bydgoszcz situation, and hence his plenum speech also included a strong defense of the media's handling of news. The Bydgoszcz actions were naturally also defended by Bydgoszcz First Secretary Henryk Bednarski, who was criticized for this by Rakowski.[37]

Some speakers made flat demands that conservatives be ousted from the Politburo. Plock worker Antoni Wrobel presented a local party resolution demanding that the plenum oust from the Politburo "those who went so far as to adopt the resolution on the Bydgoszcz events" before the government investigating commission had even completed its work. He assailed Olszowski by name for taking an early stand on the Bydgoszcz affair on television, and he read another local resolution attacking false information on the Bydgoszcz events, stating that those responsible for such information "cannot remain in the Politburo, CC, or the apparat" and calling on the plenum to "purge the party leadership of persons who are compromising it by leading its work in this way." He also read a Plock province Executive Committee resolution calling on the CC plenum to make cadre changes in the Politburo and remove "persons representing conservative positions." It endorsed "resolution of conflicts by political methods" as represented by First Secretary Kania and Premier Jaruzelski. Others reading resolutions from local organizations calling for ouster of foes of reform included Czestochowa worker Kazimierz Jarzabek, Warsaw worker Albin Siwak, and Wroclaw laboratory director Wlodzimierz Trzebiatowski.

Criticisms were directed not only against the conservatives but against the Politburo as a whole—for slowness on reform, for ineffectiveness, and for acting against the wishes of lower party organizations and the rank and file. Plock worker Antoni Wrobel read a resolution from his party organization asserting that "the huge majority of present party members do not identify with the leadership of the party." Bydgoszcz worker Jozef Blajet, criticizing the Politburo over Bydgoszcz, declared that the "CC should consider that every future step not thought through and not consulted will lead to such shrinkage of party membership that only the leadership bodies will remain. . . . Positions of the Politburo must be adopted with speedy consultation with the whole plenum of the CC," he insisted. Gdansk worker Henryk Lewandowski, criticizing the Politburo statement on Bydgoszcz, urged the Politburo, "before adopting a position on important questions, to consult in advance and seek opinions of primary party organizations." Still others—former province First Secretary Janusz Prokopiak, Siedlce First Secretary Ryszard Bryk, Krakow First Secretary Krystyn Dabrowa, and Poznan worker Stanislaw Zielinski—criticized the Politburo's report to the plenum. Warsaw worker Zygmunt Gajewski, a CC member, later told a meeting of workers that this was the first plenum to hear such "wide criticism of the Politburo's activity."[38]

Shaken by strong criticism in these local resolutions and in speeches at the plenum, the whole Politburo apparently discussed resigning. An article in the Katowice paper *Trybuna Robotnicza*, April 6, 1981, mentioned a rumor that during a 6:00 P.M. break the whole Politburo had decided to resign. Barcikowski, answering questions at a Rzeszow meeting, stated that the sharp criticism had prompted some members to submit resignations and that all Politburo members considered resigning but eventually decided that this was a poor way to solve the crisis, and so "then the idea of a vote of confidence was born."[39]

Although most other Politburo members decided against resigning, Grabski and Olszowski went ahead anyway—as a tactic to combat the attacks being made on them. At the conclusion of their plenum speeches, each placed himself "at the disposal of the CC"[40]—a loose formula implying resignation. Questioned later about use of this formula rather than outright resignation, Grabski told an audience in Tarnow: "I did not resign because no charges had been raised against me—merely incorrect insinuations were circulated."[41] Olszowski later explained his action: "Because I and Grabski in particular were attacked, we decided to raise the matter openly at the plenum, and after presenting our views we placed ourselves at the disposal of the CC."[42]

Liberal CC Secretary Roman Ney also put himself "at the disposal of the CC plenum," although for reasons entirely opposite to those of Olszowski and Grabski—as a device to force changes in the leadership and speed reform. Complaining that almost all reforms had had to be forced on the leadership from below and admitting the correctness of criticisms of the leadership at the plenum, Ney explained that he was submitting his resignation "to make it possible for the first secretary to recruit a better leadership group" and "end the party's lack of confidence in its leadership." He proposed that the plenum elect a new, better Politburo. Questioned about his motive for resigning, Ney later told an April 5 Krakow audience, "By my resignation I wanted to signal that I see the need for changes in the Politburo," and he added that there should be more factory workers in the Politburo rather than "professional party functionaries."[43] Moderate CC Secretary Kurowski, in a speech prepared for the plenum but not actually delivered, also said that he was prepared to place himself at the disposal of the CC.[44]

Although Olszowski and Grabski—both of whom had been demoted under Gierek because of their outspokenness—were apparently willing to risk a showdown vote, the moderates were not, presumbly for fear expulsion of the top conservatives would prompt Soviet intervention. To avert a showdown, a compromise was worked out. First, Kania assured the CC that all Politburo members favored dealing with the Solidarity strike threat by political means rather than by force, and hence there was no split in the Politburo and no conservatives in the Politburo.[45] Then, with Kania's support,[46] a resolution was presented by Wloclawek First Secretary Edward Szymanski stressing the need for unity (including avoidance of leadership changes) in the face of the crisis. It provided for withdrawal of all the resignations and for giving a "vote of confidence" to the Politburo and Secretariat. To pacify the rank and file it obliged Politburo and Secretariat members immediately after the plenum to meet with party organizatons of big factories where they could be questioned by party members about their attitudes. There were also vague promises of personnel changes at the next plenum. Kania in his plenum speech said that he favored retaining the present membership of the Politburo, but he added that "it seems that at the next CC plenum it may prove useful to expand it."[47] Some understood this as a firm part of the deal. Krakow First Secretary Dabrowa told a local audience that "a postulate was adopted to add workers to the Politburo at the next plenum."[48]

The resolution was adopted with near-unanimous support and enabled the leadership to get through the crisis posed by the open split and the Solidarity strike threat. Only Gdansk shipyard representative Jan Labecki voted against it, voicing his outrage at the plenum's failure to make any changes in the Politburo. He told a local paper that he had been the only one voting against it but that a "significant number" of others had abstained in "quiet protest."[49] The voting results were not announced, and Kania and Szymanski disputed claims of more opposition.[50]

The compromise infuriated many local organizations, and the resolution's order for leaders to meet local organizations after the plenum and answer questions led to unusual ordeals for many leaders. In Gdansk where there was bitterness over the "lack of personnel changes in the leadership," the province's representatives on the CC (First Secretary Tadeusz Fiszbach, shipyard worker Henryk Lewandowski, sailor Czeslaw Drozdowicz, and shipyard party first secretary Jan Labecki) went straight to a shipyard meeting to face angry constituents as soon as their plane landed.[51] According to the same account, Fiszbach had to face three other angry local meetings the same day. One important Gdansk party organization, at the Polish Ocean Lines, passed a resolution demanding that a new plenum be held to examine the work and views of Politburo members.[52]

The Gdansk shipyard party organization called a general meeting to discuss the situation and invited Kania and Olszowski to participate.[53] Kania himself showed up at the long April 9 session, listening for seven hours to criticisms of the leadership.[54] At the meeting Labecki bitterly asserted that the plenum had shown that renewal "is only a declaration on paper and will not be implemented in practice," since the plenum had failed to punish those responsible for the Bydgoszcz events, despite the demands of many CC members. He declared that the CC "in its present composition in large part represents no one," since it still included over thirty former province secretaries and a number of ministers who had been removed.[55] At the end, Kania spoke, acknowledging that the March plenum had fallen short of expectations because of the lack of cadre changes but promising that the next plenum would take up cadre matters.[56]

Hard-liners came in for tough questioning by some local party organizations. Olszowski and Grabski were asked at local meetings why they had submitted their resignations, and they defended themselves as victims of unfair and vicious maneuvers. Olszowski told Warsaw workers that "the division between supposed hard-liners and advocates of renewal is invented" and assailed Bratkowski's letter for asserting the existence of hard-liners.[57] Grabski told an audience in Tarnow that Bratkowski's letter, "read over Radio Free Europe," as well as various rumors, had listed him among the "so-called 'hard-liners.'" He snapped: "If you consider the content of my speech at the 9th plenum to have been sharp, you must remember that I was not being treated gently either."[58]

The compromise resolution produced a special backlash against its author. Edward Szymanski, who was accused of trying to whitewash the Politburo, was subjected to intensive questioning, and soon lost his post as Wloclawek first secretary. In numerous talks with reporters and at local meetings he sought to justify his actions and argued that the press had distorted his position.[59] In an interview entitled "Obviously You Don't Know the Whole Resolution," he maintained that the press had misrepresented his views by not printing his plenum speech or the full text of his resolution.[60] Denying that his resolution gave a positive evaluation of all Politburo actions, he stated that "obviously you don't know

LEADERS OF KANIA-JARUZELSKI REGIME

Stanislaw Kania

Wojciech Jaruzelski

Kazimierz Barcikowski

LEADING REFORMERS

Mieczyslaw Rakowski

Hieronim Kubiak

Tadeusz Fiszbach

Jan Labecki

LEADING HARDLINERS

Stefan Olszowski

Tadeusz Grabski

Andrzej Zabinski

Albin Siwak

Photos from Polish newspapers and television, August 1980–June 1986

the whole resolution," and "unfortunately" the "fragment" reported by the Polish Press Agency (PAP) "does not fully convey the sense of my speech." He explained that PAP had prepared the version in a hurry since it was "about 4:00 A.M.," and naturally such a version was not very accurate. Unfortunately, he complained, this initial version had provoked attacks on him "even before I managed to get back to Wloclawek from the plenum." He read the full text of his plenum speech and resolution to local meetings and got some papers to print it.[61]

In the course of defending himself, Szymanski revealed additional details of what happened at the plenum. In a long interview entitled "I Have Nothing To Hide," he insisted that he had written his plenum speech himself and had not been "manipulated" by anyone.[62] He related that at 6:00 P.M. on the first day of the plenum Zbigniew Glowacki had interrupted the debate to propose an immediate vote in view of the approaching strike deadline, after which Kania, who was presiding, announced a recess. According to Szymanski, there apparently was a Politburo meeting during this recess, "although we have no official communiqué about this." Glowacki's proposal for a vote was brushed aside, however (judging by *Trybuna Ludu*'s account), and debate continued. During this and later recesses, said Szymanski, CC members discussed their attitude toward the Politburo and Secretariat among themselves and he got the impression that despite the important criticisms the majority was positive toward the Politburo and felt that no Politburo members wanted to use force to resolve the crisis. They also felt the pressure from below, for example, the Gdansk resolution demanding the resignation of some leaders. On the basis of the consensus for unity he detected, he wrote out his resolution and presented it at 3:00 A.M. "I absolutely reject the rumors that I was manipulated by anyone in this matter. This was my personal, deep conviction. I wrote the text of my speech myself." He declared, "I have nothing to hide," and he complained about the fact that his speech and resolution were not included in the published reports on the plenum, leading to misinterpretations. "I even phoned the chief editor of *Trybuna Ludu* on this matter, but he told me that the report had been prepared not by his editorial staff but by PAP."

PAP's abridgment of his resolution distorted his position, he claimed. His proposals, far from whitewashing the Politburo, had called for a "critical evaluation of the Politburo and Secretariat," he said.[63] Moreover, he told journalists on April 3, he too wanted changes in the lead-ership—specifically the removal of Jerzy Waszczuk, Emil Wojtaszek, and Jozef Pinkowski from the Politburo—but had argued for delaying this until after the March 31 strike threat.[64]

Szymanski continued his efforts at the April 29 CC plenum, raising the matter of his March plenum resolution, "which aroused so much controversy, conjecture, and rumors in the party." Then, he argued, the CC had been facing a crisis (the general strike) and could not shake up the leadership; now, at this plenum, conditions are different and changes can be made, he said.[65] But despite his efforts to justify his actions, the beleaguered Szymanski was not reelected first secretary at his province party conference on May 30. The appreciative leadership soon found a job for him in Warsaw, however. *Trybuna Ludu* on August 14 identified him as head of the CC's Bureau for Sejm Affairs.

In the face of such dissatisfaction over the March plenum compromise, a Politburo session on April 7 scheduled a new CC plenum for late April and speeded work on a new party program and statute.[66] When the next plenum opened on April 29, pressures for changes in the Politburo were still strong,[67] but were not posed in such confrontational terms as at the March plenum. Kania sought to appease the reformers by finally coming up with things they had been urgently demanding and by sacrificing several less important leaders and adding some workers to the Politburo.

Kania opened the plenum with a report finally proposing exact dates for the party congress (July 14–18) and presenting draft theses for a party program and a draft of a revised party statute for party-wide discussion. He stressed that the new statute would strengthen intraparty democracy through such principles as secret balloting, reduction of the role of the apparat, and limitation on terms of office, even specifying that the CC first secretary himself would be limited to two terms. Some innovations in franker and fuller media coverage were also made at this plenum. For the first time, radio carried a running account of plenum speeches as they occurred,[68] and the results of plenum votes were an-nounced in detail (see below).

Kania's report mollified and disarmed at least some of the reformers. Labecki, so outspokenly critical after the March plenum, declared in his April plenum speech that "for the first time since August" a Politburo report to a large degree had satisfied him. He said that it outlined a program "which one can boldly take to party members and say this is now more or less what we would like to expect in the future."[69]

The main demand by speakers at the plenum was for changes in the Politburo, a subject left over from the March plenum. Most outspoken at this plenum were rank and file workers on the CC, especially in calling for the addition of workers to the Politburo[70] or simply changes in the Politburo.[71] Warsaw worker Zygmunt Wronski read a resolution from local Warsaw organizations urging the public disclosure of which primary party organizations individual Politburo members belonged to, so that pressure could be applied to these organizations to influence the leaders belonging to them.[72]

To demonstrate the Politburo's responsiveness to these demands, Kania proposed accepting the resignation of Jozef Pinkowski from the Politburo, Emil Wojtaszek as Politburo candidate member and CC secretary, Jerzy Wojtecki as CC secretary, and Zbigniew Zielinski as Secretariat member, and nominated two workers—Gerard Gabrys and Zygmunt Wronski— as full Politburo members, as well as Opole First Secretary Jozef Masny as Politburo candidate member and Szczecin First Secretary Kazimierz Cypryniak as CC secretary. The CC accepted the resignations,[73] and then in a secret vote elected the four nominated by Kania. In a striking departure from past practice, the communiqué on the plenum announced the results of the vote: Of 123 valid votes, Gabrys was elected with 111, Wronski with 110, Masny with 107, and Cypryniak with 87.

The changes in the Politburo—especially the addition of two rank and file workers—were clearly intended to demonstrate the Politburo's willingness to respond to the grass-roots pressure for "democratizing" the leadership. The two workers were to remain in their local jobs with no specific Politburo responsibilities,[74] and they would thus continue to represent the rank and file.

However, Gabrys and Wronski were by no means real representatives of the rank and file pushed into the leadership to represent reformist or radical views. Not only were they nominated by the Politburo and elected without opposition, but they appeared chosen on carefully weighed political factors and appeared more conservative than most workers. They represented the two biggest party organizations in the country, Katowice and Warsaw: Gabrys, a miner from Katowice, and Wronski, a worker at Warsaw's big Ursus tractor plant. Wronski had harshly attacked the leaders of KOR (the "Workers' Defense Committee," which defended victims of repression) and Solidarity in his February plenum speech.[75] Gabrys, one of the least outspoken workers on the CC, had frequent contact with Katowice officials, including conservative Katowice First Secretary Zabinski.[76] He was chosen by ultraconservatives to head a mid-May Katowice "forum" which attacked the Politburo for softness toward revisionism (although he later dissociated himself from it—see below). Although given much publicity as workers in the Politburo, Gabrys and Wronski apparently were not highly regarded by other workers. Neither were even elected delegates to the July congress by their local primary party organizations, and so they were left out of the Politburo elected at the congress.

Although the plenum appeared very subdued, especially in comparison with the rebellious March plenum, and Gabrys and Wronski won election by overwhelming votes, local papers carried hints that not everyone approved of the choice of those elevated and of the procedure used at the plenum. A May 6 *Dziennik Baltycki* article by Z. Wojmar, based on statements by CC member Labecki, concluded that the April plenum had been "far more interesting and colorful than the boring communiqués and reports of the Polish Press Agency suggest to us." It stated that "controversy had flared up" at the plenum "over the election procedure adopted in expanding the Politburo and Secretariat." Responding to workers' complaints about the plenum's failure to deal with critical issues, the article stated that some speeches—such as those by Mieczyslaw Moczar and Mieczyslaw Rakowski—had contained "juicy" and "striking" polemics excluded from PAP reports and that the audience had strongly reacted against some plenum speeches, indicating "existing lines of division."[77] Hence, it noted there were real grounds for the refusal to televise the plenum. (Some party members had insisted on live television coverage of the plenum.)[78]

The April plenum appeared to reflect successful maneuvering by Kania to satisfy both sides. He avoided the ouster of Olszowski and Grabski, which would have aggravated the Soviets,[79] yet reaction in the party to the April plenum appeared to be much milder than to the March plenum, and Politburo members faced less hostile questioning when they appeared at local party organizations during May. Party organizations appeared to be looking forward to the party-wide elections and July congress for further personnel changes, and hence the leadership was able to weather the storm during March and April.

CONSERVATIVE COUNTEROFFENSIVE

Conservatives, losing most leadership positions during the precongress elections and increasingly unable to hold back the tide of reform, began organizing a counteroffensive during May and June. One of the first signs was the appearance of the "Katowice Party Forum"—a small group of obscure party members which won national attention by making shrill attacks on the party's moderate leadership. In early June the Soviet leaders publicly attacked Kania for allowing the party to slide to the right, and conservatives felt strong enough (or desperate enough) to launch a frontal assault on Kania and try to oust him from leadership.

The conservative challenge was plagued by division, however, undermining its effect. Although the Soviets and a few more daring leaders like Grabski gave support to the Katowice Forum, more cautious conservatives like Olszowski and Zabinski avoided it or even criticized it. When the early June CC plenum opened, Grabski and several allies, bolstered by a Soviet letter attacking Kania, openly proposed removing Kania as first secretary. But Kania not only was able to rally reformers and moderates fearful of a hard-line takeover but also had forged a loose alliance with conservatives Olszowski and Zabinski, who refused to join the attacks on Kania.

Conservatives went down to public defeat at the plenum, but Kania cautiously did not force the ouster of his challenger Grabski. Moreover, he moved to undercut Soviet complaints about the Polish press and also cement his relations with Olszowski by removing liberal media chief Jozef Klasa—special target of the conservatives.

The new phase of conservative activism was heralded by the creation of the so-called "Katowice Party Forum" at a May 15 meeting of sixty obscure party members. It quickly gained notoriety by issuing statements asserting that the national leadership was allowing rightists and revisionists to operate in the party and that there was a "growing threat of a revisionist putsch in the party."[80] At a second meeting later in May, some forum speakers called Kania "unfit for the post of first secretary of the party."[81]

Soviet approval of the forum was indicated when *Pravda* printed excerpts from its statements on June 2. However, the forum's links to Polish leaders were always unclear. When the group formally constituted itself a "forum" on May 15, it sent messages announcing this to Olszowski and Grabski,[82] clearly indicating who they looked to for support. But neither did much for it, at least publicly, and Olszowski later criticized the forum (see below). Even Katowice First Secretary Zabinski carefully kept his distance.

As soon as the forum's radical statements were published, the little-known group was subjected to intense investigation by enterprising reporters from liberal papers in Krakow and Gdansk, as well as by Katowice's own *Dziennik Zachodni*. As *Gazeta Krakowska* on June 1 said, "Everyone was bothered by one thing: who its members were and who is behind them." Gdansk's *Glos Wybrzeza* sent a team of reporters down to Katowice to find out who belonged to the forum and whether it was connected to the Katowice province committee or any prominent figures. The paper's reporters found the forum's cofounder and deputy chairman Wsiewolod Wolczew, a teacher of the theory of politics at a local scientific institute, at his home and quizzed him for two hours, and then tried to find local party leaders to question about their relationship to the forum.

Judging by the extensive information in the June 1 *Glos Wybrzeza*, the ambitious forum organizers appear to have continually sought to establish ties with local authorities and leading conservatives but were largely spurned. Katowice First Secretary Zabinski had attended an informal December meeting of the group but thereafter never associated himself with it. The group sought the province committee's sponsorship, but in vain, according to forum secretary Stefan Owczarz.[83] The most province officials would do is talk with forum leaders and allow them to use the title "Katowice Party Forum under [*przy*] the Province Committee." Nevertheless, Barcikowski later accused the Katowice province committee of providing material support. Asked in Lodz who was linked to the forum, he stated that "although there are no province committee figures in the forum, it [the forum] nevertheless meets in province committee facilities," and "in connection with this there are serious claims against that body."[84]

The forum even had difficulty getting Katowice's press to carry their statements, however. Initially they could only get their statements into the city paper *Dziennik Zachodni*. Only after persuading the province committee propaganda secretary to call the *Trybuna Robotnicza* editor did they finally get the province's main party organ to carry their statements (on May 25 and 29–31). And even then *Trybuna Robotnicza* ran them with an editorial note that the editors did not agree with the statements and that the statements did "not correspond to the spirit of socialist renewal."

In the meantime they managed to get their statements to the Polish Press Agency in Warsaw, which apparently distributed them to several papers. The main party daily, *Trybuna Ludu*, did not publish them, but the central youth paper *Sztandar Mlodych* (on May 28) and regional papers *Gazeta Krakowska* (May 28), *Gazeta Pomorska* (May 29), and *Trybuna Opolska* (June 1) did. However, these papers appeared to publish the statements only to hold them up for criticism.

After the statements were published nationally, various papers and party organizations around the country began attacking the forum, and the Katowice authorities completely disavowed them. Katowice television immediately announced that the Katowice Executive Committee was not the "initiator" of the forum and "did not work closely with it,"[85] and the May 29–31 issue of *Trybuna Robotnicza* published an announcement from the Executive Committee that it "does not identify itself" with all the views expressed in the resolutions. When a *Glos Wybrzeza* reporter went to three Katowice leaders (the province first secretary was away) to ask about the forum, all of them (the province organizational and propaganda secretaries and the city first secretary) claimed to know virtually nothing about the forum and broke off the interviews. The group had latched onto Katowice miner and newly elected Politburo member Gerard Gabrys, inviting him to chair their May 15 meeting and repeatedly referring to him as their chairman.[86] But when reporters asked him on May 26 about his chairmanship of the forum he said he had been invited to the May 15 meeting but had not been able to attend and thus had no connection to the forum's statements.[87] Moreover, after the Politburo criticism of the forum Gabrys denied that he had ever "participated in any meeting or expressed agreement to lead the program council" of the forum and that he fully agreed with the June 2 Politburo statement on the forum.[88]

The Politburo quickly joined in the attacks on the forum. On June 3 *Trybuna Ludu* reported that a June 2 Politburo meeting had discussed the forum's declaration and had declared that it does not aid "party unity" with its "extreme positions" and "unfounded generalizations." On June 5 *Trybuna Ludu* reported a message from the forum stating that because of the Politburo's evaluation of the forum's statements and activities it will follow "principles of democratic centralism" and hold no further meetings until the Politburo gives its consent.

The Politburo's position itself became the subject of a curious controversy at the June 9–10 plenum. Conservative Katowice First Secretary Zabinski in his plenum speech stated that he agreed with the Politburo position "published in the press" and praised the forum for "subordinating itself to the Politburo position."[89] However, others disputed whether the Politburo had in fact ever even discussed the forum. Poznan worker Stanislaw Zielinski flatly stated: "I know that the Politburo did not take up the matter and did not condemn it; nevertheless, Comrade Zabinski asserted that it had. I would like to ask one of the comrades from the Politburo to explain this matter to us openly and frankly."[90] Grabski, complaining that some leadership decisions were being taken outside of the Politburo contrary to its wishes and that misinformation was appearing in the press, declared: "On June 3 we read in some papers about the Politburo's condemnation of the Katowice Forum. I want to declare with full responsibility that the Politburo did not take such a stand; the matter of the Katowice Forum was not considered in the Politburo."[91] Barcikowski, who just happened to be the one who had explained to the press that the Politburo session had censured the forum,[92] then spoke up to derisively "congratulate Comrade Grabski on being so uninformed."[93]

Among other conservatives, only worker Albin Siwak voiced support for the forum at the plenum.[94] Olszowski did not speak at the plenum but had criticized the forum before the plenum. In a May 31 Wloclawek speech he criticized the forum for attacking the Politburo from "dogmatic positions,"[95] and in a speech reported in the June 5 *Trybuna Ludu* he criticized the forum declaration for calling the draft party program a "retreat from Marxism" and the resolutions of the April plenum a "compromise with the right and revisionism."

The Katowice Forum, with its sharp statements, produced more of a political backlash against conservatives than any gains. But the Soviets soon stepped in to try to bolster their friends, sending a June 5 letter to the Polish leadership criticizing Kania and Jaruzelski by name for failing to defend communist principles. The letter was used by conservatives to argue that there was an immediate threat of Soviet intervention if the CC did not end Kania's permissive leadership and halt the slide into liberalism and reform. At a CC plenum to discuss the letter four days later, conservatives, citing the Soviet letter, assailed the breakdown of discipline, the type of candidates being elected at the local party conferences, and the press for being out of control.

The Soviet letter, as published in *Trybuna Ludu* on June 11, complained of "continual concessions to antisocialist forces," that the "predominant part" of the mass media had become "an instrument of antisocialist activity and is being used to undermine socialism," and that "security organs" were being run down. It complained that while Kania and Jaruzelski "agreed with our views in all these questions . . . there have been no changes in the policy of concessions and compromise" and "no steps have been taken to fight" the counterrevolutionary threat. What is worse, in the party itself "forces hostile to socialism more and more are setting the tone in the election campaign," and "people openly expressing opportunistic views" are being elected to head regional organizations and to be delegates to the congress. It asserted that the "horizontal structures" movement is being used to influence the congress, and "it is not to be excluded that at the congress itself there may be an attempt to deal a decisive defeat to the Marxist-Leninist forces of the party and produce its liquidation."

When the plenum opened on June 9, party ranks were unnerved by the new Soviet threat, and this time it was the conservatives who agitated for a shake-up in the Politburo, on grounds that a crackdown was required to avert Soviet intervention. They proposed a change in Kania's policy of peaceful resolution of conflicts, which they claimed in practice usually meant concessions, prescribing instead a policy of resolving social conflicts "at any cost," by force if necessary. Several speakers—especially Torun First Secretary Zygmunt Najdowski, former Radom First Secretary

Janusz Prokopiak, and Ostroleka First Secretary Henryk Szablak—suggested that the Kania leadership was too soft to restore social order, and finally Grabski brought the issue to a head by directly challenging Kania's leadership.

Torun First Secretary Najdowski, again feuding with his province's horizontal movement and reformers, led off by directly proposing "replacement of the present formula of overcoming the crisis by peaceful means and by our own forces with a new formula of overcoming the crisis at any cost by our own forces." He complained that the old formula often just meant concessions. Furthermore, "if you comrades share the view that the formula on the method of resolving the crisis should be replaced, I propose considering making changes in the Politburo so that it would contain comrades who will be able to lead the party in action and struggle." He assailed "social democratic tendencies" in the party and, probably alluding to the Iwanow case, insisted that violations of the party statute must be punished by expulsion from the party, because "our party is in a serious struggle and cannot tolerate anarchy in its ranks."[96]

The second speaker, Gorzow First Secretary Ryszard Labus, continued in the same vein. "I think that we all share the view that our Soviet comrades are right, that we make one concession after another." "I cannot agree" with the Politburo's "positive assessment" of the current election campaign because many party organizations are ignoring the party statute and election rules and "elements" from outside the party have been penetrating the party. He warned that some horizontal units were trying to use the elections to take over by making lists of candidates to vote against in order to ensure victory of their own sympathizers, and he said that the "destructive activity of some horizontal structures" must be "recognized as factional activity."[97]

Janusz Brych, who as head of the CC's Social-Professional Department handled such matters as strike disputes,[98] declared that up to now they had used "only the political method of resolving conflicts" but that this was "too little" to resolve conflicts, which were constantly multiplying. This state of affairs was the fault of CC members and "especially our leadership."[99] Former Radom First Secretary Janusz Prokopiak declared his agreement with the Soviet letter but asked why it was necessary for "our Soviet comrades to open our eyes to what is happening here."

Criticizing the existing "anarchy and chaos," he "formally" proposed "that our present 11th CC plenum in a secret vote express its attitude toward the leadership, precisely to the whole leadership, including the first secretary." If this proposal was approved by the CC, he said, "we will at least in part be able to change the leadership of the party."[100] Poznan First Secretary Jerzy Kusiak declared the "line of political resolution" of conflicts correct but asserted that failure to clearly define the enemy was "an error of the Politburo and Comrade Kania personally."[101] Criticizing the "opportunism" in implementing the line of accord and criticizing Kania's CC report, conservative Ostroleka First Secretary Henryk Szablak urged changes in the Politburo and disputed those (naming Fiszbach and Ney) who spoke out against such changes.[102]

Kania himself later acknowledged that all these attacks were directed against him. In his closing speech, he said that he interpreted the proposals for changes in the Politburo "as directed first and foremost at myself," since "the role and position of the first secretary in such a collective is special and his responsibility is special."[103]

Although a couple of speakers on the first day did speak out against the move to make changes in the Politburo,[104] the main counterattack by liberals and moderates came on the plenum's second day. The first speaker, Rakowski, implicitly questioned critics' commitment to peaceful settlement, stating that "listening to yesterday's debate I could not always see the precise boundary between criticism of the line of accord and criticism of its implementation." He asked Najdowski whether his proposed new formula meant "use of force to resolve this crisis," and he stressed that because of following the line of "political solutions," since August "not one Pole has died." Rakowski, who was doing most of the negotiating with Solidarity since being appointed deputy premier, snapped back at the critics of compromise, noting with irony that when faced with a crisis everyone agrees that compromise is necessary, but as soon as the crisis passes "the criticism begins: Again we've gone to concessions. Compromise changes into concessions, and in fantasy, into opportunism and capitulationism." He challenged his critics: "I would like to know what we should do if we do not resort to this kind of solution." He flatly opposed the motion to shake up the Politburo, saying that "personnel changes in the Politburo will bring nothing good," especially only "one month before the congress."[105]

CC Secretary Ney, who had urged changes at the March plenum, this time opposed changes. "A change in the composition of the Politburo made today will be considered—I am deeply convinced of this—by the whole party and society as a change forced by our allies" and as "a turn away from socialist renewal."[106] The third speaker, Szczecin worker Edward Pustelnik, declared it would be "silly" to shake up the Politburo after giving it a vote of confidence at the March plenum and with the congress so close, so "I will vote against."[107] Gdansk First Secretary Tadeusz Fiszbach gave strong support to Kania, insisting "we must rally around the leadership of the party and government and not seek to change it," especially one month before the congress. He stated that the "huge majority of the people" see in Kania and Jaruzelski "a guarantee of continuation of the policy of social accord and socialist renewal."[108] CC Secretary Barcikowski defiantly assailed critics of the line of accord and accused some of dumping responsibility for their own shortcomings on Kania. He stated that he considered the present line "the best possible for the party and for Poland," and "despite what is often said, this is not a line of capitulation."[109]

The attack on Kania peaked when Grabski directly challenged Kania. Assailing the "sliding from one concession to another" and declaring his "full" agreement with the Soviet letter, Grabski asked: "Are the members of the Politburo capable of leading the country out of the political crisis with the present membership under the leadership of First Secretary Comrade Kania? I do not see this possibility."[110]

The speaker following Grabski, Zygmunt Rybicki, put aside his prepared speech and asked the Politburo to call a recess after which Kania should respond to Grabski. "Because either what Comrade Grabski said will turn out to have no foundation and we can then continue the debate, or what he said is well-founded and then we must find a unifying solution, first of all in the program sphere."[111]

There was then a recess and the Politburo met.[112] According to Western news reports, Kania used the recess to lobby for support among provincial party leaders and military leaders.[113] Then Kania announced to the plenum that the Politburo, in accord with the proposals made at the plenum, had decided to propose that the plenum take a vote of confidence in the Politburo. According to Warsaw television on June 10, this was to be a "vote on confirmation of individual Politburo members, on the assumption that if someone fails to gain at least 50 percent of the votes he will no longer keep his post in the Politburo."[114]

This maneuver appeared to put Grabski in jeopardy, since he as well as Kania would be subject to removal, and if Kania could gather the majority Grabski would be voted out. Subsequent statements suggested that Kania in fact did have the majority. *Trybuna Ludu* gave virtually no details of the "lengthy, lively debate" on this proposal but did say that those "expressing confidence" in Kania and Jaruzelski "dominated," that Plock worker Antoni Wrobel, representing Kania's home party organization, expressed his organization's "full confidence" in the first secretary, and that various military leaders also expressed their "full confidence" in Kania and Jaruzelski.[115]

But again a compromise developed in time to avoid a showdown. During the debate, according to *Trybuna Ludu*, "many speakers questioned the advisability" of making changes in the leadership, and, according to Stockholm radio on June 10, most regional leaders also demanded that no changes be made in the Politburo.[116] Another recess was held and the Politburo apparently decided to try to avert a showdown vote. After the recess Kania proposed that the CC take a vote on whether or not to vote on his earlier proposal for a vote of confidence. In the ensuing vote, only 24 voted for holding a vote of confidence, while 89 voted against and 5 abstained.[117]

As a result, Kania remained in office and the conservative challenge was defeated. The failure of the conservatives' move against Kania was partly a result of division in their ranks. Although Grabski boldly challenged Kania, his two conservative colleagues in the Politburo—Katowice First Secretary Zabinski and CC Secretary Olszowski—did not. Zabinski in his plenum speech tried to depict himself as a friend of reform: "I am constantly accused of hostility to Solidarity and to so-called democratization of public life by some leaders, and not only Solidarity leaders, but also party leaders." Reminding his audience that "I signed the accords in Szczecin and Jastrzebie," he declared himself "against any kind of adventurism," apparently meaning resort to force. While partially repeating his February plenum statement that "the limit of concessions on the part of the leadership has been reached," his cautious statements nowhere questioned Kania's leadership.[118] Olszowski did not speak at the June plenum, but had indicated his refusal to go along with conservative attacks on Kania by criticizing the Katowice Forum in speeches on May 31 and June 4. Moreover, soon after the plenum, in a speech at a Wroclaw plant, he flatly declared that it "would be silly to change the Politburo a month before the congress."[119]

The June plenum vote thus again averted a dangerous showdown in which one side or the other might have been ousted from the Politburo. Although hard-liners had directly challenged Kania and the moderates, the victors took no action against the conservatives—presumably to avoid angering the Soviets, who would be already smarting over the fact that their letter had backfired, strengthening the position of Kania and the moderates.

At the same time, Kania made an important concession to the Soviets and conservatives: He removed liberal media chief Jozef Klasa, whom he had installed as chief of the CC's Department for Press, Radio, and Television. It was Klasa who was to a considerable extent responsible for the liberalization of the media, and his removal opened the door for other ousters and for tightening up on the media. His replacement undercut Soviet charges that the media were out of control and acceded to Olszowski's calls for a crackdown on the media and Grabski's direct demands for Klasa's ouster.

Klasa was well known for his outspoken views and independent ways. He had become first secretary in Krakow in the "wave of renewal" after the 1970 strikes,[120] and had been popular there but unpopular with CC First Secretary Gierek and other Warsaw leaders. In interviews in the April 22 and 23, 1981 *Gazeta Krakowska*, he told of conflicts with Gierek and Premier Piotr Jaroszewicz during the 1970s, for example, because of his refusal to use force against a local strike and to build luxurious rest houses for Warsaw officials. Eventually, in 1975, they ousted Klasa and sent him into "emigration" as ambassador to Mexico.

As soon as Kania succeeded Gierek, he invited Klasa back and offered him the job of media chief. Klasa explained that he accepted the job "only because I know for certain that Stanislaw Kania, who proposed it to me, from the beginning up to today has been an advocate of resolving our conflicts by political methods. He talked with me about this already before he became CC first secretary—and then afterward. He told me very clearly that as long as he held this post he would not allow workers to be fired on. And that is for me his most important statement. Therefore,

I decided to return to the party apparat, to help the idea of resolving our problems by political methods, on the path of social accord."[121]

In the April 23, 1981 *Gazeta Krakowska* interview, Klasa spelled out his concept of the role of the media and indicated that he intended to change the press from a propaganda tool to an objective source of information. Criticizing the present role of the press, radio, and television, he declared that they must not be just transmission belts from the leadership to society but must seek to educate the leaders as well. Moreover, winning the confidence of the public in the press is impossible "without democratizing the party and government." Further, in a May 25, 1981 *Gazeta Krakowska* interview, he spoke of developing a press that would actually help democratize the party and government so that leadership of the party would not be "exercised in an arbitrary way."

With these views, Klasa opened the door for unprecedent freedom of action in the press. He began in his old bailiwick of Krakow, where his old ally forty-two-year-old Maciej Szumowski became *Gazeta Krakowska* chief editor and soon made the paper a symbol of independence and initiative.[122] Szumowski angered conservatives by such acts as publishing critical accounts of the March police beating of demonstrators in Bydgoszcz that contradicted and discredited the official version.[123] In a May 14, 1981 interview in the Wroclaw paper *Gazeta Robotnicza*, Szumowski acknowledged that his paper had been attacked in Warsaw for its "dubious liberties" and for being "dominated by Solidarity," but he defended and even boasted of his reporting on the Bydgoszcz affair. "The authorities must come to understand," he said, that the "era" of newspapers' "dependence on one or two officials" has ended.

Among newspapers, *Gazeta Krakowska* became the leading target of conservatives. Olszowski, who as CC secretary for ideology supervised Klasa and the press, attacked *Gazeta Krakowska* in an early April speech and at the late April plenum declared that "freedom of speech" had exceeded "sensible bounds." His criticisms were questioned at a local question-and-answer session in Krakow, and Olszowski denied having directly accused *Gazeta Krakowska* of exercising "dubious liberties," but he admitted that he had "reservations about *Gazeta Krakowska*'s line." He added "jokingly" (as he said) that the paper had become "in a certain sense the newspaper of the Metropolitan [Krakow] Curia." Hostile local questioners asked Olszowski what right he had to "take upon himself the right to function as 'supercensor.' " He responded: "For several months I have worked with or led the press organs and have never taken upon myself the function of supercensor."[124]

At the same time, leading liberals or moderates defended *Gazeta Krakowska*. In the May 21, 1981 *Gazeta Krakowska*, CC Secretary Ney stated that he and Krakow First Secretary Dabrowa had been "investing very much time and energy in protecting *Gazeta Krakowska*," which was being criticized "not only by central authorities but also by part of the aktiv in neighboring provinces, which see it as a hotbed of evil."[125] In an April 16, 1981 *Gazeta Krakowska* interview, Deputy Premier Rakowski characterized the paper as leading the way for other Polish papers.

Conservatives finally got their chance to open a concentrated attack on the indiscipline in the press and on Klasa after the June 5 Soviet letter harshly assailed the Polish press. The lack of tight party control over the press and Klasa's personal role were attacked in speeches at the June plenum. Former Radom First Secretary Prokopiak declared that "the mass media are acting against the party, against socialism," and "this situation must change."[126] Many others echoed his sentiments, and a few singled out Klasa more specifically. Poznan First Secretary Kusiak declared that some comrades, ignoring "their obligation to the party to defend party positions in the mass media, are acting like prima donnas, as if making their own policy, and are seeking cheap popularity," and he asked the plenum to "critically evalute the work of the CC's Press, Radio, and Television Department."[127] Grabski was even more pointed: "Despite three proposals by me, starting in February, to fire Comrade Klasa as the one responsible for allowing, tolerating—I will say more— for instigating attacks on the party and its leaders, this matter has still not been decided. Moreover, in two of the three cases when I proposed this the Politburo did not even take any position."[128]

In a speech published in the record of the plenum, Klasa defended himself and the media, arguing that the media were fighting to win public confidence and recalling that when the media used to please the leadership "nothing good resulted." "Who today provides the most information? Not the party, not the leadership, but Solidarity."[129] In a separate statement delivered at the end of the plenum, Klasa noted the "very harsh evaluations of the mass media" at this plenum, and he rejected the accusations that his department had made no efforts to restrain the media.

He blamed his department's inability to effectively control the media on lack of "help and support" from party organs and complained of "campaigns against me which use any means." "I think that in such a situation it will be better" to appoint someone else head of the department, and hence "I put myself at the disposal of the Politburo."[130]

The plenum ended, however, with no indication of whether his resignation was accepted or not, and *Trybuna Ludu* on June 15 still identified him as head of the department. But Olszowski soon had the pleasure of announcing Klasa's departure. In a speech at the June 17 Jelenia Gora party conference, Olszowski, after describing the June plenum's "sharp criticism" of the media, stated that Klasa had resigned and that the Politburo had named Leslaw Tokarski to replace him.[131] It was apparent that Olszowski's assessment of the political situation immediately took a turn toward optimism. He told an interviewer in the June 16, 1981 *Gazeta Robotnicza* that after the June plenum and the June 5 CPSU letter, "I am not so pessimistic regarding ideological unity. . . . I think that ideological consolidation is now more possible than it was before." Later, at the Gorzow party conference, he declared that the June plenum had decided to ensure that the media acted "in the interests of society and the socialist state" and that "changes in the media in this spirit are now being carried out."[132]

Further changes in the media followed, also apparently on Olszowski's initiative. For example, *Trybuna Ludu* on July 8 announced that Zdzislaw Balicki had been removed as chairman of the State Committee for Radio and Television and was being transferred to diplomatic work. He was replaced with Wladyslaw Loranc, a former chief editor of the radio station in Krakow and a former first deputy chairman of the national radio-television committee. Both Olszowski and Rakowski (who apparently shared some control over the media) attended the meeting of the state committee's presidium which installed Loranc.

The changes in the press were raised at the July congress, in its working group on the media. According to a July 25 *Polityka* account, Krakow Secretary Jan Broniek asked Olszowski "as the person responsible for propaganda" about the intention behind the "restrictive wave of changes in the posts of chief editors (*Kurier Polski, ltd,* etc.)." Olszowski countered that "he knew of no such wave nor planned any."[133]

Olszowski emerged from the congress with much enhanced power over the press. Whereas earlier he had had formal supervisory responsibility for the CC's press and ideology departments, but not *Trybuna Ludu* or *Nowe Drogi*,[134] after the congress he added these two most important CC organs to his sphere of responsibility. Lodz First Secretary and Politburo member Czechowicz, asked about Secretariat responsibilities in the August 5 Lodz paper *Glos Robotniczy*, revealed that Olszowski now had "supervision" over *Trybuna Ludu* and *Nowe Drogi*.[135]

The removal of Klasa appeared to help seal a deal between some conservatives, especially Olszowski, and Kania. Olszowski and Zabinski had refrained from joining Grabski's attack on Kania at the June plenum. During the election campaign Kania personally went to the province conferences where Olszowski and Zabinski were running for election and made a strong appeal to delegates to elect them. At the June 25 Katowice conference he backed Zabinski for reelection as province first secretary, saying "everybody knows" he [Kania] was the one who proposed Zabinski for Katowice first secretary last year and if the conference reelects him "I and the PZPR CC Politburo will be very satisfied."[136] At the June 27 Warsaw party conference he endorsed Olszowski for delegate.[137] He made no effort to help Grabski, however, when the latter ran for delegate in Konin.

Thus with the new pluralism and the breakdown of discipline in the party, the sharp issues of how to deal with Solidarity and with demands for reform produced ever more obvious splits. As Rakowski said at the June plenum, "In general it is hard to imagine that in such critical days and months one could reach any uniformity of views. That is simply impossible."[138] By mid-year the ideological differences between moderates led by Kania, Jaruzelski, and Barcikowski and conservatives led by Olszowski, Grabski, and Zabinski had become obvious, and rank and file party members and reporters increasingly harassed the hard-liners. Olszowski became defensive over his conservative reputation. At a Krakow university question-and-answer session, he denied accusations of joining with Grabski: "Neither Grabski nor I are creating any group in the party. We each speak out in our own name. . . . You have no right to say that I and Grabski want to torpedo reforms."[139] At a late May Bogatynia town conference in Jelenia Gora province, someone proposed a "vote of no confidence" in Olszowski and the majority favored it, even though the minority pointed out that the delegates' complaints mainly concerned matters that Barcikowski rather than Olszowski was responsible for in the Politburo.[140] In a Krakow speech Olszowski acknowledged that some called his views "conservative."[141] Jokes even circulated about Olszowski as a hard-liner (*twardoglowa*, or hardhead, in Polish). A reporter noted the widespread opinion that Olszowski was *beton* (concrete, another word used for hard-liners) and asked him if he had heard the story "that you wanted to commit suicide but the bullet just bounced off your head."[142] In remarks at the Piotrkow Trybunalski party conference, he asserted that "his activity has won him more enemies than supporters."[143]

As the congress approached in mid-July, Kania was in a relatively strong position. In the Politburo moderates such as Premier Jaruzelski, Organizational Secretary Barcikowski, Deputy Premier Jagielski, and President Jablonski clearly backed him, while Moczar, a prominent independent member, also gave his strong support to Kania and directly criticized Grabski's plenum attack on Kania. Answering questions at the June 17 Kielce conference, Moczar criticized Grabski's June plenum speech because, he said, "unity in the party and continuation of the process of renewal" were the "most important thing" and CC members supported Kania.[144] Liberals, such as Politburo candidate members Fiszbach and Ney, backed Kania as preferable to a hard-liner, especially after the June CPSU letter and Grabski's challenge. Even conservatives Olszowski and Zabinski appeared to be at least temporarily supporting Kania, who had helped them survive attacks by militant reformers. Meanwhile, Grabski, who had openly challenged Kania, appeared isolated and on the defensive. At the Leszno party conference he assailed the press for manipulating reports of the June plenum speeches to set him and Barcikowski against each other, and he insisted that Politburo disagreements only involved implementation of renewal, not renewal itself.[145] At the Konin party conference he defended his plenum speech and declared: "I am not an opponent of renewal."[146]

CHAPTER 4

THE UNCONTROLLED CONGRESS

THE DEMOCRATIZATION of party election rules and loss of control over the selection of delegates turned the July 1981 party congress into a gathering virtually unique among communist party congresses: a congress controlled to a considerable extent by the delegates themselves, rather than by the party leaders. While the congress' activities were well enough organized to run fairly smoothly, delegates were able to actually make many decisions rather than just ratify proposals of the leadership, and the results of the election contests were not predetermined by leadership manipulation. The breakdown of traditional control was also evident in the inability of the leadership to keep the usual veil of secrecy over inner workings of the congress and over politicking by groups and individuals.

The efforts to control media coverage of the congress—led by Ideology Secretary Olszowski—were largely unsuccessful. Traditionally, party leaders keep most congress deliberations secret and only issue carefully edited reports on congress activities. To this end, there were initial attempts to isolate journalists from the proceedings and control what information they received, as well as limiting what appeared in the media. But aggressive reporters overcame many restrictions and were aided by sympathetic delegates who passed on embargoed information to reporters who then published it in local papers. While Olszowski could keep tight control over central television, radio, and press, local papers often went ahead and published what they wished. This made central media look bad and led to criticisms of central media for poorly reporting the congress. The inability to prevent local papers from publishing inside information on the congress provided an unprecedented opportunity to view the inner workings of the congress in detail.

The efforts to organize the congress were led by Organizational Secretary Barcikowski and were generally successful in preventing the session from sliding into anarchy. Many delegates came to the congress extremely distrustful of the leadership and eager to press for punishment of former leaders and ouster of any incumbents who showed signs of wanting to manipulate the congress or hinder change. Careful leadership negotiations with delegation leaders helped develop consensus on most subjects and kept the proceedings orderly, but did not prevent delegates from voicing their views, voting as they wished, and occasionally dealing the leadership clear defeats. Most delegates appear to have left the congress with the conviction that the congress had been democratic and not manipulated.

Congress delegates demonstrated their independence repeatedly during the congress: in voting down the decision to elect the first secretary on the first day, in voting to expel Gierek and other former leaders from the party, in sharply challenging candidates for the CC and for first secretary, and in vigorously debating the draft party statute. However, it was the main act of the congress—the election of a new CC—which was by far the most striking demonstration of independence. Voting in secret, delegates surprised even themselves by effectively taking advantage of just a limited choice (279 candidates for 200 seats) to defeat most of the established leaders and elect a new kind of CC—a CC made up mainly of rank and file workers and farmers and excluding almost all prominent party and government figures. These new CC members, beholden to their constituents rather than to party leaders, appeared likely to exercise effective control over the Politburo and Secretariat.

Perhaps the main achievement of the congress was to demonstrate that such a democratic system could really function effectively, without falling into chaos, and to demonstrate that the party rank and file could oust most of the incumbent CC members and Politburo members and peacefully carry out a virtual revolution in the leadership—all within the party rules. The party leaders had taken their chances in uncontrolled elections, and those that survived the ordeal appeared to accept the value of this new, more democratic system. The congress devastated conservatives and incumbents, but provided a resounding mandate for First Secretary Kania, who emerged from the congress stronger than ever before and presumably able to give firmer leadership. Following the successful exercise in deinocracy, there was hope that the party could persuade a still-suspicious public that it had reformed itself and gotten rid of the features that had so alienated most Poles.

EFFORTS TO CONTROL MEDIA COVERAGE

One of the keys to controlling the congress was control of public information about it. Traditionally, media accounts of party congresses are limited to edited versions of the official reports and other speeches and skimpy details on the resolutions and election of leaders, with absolutely nothing about the inner workings and any political disputes. Indeed, it is difficult to judge if any political issues are really debated and thrashed out; the appearance is of a unified congress obediently approving all proposals made by the party leadership and reelecting the incumbent leaders unanimously.

This time, however, the Polish leadership was operating with unusual handicaps: censorship had largely broken down except for the central media, local party organizations were demanding more information, local papers were acting independently, and reporters were asserting their right to know and report details of party activity. Unable to censor all reporters' accounts, Olszowski, who was in overall charge of the media, issued orders to isolate journalists from congress delegates and also to limit television coverage. But reporters published embarrassing accounts of these restrictions and protested them so strongly that Olszowski soon had to back down.

Meanwhile, even traditional devices such as holding closed sessions of the congress began to fail. Although leaders bound delegates not to reveal details to reporters, some rebellious delegates soon passed on inside information to aggressive reporters, who published it in local papers.

The failure to control information about the congress resulted in an unprecedented wealth of material about the inner workings of the congress and politicking by groups and individuals. This material—mainly from local papers—makes it possible to present a more detailed analysis of a communist party congress than ever before.

The breakdown of the normal veil of secrecy began already during precongress preparations. Local papers reported meetings of their province delegations which discussed negotiations with Warsaw leaders on congress affairs. These accounts revealed secret proposals by the central leadership on how to conduct the congress and also reported that some province delegations had rejected some of the Warsaw proposals (see following section).

When the congress itself opened, the usual censorship of journalists' reports was missing. Reporter Jerzy Sadecki wrote in the July 24–26, 1981 *Gazeta Krakowska* that at previous congresses the censor "had to check every line of a report" and "without his approval none of the congress telexes had the right to accept the text," but "this time there was no censor." Instead of censoring journalists' writings, the authorities sought to restrict their sources of information to the officially selected and edited material. To this end, reporters were banned not only from the hall where the congress was held but even from the adjoining lobbies and corridors where they might be able to question delegates. As one reporter wrote, on the first day reporters were "stunned" to find that their credentials did not allow them "contact with delegates in the lobbies [*kuluary*] of the Congress Hall and that they were in general isolated from the delegations from their provinces."[1] Moreover, he wrote that "someone had the 'brilliant' idea of establishing go-betweens from the CC Press Department who were to ask specific delegates for interviews when journalists desired a conversation."[2] Journalists were assigned to a special hall (the "Marble Hall") of the Palace of Culture (where the congress was held) to observe the open sessions of the congress through television monitors. A reporter from a Lublin paper wrote that "they sat us down in the Marble Hall of the palace in front of color receivers for the internal television system, but we were separated from the delegates and the lobbies by glass doors guarded by so-called 'goalkeepers.' "[3]

Olszowski, the supervisor of the press and information, apparently was the leader responsible for this, and, according to the July 15 *Gazeta Krakowska,* he defended these restrictions, arguing that giving six hundred reporters access to the delegates "could hinder their work." One reporter wrote that "we protested sharply and collectively" to the congress authorities,[4] and according to others, by later the same day reporters were allowed to roam the lobbies.[5]

The reporters were aided by sympathetic delegates. Wroclaw delegates protested the exclusion of reporters, and delegate Jerzy Jankowski later boasted that "we got the journalists admitted to the lobbies of the congress."[6]

Toward the end of the congress, however, journalists' access was again cut off, at least temporarily. After a reporter was caught inside Saturday night's closed session, reporters were again banned from lobbies on July 19.[7] The new restrictions were applied by the authorities, and the delegates themselves knew of no congress decision on this.[8] Journalists again protested after Saturday's new restrictions,[9] and some complained that conservatives—those from the publications *Rzeczywistosc* and *Plomien* and representatives from the Katowice Party Forum—were exempted from the restrictions on other reporters.[10]

Olszowski also sought to restrict television coverage. On the first day of the congress some Wroclaw delegates proposed that television "fully transmit the congress proceedings," but Olszowski spoke against this, arguing that it already was planned to have five to six hours of telecasts each day and as much as eight hours on the first day.[11] He stated that "full broadcasting of the proceedings would create enormous technical difficulties." One Wroclaw delegate admitted that there were frequent radio and television reports on the congress but complained that "they continually repeat the same thing and give little new."[12] The Wroclaw proposal was then defeated in a vote, with only 115 delegates voting in favor.[13]

The main methods of limiting information on the congress were the holding of closed sessions of the congress, the appointment of an official press spokesman for the congress—conservative *Trybuna Ludu* chief editor Wieslaw Bek—and the tight editing of reports in the central party paper *Trybuna Ludu* and on central television and radio.

While open sessions of the congress were devoted mainly to relatively innocuous speeches, the most important actions—including nomination of candidates, debate over candidates, and the elections themselves—were held in closed sessions, from which reporters and other outsiders were excluded. The congress began on July 14 with a closed session from 9 A.M. to 12 noon to elect the Presidium and other congress bodies and to vote on rules. The second day also began with a closed session, from 8:30 to 10:30, to resolve more of the questions over rules for electing the CC and first secretary. Another closed session, to hear Grabski's report on the investigations of former leaders, was held in the evening, lasting until after midnight. The third day, July 16, began at 8:30 with a closed meeting which discussed candidates for the CC and other bodies and at which some candidates were questioned. Another closed session—to cast the votes for the CC—started at 10 P.M. On July 17 there was a late evening closed session at which the results of the CC election were announced. On Saturday, July 18, after a morning plenum of the new CC to nominate candidates for first secretary, a 5 P.M. closed session of the congress heard and discussed nominees for first secretary. After voting, the session adjourned and then resumed at 10 P.M. in open session to hear the results of the vote for first secretary.

The reports on these closed sessions in *Trybuna Ludu* and on radio and television were very brief and provided only the minimal information. Even official spokesman Bek, who did sometimes provide a little additional information in response to reporters' requests, told them when outlining the reelection of Kania on July 18: "Don't ask me about details because I cannot reveal them."[14]

Strenuous efforts were made to bind all delegates to secrecy about the closed sessions. Nevertheless, some did leak details—including details about the efforts to enforce secrecy—to reporters. Reporter Ryszard Fedorowski in the July 20 *Trybuna Robotnicza* (Katowice) wrote that a resolution was passed at the opening of the congress "binding all delegates not to pass on details to reporters" and that delegates had to turn in their tape recorders during closed sessions. Henryk Sroczynski in the July 24–26 *Glos Robotniczy* (Lodz) also wrote that delegates were bound not to tell details to reporters and had to deposit their recorders. He declared that "as a journalist, I cannot persuade anyone to violate these secrets," but, he added, journalists with "good contacts with delegates from their provinces" were well informed about the closed sessions.[15] In reality, he wrote, "the journalists themselves" decided whether or not to disclose particular details.

The maintenance of secrecy was also complicated by the fact that *Gazeta Krakowska's* reformist chief editor Maciej Szumowski was himself a delegate and entitled to attend all closed sessions. Some of his reporters later wrote that Szumowski phoned his paper "several times a day" to give instructions on how to report the congress and to pass on information and that he was the paper's first informant, "taking advantage of his delegate's mandate." They noted that conservative delegates demanded the ejection of some liberal reporters from the congress, but "Szumowski was a delegate and therefore he could not be expelled from the hall." *Gazeta Krakowska* even carried a column entitled "From Behind Closed Doors at the Congress."[16]

Armed with inside information, reporters from local papers wrote lively accounts including unique details about what went on in closed sessions and about political maneuvering. Zdzislaw Grzyb in the July 16 *Gazeta Lubuska,* for example, wrote about speculation over candidates for first secretary. Others wrote about the campaigns to defeat various leaders and about the reasons for the defeat of specific candidates in congress voting. The provincial reports described active campaigning by the Katowice Party Forum and other conservative groups against Kania, Rakowski, and others, and revealed that there was much more political infighting and controversy than the official accounts admitted. Krakow's *Gazeta Krakowska* and Katowice's *Trybuna Robotnicza* particularly stood out for playing up dramatic aspects of the congress.

The lively local reports, as well as comments by delegates, helped stimulate complaints against national media coverage. Henryk Sroczynski in the July 24–26 *Glos Robotniczy* wrote of widespread complaints about the "narrow and one-sided reports" by PAP, television, and some papers. The Lodz division of the Academy of Sciences sent a telex to the congress Presidium stating that "judging by information from delegates, radio, television, and press reporting is not conveying the stormy atmosphere of congress proceedings."[17] Reporters complained about the "enigmatic" PAP communiqués on the congress and asked delegates what really happened.[18] Wroclaw delegates complained about news coverage, saying they were getting phone calls from home asking, "What is happening in Warsaw?"[19] Legnica party members complained that the short reports "create a mosaic hindering understanding," although "from these fragments one could see that the debate was lively and interesting."[20] Krakow party members later asked "why television in particular showed so poorly what was happening at the congress" and compared its coverage with the "high-quality reports of *Gazeta Krakowska*." (Jerzy Sadecki wrote in the July 24–26, 1981 *Gazeta Krakowska* that the kiosk which sold Krakow papers was the busiest kiosk at the congress.) After seeing the television editing of his congress speech, Krakow delegate

Kazimierz Miniur said that if they "wanted to damage someone or compromise someone, that was precisely the way to cut up his speech."[21]

After the decision not to broadcast the full (open) proceedings, according to spokesman Bek, petitions began arriving from various party organizations urging expansion of television information.[22] The complaints eventually had some effect. The congress' working group on the media heard and discussed local complaints about coverage, and when the congress session opened on July 17, the chairman of the working group, *Glos Robotniczy* chief editor Lucjusz Wlodkowski, said that his group had come to the conclusion that the kind of television reporting being practiced "is causing serious reservations." On behalf of his group, he urged immediate allocation of television time for live coverage of the open sessions.[23] Press spokesman Bek, after consulting with the State Committee for Radio and Television, said that starting Saturday, television would allot more time, up to six to nine hours on the first or second channel.[24] T. Kwasniewski in the July 29 *Sztandar Ludu* reported that on July 18 local dissatisfaction with "the selective method of reporting the congress in the media, especially on television," had led to a change to full transmission of open proceedings.

After the congress, it was pointed out to beleaguered official press spokesman Bek that various articles in the press were telling much more about the closed sessions than he had, and he responded with irritation that these articles were violating the congress' right to keep its internal business secret. Asked if delegates were not expressing dissatisfaction about his performance, he defended himself against accusations of providing too little information.[25]

The resentment against the central press leaders was expressed again when the July 19 plenum reconfirmed Bek as *Trybuna Ludu* chief editor, Stanislaw Wronski as *Nowe Drogi* editor, and Mieczyslaw Rog-Swiostek as *Chlopska Droga* editor. Krakow party members, noting that all three had been defeated as candidates for the CC, called their reappointment "a slap in the face for all of us."[26]

EFFORTS TO ORGANIZE THE CONGRESS

In addition to lack of control over the press, the leadership faced another unaccustomed problem in preparing the congress: With the collapse of democratic centralism the party's provincial organizations no longer obeyed orders from Warsaw. In fact, provincial delegations around the country were caucusing before the congress and working out positions on issues and candidates—positions often at odds with Politburo positions. To avoid disruptive disputes at the congress the leadership sought to negotiate with delegations and develop consensus on as many issues as possible before the congress opened. It established a body called the Central Group of Delegates (Centralny Zespol Delegatow—CZD) to hold meetings with representatives of all delegations to "prediscuss" and come to preliminary agreement on rules for the congress and on other controversial matters. This body also compiled lists of candidates for the CC and other elective bodies from lists submitted by province delegations.

The CZD, guided by Organizational Secretary Barcikowski, managed to get delegations to accept many proposals on organizing the congress, making it possible to move the congress relatively well on schedule. In addition, allowing delegates to play such a large role in selecting candidates successfully defused much potential conflict. But with so many reform-minded and anti-establishment delegates, the congress could hardly avoid all conflict. Despite careful preparations, rebellious delegates rejected some leadership proposals, changed some items on the agenda, vented their anger against Gierek and other former leaders, carried on long, heated debates over candidates and issues, and finally, surprised the leadership by voting out many Politburo members and other prominent figures in the CC election. The leadership (or better, part of it) survived the congress, but it was an unprecedented ordeal for most of them—especially those directly challenged and criticized, not to mention those voted out of office.

The congress delegates elected during the May-June province conferences (and factory conferences) met repeatedly in provincial caucuses during June and July, organizing themselves for the congress and deciding among themselves what positions they wished to take on issues. They elected chairmen—usually the province first secretary[27]—and sometimes secretariats or presidiums.[28] They designated the chairman or certain delegates to represent the delegation in dealing with central party authorities,[29] and these men became the key figures in negotiations with central leaders and other delegations—the closest thing to power brokers.

Many delegations worked out firm positions on candidates or issues before the congress, defying "democratic centralism" and limiting the Politburo's influence. For example, delegations from Katowice, Poznan, Gdansk, and Torun reportedly came "with extensive prepared drafts" of resolutions.[30] Some delegates had been given specific orders by their home party organizations, leading Olsztyn First Secretary Mokrzyszczak to later complain about the fact that "some delegates were formally bound by resolutions of their organizations to take specific positions at the congress."[31] Caucuses of delegations discussed which candidates to support for central leadership posts (for example, the Gdansk delegation)[32] or discussed draft election rules (the Krakow delegation)[33] or other documents.

Some of the delegations' stands were clearly aimed against possible manipulation by the leadership. For example, the Kielce delegation adopted the position that the Politburo should not propose any candidates for the congress' election and vote-tallying commissions, leaving this entirely to province delegations.[34] The Legnica delegation decided that government representatives and province first secretaries should not be nominated for central bodies except in "sporadic, specific cases."[35] The Krakow delegation proposed that a rule be adopted that there had to be at least two candidates for first secretary.[36] The Lublin delegation· also insisted on at least two candidates for first secretary, [37] while the Elblag delegation insisted there should be more than three.[38]

To help counter the centrifugal forces developing in the province delegations and to defuse open squabbles, Kania and Barcikowski called together the leaders of all delegations to reach agreement on as many subjects as possible before the mass of delegates arrived at the congress itself. The first meeting of this "Central Group of Delegates" (CZD), consisting of three representatives from each delegation, was opened on June 29 by Kania, who noted that its purpose was to work out "a common position on matters of procedure and rules, and on the method of selecting candidates for central party leadership bodies."[39] Barcikowski in his speech stated that "the more that detailed matters can be prediscussed before the congress, the more effective will be its proceedings." The meeting elected a presidium for the CZD, including members of the Politburo and chairmen of all province delegations.

The CZD meeting reached agreement on a number of important organizational decisions—subject to confirmation by the congress, of course. According to comments in local papers, the CZD decided to increase the number of CC members to 200 and decrease the number of candidate members to 70 (versus the 143 members and 108 candidate members elected at the 1980 congress),[40] that the Electoral Commission would present a list of candidates exactly equal to the number of seats available,[41] that nominations additional to the Electoral Commission's would be made via province delegations rather than directly from the floor,[42] that province delegations would be allowed to nominate a number of candidates for the CC and other bodies proportionate to the size of the delegation,[43] that provinces could nominate additional candidates up to 50 percent of their basic quotas,[44] and that if the first vote for the CC failed to produce enough winners (with over 50 percent of the vote) succeeding ballots would eliminate the lowest 20 percent until enough candidates were elected.[45] One paper reported that the Politburo had proposed that only 15–16 province first secretaries be elected to the CC.[46]

Almost all these details on the CZD decisions appeared only in the local papers. *Trybuna Ludu* only reported that the CZD had decided to propose to the congress an increase in the number of CC members and decrease in the number of candidate members and that there would be speakers from every province and that the time for speeches would be allotted according to the size of each delegation.[47] But with central control weakened, delegates passed on details to local reporters, who published them. One elated local reporter wrote that this was the "first time in the history of the PZPR that we have been informed before the congress about which organizational principles it will adopt concerning the conduct of the congress, which principles will determine the size of representation in the leadership bodies, and finally, what is discussed during meetings of groups of delegates."[48]

How the above principles were implemented could also be observed from the local press accounts of the number of candidates nominated for the CC by various delegations. These indicate that provinces were entitled to nominate roughly 1 candidate for CC membership per 10 congress delegates, plus additional or "reserve" candidates. Thus, Krakow, with 58 delegates, nominated 5 candidates for CC seats "plus 3 reserve," and 3 for CC candidate members, 3 each for the Central Auditing Commission and Central Party Control Commisssion, plus 6 for the congress Presidium, 1 for the Secretariat, etc.[49] Warsaw, with 125 delegates, nominated 15 candidates for the CC;[50] Lodz, with 79 delegates, ran 10 candidates for CC members and 2 for candidate members;[51] Bydgoszcz, with 65 delegates, ran 7 for full members and 3 for candidate members;[52] Gdansk, with 62 delegates, ran 8 for CC members;[53] Wroclaw, with 58 delegates, ran 5 for CC members and 2 for candidate members;[54] and Torun, with 34 delegates, ran 4 for members and 1 for candidate member.[55]

But on some issues the CZD could not reach agreement and had delegation representatives relay Politburo proposals down to their delegations for discussion. Most sensitive was a Politburo proposal to give the right to run for the CC and other bodies (the "passive election right"— *bierne prawo wyborcze*) to ten "veterans of the workers' movement" and six province first secretaries who had not been elected delegates. This proposal was not mentioned in *Trybuna Ludu*, but was cited and explained in local accounts of several province caucuses where it stirred hot debate.[56] The province representatives to the CZD reported on this proposal at their delegation meetings and tried to persuade their delegations to accept it, arguing that the veterans were "bearers of the traditions and continuity of party policy" and that the six province first secretaries had been elected after their province conferences had already chosen their delegations and hence had simply missed the chance to be elected delegates.[57]

Some delegations reluctantly agreed; others flatly refused to grant the right to run for the CC to anyone not elected a delegate. In Bydgoszcz, First Secretary Bednarski, speaking "in the name" of Kania and the Politburo, persuaded his delegates to accept this—although they insisted that this was acceptable only if the persons had not run for delegate anywhere and been defeated.[58] The Katowice delegation took the reserved position that the congress could decide "in justified cases" to give the passive election right to persons who had not run for delegate,[59] while the Lublin delegation approved giving the right to run to the veterans but postponed a decision on whether to give it to the six first secretaries.[60] On the other hand, the Bialystok delegates declared themselves flatly against giving the "passive right" to nondelegates, and First Secretary Zawodzinski as a compromise suggested the delegation propose to the CZD giving veterans the "title of honorary CC members."[61] The Krakow and some other delegations declared themselves "in a decisive manner against making any exceptions" to limiting election rights to delegates,[62] and the Elblag, Gdansk, and Torun delegations also opposed the proposal.[63] The Walbrzych delegation voted against letting the six province secretaries run and decided that the congress should vote individually on the veterans,[64] while the Lodz delegation specified its opposition to one of the veterans, outspoken conservative writer and editor Jerzy Putrament.[65] Poznan initially opposed extending election rights to any nondelegates, but later agreed to let five of the veterans run as exceptions—Marshal Michal Rola-Zymierski, Felicia Fornalska, Gen. Franciszek Ksiezarczyk, Feliks Baranowski, and Putrament.[66] These five were also approved for the passive right by the Gorzow delegation.[67]

This matter was resolved finally at the congress itself, where, according to a delegate quoted in the July 16 *Sztandar Mlodych,* it stirred hot debate. Eventually, the congress agreed to allow the five above-named veterans to run for the CC or other bodies.[68] Four were later elected, but conservative Putrament was defeated.[69]

On one issue the CZD adopted a decision only to have delegates vote against it at the congress itself. At the first CZD meeting the Politburo presented three "variants" for election of the CC first secretary:[70] having the congress elect the first secretary by secret ballot before electing the CC (in which case he would automatically become a member of the new CC and Politburo); having the newly elected CC elect the first secretary in a secret ballot (the closest to the traditional manner); and having the newly elected CC select candidates for first secretary and present these for the congress itself to vote on by secret ballot.

These variants were relayed to province delegations for discussion. Most province party conferences had followed the first variant in electing their local first secretaries—i.e., they had elected him directly by the conference before electing the province committee. But when delegations discussed these variants for the congress, most of those whose stands were reported in the local press—including Katowice, Elblag, Bydgoszcz, Lublin, Lodz, Legnica, Walbrzych, and Gorzow[71]—clearly favored the third variant. Krakow was the main supporter of the first variant: a "decisive majority" of the Krakow delegation voted for election of the first secretary before electing the CC.[72] Poznan initially took an ambiguous position, but later joined Krakow in favor of electing the first secretary on the first day.[73] The position of some, such as Wroclaw and Przemysl, was ambiguous.[74] The second biggest delegation—from Warsaw—split, 60 percent for electing the CC first and 40 percent for electing the first secretary first.[75]

Maneuvering over this issue continued, however, and at the second meeting of the CZD, on July 11—the last meeting before the congress—someone proposed electing the first secretary on the first day, and despite the apparent sentiment against this in delegation meetings after the June 29 CZD meeting, the motion carried. This decision was not reported in *Trybuna Ludu's* account (July 13) but was mentioned in some province papers and on the radio.[76]

The July 11 CZD action had the appearance of a move to ensure Kania's election right at the outset of the congress. Although no source has mentioned who initiated the proposal, Kania himself chaired the CZD session that adopted it, and his friends in Krakow were among those pressing for it. The move not only would have ensured Kania's election but would have given him a position of dominance at the congress and also a position of independence and superiority vis-à-vis his Politburo colleagues. In fact, delegate Jerzy Majka later said that foes of the move argued that such immediate election would "strengthen his position so much that he will stop paying heed to the leadership collective" and will "move out of any kind of control."[77]

However, on the first day of the congress when Krakow delegates proposed immediate election of the first secretary the CZD decision was overturned.[78] The reversal was the result of using a different voting procedure which gave more weight to the big delegations, most of which opposed immediate election of the first secretary. In the CZD each delegation had had one vote,[79] giving small delegations more influence, and "a majority of delegations" had favored immediate election.[80] The July 15 *New York Times* reported that the CZD vote had been 32 delegations for immediate elections, 14—including the big provinces Warsaw, Katowice, Poznan, and Wroclaw—against. At the congress itself, the voting weight of the big delegations reversed the majority, as the third variant was approved 925 to 872.[81] For example, a Lodz reporter wrote that his province's big delegation—which opposed immediate election—had been in the minority at the CZD meeting but was on the winning side at the congress.[82] He later added that after the big delegations had reversed the CZD vote "some representatives of smaller provinces became convinced that big party organizations want to dominate the small provinces."[83]

Not only the precongress meetings but also the course of the congress itself reflected a balance between organizational control by the leadership and independence of the delegates. Leadership efforts to work out procedures and lists of candidates in advance with delegations kept sessions orderly. But virtually every day saw the delegates asserting themselves, forcing their will on the congress. Almost all these outbursts took place in the closed sessions, where the most important matters were decided.

The congress opened on July 14 with a three-hour closed session which first elected a 203-member Presidium, a 64-member Secretariat, and five commissions (a 54-member Mandate Commission, a 142-member Commission on Decisions and Resolutions, an 81-member Statute Commission, an 81-member Electoral Commission, and a 53-member Appeals [Odwolan] Commission).[84] This process went smoothly, as delegates voted on lists based on nominations submitted to the CZD by the delegations themselves.[85] As one paper wrote, the candidates "had been cleared earlier with provincial congress groups" and "were quickly confirmed by the delegates."[86] Debate did erupt, however, over the principles for electing leadership bodies, and, as indicated above, the congress voted against the CZD recommendation of immediate election of the first secretary. The rest of the day, starting at noon, was devoted to an open session which heard Kania's CC report and several other speeches.

The second day opened with a short closed session at 8:30 to finish the procedural decisions left over from the July 14 closed session. It approved the number of seats on the CC (200 members and 70 candidate members), Central Auditing Commission (70), and Central Party Control Commission (90), the number of votes needed to be elected, the system for electing the first secretary, the system for nominating candidates for the CC and other bodies, and the system for nominating Politburo and Secretariat members, and extended the passive election right to 5 veteran party members. The open session, from 10:30 A.M. until evening, was devoted to speeches, capped by a rousing evening address by Rakowski attacking conservatives.[87] But when the closed evening session began delegates seized control of the congress over the emotional issue of punishing former leaders. The session debated the Grabski commission report on the responsibility of former leaders—a document supported by 1,700 pages of testimony and material about the Gierek regime. Discussion of the Grabski report was apparently not even on the original schedule, but had been added at the insistence of delegates anxious for action against the former leaders. A motion to add this item to the agenda had been adopted 1,455 to 33 on the opening day.[88] The debate became very emotional,[89] and delegates criticized Grabski's commission for not presenting proposals to expel Gierek and others from the party.[90] Finally, someone proposed that the congress present a formal proposal on expulsion, and a break was called during which the Presidium formulated proposals to expel the former leaders. The session finally ended at about midnight by voting to expel Gierek, Edward Babiuch, Jerzy Lukaszewicz, Tadeusz Pyka, Jan Szydlak, Zdzislaw Zandarowski, and Zdzislaw Grudzien from the party.[91]

The July 16 proceedings again began with an 8:30 closed session at which chairman of the Electoral Commission Bednarski presented a report announcing the candidates for central bodies. However, this session quickly turned "stormy"[92] as delegates argued over the list of candidates for the CC and other bodies. Grabski (chairman of the investigating commission), Jerzy Urbanski (deputy chairman of the Central Party Control Commission), Mieczyslaw Moczar (chairman of the Supreme Chamber of Control), and Prosecutor General Lucjan Czubinski all answered questions about whether there was incriminating evidence against any candidates.[93] Moczar, questioned whether any candidates had misused their positions for profit, swore that they were all clean: "I give my word as a communist."[94] Delegates questioned Kania, Jablonski, Jagielski, and others.[95] Olszowski also came under fire for some of his stands and defended himself, saying that leaders "must say the truth, including unpopular things."[96] Finally, by open vote the congress approved a list of candidates for the CC and other bodies—a list totaling 618 names (31 percent of all delegates) from which the congress would choose 200 CC members, 70 candidate members, 70 Central Auditing Commission members, and 90 Central Party Control Commission members (430 in all). It also elected a 130-member Vote Tallying Commission (Komisja Skrutacyjna). After breaking up into subgroups in the afternoon,[97] the congress resumed in closed session at 10 P.M. to cast votes for the CC and other leadership bodies.

Friday, July 17, was relatively uneventful, except for the shock of the announcement of the CC vote and the defeat of many prominent leaders. From 9 A.M. until late afternoon the delegates continued meeting in problem groups, then the congress resumed in open session at 3:30 P.M. for more speeches, and late in the day it went back into closed session to hear the announcement of the results of the vote for the CC and other bodies. After more speeches in open session, the congress adjourned at 11 P.M.

On Saturday morning, the problem groups finished their discussions and formulated proposals to submit to the congress bodies. At 2 P.M. the newly elected CC held its first plenum and selected candidates for first secretary, while the congress in open session heard more speeches.[98] At 5 P.M. the congress returned to closed session and presiding officer Jaruzelski presented the candidates for first secretary. Then a lively two-hour debate began, including a grilling of the candidates which was dubbed the "hour of truth" by some reporters.[99] Delegates questioned not only Kania and Barcikowski who ran for first secretary, but also Olszowski and Rakowski who had declined. After a break, delegates voted.[100] When proceedings resumed at 10 P.M., the results (1,311 for Kania, 568 for Barcikowski, 60 against both) were announced.[101]

After the election of the CC and first secretary, the rest of the congress was largely an anticlimax, although there still was one controversial matter to finish—adoption of the new party statute. All day Sunday was devoted to speeches, while at about 5 P.M. a second CC plenum was held to elect the new Politburo and Secretariat. At 7:35 P.M. the congress resumed its open session to hear Kania announce the results of the election of Politburo and Secretariat members. Then at 10 P.M. a long, hard debate on the statute began. Kurowski, on behalf of the Statute Commission, presented the proposed changes in the party statute and answered questions. The debate over these changes lasted until 3 A.M.[102] and involved much exchange of views.[103] During the debate reformers pressed to further liberalize the statute, but were largely frustrated. Delegates from Krakow and Gdansk fought to add to the statute a clause that "primary party organizations have the right to conclude horizontal arrangements."

A Krakow delegate later complained that others in the Statute Commission had opposed everything and revealed that he had threatened to quit the party if nobody would do anything. He also accused Kurowski of trying to prevent the commission from working out new election rules.[104] Legnica delegate Adam Butynski, head of the relatively extreme Legnica Forum,[105] declared that "I would favor more radical propositions" in the statute but was outvoted.[106] The statute wound up saying nothing about horizontal structures[107] or about the status of believers in the party, a "subject which stirred great emotion."[108]

The vote on the statute finally occurred at 11 A.M. Monday, July 20. The weary delegates voted to adopt the new statute, with 38 against and 53 abstaining.[109] The congress did not manage to adopt new election rules. It simply voted to order the CC to work out new rules based on the new statute and to present these new rules to a national conference of delegates for approval. Finally, after a "lively debate" over a program resolution, the congress concluded its work.[110]

ELECTION OF A NEW CENTRAL COMMITTEE

The most stunning expression of lack of control at the congress was the surprising results of the election of a new CC. Although given only a limited choice of candidates, a majority of delegates crossed off most of the Politburo and Secretariat members, carrying out a striking purge of the top leadership. The antileader sentiment had been signaled by the sharp questioning of several Politburo members just prior to the vote, but apparently no one expected such a drastic result. The decimation of the party's national leadership appropriately crowned the whole spring election process, which had thrown out leaders on a massive scale at the local and provincial level. It also virtually settled the contest for first secretary—which had seemed exciting up to that point—by simply eliminating some of Kania's key rivals from CC membership.

The vote not only was directed at the top leaders but also had a general thrust against all incumbents and leaders. Many delegates voted against anyone identified as a party leader, even at the local level. As a result, very few officials, central or provincial, were elected, and the new CC became a body mainly of workers and farmers and other rank and file members.

The uncontrolled nature of the congress was also reflected in other unusual aspects of the CC election. Conservative groups openly campaigned against liberal leaders, and reformers appeared to target conservative leaders and incumbents in general. As a result, almost everyone with a clear political profile—outspokenly conservative or liberal or just controversial—was defeated. The CC became a body of relatively inoffensive moderates and novices with obscure or unformed views.

The election produced a new kind of CC. Instead of a who's who of officeholders, it became a body of representatives of local party organizations not beholden to the Politburo and hence able to act as a check on the top leaders. Though some reformers had called for this kind of change, the delegates themselves were initially surprised at what they had wrought.

Although the CZD and the coordinating process were rather successful at producing an orderly congress and avoiding messy conflicts, they failed to control the selection of CC members and guarantee the election of most key officials despite carefully developing a list of candidates cleared with the delegations and presenting only a limited range of choice to the delegates. The list of candidates for the CC and other bodies was made up from the nominees submitted to the CZD by province delegations, and was compiled by and presented to the congress by the congress' Electoral Commission. The basic list for full CC members consisted of only 200 names[111]—the exact number of seats to be filled—but according to commission chairman Bednarski, provincial delegations added some nominations after examining the initial list, and then a 279-member list was presented to the congress on the third day.[112] There were 105 candidates for the 70 positions of CC candidate members.[113] Delegates were given ballots listing the 279 candidates for CC membership, for example, and voted in secret for 200 members by crossing off 79 names.[114]

The opportunity for choice was thus fairly limited: With only 79 extra names for members and 35 extra for candidate members, most candidates agreed upon during preliminary negotiations surely would be elected. Nevertheless, despite the careful organization and limited choice, the delegates succeeded in defeating a remarkable number of leading figures on the list they received: 11 of the 15 incumbent Politburo and Secretariat members who were on the list were voted down.[115] An absolute majority of delegates struck off the names of Politburo members Grabski, Jablonski, Jagielski, Moczar, and Zabinski, Politburo candidate members Fiszback, Kruk, and Ney, CC secretaries Kurowski and Cypryniak, Secretariat member Gabrielski, and the first secretaries of almost all big provinces: Katowice's Zabinski, Warsaw's Kociolek, Poznan's Skrzypczak, Bydgoszcz's Bednarski (chairman of the Electoral Commission), Gdansk's Fiszbach, and Krakow's Dabrowa. Only 18 members of the previous CC were reelected.

The vote totals for top leaders show that Premier Jaruzelski received far more votes than First Secretary Kania or other Politburo members, and that many leaders received far less than the required 50 percent. Based on the available tallies, the most prominent candidates for CC member scored as table 4.1 shows.[116]

TABLE 4.1

Successful		Unsuccessful	
Jaruzelski	1,615	Fiszbach	951
Kania	1,335	Grabski	899
Barcikowski	1,262	Dabrowa	790
Olszowski	1,090	Moczar	764
Rakowski	1,085	Jablonski	645
		Kociolek	611
		Jagielski	580
		Zabinski	533

The most notable feature of the results was that delegates voted against prominent persons, conservatives and liberals alike.[117] They struck out against anyone in a position of authority, nationally or locally, systematically crossing off the names of delegation heads and well-known candidates in favor of unknown workers and rank and file candidates.[118] This trend is very clear from examining the results among candidates from specific provinces where the names of both successful and unsuccessful candidates were mentioned in the press:

- Of Bialystok's three candidates for the CC, the province first secretary (Zawodzinski) was defeated, while a factory party first secretary and a veterinarian were elected.[119]

- Of Krakow's eight candidates, First Secretary Dabrowa, former CC Press Department head Jozef Klasa, and a doctor were defeated, while three workers, a local party secretary, and university professor Hieronim Kubiak were elected.[120]
- The only one of Elblag's four candidates who lost was Deputy Premier and Politburo member Jagielski.[121]
- Of the eight Gdansk candidates for CC member, First Secretary Fiszbach, province Secretary Andrzej Surowiec, and factory party committee secretary Zbigniew Dula were defeated, while an actor, farmer, two workers, and shipyard party secretary Jan Labecki were elected.[122]
- Only one of Lodz's ten candidates, a plant committee secretary, was defeated, but province First Secretary Czechowicz, even though elected, received fewer votes (1,151) than seven of the eight other successful candidates (six workers and the director of a political science institute).[123]
- Of the seven Bydgoszcz candidates, First Secretary Bednarski and one other were defeated.[124]
- Of the seven Jelenia Gora candidates for the CC and other bodies, only province First Secretary Jerzy Golis (candidate for CC candidate member) and city police chief Stanislaw Bryndza (candidate for the Central Party Control Commisssion) lost.[125]
- Of Wloclawek's three candidates for CC member, former First Secretary Edward Szymanski and one other were defeated.[126]
- Of the four Torun candidates for full members, only First Secretary Edmund Heza and one other were defeated.[127]

In all, only 8 provincial first secretaries were elected full CC members and 10 as candidate members (and this included the leaders of only two of the eight biggest provinces—Lodz and Wroclaw).[128] According to various reporters in local papers, 27 or 28 province first secretaries had run for full member and 13 for candidate member—indicating that about 22 or 23 were defeated.[129] These defeats were not accidental. Olsztyn First Secretary Mokrzyszczak declared that he had heard delegates telling each other: "Cut off all aparatchiks higher than first secretary of a plant committee."[130] Torun First Secretary Heza complained about the "phenomenon of mechanical 'cutting off' of province first secretaries in the election,"[131] and commentator Helena Lazar wrote about the widespread "motto 'cross off the party apparat.' "[132] Such negative voting was facilitated by the fact that the election ballot identified candidates by position. Former press chief Klasa, in explaining various reasons for his defeat, mentioned that he had been listed on the ballot as a "central party figure."[133] In contrast, apparently nobody voted against the little-known workers and farmers on the ballot. All 80 workers running for CC membership won, as well as 28 of the 34 farmers.[134]

The reaction against officialdom may have been unintentionally aggravated by the form in which the election lists were presented to the delegates. The Electoral Commission compiled the list of candidates from nominations from provinces and sent the list to delegates in the form of two lists: a "main" list of 200 candidates for CC members, including only 60 workers, and a "supplemental" list in which workers and farmers predominated.[135] This stirred considerable resentment, judging by descriptions in the July 16 and 17 *Gazeta Robotnicza,* as delegates viewed the first as the official list and the second—apparently consisting of nominations made by rank and file delegates—as more democratic and anti-establishment. Wroclaw delegate Jankowski complained that there were too many candidates from the party and government apparat and few workers and farmers, and other delegates objected to the fact that 13 of the candidates were from the central government.

Responding to the complaints about too many "representatives of central organs," Barcikowski argued the need for continuity in leadership.[136] Suspicious delegates demanded a full list of those recommended by the Politburo.[137] After debating over the lists and questioning the leaders all morning on July 16, the congress finally decided to merge the lists.[138]

The net result of all this was that the new CC wound up with few central and even provincial officials among its full members. It became a body of unknowns representing various social elements but holding no positions of authority. Thus, there were only five ministers and deputy ministers, one deputy premier, three CC secretaries, and no CC officials among the members. T. Kwasniewski in the July 27 *Sztandar Ludu* (Lublin) counted only 12 members of the CC, Central Auditing Commission, and Central Party Control Commission who "exercise real leadership functions in the central government and party apparat." The pattern also was apparent among the military: Generals lost representation, as conservative Main Political Administration chief Jozef Baryla and some deputy ministers of defense dropped out of the CC, while five lower-ranking officers were elected. Several newspaper articles pointed out that the new CC had 80 workers and 28 farmers among its 200 members—an actual majority—as against only 58 workers and farmers in the previous CC.[139] Moreover, 41 of the 200 CC members were members of Solidarity.[140]

In addition to the general anti-official factor in the vote, local press accounts revealed that there had been attacks on many individual leaders during the congress questioning of candidates just prior to the vote. According to reports in local papers, Kania had to explain his role in the 1970 suppression of workers in Gdansk,[141] Jablonski had to explain why he had announced that he would not run for delegate and then changed his mind, and Olszowski had to explain his "political line."[142]

Deputy Premier Jagielski, despite his close association with reform, was particularly badgered, mainly because of his role under Gierek in the purchase of foreign licenses, which had helped get Poland so deeply into international debt. According to one delegate,[143] he first tried to blame various ministries, but then was forced to speak again and finally accepted "part" of the responsibility. He was defeated for election to the CC, and according to the delegate, received fewer votes than anyone except Zabinski. A July 20 *Glos Wybrzeza* (Gdansk) article also attributed Jagielski's defeat to his having signed so many license purchases.

Other leaders, both conservative and liberal, were targets of attacks at various times during the congress. Zabinski may have been hurt when one of his own Katowice delegates asserted during the prevote discussion that Zabinski had selected Katowice's candidates for the CC single-handedly without consulting the members of the delegation.[144] Zabinski and others objected and after hurried caucusing, forced the delegate to partially retract his accusation.[145] Questioned later by local constituents about his defeat for CC member, Zabinski called the defeat of province first secretaries a "general tendency" but acknowledged that the defeat "is not pleasant for me personally and without doubt forces personal analysis and reflection."[146]

Liberal spokesman Rakowski was also attacked during the discussion of candidates, but most of the attacks on him occurred in the cloakrooms. Rakowski had given a rousing speech on the second day of the congress, which had appeared to make his popularity among delegates grow.[147] Delegates described his speech as "the first speech in the impending election campaign,"[148] and there was reportedly a "long line" to get his autograph.[149] At the same time, attacks on him increased following his July 15 speech, according to a Lodz paper.[150] Other reports indicate that during the discussion of candidates at a July 15 late evening congress session, one Szczecin delegate assailed Rakowski for conducting an "election campaign in the corridors."[151] A delegate sympathetic to Rakowski complained that for a "full hour" before the selection of candidates for first secretary, Rakowski was being attacked "furiously" in the lobbies.[152] A Lodz reporter wrote that "in general" Rakowski "was the subject of the sharpest attacks," including a pamphlet asserting that he had been "walking with Werblan in the corridors, holding him by the arm."[153] Reporter Jerzy Sadecki in the July 24–26 *Gazeta Krakowska* asserted that it was mainly "invited guests" rather than elected delegates who were attacking Rakowski.

After the congress, delegates were besieged with questions about the defeat of well-known figures and offered their own speculation on the reasons. Expressing astonishment at the defeat of Politburo member Moczar, Klasa told *Gazeta Krakowska* that Moczar's enemies "had unloosed an exceptionally perfidious campaign" against him, and he speculated that "probably many of them were after his hide" because he was chairman of the Supreme Chamber of Control (which conducted investigations of many leaders). Regarding his own defeat, Klasa, stating that "I received the fewest votes" among all candidates, blamed this on the widespread criticism of the media and attacks on him as the one responsible for media abuses, as well as on personal attacks by conservative groups (the Katowice Forum, the publication *Rzeczywistosc*, the "Grunwald" association, and "various Mafia groups") and the fact that he had been placed on the "supplemental" list of candidates for CC member rather than on the main list.[154] A Gdansk delegate, noting that their First Secretary Fiszbach had fallen short by 120 votes, expressed regret that the delegation had not lobbied more with other delegations and suggested that "guests invited by who knows whom" had campaigned hard against him.[155]

There was also evidence of organized campaigning, especially by conservative groups, in and around the congress hall. Commentator Helena Lazar in the July 24–26 *Gazeta Krakowska* wrote that a virtual propaganda battle had occurred, with literature from the Katowice and other forums, the conservative "Grunwald" association, and the conservative magazine *Rzeczywistosc* being passed out to delegates. Olsztyn First Secretary Mokrzyszczak stated that "literature of the Katowice Party Forum" was being circulated and that some delegates were "upset" over this.[156] Editor T. Kwasniewski in the July 20 *Sztandar Ludu* (Lublin) reported that various "bulletins" with personal attacks were circulating in the cloakrooms.

Much of this propaganda and campaigning was aimed at defeating specific liberal leaders. An Interpress reporter complained that copies of the weekly *Rzeczywistosc* attacking Rakowski and liberal Krakow editor Maciej Szumowski were circulating in the cloakrooms.[157] *Gazeta Krakowska* reported finding someone passing out 250 issues of *Rzeczywistosc* containing attacks on Rakowski, Klasa, and Szumowski.[158] The Katowice paper reported that cards were circulating listing names to cross off—including Rakowski, Kania, Zabinski, Fiszbach, Moczar, Klasa—as well as pamphlets attacking Kania, Rakowski, and others.[159] One delegate blamed the defeat of liberals Fiszbach, Dabrowa, and Klasa on attacks by *Rzeczywistosc* and other groups,[160] while Klasa criticized the conservative campaign against Rakowski, Dabrowa, Fiszbach, Szumowski, and himself.[161]

Some reporters asserted that these conservative groups were being aided by some of the congress organizers. Ryszard Fedorowski in the July 20 *Trybuna Robotnicza* and Henryk Sroczynski in the July 24–26 *Glos Robotniczy* complained that representatives of conservative publications like *Rzeczywistosc* and *Plomien* and members of the Katowice Forum had been specially favored by being exempted from restrictions applied to other reporters. In fact, Sroczynski asserted that reporters pointing out these conservatives' activities were punished by being banned from the lobbies.

The Katowice Forum was active at the congress and appeared to be specially favored by some unidentified people in authority. Congress spokeman Bek acknowledged that one of the forum leaders, Wsiewolod Wolczew, was invited to the congress as a guest by the Congress Organizing Committee.[162] *Gazeta Krakowska* claimed that Wolczew was "very active, you saw him everywhere" and that he had been invited "on the inspiration of Comrade Grabski."[163] Newspapers exposed forum members among the Katowice delegates and publicized opposition to them. The July 15 *Gazeta Krakowska* identified Katowice delegate Roman Grebosz as a member of the forum's leadership, and the July 27 *Gazeta Lubuska* reported that the Katowice delegation included four forum members. After a Katowice Forum member made a speech to the congress in which he allegedly tried to promote the organization's views, other Katowice delegates reportedly declared that he did not speak for the delegation.[164] The editor of *Gazeta Krakowska* gleefully noted in the July 21–22 issue of his paper that representatives of the forum were often opposed "by the Katowice delegation itself."

With the conclusion of the congress, pressure increased to end the Katowice and other such forums, as well as horizontal units, on grounds that the intraparty discussion was concluded and the congress had adopted the party's position. At the end of the congress, Resolutions Commission chairman Kubiak told delegates that "all forums which threaten the unity of the party should cease operation."[165] Katowice First Secretary Zabinski told a local audience after the congress that "next Saturday the Katowice Forum is to have its final farewell meeting and cease operations."[166] The Katowice and other forums did not cease their activity, however. A meeting of representatives of party forums and debate clubs, including the conservative Katowice Forum and Poznan Forum of Communists, was held in Poznan in late July, but the reports on it did not indicate whether it discussed disbanding or conducting further activity.[167] The liberal Poznan Forum of Political Thought met again after the congress, with Poznan First Secretary Skrzypczak participating, and outlined plans for further "anticonservative" activity.[168] In October the Szczecin province party control commission adopted the position that the activities of the Szczecin Movement of Communists and Szczecin Party Debate Forum were "harmful for unity" of the party because of "maintaining extrastatutory organizational forms conducting their own party activity." An October 29 Szczecin party conference debated this report and voted to order the forums to cease operations.[169]

ELECTION OF THE FIRST SECRETARY AND POLITBURO

The election of the first secretary, Politburo, and Secretariat turned out to be unexciting compared with the CC election, but delegates also played a significant part in these events. The once-exciting contest for first secretary virtually ended after the CC election defeated many of Kania's rivals and the others refused to run against him. Eventually there was only a sham contest as Kania-ally Barcikowski ran against him just to provide the semblance of a choice. However, delegates had already played an active role in picking the first secretary. Not only did they eliminate Grabski and other candidates in the CC election, but they had voted down the motion for an opening day election, they had actively and openly debated candidates other than Kania, they had questioned Kania and other potential candidates before the vote, and they had campaigned for and against various candidates. And they themselves cast the votes for first secretary, rather than letting the CC do this as in the past.

The election of the new Politburo and Secretariat was carried out in the more traditional way—at a CC plenum—but even in this case representatives of the rank and file insisted on having at least some alternative candidates nominated from the floor. Moreover, to placate the various wings of the party, Kania had proposed a Politburo balanced between liberals, moderates, and conservatives, and including rank and file workers (four) and regional leaders (five) and only a minimum of central leaders (five).

As the congress opened, a contest for first secretary had appeared imminent. The *New York Times* on July 13 and 15 reported that the leadership had decided to present four candidates for first secretary: Kania, Olszowski, Grabski, and Rakowski—the four who had been most often suggested by province delegations. Although Olszowski, who had been cooperating more closely with Kania since early June, reportedly planned to withdraw, the daring Grabski, who had openly challenged Kania at the June plenum, probably would have stayed in the race. That Grabski's cause might not be as hopeless as it would seem was suggested by a July 15 *New York Times* report that the Warsaw party organization in a preference vote had given Grabski the most votes, followed by Olszowski, Zabinski, and only fourth, Kania.

There was considerable speculation over possible candidates among delegates and even in a few Polish provincial papers. Zdzislaw Grzyb in a July 16 *Gazeta Lubuska* article entitled "Who Will Be First [Secretary]?" reported on discussions among delegates over whom to vote for and the prospects of different candidates. Delegates "give Comrade Stanislaw Kania the best chance" because "he has support not only of the majority of party members but of all progressive social forces." But, wrote Grzyb, there are also "reservations" about him: "that he has led the party too inconsistently and ineffectively, that his position during social conflicts was too conciliatory." Grzyb reported much talk about Olszowski, Grabski, Rakowski, and Fiszbach, and added that the Wroclaw delegation "apparently intends to nominate its First Secretary Tadeusz Porebski." Jacek Grazewicz reported in the July 16 *Kurier Szczecinski* that delegates were saying that three to six persons would run for first secretary, while a Szczecin delegate in a July 30 *Kurier Szczecinski* article revealed that Kania and Olszowski had proved to be the favorites in a "secret 'pre-election'" vote among Szczecin delegates. One reporter, Henryk Sroczynski, reported already at the opening, however, that Olszowski, Rakowski, and Fiszbach would not run.[170]

The first day's vote to postpone the election until after the election of the new CC changed the picture, however. Grabski, the most likely candidate to challenge Kania, as well as some other possible candidates (Fiszbach, Zabinski, Moczar) were defeated for election to the CC, eliminating them as candidates. So when the CC met on July 18 to select candidates, it was difficult to find anyone willing to run against Kania. Four candidates were nominated—Kania, Olszowski, Barcikowski, and Rakowski (in that order)—but Olszowski and Rakowski quickly withdrew.[171] One delegate later reported that the plenum had spent over an hour discussing whether Olszowski and Rakowski should run and that both had insisted that Kania was the best candidate.[172] Barcikowski also initially refused to run, but eventually agreed just so that there would be a second candidate.[173] At the outset of the plenum CC members had been insistent that at least two candidates had to be presented to the congress.[174]

When the plenum presented the congress with the candidates on July 18, delegates questioned Kania and Barcikowski—and even noncandidates Olszowski and Rakowski—at length. Local reporters wrote that delegates later described this as a "jarring hour of truth for our party and our leaders."[175] The discussion of candidates lasted two hours, and during this congress session other candidates were reportedly nominated but also refused to run.[176]

Although the reelection of Kania occurred with no real contest, there were some efforts to defeat him on the part of conservatives. Olsztyn First Secretary Mokrzyszczak later told an Olsztyn paper that the Katowice Forum was circulating literature, and Olsztyn delegate Tadeusz Krzymowski said that after the election of the CC, defeated candidates formed a "second opposition group" and "mobilized" during the night. According to this account, they took advantage of the interrogation of the candidates for first secretary on the evening of July 18 to "launch an attack on Kania and Barcikowski." The supporters of the Katowice Forum "did not sit quietly but distributed thousands of pamphlets of that forum and others." One could have no doubt that it was "an organized attack on Comrade Kania," said Krzymowski.[177]

There was also an attempt to discredit Kania by circulating a letter from Gomulka (or at least the rumor that there was such a letter) claiming that Kania was partly responsible for the decision to repress strikers in Gdansk in December 1970 and hinting that this was the reason Kania was so active in defending Kociolek's Gdansk role. According to AFP (the French Press Agency), the Gomulka letter was to be published in the hard-line weekly *Rzeczywistosc* on the eve of the congress but had been stopped by censors.[178] Congress spokesman Bek denied knowledge of such a letter.[179]

After his reelection, Kania repeated what he had said upon becoming first secretary in 1980, in effect, promising to be a nondictatorial leader in the spirit of the new democratization. He stated that "the party does not need a leader, a leader understood as an idol, a powerful individual dominating the party, a leader who by reason of his position, as it were, sets norms and rules."[180]

In contrast to the voting for the CC, the election of the new Politburo and Secretariat was carried out in a more traditional way—although also more democratically than usual. While the CC and first secretary were elected by the whole congress, the Politburo and Secretariat were elected by the CC, at its second plenum, on July 19. In accordance with the election rules, newly elected First Secretary Kania compiled a list of candidates and presented it to the CC plenum. The list provided no choices: 14 candidates for the 14 Politburo seats, 2 for the 2 candidate members, and 7 for the 7 Secretariat slots. (Kania himself automatically became a Politburo and Secretariat member upon election as first secretary, as the rules stipulated.)

The list apparently had been worked out and cleared with various groups or individuals,[181] and represented various segments of the party. Kania himself, in presenting the list, argued that it provided representation for various units, expanded the number of workers, and for the first time even included a woman and province people's council chairman in the Politburo. He "stressed also" that the list "considers varying shades of opinion within the framework of the line of socialist renewal which should serve well to unite the whole party."[182] In accord with the statute's provisions for separating government and party leadership posts, he said, the premier was the only government official proposed for Politburo membership.[183]

Some CC members nevertheless were dissatisfied with the list, apparently on grounds that it contained too few workers and farmers, and using their new rights, nominated candidates from the floor: Koszalin farmer Mieczyslaw Maksymowicz, Krakow steel mill party secretary Kazimierz Miniur, Szczecin shipyard worker Jozef Mitak, and Walbrzych miner Stefan Paterek for full Politburo members, and Poznan worker Stanislaw Kalkus and Lodz worker Jadwiga Nowakowska for candidate members.[184] (No one was nominated from the floor for the Secretariat.)

CC members then questioned the candidates and then by secret ballot proceeded to elect the slate proposed by Kania. Although the vote totals for individual CC members in Thursday's election of the CC had been withheld from the public, the tallies for Politburo and Secretariat members at Sunday's CC plenum were published in the June 20 *Trybuna Ludu* (table 4.2).

The new Politburo was clearly a balanced group. The two most liberal members were Gdansk shipyard party first secretary Labecki, a nationally known spokesman for reform who had cast the only vote at the March plenum against the compromise which saved the positions of Grabski and Olszowski, and Professor Kubiak, who represented the reform center of Krakow and who soon became a favorite target of conservatives.[185] Worker Zofia Grzyb had pressed for reform in various plenum speeches and was even a member of Solidarity, although she later turned out to be somewhat more conservative. There were three outspoken conserv-

TABLE 4.2

Vote for Politburo Members

	Of 191 valid votes
Successful Candidates (proposed by Kania):	
Wojciech Jaruzelski (premier)	189
Jozef Czyrek (foreign minister)	187
Kazimierz Barcikowski (CC secretary)	186
Stefan Olszowski (CC secretary)	186
Zofia Grzyb (Radom worker)	177
Zbigniew Messner (Katowice academy rector and people's council chairman)	176
Tadeusz Czechowicz (Lodz first secretary)	170
Tadeusz Porebski (Wroclaw first secretary)	170
Stanislaw Opalko (Tarnow first secretary)	168
Miroslaw Milewski (internal affairs minister)	167
Jerzy Romanik (Katowice worker)	166
Jan Labecki (Gdansk local party leader)	162
Hieronim Kubiak (Krakow professor)	150
Albin Siwak (Warsaw worker)	133
Unsuccessful Candidates (nominated from the floor):	
Kazimierz Miniur (Krakow plant secretary)	57
Jozef Mitak (Szczecin shipyard worker)	45
Mieczyslaw Maksymowicz (Koszalin farmer)	42
Stefan Paterek (Walbrzych miner)	35

Vote for Politburo Candidate Members

	Of 192 valid votes
Successful (proposed by Kania):	
Jan Glowczyk (editor of *Zycie Gospodarcze*)	151
Wlodzimierz Mokrzyszczak (Olsztyn first secretary)	126
Unsuccessful (nominated from the floor):	
Jadwiga Nowakowska (Lodz worker)	49
Stanislaw Kalkus (Poznan worker)	46

Vote for Secretariat Members

	Of 192 valid votes
Successful (proposed by Kania):	
Josef Czyrek (foreign minister)	189
Kazimierz Barcikowski (CC secretary)	187
Stefan Olszowski (CC secretary)	187
Zbigniew Michalek (state farm director)	183
Marian Wozniak (Siedlce first secretary)	178
Miroslaw Milewski (internal affairs minister)	178
Hieronim Kubiak (Krakow university professor)	164
Unsuccessful (no one nominated)	

ative members: CC Ideology Secretary Olszowski, Internal Affairs Minister Milewski, who had repeatedly warned against subversion and disorder, and hard-line worker Siwak, who constantly was engaged in polemics with Solidarity and various liberals and who praised the Katowice Forum and other conservative groups.

The four workers and two academics among full members represented a careful balance: The workers were from the two biggest party organizations—Katowice and Warsaw—plus Gdansk and Radom, and the academics were from the rival provinces of Katowice[186] and Krakow. This balancing also helped give representation to the provinces whose party leaders had been defeated in the CC election and hence could not be in the Politburo. The choice of province first secretaries for Politburo membership was largely determined by the elimination of the leaders of virtually all big provinces from the CC. Hence, the few province first secretaries who made it to the CC had a good chance to join the top leadership as well: Of the eight who became CC members, three became Politburo members, one a candidate member, and one a CC secretary. Between the workers, academics, and province first secretaries, Katowice, the biggest organization, got two representatives, Warsaw (the second biggest), Lodz (the third largest), Gdansk (the sixth), and Krakow and Wroclaw (the seventh and eighth) each got one representative. Poznan (the fourth largest) and Bydgoszcz (the fifth) got none.

The July congress carried the democratized procedures up to the party leadership itself. Despite being given only limited choice in electing CC members, delegates exercised their right to choose in a stunningly effective manner. Overriding Politburo efforts to protect incumbents, they chose a CC almost devoid of officials and filled largely with unknown and unpredictable rank and file members. In this unique CC, members appeared to feel mainly beholden to their constituents—the local party organizations which had raised them up as delegates and then as candidates for the CC—and appeared wary of and critical of central leaders.

First Secretary Kania, who successfully rode out the wave of democratization, saw his policy of peaceful resolution of conflicts win widespread support, and he emerged from the congress stronger than ever before. However, just how unpredictable this new CC elected by an uncontrolled congress was was demonstrated only a few months later when attitudes shifted against Kania and this same CC voted to replace him. The new CC appeared on its way to developing into an independent citizens' body intent on scrutinizing the work of party officials and reacting against any perceived abuse of power by party leaders. The unreliability of the CC and even its Politburo prompted Kania's successor Jaruzelski to totally bypass those bodies when he imposed martial law in December 1981.

CHAPTER 5

KANIA'S FALL;
JARUZELSKI'S TAKEOVER

THE WITHERING OF control from above and transformation of the PZPR into a communist party responsive to the rank and file was demonstrated in a final dramatic act when the first secretary himself was forced out of office in October 1981. Support for First Secretary Kania had risen after the threatening Soviet letter and the clumsy challenge to him by hard-liners in June, and he had gained new stature by winning an overwhelming reelection at the unprecedentedly democratic party congress in July. But Kania's power was now based on support from independent-minded party organizations and members rather than the traditional political machine and party discipline, and this support proved fickle in the face of adverse trends.

Kania's removal as first secretary appears to have been the direct result of the new democratic features of the party—freedom for the rank and file to criticize leaders, absence of the traditional control over the CC, and leaders' new dependence on their electors—rather than of the traditional plotting and manipulation of communist power politics. A communist party first secretary is normally too powerful for anyone to openly challenge, and on those rare occasions when a first secretary has been ousted the move has begun at the top, with a conspiracy among top leaders who control some of the levers of power. The CC, made up of party and government officials who usually depend on those above them, obediently follows the lead of the victorious group of leaders. In Kania's case, there appears no evidence of conspiracy by his Politburo colleagues, most of whom still appeared to support him to the end.

Another factor occasionally important in the replacement of communist party first secretaries in East Europe (Rakosi in Hungary, Ulbricht in East Germany, Dubcek in Czechoslovakia) has been Soviet pressure or intervention. It is clear that Soviet leaders sought Kania's removal, but their public moves against him had not worked earlier and appeared to play no decisive role in October either. Secret Soviet moves are harder to judge but presumably depended on an effective hard-line party group or powerful secret police force to act on behalf of the Soviets. However, such earlier moves as Grabski's challenge and the Bydgoszcz beatings had simply backfired.

In the replacement of Kania the impetus came from dramatically shifting sentiment in the party, a sudden upwelling of anger and frustration following Solidarity's national congress. The optimism generated by the successful holding of the most uncontrolled party congress ever and its demonstration of the party's new democratized and responsive character had begun to dissipate already during August as strikes and government-Solidarity tension resumed. Kania himself at the September 2–3 CC plenum had to hint that invoking a state of emergency might be necessary if strikes got worse. The Soviets started large-scale military exercises on the border with Poland on September 4, apparently to put on pressure as Solidarity's national congress gathered to open on September 5. The September 5–10 Solidarity congress proved more aggressive than many leaders had hoped, in particular in its adoption of an appeal to workers in other bloc countries to strive to create their own free trade unions. This in turn provoked new attacks from Moscow, and following a new, sharp letter delivered by the Soviet ambassador, the Polish Politburo and Council of Ministers issued criticisms of Solidarity's congress and apparently discussed the possibility of a state of emergency.

Meanwhile, Kania apparently fell ill in early August and appeared to play a relatively inconspicuous role during much of the month, conveying an impression of weakness and passivity. During September and October frustration over growing economic difficulties and anger at Solidarity's assertiveness and extremism began turning against Kania this time. Low-level party secretaries and rank and file members fighting aggressive Solidarity organizations spoke out bitterly against weak party leadership, and hard-liners, now finding more support, became more vocal. Moderates and liberals, who had defended Kania through the first half of 1981, also appeared disaffected and fell silent. The frustration and anger translated into open criticism of Kania at the October plenum. Finally,

Kania, harassed by criticism, submitted his resignation, which was narrowly accepted by an apparently surprised plenum. As a crowning achievement of the new, more democratic system, the first secretary himself was replaced with no turmoil or conspiracy—precisely fulfilling the vision of those who in September-October 1980 had called for a system whereby the top leaders could be replaced routinely, whenever constituents had lost confidence in their leadership ability or their policies.

This development depended on the new type of CC elected by the congress: a collection of representatives who largely felt themselves obliged to follow the wishes of their local party organizations, rather than the traditional assemblage of officials beholden to their superiors. As with the rest of the party structure, power no longer flowed downward from the top, and no leader, even First Secretary Kania, could secure his position just by pleasing the elite. The democratic election of these CC members did not mean that they were overwhelmingly liberal or reformist; as the reaction after Solidarity's September congress and the anger and frustration over Kania's inability to control the situation demonstrated, this uncontrolled CC—reflecting the rank and file it represented—was subject to sharp swings in attitude and was capable of temporarily swinging in favor of a more hard-line, aggressive policy.

This new kind of CC also presented a basic problem for Kania's successor, who was expected to provide strong leadership despite an undisciplined and divided CC. The CC wanted a strong leader but not a hard-liner, so it turned to Jaruzelski, a trusted moderate who also was a respected military man. Jaruzelski initially attempted to keep to Kania's line of accord and seek an understanding with Solidarity, but he soon gave up on this. With an uncontrolled CC divided between liberals, moderates, and conservatives, it was clearly unrealistic to expect the CC (and even its divided Politburo) to endorse any decisive action. So Jaruzelski bypassed the CC and Politburo, prepared for martial law in secrecy, and then imposed it on the party along with the rest of the country through his armed forces. Martial law had to be prepared behind the back of the CC not only because it would have been difficult to win approval from the CC but because it would have been impossible to maintain secrecy—and the element of surprise was the key to the success of martial law.

SURGE OF CRITICISM OF KANIA

Kania's resignation was a direct response to a surge of criticism of him within the party which built up suddenly after the Solidarity congress. Party leaders appeared to play virtually no role in this developing criticism; in fact, they resisted it. The key Politburo members Barcikowski, Olszowski and Jaruzelski and Warsaw First Secretary Kociolek defended Kania's leadership right down to the CC plenum, which voted him out. Far from plotting to remove Kania, the most influential party leaders were caught on the losing side with him.

The surge of criticism started in local party organizations and was voiced at the October plenum by their representatives in the CC. The criticism surfaced first in outspoken reform strongholds such as Gdansk and Szczecin, which presumably were sympathetic to Kania, although the sharpest and most weighty attacks emerged in the relatively conservative Warsaw party organization. In fact, if there were any elements of an organized campaign against Kania, it surely was based in the Warsaw organization, which had repeatedly demonstrated anti-Kania sentiment before.

The dissatisfaction with Kania that CC members expressed at the October plenum appears to have built up relatively suddenly before the plenum, since there had been very few signs of criticism of the Politburo or Kania in the central or local press during September and early October. It followed close on the heels of the September 5–October 7 Solidarity congress, the provocative actions of which left many party members clamoring for a tougher response by party leaders. The congress, dominated by relatively radical grass-roots representatives, shocked party members and appeared to confirm the warnings of hard-liners that Solidarity was out to destroy the party and take power. The first session of the two-part congress, from September 5 to 10, adopted several stands aimed at reducing party powers and, in its most provocative action, issued a message to workers in the Soviet Union and other bloc countries encouraging them to create free trade unions like Solidarity in their own countries. The Soviet press agency TASS reacted by labeling this an appeal to "fight against the socialist system" internationally as well as in Poland,[1] and the Soviet ambassador gave Kania and Jaruzelski a sharply worded letter from Soviet leaders attacking the Solidarity congress for "slander and insults" against the USSR, calling the congress message to workers abroad an "outrageous provocation," and calling on Polish leaders to take steps against the growing "anti-Sovietism" in Poland.[2] The Polish leadership, upset and prodded by the Soviet protest, reacted sharply also. The Council of Ministers met on September 14 and 17 and the Politburo on September 16, and both issued statements harshly criticizing the Solidarity congress for provoking Poland's allies and for aiming to seize power and change the communist system in Poland.[3]

These warnings may have worried the more cautious Solidarity leaders, but they had limited effect on the determined rank and file delegates. When the second stage of the Solidarity congress was held, from September 26 to October 7, radicals directly challenged the leadership of Lech Walesa and other moderates. Although Walesa won by a solid majority, many of the more radical regional leaders, enjoying strong grass-roots support, were elected to the union's national leadership—indicating that the union would be difficult to deal with.[4] In addition, the program adopted by the congress presented a new series of troublesome demands. While Solidarity pressure in the fall of 1980 had prodded the party into reform, the pressure in the fall of 1981 provoked a reaction against reform. And Kania was perceived by many as being too soft in dealing with Solidarity.

The criticism of Kania, direct or indirect, ironically began appearing mainly in provinces headed by Kania allies—Gdansk, Szczecin, and Warsaw—rather than in provinces where anti-Kania activity had been evident earlier (such as Katowice). The first hints of criticism appeared when the Gdansk province committee's Executive Committee met on October 9 and adopted a resolution frankly recognizing a new wave of rank and file dissatisfaction with the leadership—although without naming Kania. The resolution, published in the October 12 *Glos Wybrzeza* and October 13 *Dziennik Baltycki*, noted that "among members of the Gdansk province party organization critical views regarding the functioning of party leadership at all levels have been growing lately," and "the most critical remarks" are being directed at the "central authorities." The resolution's description of the criticisms matched those later made at the CC plenum: "The criticism concerns mainly the lack of an effective concept for leading the country out of the crisis, the inconsistent carrying out of resolutions, and adopting of decisions mistaken in the public view or causing a harmful growth of social tension." The Executive Committee declared that these criticisms had foundation and that it understood the "tiredness, bitterness, and impatience" of party members, but it disagreed with some of the "radical and even drastic" solutions proposed, since "there is no sensible alternative to the line of social accord."

The outspoken moderates who led Gdansk—First Secretary Fiszbach and Politburo member Labecki—continued to defend moderation at a local plenum and at the CC plenum, but ignored Kania in their speeches. Labecki stated at an October 14 Gdansk plenum that he viewed the upcoming CC plenum with great alarm, because he felt that things could not continue the way they were going and that the plenum would have to do something to restore order. In seeking solutions to the crisis, he said, "a certain part of the party and a certain part of the leadership apparat" is seeking to roll back the line of accord, and "we have fewer and fewer arguments" to counter this. "For the first time I'm greatly alarmed by this," he declared.[5]

Szczecin's moderate leaders even went so far as to take a stand criticizing Kania by name, although this was not publicized before the plenum. In his CC plenum speech, Szczecin shipyard worker Jozef Mitak told Kania that the Szczecin Executive Committee "expresses its disapproval of the present practice of the Politburo under your leadership, Comrade Kania."[6] The stand presumably was supported by moderate Szczecin First Secretary Miskiewicz, who said nothing at the CC plenum.

Bitter criticism of the leadership also broke out at a Lodz meeting of delegates to the party congress. Delegates assailed the Politburo for a variety of shortcomings and criticized Kania's "disappearance" for causing "rumors and ironic remarks" about the leadership.[7]

The anti-Kania sentiment broke out most openly at an October 13–14 plenum of the Warsaw city organization, where there had long been a well-established anti-Kania faction. Warsaw Secretary Jerzy Boleslawski, who delivered the main report, turned from attacking Solidarity's intransigence to complaining bitterly about the party leadership. Warning that rightist forces were moving against the party, he complained that the Warsaw party aktiv "often was fighting alone," without sufficient support and hampered by "mistaken decisions or unconvincing explanations by the leadership." He assailed the leadership for "vacillation" and "readiness to concede" and declared that the party has "had enough of anarchy and chaos."[8] First Secretary of the big Ursus tractor plant Marian Wall complained of too many concessions, declaring that we give in to everyone who "stamps on us."[9] *Trybuna Ludu* reported that "many speakers criticized the leadership" for being "isolated" from the party membership and for not providing activists at the local level with viable arguments to use in fighting hostile rumors and propaganda.[10] Reports in East Germany's *Neues Deutschland*, based on Interpress material from Warsaw, contained much more pointed quotes than the watered down versions in *Trybuna Ludu* and the Warsaw papers *Zycie Warszawy* and *Trybuna Mazowiecka*. On October 16 *Neues Deutschland* reported that Wall's speech had proposed calling the delegates to the July party congress back into session in order to make changes in the leadership and that another speaker, Professor Jan Rychlewski, had stated that "I am ready to fight for the party but under a different leadership." The German paper declared that "the majority of speakers" directed "sharp criticism at the activity of the top party organs," accusing them of "caving in and liberalism." Dan Fisher in the October 15 *Los Angeles Times* also reported that an Interpress account had said that the top leadership had been attacked for "liberalism" at the Warsaw plenum. Fisher added that "reliable sources" said that there had been open calls for Kania's ouster at the Warsaw plenum.

On the Warsaw plenum's second day, October 14, more speakers attacked the leadership for "ineffectiveness and incompetence," but Kania's allies Kociolek and Barcikowski spoke up in his defense.[11] First Secretary Kociolek, who was presiding, took the floor and "was among those to take issue with these statement" and defend the leadership.[12] Later, in his October 16 CC plenum speech, Kociolek recalled that he had spoken up in the "very sharp debate" at the Warsaw plenum in order to call for "balance in assessing the leadership" and avoidance of personal accusations against "leading figures of our party."[13] Other pro-Kania speakers objected to the call for a national conference to shake up the leadership, and then Barcikowski, who was attending the plenum, spoke and sought to deflect criticism from Kania by blaming the party's weakness on Gierek's mistakes.[14] Saying that he "respected the right of party members to criticize the leadership," he reminded the audience how difficult it was to lead now.[15] The hard-liners appeared to prevail, however, as the plenum adopted a resolution condemning the "inconsistency" and "lack of resolve" by the central party leadership and declaring that confidence in the leadership was decreasing.[16]

The Warsaw attack on Kania appeared to catch First Secretary Kociolek by surprise, even though the attacks were led by his own subordinates, Warsaw Secretary Boleslawski and other city committee secretaries.[17] There had long been opposition to Kania and Kociolek in Warsaw, apparently coming both from liberal and conservative sides. When Kania initially proposed Kociolek for first secretary at a November 17, 1980 Warsaw plenum, he had defended Kociolek's role in the bloody crackdown on Gdansk workers in December 1970, insisting that Kociolek had "stubbornly" argued for avoiding use of force.[18] The Kociolek appointment appears to have alienated some Warsaw party members, who continued to suggest that Kociolek, and perhaps Kania himself, was really responsible for resort to force in 1970. When Kociolek was nominated as a candidate for reelection as first secretary at the June 27–29 Warsaw conference, "many delegates" again demanded an explanation of Kociolek's role in putting down the Gdansk demonstrations and forced Kania into a long defense of Kociolek.[19] There appeared to be a persistent belief that Kociolek was really a hard-liner, and Kania and Kociolek devoted their arguments to proving that Kociolek was a true moderate. There had also been strong conservative opposition as well. Bratkowski had claimed in his March 23 letter that the Warsaw party organization was the center of opposition to Kania. Moreover, a precongress Warsaw party organization vote had reportedly favored Grabski, Olszowski, and Zabinski over Kania.[20] In October the attack was clearly from the conservative side.

The Warsaw plenum's attacks so angered Barcikowski that in comments at the end of the plenum he called the whole plenum "splitting and sectarian."[21] This led to a bitter squabble at a Politburo meeting the next day (October 15), as well as at the CC plenum itself on October 16. This pitted Kania supporters Barcikowski and Kociolek against outspoken hard-liner Albin Siwak and some other Warsaw officials.[22] In the Politburo meeting, Politburo member Siwak, who was a member of Warsaw's Executive Committee and had participated in the Warsaw plenum, attacked Barcikowski for criticizing the plenum's work.[23] Kociolek apparently tried to placate conservatives in his organization by stating that he disagreed with Barcikowski's overly sharp characterization of the Warsaw plenum.[24]

At the plenum itself, the dispute flared again, with Barcikowski, Kociolek, and even Olszowski arguing with Siwak and one of the Warsaw secretaries. The irrepressible Siwak raised the dispute in his plenum speech, praising the Warsaw plenum for "defending and strengthening the Marxist-Leninist line of the party" and adding that "unfortunately" Barcikowski had called it "splitting and sectarian." He compounded his attack on Barcikowski by accusing him of proposing an accord with Solidarity and the Church which amounted to "sharing power with Solidarity and the Church, namely with those who are doing everything to overthrow the party and seize power."[25] Kociolek defended Barcikowski, saying that the interpretation of Barcikowski's attitude toward the Church and Solidarity given by Siwak was a "misunderstanding." He also indicated his disagreement with the Warsaw attacks on Kania: Recalling the "sharp, even very sharp" debate at the Warsaw session, Kociolek said that he had spoken up at the local plenum in order to call for "balance in evaluating the leadership" and to caution that imputing bad intentions to leaders is "impermissible." At the same time, he again disassociated himself from Barcikowski's attack on the plenum as "sectarian."[26]

Kociolek's statement angered Siwak, who then broke in to turn his attack to Kociolek. Although stating that "I deeply respect Comrade Kociolek," he asked: "What happened to you during the night? After all, yesterday in the Politburo when we discussed this fully, you agreed, you even added that you had to explain several things, such as the matter of Grudzien's house, etc., for Comrade Barcikowski. Really, comrades, I don't know what's happening; there is a stenographic record of what Comrade Stanislaw Kociolek said. . . . It is not the way it was said here."[27] However, Kociolek defended himself, and some others backed up Kociolek's version.[28]

Barcikowski then spoke, thanking Kociolek (and also Olszowski) for backing up the true meaning of his speech and opening his own attack on Siwak. Barcikowski declared that "what Comrade Siwak said was an ordinary insinuation" and indirectly accused Siwak of acting as a stooge for someone else by stating that "the authors of his remarks apparently had some purpose in this." Barcikowski stubbornly reasserted his judgment that the Warsaw plenum had been "dominated by sectarian attitudes." He indicated that this was his opinion and that Politburo members did not have to publicly all say the same thing.

One of Siwak's Warsaw colleagues, Zygmunt Galecki, then spoke in rebuttal to Barcikowski. He reproved Barcikowski for using the "expression 'authors of his remarks' " in replying to Siwak. Galecki insisted that Siwak was right about the Warsaw plenum and about Barcikowski's support for dialogue with the Church and Solidarity, which amounted to "the line of accord at any price."[29]

The surge of criticism of Kania was resisted not only by Barcikowski and Kociolek but apparently even by the two most prominent conservatives still in leadership posts—CC Secretary Olszowski and Katowice First Secretary Zabinski. Although both had shown signs of discontent with Kania's overly liberal policies in early 1981, they did not lead the move against Kania or even assist it. Their speeches during September and early October contained no public criticism of Kania, and judging from plenum reports, they said nothing against Kania at the plenum either. In fact, Olszowski, who had been cooperating with Kania since June, appeared to be defending his leadership right up to the plenum itself. In a speech at a September 11 Sieradz plenum, Olszowski stated that while Politburo actions before the congress had been notable for "many concessions and compromises toward Solidarity," since the congress they have been "characterized by decisiveness."[30] In a September 4 speech in Wroclaw, he boasted that since the congress "there have been no concessions," and "policy has been conducted consistently despite the existing tension."[31] Moreover, on the very eve of the plenum, during a question-and-answer session in Katowice, an area where there had been much anti-Kania activity, he appeared to defend the leadership, stating that the "consistent implementation of the line of accord is not a result of the leadership's weakness" but an expression of "well-considered tactics."[32] In fact, speakers at the Warsaw plenum reportedly criticized Olszowski for being "too liberal."[33]

The criticism of Kania thus came from below, rather than from leaders, even conservative leaders. Kania's inability to counter it this time stemmed to a considerable extent from a loss of enthusiastic support from many moderates and liberals. Although Barcikowski vigorously defended Kania before the plenum and Jaruzelski spoke at the plenum against replacing

Kania,[34] most other moderates and liberals stood on the sidelines, apparently disenchanted or cowed by the tide of criticism in the ranks. Deputy Premier Rakowski[35] and Gdansk First Secretary Fiszbach, who with Barcikowski had spearheaded Kania's defense at the June plenum, failed to defend Kania in speeches at the October plenum. Nor did Krakow First Secretary Dabrowa, Szczecin First Secretary Miskiewicz, or Gdansk leader Labecki. In general, central and regional party leaders played little role at the October plenum, either in attacking or defending Kania. In contrast, they had played the main roles at the June plenum, Grabski and various province first secretaries attacking Kania, while Barcikowski, Rakowski, and Fiszbach defended him. This time few of these leaders were even on the CC—since the congress had so radically changed the CC membership. Only three province first secretaries spoke at the October plenum, and most of them were only invited guests. None of them attacked or defended Kania.

Those that did play the leading role in Kania's removal were CC members representing the rank and file and lower party organizations. CC members had come to see themselves as representatives of the party organizations that elected them and felt a strong obligation to reflect their sentiments. Poznan worker and CC member Stanislaw Kalkus stated that during the three-day October plenum, "I maintained constant telephone contact with my home plant committee," and "I was obligated to do this and cannot imagine voting or speaking at the CC plenum without knowing the attitude of my comrades at the plant."[36]

This representative concept had developed already by early 1981 and had played a key role in the attacks on hard-liners at the March plenum. Virtually all the workers and some others who addressed that plenum stated that they represented specific local organizations and had been instructed to present resolutions adopted by their organizations on issues or personalities. For example, worker Jadwiga Nowakowska stressed that what she was saying represented not "just my own feelings" but positions adopted by "the fifty biggest industrial factories" in Lodz— "the voice of the communist worker milieu of Lodz." Poznan worker Stanislaw Zielinski explained that he was speaking "in the name" of 3,500 workers of a Poznan factory who had just sent him a telex message ordering him not to come home until he had presented their views to the plenum. Worker Antoni Pierz stated that members of the Gorzow party organization had ordered him to "convey their position regarding the central authorities of our party" and that they "do not ask but demand resolute action." Wroclaw worker Janina Kostrzewska stated that her local party organization "had bound me to declare" that the March 22 Politburo statement on Bydgoszcz was "premature" and was opposed by members of her organization. Wlodzimierz Trzebiatowski (director of a scientific laboratory) indicated that he was bringing many resolutions from local Wroclaw organizations demanding personnel changes in the leadership.[37]

While CC representatives had thus conveyed local attacks on conservatives at the March plenum, prompting Olszowski and Grabski to offer their resignations, similar local attacks presented at the October plenum prompted Kania to present his resignation.

KANIA'S DECISION TO RESIGN

It appears that Kania had no intention of resigning when the plenum opened on Friday, but that two days of criticism—in formal plenum speeches and informal plenum gatherings—coupled with loss of support from key provincial organizations and adoption of a resolution critical of his leadership prompted him to decide to submit his resignation on Sunday morning. It is not clear whether he expected his resignation to be rejected or really desired to leave, either to avoid having to eventually resort to force against Solidarity or, like some provincial leaders in 1980–81, to be rid of a thankless job with little power. It does seem clear that his Politburo colleagues did not push him out; in fact some accounts indicate that Jaruzelski and Barcikowski opposed Kania's resignation at the plenum and that even Olszowski had refused to be a candidate to succeed him. In any case, only three months after Kania's resounding reelection at the congress, a narrow majority of the CC voted to accept his resignation.

When the CC plenum opened on October 16, the representatives of the Warsaw party organization played a key role in initiating criticism of Kania, even though some others were even more aggressive.[38] A local

Warsaw factory party secretary, Ryszard Kucharski, the first to speak, kicked off the criticism of Kania by saying that parts of his report to the plenum "simply smacked of fantasy." Hard-line Warsaw worker Siwak, the eleventh to speak, called for strong leadership and declared that people were "ceasing to believe in Comrade Kania." The third Warsaw representative to speak, First Secretary Kociolek, cautiously waffled, recalling his efforts to restrain the sharp criticism at the Warsaw plenum but expressing his disagreement with Barcikowski's harsh assessment of the Warsaw plenum.

Some other speakers on the first day—Radom worker and Politburo member Zofia Grzyb, Opole First Secretary Eugeniusz Mroz, and Koszalin farmer Mieczyslaw Maksymowicz—expressed pessimism and called for decisive action by the Politburo, and a worker proposed adding "assessment of the work of the Politburo" to the agenda.[39] Szczecin shipyard worker Jozef Mitak announced that the Szczecin Executive Committee had expressed its "disapproval" of the Politburo work "under your leadership, Comrade Kania." The sharpest challenge came from Czestochowa worker Zofia Stepien, who declared that "many" workers were beginning to wonder if "Grabski was not right" in saying that the present leadership could not lead the country out of crisis.[40] She asked Kania whether "you, Comrade First Secretary, know what difficult party work we have in the factories, how they call us various names, [blame] us for the crisis in the country, for our helplessness and lack of consistency," and for his lack of public appearances and unwillingness "to talk to the people." The first day ended with no one defending Kania or the Politburo.

When the plenum reconvened on Saturday, October 17, so many members clamored to speak that it was decided to extend the plenum to a third day. The second speaker, Konin worker Czeslaw Borowski, proposed calling the congress delegates back into session in a national conference—apparently to reconsider the congress' decisions on the leadership. Jelenia Gora miner Jozef Jarmala, assailing repeated concessions to Solidarity, declared that the work of the "first secretary must be energetic and effective" and that "it is high time for one who is unable to or is afraid to adopt an effective decision, to retire." Wroclaw worker Marian Kasprzycki boldly stated: "Comrade Kania! . . . You are responsible for carrying out Politburo resolutions. Tell us at today's plenum who does not want to carry out the resolutions. . . . Is the present Politburo headed by you in a condition to lead the party along the straight road? We cannot allow ourselves the luxury . . . of incompetence and lack of consistency in the work of the Politburo," because this leaves local party activists defenseless. Again no one defended the leadership.[41] Liberal Politburo member Labecki made a point of denying that the Politburo was split, but as for the Politburo's "competence or incompetence," he said, that is "another problem" and for the CC to judge. Representatives from the reform centers of Gdansk and Krakow continued to counsel moderate policies but ignored Kania.[42]

In addition to the criticism in the plenum speeches, the Politburo heard criticism of itself and Kania in informal polling of CC members during the plenum and in working group sessions on Saturday, judging from subsequent statements by individual CC members. A Poznan representative said that during a break in the plenum, Politburo members met with representatives of individual provinces and "asked us . . . for objective evaluation of the leadership's work." He added that "I think these meetings predetermined comrade Stanislaw Kania's decision."[43] A Bydgoszcz official stated that "group consultations between CC members and comrades from the Politburo during a break in the proceedings showed that a basic change in the style of work of the Politburo and its members was needed to carry out the resolutions of the 9th congress."[44] An Opole participant related that "working groups" had held discussions on Saturday, and participants had expressed themselves considerably "more concretely" than was possible at the plenum itself and that the Politburo early on Sunday had met and analyzed these discussions. He stated that Kania decided to resign "on the basis" of these "critical statements" about his work.[45]

The discontent came to a head on the third day of the extended plenum, when CC members voted to adopt a resolution sharply critical of the leadership. The official accounts of the decisive day of the plenum are exceedingly skimpy,[46] but the events can be reconstructed from comments made later by plenum participants at local question-and-answer sessions reported in province papers. The Sunday session began by adopting a resolution critical of the leadership, although without naming Kania. As published in the October 19 *Trybuna Ludu*, it criticized the leadership for "lack of consistency" and "lack of decisiveness," called on the leadership to more actively fight "the foes of socialism," and declared that

Politburo and Secretariat methods have had "little effect." The chairman of the commission which produced the resolution, Wroclaw university professor Marian Orzechowski, explaining the resolution later in an interview, said drafters felt the Politburo was not fighting the opposition hard enough and that the resolution was a "proper criticism" of the leadership. He directly linked Kania's resignation to the resolution, stating that in the light of the resolution's criticisms "the change in the post of CC first secretary becomes understandable."[47]

Taking the resolution as a repudiation of his leadership, Kania then offered his resignation. It was apparently not forced or even suggested by anyone else. A Poznan representative later said, "I did not hear any speaker in the discussion assert that Comrade Stanislaw Kania should leave the post of CC first secretary," but "he himself said that he understood the criticism of the Politburo in this way and precisely for this reason decided to resign"—something "unprecedented" in the party.[48] Politburo member Kubiak told a local meeting that Kania had submitted his resignation "even though the Politburo had not made such a proposal."[49] The result appeared to surprise even those unhappy with his leadership. One CC member stated that "from the very start of the plenum we calculated that during the 4th plenum there must be some kind of change, although we still did not know about Comrade Kania's resignation."[50]

Barcikowski then took over as presiding officer at the plenum and gave the floor to Jaruzelski. Jaruzelski argued against any leadership changes on the grounds that the congress had been held only three months earlier and changes could evoke an "unhealthy sensation" and disrupt the "substantive work of the plenum." Despite this, criticism continued and finally Barcikowski interrupted the discussion and proposed a vote.[51] In a secret vote, the CC narrowly voted in favor of accepting Kania's resignation, 104 for, 79 against.[52]

Faced with Kania's departure, the Politburo quickly settled on Jaruzelski as his successor, seeing him as the only candidate who could rally the country and who could reassure the reformers. A Lodz representative later stated that "a majority of provinces" urged Jaruzelski's candidacy and that the choice of Jaruzelski was "perhaps dictated by the fact that there was fear about whether the line of the 9th congress would be retained after S. Kania's departure."[53] Jaruzelski was nominated unanimously by the Politburo.[54] Conservatives made no bid for party leadership themselves. One participant stated flatly that Jaruzelski was the "only candidate,"[55] and another stated that Olszowski had "indicated in advance that if he were nominated he would not consent" to run.[56] By secret vote, Jaruzelski was elected 180 to 4.[57]

Plenum participants all appeared to agree in later statements that Kania's resignation had been caused by the criticism. In addition to the statements cited above, CC candidate member Marek Bartosik stated: Kania's departure was "a result of the very harsh evaluation of the work of the Politburo and its chief. I would say, of the style of work. Comrade Kania left not because of what he did, but because of what he didn't do. The Politburo received very many criticisms addressed to the first secretary and that influenced him to resign."[58] Bydgoszcz worker Zbigniew Szadkowski said that Kania resigned after the CC questioned whether he was "capable of fulfilling his function,"[59] while a local secretary in Lodz stated that Kania had been replaced following criticism of him "for being not visible enough in the party leadership."[60]

Despite all the criticism, the vote to accept his resignation was relatively close and he left in relatively little disgrace. Kubiak stressed that Kania had remained at the plenum after his resignation, and "no one pretended that he was ill" (as they had pretended that Gierek was ill when he resigned). "This method of departure is a valuable element of political culture and a new style in the practice of politics," Kubiak contended.[61] CC member Zbigniew Szadkowski stated that "in my opinion, he left with honor."[62]

CC member Jozef Gwozdz revealed that Kania had submitted his resignation from the Politburo as well.[63] Official accounts only mention him resigning his Secretariat post, but his resignation as first secretary apparently meant his departure from the Politburo and Secretariat as well—just as his election as first secretary had automatically made him a member of those bodies also. This was never spelled out officially, however, and some local party members later asked whether Kania was still a Politburo member after the plenum.[64] The main confirmation of his departure appeared when he was identified only as "former first secretary" and a "CC member" when he participated in the working groups at the November 27–28 plenum.[65] Kania also was not listed with Politburo members at any post-October events.

Even though Kania had led the party through a long and difficult year and did not leave his post in disgrace, there were few expressions of regret at his departure. Katowice's *Trybuna Robotnicza* was openly negative about Kania, reporting many comments by local activists criticizing Kania's inconsistency and ineffectiveness and stating that it was "high time" for this change.[66] Even the areas most supportive of him in the past—Krakow and Gdansk—appeared satisfied that Jaruzelski would be just as moderate as Kania and perhaps more effective. The Elblag Executive Committee expressed approval of the change of first secretary because "it expects that now the Politburo will act more decisively, while continuing to maintain the line of social accord."[67]

Only Jaruzelski and a couple of liberal publications paid tribute to Kania. Jaruzelski, upon being elected first secretary, praised Kania as "my close, warm friend of many years" and as leader during a tough year and declared that "Comrade Kania will remain with us in the ranks of active work and service for the party and Poland."[68] The chief editor of the Warsaw weekly *Kultura*, Dominik Horodynski, wrote: "Stanislaw Kania was first secretary in a very difficult period in the history of People's Poland. His sense of responsibility, his honesty and caution, his inclination to delay decisions were seen as excessive vacillation or as lack of consistency. For this he was criticized from various sides. In essence, the historic service of Comrade Kania was to keep Poland from spilling blood. And that counts for a great deal."[69] The outspoken liberal Krakow paper *Gazeta Krakowska* printed a glowing tribute to Kania on October 19, thanking him for his "courage" in carrying out "political solution of conflicts" since renewal began and for the fact that "as of today, Poland is a country in which we debate but don't fight. . . . And for this policy, which had and has many enemies, Stanislaw Kania has his place in history."

JARUZELSKI IN CONTROL

The party and its CC clearly wanted a strong leader, someone to lead it out of the frustrating morass, and so it turned to the most respected state figure, armed forces chief Jaruzelski. In the wave of discontent with Kania and weak leadership, conservatives sought to oust liberals and moderates and regain some of their lost influence. But the CC appeared to want continuation of moderation, of Kania's line of accord—just with more effective leadership. Jaruzelski represented that line to most CC members, and he blocked conservative efforts to oust those who, with him and Kania, had pressed for moderate reform. The limited personnel changes that did occur during late October and November mainly strengthened Jaruzelski—something that frustrated the conservatives but which eventually also proved to be ominous in preparing the ground for Jaruzelski to impose dictatorial rule in December.

Initially, as Kania lost control in mid-October, conservatives were able to score some notable successes in purging outspoken reformers. As the plenum opened, liberal Journalists Union chairman Stefan Bratkowski was expelled from the party and liberal Jacek Nachyla was fired as editor of the youth paper *Sztandar Mlodych*. These actions were announced by conservatives on the very opening day of the plenum, in the midst of the growing attacks on Kania. Outspoken hard-liner Siwak raised the subject in his October 16 plenum speech, complaining that Bratkowski had ignored the Central Party Control Commission and was not being punished, and that *Sztandar Mlodych* had printed an interview with dissident Jacek Kuron and let him represent himself as a "hero of renewal." He also asked impatiently when the editors of *Gazeta Krakowska, Glos Wybrzeza,* and *Gazeta Wspolczesna* would finally be changed.[70] Responding immediately to Siwak's speech, Central Party Control Commission chairman Jerzy Urbanski rose to announce that on that very day a unit of the Central Party Control Commission had expelled Bratkowski from the party.[71] On the same day, Olszowski announced to the plenum that editor Nachyla had been fired for the Kuron interview.[72] Olszowski, the CC secretary in charge of the press, later declared himself personally "responsible for Nachyla's dismissal."[73]

These moves stirred loud protests from liberals and moderates. On October 19, *Gazeta Krakowska* editor Maciej Szumowski signed a long "open letter" in his paper angrily protesting the Bratkowski expulsion, arguing that this act played into the hands of those who argued that the party is "not reformable."[74] The following day *Gazeta Krakowska* reported that a meeting of the paper's primary party organization, to which all Krakow party journalists were invited, had sent a letter to Jaruzelski protesting the expulsion. On October 30 the Warsaw writers union's primary party organization—of which Bratkowski was a member—met and protested his expulsion.[75] Gdansk journalists also sent a protest to Jaruzelski,[76] and the expulsion was criticized at a number of local party meetings.[77] Nachyla's firing caused a storm of protest among *Sztandar Mlodych* employees,[78] and complaints at various party meetings.[79]

In addition to their moves in Warsaw, conservatives mounted new campaigns against liberals in several provinces. Conservatives in Gdansk— though a clear minority—launched an attack on the liberal paper *Glos Wybrzeza* and at an October 14 Gdansk plenum called for the dismissal of chief editor Tadeusz Kuta and also attacked First Secretary Fiszbach "and the line of accord he represents." Liberals responded by labeling them "officials of the old party apparat, who lost in democratic elections and who are against renewal and the line of understanding represented by Comrade Fiszbach."[80] A "Marxist-Leninist Party Forum" in Walbrzych on October 16 "expressed sharp disapproval of the Politburo's work and especially of Comrades Kania and Barcikowski for not resisting the counterrevolutionary threat and for permitting dramatic worsening of the economic situation. . . . On the other hand, it expressed recognition of the position of Comrade Olszowski."[81] However, central authorities took action to suppress the latter group. Marian Orzechowski, named CC ideology secretary (under Olszowski) at the late October plenum, went to Walbrzych and at a November plenum asked the forum to close down on grounds that it was dividing and weakening the party.[82]

On October 20 a group of extreme hard-liners, calling themselves a "Marxist-Leninist Seminar," resorted to force, seizing a local party building in Katowice and sending a letter to newly elected First Secretary Jaruzelski calling for the October 28 plenum to take action against Kania and other moderates. The October 21 *Trybuna Ludu* reported that the group had seized the factory party committee headquarters at the Katowice steel works and had presented complaints against the local party committee and "against some members of the central leadership" (the latter complaints were not specified). The group soon surrendered and its complaints were not given much publicity, but a long letter circulated by the group was read at an (unsympathetic) October 23 meeting at the Lenin shipyard in Gdansk, and its contents were published in the October

26 *Glos Wybrzeza*. It called on the party control commission to investigate the activities of Kania, Barcikowski, Kubiak, and Rakowski, and
demanded a discussion of the question of whether they should belong to
the leadership or even to the party. It also urged the return to "active
political life" of former Politburo member and Kania foe Grabski, "who
by his uncompromising position" had won "confidence and support as
a true son of the working class." *Gazeta Krakowska* on November 9
reported that the group had also sent a letter to East German leader
Erich Honecker warning that counterrevolution was gaining the upper
hand in Poland.

The ultraconservative magazine *Rzeczywistosc* meanwhile began a smear
campaign against liberal Politburo member Kubiak, reporting that people
were writing about the "Krakowiak from the CIA" (*Krakowiaczek z
CIA*) on walls in Kubiak's native Krakow.[83] The use of this epithet against
Kubiak by *Rzeczywistosc* came under attack at a Lodz meeting[84] and
also in an October 31 article in Rakowski's *Polityka*. On November 10
Trybuna Ludu reported that the Central Party Control Commission had
ordered *Rzeczywistosc*'s chief editor to apologize to Kubiak.[85]

Liberals attacked *Rzeczywistosc*, but could get no real action against
the weekly, probably because it was protected by Olszowski. At the
November 27–28 plenum, Torun factory party committee first secretary
Marian Arendt cited *Rzeczywistosc*'s "perfidious slandering" of Kubiak
and criticized the soft rebuke by the Central Party Control Commission,
saying the state prosecutor should take up this case. Declaring that *Rzeczywistosc* must be a party paper because it was created on the basis of
a decision by the CC Secretariat, he asked Olszowski why it was allowed
to pursue "its own political line," often contradicting the congress' decisions, and he called for the CC to vote on whether the magazine should
continue.[86] Olszowski replied, revealing that he himself had presented
the proposal to create *Rzeczywistosc* to the CC Secretariat and praising
its consistent campaigning against "antisocialist forces." He termed the
Kubiak incident just a "mistake" by the magazine and said that editor
Henryk Tycner "had been punished by the Central Party Control Commission" and that he (Olszowski) and the Press Department had called
Rzeczywistosc's editors in for an "appropriate talk" about this. But he
defended the magazine's continuing on the same basis.[87]

Meanwhile, liberals began some attacks on Olszowski and other conservatives. A speaker at an October 23 Gdansk shipyard party meeting criticized Olszowski for trying to pull the party away from the line of accord and also for his management of propaganda.[88] At an October 24 meeting of Krakow leaders devoted to the upcoming October 28 CC plenum, speakers called for removal from the CC leadership of those favoring confrontation.[89] *Gazeta Krakowska* on October 29 also reported party members calling for the ouster of Politburo members who criticize the line of accord. A letter to the Politburo from the first secretaries of the fifteen biggest party organizations in Tarnow called for "elimination" from leadership "of persons carrying out a policy of confrontation and not recognizing dialogue and the line of social accord as obligatory."[90] Deputy chief editor of *Nowe Drogi* Ludwik Krasucki at a Torun meeting "sharply attacked 'the citadel of aggressive conservatism'—as he called it—which has been operating very offensively recently in the party."[91]

Although there were signs that conservatives were in the ascendancy—the ouster of Kania, party-wide demands for more assertive leadership, punitive actions against Bratkowski and Nachyla, and hard-liners' bold attacks on liberal and even moderate Politburo members—Jaruzelski blocked further actions against liberals and kept conservatives from gaining much more power in the leadership. Jaruzelski himself had promised leadership changes when elected first secretary at the mid-October plenum,[92] but when the next plenum was held on October 28 no one was dropped from the leadership and only minimal alterations in the Politburo and Secretariat were made. The plenum's main personnel actions—all additions—strengthened Jaruzelski and, to a lesser extent, Olszowski. Chief of the General Staff Florian Siwicki was elected a Politburo candidate member, and Olsztyn First Secretary Wlodzimierz Mokrzyszczak and Wroclaw university professor Marian Orzechowski were elected CC secretaries.[93] The addition of Siwicki bolstered Jaruzelski, since he had long been Jaruzelski's deputy as deputy defense minister and (as Jaruzelski indicated in his October 30 speech to the Sejm) would now carry out the day-to-day management of the defense ministry in Jaruzelski's stead.[94] Orzechowski's promotion may have strengthened Olszowski, since he was Olszowski's deputy in the CC's Ideological Commission,[95] and subsequently, as CC secretary, he was assigned to handle ideological matters under Olszowski's supervision.[96]

The plenum also reorganized the CC apparat, strengthening Jaruzelski and Olszowski by adding two new officials who had worked under them. General Tadeusz Dziekan, deputy chief of the armed forces' Main Political Administration, was named head of the Cadres Department, while Jerzy Majka, party secretary in the "Prasa" Publishing House,[97] was named head of the newly created Information Department. Majka had worked under Olszowski's jurisdiction, and Olszowski had announced plans to create the Information Department at the October 16–18 plenum.

The appointment of Olszowski's associates Orzechowski and Majka probably partially reflected the fact that he was cooperating with Jaruzelski against the more aggressive hard-liners. He appears to have cooperated, for example, in discouraging the Walbrzych forum which had openly backed him and in admonishing the *Rzeczywistosc* editor to tone down his attacks on Kubiak (see above). In contrast, Jaruzelski did nothing to bring back other conservatives like Grabski and Zabinski.

At the same time, Jaruzelski himself was further strengthened by the promotion of Siwicki and Dziekan. The naming of a general to head the Cadres Department—probably an unprecedented step in a communist party—put a Jaruzelski man in direct control of party appointments. As premier, Jaruzelski had earlier named several generals to ministerial posts (including Internal Affairs Minister Czeslaw Kiszczak). Jaruzelski now not only personally headed the party, government, and defense ministry, but had close military associates in direct control of key levers of power: General Siwicki running the defense ministry, General Dziekan running party cadres, and General Kiszczak running the police.

DECISION TO IMPOSE MARTIAL LAW

In his new role as party leader Jaruzelski initially followed Kania's line of trying to deal with Solidarity. Despite new strikes and pessimism in the party over Solidarity's good faith, Jaruzelski in late October proposed a new approach to overcome confrontation and facilitate cooperation in solving the country's problems: a grand coalition of social forces, including the Church and Solidarity—a "Front of National Accord." Negotiations between leaders of the three main forces—General Jaruzelski, Cardinal Jozef Glemp, and Solidarity leader Lech Walesa—began in early

November, but agreement proved elusive. The party was badly divided over how far to go in making concessions, and it was dubious whether the regime could really bring itself to share power with Solidarity. Solidarity meanwhile was also sharply divided between moderates interested in some cooperation with the regime and radicals totally hostile to the authorities. Moreover, Solidarity's leaders were having great difficulties in controlling local branches which sometimes insisted on resorting to strikes against the wishes of the national leadership. Meanwhile, economic conditions continued to deteriorate.

While pursuing "national accord," Jaruzelski also initiated plans for imposing martial law, apparently as an alternative in case accord proved unreachable (assuming his efforts for accord were sincere in the first place). Planning for martial law was already well along by early November, but no final decision apparently had been made at that point and no date set. Nevertheless, the need for releasing many army recruits whose terms expired in December—plus later Solidarity talk of holding a national demonstration on December 17—made it increasingly clear to Jaruzelski and his fellow planners that if they were going to use martial law they would have to do so by mid-December.

The decision to impose martial law appears to have evolved gradually during November, but only became firm in early December. Later statements by insiders—Rakowski, Kiszczak, Kubiak—portray a growing pessimism about national accord after the early November efforts and a feeling that martial law was inevitable after Solidarity's December 3 Radom meeting. By early December there were signs that the regime was resigned to confronting Solidarity: On December 2 it used force against striking fire-fighting cadets who were backed by Solidarity, and on December 7 it broadcast tape recordings of belligerent statements by Solidarity leaders at Radom supposedly proving that the union's leadership was bent on confrontation and bringing down the communist system. Statements by regime leaders, however, argue that the actual decision was adopted only at the last minute—on December 11 or 12—and indeed the intentions of the regime were still unclear enough so that Solidarity leaders were caught by surprise when Jaruzelski finally did move during the night of December 12–13.

The plans for martial law were worked out by Jaruzelski, Defense Minister Siwicki, Internal Affairs Minister Kiszczak, and a few others, and the decision to implement appears to have been made more or less by Jaruzelski alone. The Politburo and CC were apparently not asked to adopt martial law, both because the element of surprise (which proved so effective in seizing Solidarity's leaders and breaking its power) would have been lost and also because there was considerable doubt that they would easily agree to this. The possibility of adopting a state of emergency had apparently been discussed and rejected by the Politburo in September. The mid-October CC plenum had debated resorting to emergency powers, and the result had been a compromise formula so watered down as to be meaningless. Clearly neither the CC nor even the Politburo—made up of a range of liberals, moderates, and conservatives—could be relied upon to approve a state of emergency or martial law. Hence, Jaruzelski, who held an unprecedented combination of posts—direct leader of the party, government, and armed forces—used his authority to set up a new ruling body made up exclusively of military men and had his military units carry out the martial law provisions. He did not even claim Politburo or CC authorization. The Politburo and other party bodies became inactive and only gradually resumed limited functions.

There appears to have been some discussion of adopting a state of emergency already during September, but with negative results. Kania at the September 2–3 CC plenum had publicly warned that those who threaten national strikes saying "that the authorities will definitely not declare a state of emergency" (*stan wyjatkowy*) are deluding themselves, because the regime does have the will to resort to this if it really becomes necessary. Following the aggressive positions taken at the September 5–10 Solidarity congress and receipt of a new letter from the Soviet leadership shortly after the congress, this step apparently was discussed in the Council of Ministers and the Politburo, but the leadership decided against any such action. John Darnton reported in the *New York Times* on September 27, 1981 that following the new Soviet letter the Politburo had debated declaring a state of emergency. According to his account, the session lasted late into the night, but eventually the Politburo followed Kania's lead and rejected this course. There was no official information to support this,[98] but the sequence of events following the Solidarity congress suggest serious discussions. According to announcements in *Trybuna Ludu*, the Council of Ministers met on September 14, the Politburo on September 16, and the Council of Ministers again on September 17. All these meetings dealt with the current crisis and relations with Solidarity, judging by the Council of Ministers and Politburo statements published in the September 17 and 18 *Trybuna Ludu*.

Whatever happened in September, the CC clearly took up the general question of action against Solidarity at the mid-October plenum where Kania resigned. It discussed a proposal to adopt something in the nature of a state of emergency and also a proposal to force the hundreds of thousands of party members in Solidarity to either quit Solidarity or quit the party. There clearly was no consensus for firm action, however, so a compromise was settled on and ambiguous formulas were inserted into the plenum's resolution. After the plenum, liberals and conservatives chose to interpret these provisions as they wished.

The question of the proper attitude of party members toward Solidarity was debated sharply at the plenum. Politburo member Zofia Grzyb announced that she was resigning from Solidarity in protest after observing the radical orientation of the Solidarity congress. Nine other CC members and one candidate member also quit Solidarity at the plenum. Katowice worker Franciszek Banko argued that party members are not able to follow the party line while belonging to Solidarity and that party leaders in particular "cannot be in Solidarity."[99] On the other side, Leszno worker and CC member Edward Banicki declared that despite those resignations he was not ready to quit Solidarity, and Jerzy Zieba, first secretary of a factory party committee in Krakow, criticized the Politburo's statement on the Solidarity congress as not "objective" and insisted that "we can't go to workers with the one-sided thesis that the whole program and all resolutions of the Solidarity congress are only and exclusively counter-revolutionary."[100]

Similarly, there were two sides on what to do about Solidarity and the strikes plaguing the nation. Wroclaw university professor and CC member Marian Orzechowski later declared that one side felt that "all means of accord had been exhausted," and the other side stressed the need to continue the line of accord.[101] Bielsko-Biala First Secretary Andrzej Gdula in his plenum speech declared that there were two paths to follow: "consistent carrying out of the 9th Congress program and the reforms outlined in it" or "introduction of a state of emergency" (*stan wyjatkowy*), which would mean an end to "reforms, to expanding democracy and civil freedoms" in order to guarantee food supplies and social order. Gdula took the moderate side, stressing the serious consequences of the latter choice.[102] In a like vein, CC member Marian Arendt complained at the plenum that "reactionary forces in the party who call themselves 'the only authentic communists' are mobilizing more and more openly."[103] Orzechowski appeared to favor tough measures and spoke of fighting anti-socialist forces "not only with the force of arguments but also with the argument of force, which our state possesses."[104] Judging by the apparently full versions of the plenum speeches in the November *Nowe Drogi*, the only speaker who directly advocated a state of emergency or martial law was Katowice worker Franciszek Banko, who declared: "I don't want blood spilt, but the only way to avoid spilling blood is for us to obligate the government to introduce a state of siege [*stan zagrozenia panstwa*] or state of war [*stan wojny*]. In this framework, I introduce a proposal that the CC transfer power for the period of a year to the hands of the Polish people's army with leadership in the hands of General of the Army Comrade Jaruzelski."[105] No one commented on this proposal.

The plenum ended by adopting a resolution containing only this vague provision relating to a state of emergency: "In the situation of the existing threat to public life and the safety of the state, the Central Committee considers it necessary for the highest authorities of the Polish People's Republic, in the case of supreme need [*w razie wyzszej koniecznosci*], to resort to constitutional powers in order to protect the most vital interests of the state and nation."[106] It contained this provision regarding party members belonging to Solidarity: "The ideological confrontation requires an unequivocal ideological self-definition [*samookreslenie*] by party members. . . . The Central Committee especially considers it necessary that party activists, leading personnel in state institutions, and members of party leadership bodies at all levels who belong to Solidarity determine their political stance. The Central Committee recognizes the declaration by a number of CC members that they are resigning from Solidarity."

Orzechowski, chairman of the commission on resolutions and proposals which worked out the resolution adopted by the plenum, gave considerable insight into the plenum debate and the compromise nature of the resolution in an interview in the October 20 Wroclaw paper *Gazeta*

Robotnicza. He frankly acknowledged sharp divisions in the CC and explained that the original draft resolution prepared by the apparat had been rejected by the plenum[107] and that a new thirty-four member commission on resolutions and proposals, including only three Politburo members, had been elected.[108] The commission held three debates on the resolution, and then the plenum itself debated it twice. Orzechowski declared that "the resolution is a result not so much of compromise as of searching for such formulations and decisions which could be accepted by all members of the plenum. The resolution was adopted unanimously."[109] The most debate, he said, had arisen over the "formula which said that in case of great need the highest authorities of the Polish People's Republic should resort to the constitutional powers to defend the most essential interests of the people and the state." He added that this is "a very sharp formulation," but he stressed that this meant only "in case of great need" and that it meant that CC members felt that "not all possibilities for political solutions have been exhausted." Asked whether this formula meant a "state of emergency" (*stan wyjatkowy*), Orzechowski said no: "It means martial law [*stan wojenny*], because our Constitution has no provision for a state of emergency [*stan wyjatkowy*]." He stressed again that "it should be understood that the government would resort to extraordinary means when all other means of managing a national catastrophe—economic and political—have been exhausted." "No one today is in a position to predict what consequences that would bring," and "this knowledge hung over the debates and over those members of the CC and commission who proposed and defended this formulation."

He also interpreted the provision about Solidarity as a compromise. "As can be seen, a decision prevailed which does not put party members who are also in Solidarity 'up against the wall' " (i.e., force them to make a choice). "*Samookreslenie*," he explained, meant that party members in Solidarity "should represent the party line," and "whether he should leave Solidarity, when and how, depends on his specific evaluation. If he judges that he can do nothing more in Solidarity, that his activity there brings more harm than value, he should leave it."

Although the provision on emergency powers in the resolution was vague, it still stirred some uneasiness. A primary party organization first secretary in Opole complained that some "extremist forces" were striving to use force and noted that the resolution speaks about a "state of extreme need [*stan wyzszej koniecznosci*] or introducing something in the form of a state of emergency [*stan wyjatkowy*]." He added, however, that he was reassured by the election of Jaruzelski, because "Comrade Jaruzelski has proved himself in conflict situations, speaking out every time for dialogue and political solution."[110] Local Krakow party members expressed concern that the provision in the Constitution might be misused "by some groups."[111] Party members at Krakow's Jagiellonian University expressed "disquiet at the suggestion of a state of emergency [*stan wyjatkowy*]."[112] Henryk Galus, in analyzing the plenum in the October 23–25 *Glos Wybrzeza*, noted that the resolution provided for resorting to constitutional provisions in case of great need but reassuringly reaffirmed the line of accord. Opole First Secretary Mroz declared that "no one in the party leadership bodies is thinking about solutions by force, no one is raising such concepts."[113] Asked whether the plenum had discussed a "state of emergency," CC member Jozef Gwozdz told a Katowice audience that the speeches and resolution of the plenum showed that the leadership bodies would abide by the Constitution, which provides for no "state of emergency."[114]

On the other hand, conservative leader Olszowski lauded the inclusion of the provision and interpreted it as significant. He told journalists from socialist countries that "the CC had authorized the highest party and state bodies to use their constitutional powers in the event of a threat to the national existence, in the event of greatest need. This means, when it is considered really necessary, the declaration of a state of emergency with all its attendant consequences."[115]

Most people chose to interpret the clause on *samookreslenie* as not requiring party members to quit Solidarity. A Gdansk commentator wrote that the plenum did not accept proposals to call on party members to quit Solidarity and that some members even criticized the demonstrative resignations from Solidarity at the plenum by several CC members.[116] Recognizing the varied interpretation of *samookreslenie*, Opole First Secretary Mroz at an Opole city conference stated that "one cannot treat this concept mechanically, no one is calling on party members to leave Solidarity."[117] CC Secretary Zbigniew Michalek told another Opole conference that the provision does not call for party members to resign from Solidarity but rather to "represent the party program there."[118] One

Opole party member criticized the resolution for "wrongly throwing all members of the Solidarity union into one sack" and, noting that "my whole primary party organization belongs to Solidarity," declared that "I don't want to leave Solidarity" because it has played a constructive role.[119] Meetings in Katowice also debated the interpretation and decided it did not bind party members to quit Solidarity. Katowice CC member Kazimierz Konieczko said he felt no obligation to leave Solidarity.[120] Krakow First Secretary Dabrowa declared that it did not force party members to choose between the party and Solidarity but meant that party members should fight negative trends within Solidarity.[121] CC member Mieczyslaw Maksymowicz denied to a Koszalin meeting that party members had to quit Solidarity.[122]

Squabbling over whether or not party members should leave Solidarity continued at the November 27–28 CC plenum. Hard-liner Siwak attacked CC member Zbigniew Ciechan, a plant committee secretary, for refusing to quit Solidarity.[123]

In view of the lack of consensus for declaring a state of emergency, Jaruzelski moved cautiously. The resolution adopted by the CC plenum on October 18 asked PZPR members in the Sejm to propose a suspension of the right to strike.[124] Addressing the Sejm on October 30, Jaruzelski declared that he was presenting the Sejm with a draft resolution appealing for an immediate end to strikes. If this appeal is adopted but ignored by Solidarity, he said, he would appeal to the Sejm to adopt a "law on extraordinary measures of action in the interest of defending citizens and the state."[125] But with Solidarity threatening to strike if a strike ban was adopted, the Sejm did nothing.

The next plenum, on November 27–28, adopted a resolution declaring it necessary to give the government "full powers [*pelnomocnictwo*] necessary for effective combating of destructive acts ruining the country and its economy and threatening the socialist state, system, and public security" and asking the PZPR deputies in the Sejm to introduce a law "on extraordinary measures of action in the interest of defense of the citizen and the state."[126]

Meanwhile, preparations for martial law had been initiated by Jaruzelski as an alternative to the peaceful (national accord) approach. Planning was kept strictly secret by including only a tight group of Jaruzelski's closest military colleagues. Internal Affairs Minister Kiszczak, interviewed later, explained that "martial law plans were evolved by a small group" including Jaruzelski, army chief of staff Siwicki, General Kiszczak himself, General Michal Janiszewski (chief of the premier's office), and some others in the General Staff and Internal Affairs Ministry.[127] Planning was well along by early November, as became clear in 1986 when reports of the defection of one of the planners became public and were confirmed by Polish government spokesmen. According to a June 4, 1986 *Washington Post* report, Colonel Ryszard Kuklinski, a general staff officer who had been participating in planning martial law, was a CIA spy and left Poland on November 6, revealing to U.S. authorities everything about martial law plans except for a date for implementation.[128] Government press spokesman Jerzy Urban confirmed the details to the *Post* and also in press conferences,[129] as did Internal Affairs Minister Kiszczak in a June 13, 1986 *Trybuna Ludu* interview.

Although there were plans for martial law, there was apparently still no decision to implement them or any date for implementation. These apparently gradually took shape during November and were finally adopted only in December, according to the few leaders who have addressed the question.

The most detail has been provided by Rakowski, in an interview with Italian journalist Oriana Fallaci shortly after martial law was introduced (reprinted in the February 21, 1982 *Washington Post*) and later in a whole book on his dealings with Solidarity published in German (*Ein Schwieriger Dialog*, 1985). In his 1985 book he argued that it simply was untrue that the government had decided use force before November, contending that he would have conducted himself more cautiously if that had been true. He described November as a "month of intensive efforts" to reach a national accord.[130] In his initial February 1982 interview Rakowski contended that he and Jaruzelski had tried hard to avoid martial law and thus "came up with the idea of a National Conciliation Front" as a framework for cooperation between Solidarity and the regime and to end strikes and strife. Rakowski, who long had conducted negotiations with Solidarity, declared that he gradually became convinced that Solidarity would not agree to any deal with the regime but that Jaruzelski kept telling him to keep trying.

Rakowski maintained that Jaruzelski decided on martial law only after hearing Solidarity leaders' militant discussion at the December 3 Radom meeting. In his February 1982 interview he declared that the statements of Solidarity leaders at Radom "simply scared us" because they "started organizing a workers' militia in the factories and in the mines" and "announced a general strike with street demonstrations for the second week of December." In his 1985 book he describes how after reading the aggressive statements of Solidarity leaders at Radom, "it was clear to me that the dialogue between the Government and Solidarity was at an end."[131] In his 1982 interview he related that Jaruzelski had called him to his office on Friday afternoon, on December 11, and tersely told him: "It's for the day after tomorrow, the thirteenth."

Kiszczak in a 1986 interview presents a similar picture. He argued that the "realistic" elements in Solidarity were losing ground to militants "with each passing day," that the November 4 talks between Jaruzelski, Glemp, and Walesa "did not help eliminate the confrontational trends within Solidarity," and that police talks with "some more realistic Solidarity leaders were also futile," so "more radical measures" had to be prepared. He contended, however, that "preparations which would make it possible to introduce martial law by decision are one thing and making such a decision is another thing," and the decision "was made at the very last moment." After the Radom meeting on December 3 it became clear that the radical solution was needed, he said, and so Jaruzelski during the mid-afternoon on December 12 told him and Siwicki that martial law was to begin and issued corresponding messages to province police chiefs.[132]

Kubiak in a 1986 interview appeared to set the decision earlier, although he probably was not privy to the planning himself and probably was conveying an outsider's impression. Asked when, as a Politburo member with inside knowledge, he had become convinced that martial law was inevitable, he stated that "I think it was decided by the days after November 4" when the meeting between Jaruzelski, Walesa, and Glemp "failed to produce results."[133]

The timing of the decision was largely determined by events which would occur in mid-December. A large number of conscripts were due to be released from military service in mid-December and would have to be replaced by new recruits who would be more likely to have been infected by Solidarity sympathies and therefore be less reliable.[134] In addition, Solidarity leaders at their December 12 Gdansk session called for a national protest demonstration on December 17, a call interpreted as a serious threat by regime leaders.

Starting in early December, events began accelerating, mainly because of government actions. On December 2 the government used force against striking fire-fighting cadets supported by Solidarity. Kiszczak in his 1986 interview characterized this as a "warning" to militants.[135] Solidarity responded with a more militant stand, however, at its December 3 Radom meeting. The government then seized upon Solidarity leaders' belligerent statements, broadcasting tape recordings of these statements in an effort to portray Solidarity as uninterested in cooperation, thus preparing the ground to justify use of martial law. Solidarity responded with more militant discussion at its December 12 Gdansk meeting.

In the early morning hours of December 13, Jaruzelski announced martial law and had Solidarity's leaders immediately arrested. Jaruzelski based his actions on Article 33 (part 2) of the Constitution, which provides that "the Council of State may proclaim martial law . . . should this be required by considerations of the defense or security of the State." The council was summoned during the night to sign this document. According to Michael Dobbs in the December 18 *Washington Post*, the Council of State members were called at 12:15 A.M. on the morning of December 13 and assembled at 1:00 A.M., at which time they were presented with the decree declaring martial law. Jaruzelski was reportedly not present at this two-hour session, and when the final vote was taken only one of the fourteen members present voted against it.[136]

One of the striking features of the imposition of martial law was the exclusion of any party role. Jaruzelski, in his December 13 speech announcing martial law, ignored his role as party leader and declared that he was speaking as a soldier and premier. He opened by saying: "I turn to you today as a soldier and as head of the Polish government." Although he declared that "we are not striving for a military coup, a military dictatorship," he almost ignored the party. He said simply that "party people have a special role to play" and that despite errors the party "continues to be an active and creative force." Neither initially nor later did he claim CC or Politburo approval of this step.[137] He set up a twenty-one member Military Council for National Salvation (Wojskowa Rada Ocalenia Narodowego—WRON) composed exclusively of military officers.[138] Not even conservative party leaders like Olszowski were included in the new junta. Local party organizations ceased functioning as severe limits on travel, communications, and assemblage were imposed. The *Washington Post* on December 24 reported "little visible activity" at party headquarters and cited a middle-level official as saying that little was going on inside. David Binder in the *New York Times* on December 24 reported a statement by Jaruzelski's adviser Major Wieslaw Gornicki that the party had played no role in the decision to impose martial law and that party members largely were subject to the same restrictions as everyone else. CC Secretary Orzechowski acknowledged in the December 21 issue of the army paper *Zolnierz Wolnosci* that "only part of the party membership—unfortunately, the smaller portion—are withstanding the test" of martial law.

Even the Politburo and Secretariat appeared to have played little role in the decision on martial law, and they became temporarily inactive after December 13. The *New York Times* on December 24 reported Barcikowski saying that Politburo members were taking orders from the military, not giving orders, and on December 29 reported that Politburo member Kubiak had told friends that the Politburo had not learned about martial law until 4:00 A.M. on December 13, hours after it had been adopted.

The fall of Kania added yet another striking feature to the unique Polish communist system. By the available evidence, his departure appeared not a result of Soviet intervention or effective hard-line plotting, but of shifting sentiment in the party, welling up from below and swaying the uncontrollable new CC. Growing discontent over the political and economic malaise and the inability of the leadership to deal with the situation brought demands for a strong, effective leader. The change was apparently made against the wishes of the main Politburo leaders and was part of sharp criticism of Politburo effectiveness. To replace Kania, the Politburo and CC turned to the country's most popular leader, General Jaruzelski, and made him head of the party, as well as of the government and armed forces.

Jaruzelski came to office faced with the main task of providing strong leadership and decisive action. He briefly attempted to reach understanding with Solidarity, but then gave up on this. The CC and Politburo were divided on what to do, so Jaruzelski took advantage of his unusual monopoly on the levers of power to use force on his own. Despite his long adherence to Kania's line of peaceful resolution of conflicts, Jaruzelski imposed a strict martial law regime, both on Solidarity and on his badly divided party.

Although the imposition of martial law came less than two months after Jaruzelski's election, it appears unlikely that he was elected with the idea of carrying this out. Statements by many CC members after the October plenum reflected assurance that Jaruzelski would adhere faithfully to Kania's line and that use of force would not be justified. Most CC members were surely as surprised as most Solidarity leaders were.

CHAPTER 6

MARTIAL LAW
AND THE PARTY

O N December 13, 1981, martial law was suddenly imposed on a surprised and shocked nation. Though aimed mainly at ending the crippling strikes and breaking the power of the increasingly strident Solidarity, martial law also halted reform in the party. The harsh restrictions on movement and communication which brought most activity to a halt also stopped most party activity.

The party, like the rest of the system, had gotten out of control, and Jaruzelski clearly saw the task as restoring control from above so the leadership could actually run the party and the country. He used overwhelming force to arrest and suppress the key opposition forces outside the party and to intimidate and neutralize the opposition within the party. But while the naked use of force gave the appearance of reversion to Stalinism, Jaruzelski's martial law was not a return to Stalinism or even to the authoritarianism of the late Gierek period. Jaruzelski did not cancel the democratic innovations enacted in 1980 and 1981 (for example, the democratized election rules), did not invalidate the 1981 elections and displace all the liberals elected to leading posts in those elections, did not disavow the 1981 party congress and its decisions or even make discussion of these taboo (as, for example, the Soviet 20th and 22d party congresses and their anti-Stalin actions became largely taboo subjects under Khrushchev's successors), did not massively purge reformers from the party, and did not restore conservatives to positions of power. It was a hard line applied by moderates, rather than by the true hard-liners, and these moderates remained committed, in word if not in spirit, to the 1981 reforms.

Other than Solidarity leaders, the group hit hardest by martial law was probably journalists. Reestablishing control over the independent-minded media was obligatory if control over society was to be restored. To limit information, Jaruzelski immediately suspended most publications and radio and television operations; only a few carefuly controlled newspapers and broadcasts were allowed. Meanwhile, a massive purge of journalists began, and when publications and radio-television broadcasts gradually reappeared months later, many were under new people.

Jaruzelski took a more subtle approach to the trickier problem of restoring control over the party itself. To reestablish some immediate form of democratic centralism, he resorted to two temporary mechanisms bypassing normal party procedures. He issued a secret Politburo "instruction" temporarily suspending free elections and other provisions of the party rules and empowering party executive bodies to act without the approval of those who elected them. And he created "plenipotentiaries" outside the normal party structure who were to ensure that the demoralized, disobedient, and disintegrating party organizations would carry out his orders. He did not cancel or amend the democratized rules; as soon as the emergency conditions were past the "instruction" was canceled and the democratized rules were again in force.

Faced with the fact that so many party members were strongly in favor of democratic reform and so many elected party officials had come into office pledged to further reform, Jaruzelski did not attempt to purge all reformers or reverse the results of the 1981 party elections. He gradually and quietly forced the most outspoken reformers in prominent positions to resign and ordered or allowed a substantial purge of pro-Solidarity party members at the rank and file level. The overwhelming majority of party officials elected in 1981 remained in their posts, especially at higher levels.

The problem was complicated by the fact that Jaruzelski himself was committed to the reforms of 1981 and did not want to simply return to the situation under Gierek or to allow hard-liners to take over control. Moderates, rather than conservatives, surrounded Jaruzelski, producing in effect a suppression of relatively radical reformers by moderate reformers. This was probably one of the main reasons so few of the democratically elected CC members protested against martial law. Many apparently felt it was unavoidable and that Jaruzelski, with his commitment to reform, was preferable to a conservative. After a year of martial law moderates like Rakowski and Barcikowski held the top government and party posts, and a return to civilian rule appeared likely to benefit moderates rather than conservatives.

Hard-liners soon recognized the continuing predominance of moderates and their own continued exclusion from power and began agitating for a more thorough purge, especially at the higher level. The gap between hard-liners and Jaruzelski widened, despite his repression of Solidarity, and Jaruzelski soon took steps to dissolve conservative groups and neutralize conservative leaders Olszowski and Grabski.

After several months of martial law, the regime felt safe enough to begin returning to more normal party and government rule, but whether the party was really ruling the country was still questionable. Even in late 1982, party bodies from the Politburo on down still played only a limited role, as power remained basically in the hands of Jaruzelski and his group. Party bodies resumed using many of the democratic procedures provided for by the new party statute and rules, but without the democratic spirit of 1981. For example, party leaders were elected in secret balloting, but with no choice of candidates, and the single candidate was clearly chosen (or at least approved) from above. Little criticism of the leadership appeared in press accounts of party meetings, either because speakers were too intimidated to speak up or because their criticism was simply not reported by the more tightly controlled press. Party members appeared submissive and no longer eager to use their democratized rights. Exemplary expulsions of especially outspoken party members apparently cowed most others, while thousands of reformers quit the party in disgust. Despite these losses, however, many reformers apparently remained in the party waiting for better times. This is evidenced by the continued presence of reformers such as Kubiak and Rakowski in the leadership and the continued defense of Jaruzelski's regime even by moderates dropped from the leadership (such as Labecki and Kania himself).

PURGE OF THE MEDIA

In addition to Solidarity, the prime target of the new crackdown was the media, especially the press, which had undermined party and government actions, helped divide the party, and would clearly hamper any effective reimposition of discipline. Jaruzelski reestablished close censorship (under temporary military censors) and moved against the most extreme publications on both ends of the spectrum. The chief editors of the outspoken liberal papers *Gazeta Krakowska* and *Glos Wybrzeza* as well as the conservative magazine *Rzeczywistosc* were ousted. The recalcitrant Journalists Union, still headed by Bratkowski despite his expulsion from the party in October, finally was simply dissolved.

The media were one of the sectors hardest hit by martial law, although it appears that most affected newsmen were only fired and few arrested.[1] The crackdown began with a suspension of most newspapers and journals and radio and television broadcasts. It was announced that only the main party paper, *Trybuna Ludu*, and the military's conservative organ *Zolnierz Wolnosci* and sixteen local papers (one to cover each province or group of provinces) would be published and that only one television channel and one radio station would broadcast.[2] Most of the sixteen provincial papers suffered little apparent disruption in publication schedules, not even missing a day of publication[3]—although some had their editors removed immediately (with no public announcement). Most of the suspended publications gradually were allowed to reappear—but only after unreliable journalists and editors were weeded out.

The most seriously affected papers were the controversial Krakow and Gdansk papers. *Gazeta Krakowska* was combined with other Krakow papers *Echo Krakowa* and *Dziennik Polski*, and *Glos Wybrzeza* was combined with other Gdansk papers *Dziennik Baltycki* and *Wieczor Wybrzeza*. In both cases, all three titles appeared on the masthead. The new combined papers appeared already on December 14. The papers were broken up into separate papers again in early February.[4]

The temporary merger of these papers was accompanied by the ouster of their controversial editors. As former *Gazeta Krakowska* chief editor Szumowski later told a *Washington Post* reporter, he was summoned to a party meeting as soon as martial law was declared and learned that he would not even be allowed to reenter the paper's building. During the coming days, twenty of the forty permanent staffers of *Gazeta Krakowska* were dismissed by hard-liners and military commissars, according to

Szumowski.[5] Zbigniew Gazowski became editor of the combined Krakow papers on December 14, and when *Gazeta Krakowska* was reconstituted as a separate paper on February 5, Zdzislaw Les became editor.[6]

Embattled *Glos Wybrzeza* chief editor Tadeusz Kuta was fired, and chief editor of the smaller *Dziennik Baltycki* Jozef Krolikowski became editor of the combined Gdansk papers on December 14.[7] *Le Figaro*'s Bernard Margueritte indicated that, in addition to Kuta, thirteen of the paper's fifty journalists had been dismissed and that Kuta was being accused of revisionism and that the party control commission was taking up his case.[8] When the combined Gdansk papers were broken up into separate papers in early February, Krolikowski became *Glos Wybrzeza* editor.[9] The new *Glos Wybrzeza* editors had to make peace with their conservative critics. *Glos Wybrzeza* on March 2, 1982 reported its editors meeting with representatives of the Gdynia "aktiv of veterans of the workers' movement" (who had attacked the paper in September-October). The editors apologized for "distorting the intentions" of the Gdynia conservatives in *Glos Wybrzeza*'s replies to their criticism.

The main papers in Warsaw, Wroclaw, and Szczecin were also greatly affected. The prestigious Warsaw daily *Zycie Warszawy* did not resume publication until January 16–17,[10] Warsaw's evening paper *Express Wieczorny* resumed publication on January 25,[11] while *Trybuna Mazowiecka* (serving Warsaw and four adjacent provinces) ceased publication permanently.[12] In the other two provinces, the main papers were temporarily replaced by brand-new papers. The Szczecin paper, *Kurier Szczecinski*, ceased publication until January 18 and was replaced during this period by a new paper, *Wiadomosci Szczecinskie*.[13] *Gazeta Robotnicza*, which covered Wroclaw, Jelenia Gora, Legnica, and Walbrzych, ceased publication until the beginning of January and was replaced from December 14 through December 30 by a special martial law paper, *Monitor Dolnoslaski*, which labeled itself a "paper for the martial law period" (*pismo czasu stanu wojennego*) for the same four provinces.[14]

One paper, Lodz's *Glos Robotniczy*—actually described the purge of its own staff. On December 17 it announced that it had a "new staff" (*nowy zespol dziennikarski*), including some of the existing *Glos Robotniczy* staff as well as newsmen from other local papers, and that *Glos Robotniczy*'s branch offices in neighboring Piotrkow Trybunalski, Sieradz, and Skierniewice provinces were absorbing some staffers of local papers in these provinces. The remaining journalists were sent "to work with party bodies" or put on leave. On January 2–3, 1982, *Glos Robotniczy* reported that the "propaganda staff" (*sztab propagandowy*) of the Lodz party committee "in the framework of the new party structure functioning under martial law" had named an Executive Committee of the *Glos Robotniczy* primary party organization, including representatives from *Glos Robotniczy* and local radio and television and including a lieutenant colonel. The new party Executive Committee was to direct *Glos Robotniczy*. The paper's chief editor, Lucjusz Wlodkowski, remained unchanged during the shake-up.

In addition to those journalists who were purged, some quit in protest or disgust. A journalist later described "the agitation and uncertainty" bordering on "deep depression" which "reigned among our Warsaw journalists" in December 1981 and January 1982. Some "ostentatiously" renounced their profession and became taxi drivers. Many prominent journalists at the journal *Kultura* "refused to show up for the verification meetings" (where journalists were individually screened for loyalty) and simply quit the party.[15]

Central papers and journals gradually began reappearing—many (including *Nowe Drogi, Chlopska Droga, Polityka,* and *Zycie Gospodarcze*) continuing under their old editors. The Democratic Party's *Kurier Polski* resumed publication already at the end of December.[16] *Zycie Warszawy* reappeared on January 16; the economic magazine *Zycie Gospodarcze* (whose editor Jan Glowczyk was a Politburo candidate member) reappeared on January 24; agriculture journal *Chlopska Droga* on February 10; youth daily *Sztandar Mlodych* (whose editor had been purged in October) on February 12; Catholic paper *Slowo Powszechne* on February 19; *Polityka* (edited by Deputy Premier Rakowski) on February 20;[17] and the CC organizational journal *Zycie Partii* on March 3.[18] The CC's main journal, *Nowe Drogi*, also reappeared during February.[19] The reappearance of dozens of other central and local papers and journals was announced on television on January 30[20] and in *Trybuna Ludu* on February 15. A second television channel and a second radio station resumed on January 17,[21] and many local radio and television stations resumed operation at the end of January.[22] One of the last publications to resume was the outspoken conservative periodical *Rzeczywistosc*, which finally reappeared on May 23 under a new editor.[23]

The decisions over which publications to reestablish occasioned behind the scenes jockeying and some of the delay in restoring journals apparently resulted from this maneuvering. Adam Budzynski in the December 1982 *Prasa Polska* wrote that "in January and February many proposals for reactivating pre-December 13 journals and suggestions for creating entirely new ones began coming to the office of CC Secretary Stefan Olszowski." At one point, he wrote, there was talk of creating only one cultural-social weekly besides *Polityka*, but this "alarmed many people" because it would have excessively narrowed the opportunities for writers, and this plan "never saw the light of day." The "discussions and negotiations" over cultural and social periodicals continued, and Budzynski described a February 28 meeting of writers and publicists which came up with the proposal to create the new journal *Tu i Teraz*. Some wanted it to appropriate the unpurged part of *Kultura*'s staff, as well as its offices, but this was not done.

The extent of the purge in radio and television was revealed by Radio and Television Committee chairman Loranc in a March 8 private meeting. According to *Le Figaro* reporter Bernard Margueritte, Loranc said that 513 radio and television journalists—including 299 in Warsaw—had been dismissed, while another 134 (100 in Warsaw) had been put on leave at 75 percent of their pay.[24] *New York Times* reporter John Darnton cited reports that Loranc had stated that 513 of the State Committee for Radio and Television workers had been dismissed, 109 demoted, and 134 placed on special leave (out of 6,000 journalists and technicians), 404 of them from Warsaw television alone.[25] The full extent of the purge of the media is unclear, but Olszowski, according to *Los Angeles Times* reporter Dan Fisher, stated that of about 7,000 journalists in the press, radio, and television, no more than 1,500 were fit to keep their jobs.[26]

The Journalists Union was a particular sore spot for the new Jaruzelski regime. The union's activities—along with those of other professional associations—were suspended by the martial law decree, but its outspoken chairman Bratkowski, expelled from the party in October, went underground when martial law was declared and issued clandestine attacks on the new regime. In mid-March the media began reporting letters from various groups of journalists criticizing the old Journalists Union and asking Premier Jaruzelski to approve the establishment of a new association of journalists.[27] On March 20 the mayor of Warsaw, Gen.

Mieczyslaw Debicki, formally dissolved the old Journalists Union on grounds that it had backed Solidarity's strikes and dissident attacks on the state, rather than working for journalists' interests.[28] On the same day a conference of journalists formed a new "Association of Journalists of the Polish People's Republic," dissociated itself from the leaders of the old union "who tried to use the association as an instrument of antisocialist political struggle," and proceeded to elect new leaders.[29] Most of the leaders of the new association were not well known and, according to a March 22 Stockholm radio comment, were composed mainly of journalists from the conservative daily *Trybuna Ludu*.[30]

SUSPENSION OF PARTY DEMOCRACY

During 1981 the party had become so unresponsive to central direction that Jaruzelski completely bypassed it in establishing martial law. It was obvious that one of the central tasks facing Jaruzelski was to somehow regain control over the party, to reestablish democratic centralism and party discipline. Rather than reverse the party reforms adopted in 1981, Jaruzelski resorted to measures which—like martial law itself—were clearly only temporary: he temporarily suspended the party's new democratic procedures with a secret Politburo "instruction" and appointed special emissaries—most notably, military plenipotentiaries—outside the normal party structure to carry his orders down the party apparatus and make sure they were obeyed. Using these devices and various forms of less visible pressure, he ousted a relatively small number of outspoken liberals (and conservatives as well) and managed to intimidate the rest.

The "Politburo instruction" (or "instructions") on party activities under martial law was never published and was rarely even referred to.[31] Its proper title was given as "On the activities of the party in conditions of a threat to the security of the state" ("O dzialalnosci partii w warunkach zagrozenia bezpieczenstwa panstwa") in the February 2, 1982 *Trybuna Ludu*. Occasional later comments indicate that it was secretly announced to party organizations in early January. Barcikowski explained the instruction to a conference of CC lecturers on January 7, and local party meetings in the Szczecin shipyards heard explanations of it starting on January 11.[32] Jaruzelski tersely referred to it himself in his late February 1982 CC plenum speech: "The extraordinary situation inclined the Politburo to issue instructions on party activities under conditions of martial law, instructions which are known to the comrades. They had a temporary character."[33]

A March 6, 1982 *Polityka* article indicated that the instruction suspended party election rules and gave Executive Committees (the small bureaus elected by province committees) and secretaries the power to issue decrees with the force of resolutions adopted by plenums of province committees and other elective bodies, to dissolve subordinate party organizations, and to appoint or "co-opt" new leaders. The instruction was quickly used to oust undesirable party officials. For example, on January 23 the Katowice Executive Committee, "in accord with the instructions on party operations during the period of martial law," removed three of its own members and province secretaries and appointed new province committee secretaries and Executive Committee members— including General Roman Paszkowski, the local viceroy of the martial law regime.[34] Usually changes were carried out with no reference to the instruction, for example, when the Gdansk Executive Committee on January 21 removed two province committee secretaries and appointed two new secretaries and two new Executive Committee members (three of whom were military men),[35] or when the Skierniewice province Executive Committee removed a local city first secretary and "confirmed as with a commissar" (*komisarycznie zatwierdzila*) a new first secretary for the lower body.[36]

The Politburo used the instruction initially to remove three province first secretaries without holding elections or even plenums. On January 8 the Politburo accepted "resignations" from Gdansk First Secretary Fiszbach and Katowice First Secretary Zabinski and then simply appointed new first secretaries who were installed at meetings of the province Executive Committees, rather than being elected at province committee plenums.[37] The resignation of Legnica First Secretary Jasinski, the only province first secretary who was a Solidarity member, was similarly announced at a province Executive Committee session on February 5, and a Warsaw official (CC Ideology Department deputy head Jerzy Wilk) was appointed to replace him.[38]

The Politburo instruction was not always followed, however, and some changes even soon after the imposition of martial law were conducted in accord with party rules. A later article mentioned one primary party organization that could have "used the internal party instruction issued for the martial law period" to "co-opt" someone to fill a vacancy in its Executive Committee but chose instead to have a regular election meeting with a "secret vote among two candidates nominated from the floor."[39] Moreover, a January 28 Warsaw city plenum elected two new secretaries in a secret ballot.[40] In addition, the Politburo soon canceled some parts of the instruction. On May 6 a reporter for *Rzeczywistosc* asked Katowice First Secretary Messner when "the Politburo resolution known in the apparat as the CC instruction" and which "hampers the process of intraparty democratization" would be lifted. Messner replied that a Politburo decision had already done that, that "some elements of the instruction" had been canceled. He indicated that in places where "conditions exist"—including most places—the instruction was being disregarded; only where there still were "some extraordinary circumstances which make it impossible to apply the statute" was the instruction being applied. He noted that while he and three other Katowice province secretaries had been installed on the basis of the instruction, the next Katowice province secretary had been elected by secret ballot at a plenum.[41] A review of 1981–82 events published in the February 21, 1983 Katowice paper *Trybuna Robotnicza* stated that the Politburo instruction on leading the party under martial law had been used in 31 percent of the removals of party officials in Katowice but in only 1.5 percent of the appointments of new officials.

Jaruzelski still used the undemocratic methods later in May in ousting Poznan First Secretary Skrzypczak, who apparently displeased Warsaw and then refused to submit a resignation.[42] Skrzypczak was removed at a May 28 province Executive Committee meeting with no mention of a resignation, and a new first secretary from Warsaw—General Edward Lukasik, the deputy commander of the air force—was "appointed" by the Politburo with no election whatever. The removal of Skrzypczak and appointment of Lukasik were announced to Poznan leaders by CC Organizational Secretary Mokrzyszczak and CC Cadres Department head Dziekan.[43] This procedure may have been partly necessitated by refusal of the Poznan province committee to cooperate. Mokrzyszczak and Dziekan returned to Poznan on June 2 to explain to a plenum of the province committee the "motives" for the Politburo decision and respond to "questions and doubts raised in the course of the discussion"[44] *Le Figaro's* Bernard Margueritte reported that the Poznan province committee had adopted a resolution protesting the removal of Skrzypczak and calling the reasons given for his removal "not convincing" and "regarded as erroneous by workers."[45] Skrzypczak was sent to a "suitable position in industry."[46]

The instruction appears to have been unnecessary thereafter. Other methods were used to get rid of undesired first secretaries, while respecting democratic forms. For example, Torun First Secretary Heza was forced out after an inspection by a military group. Jaruzelski fired the province *wojewoda* (governor) and deputy *wojewoda* of Torun after a military inspection had exposed profiteering and abuse of position and lax administration by local government officials.[47] During a September 13 Politburo discussion of the results of the Torun inspection, Heza submitted his resignation to the Politburo.[48] At a September 23 Torun plenum Heza said he was resigning because of his "personal responsibility" for "negligence" and the "ineffectiveness" of the local leadership exposed during an inspection by a military group.[49]

In the case of the most liberal remaining province first secretary—Krakow's Dabrowa—it is unclear whether he resigned more because of pressure to leave or out of protest against the regime's repressive actions. Krakow, although the most reform-minded of Poland's provinces, had not produced the violent protests against martial law which occurred in Gdansk, Katowice, and elsewhere, and its liberal leaders were untouched by Jaruzelski for many months. Finally, on October 13, 1982, demonstrations in Nowa Huta to protest the banning of Solidarity led to a police crackdown which left one worker dead. Dabrowa's resignation followed within two weeks.

Dabrowa's October 26 resignation speech, as carried in the October 27 *Gazeta Krakowska*, indicated that he had felt pressure to leave. He noted that there had been many complaints in party circles about leaders who fail to "leave at the right moment" and who "get stuck to their chairs." He indicated that the Nowa Huta events had been a heavy blow to him. He recalled that despite the turmoil throughout Poland in recent months, "Krakow had been a quiet city where there was hot debate but where matters did not come to dangerous confrontations." But in recent weeks, he continued, tragedy had struck in Nowa Huta and he felt he "should not lead the Krakow party organization any longer." The account in the October 27 *Dziennik Polski* (another Krakow paper) stated that he spoke at the plenum "with a candor not often noted in politicians" and suggested that he had hinted criticism of the regime's harsh policies. The reporter wrote that events such as the Nowa Huta disorders had been "averted effectively for many months by use of political methods." *Gazeta Krakowska*'s account, directly quoting Dabrowa, reported him arguing that the Nowa Huta events were not a "defeat for the line of accord" or "the line of the 9th PZPR Congress." Dabrowa also appeared to assert some independence by getting the Politburo to approve an apparently reform-oriented local man as his successor. He called Jozef Gajewicz "the most natural candidate," "one of us," and said that he "gives a guarantee that the line established at the 9th PZPR Congress will continue."[50]

After the Poznan ouster, province plenums used the following procedure in replacing first secretaries: a plenum was held which voted in open ballot on accepting the retiring first secretary's resignation; a candidate for first secretary—often a local official—was cleared with local party officials in preplenum "consultations"; a secret, plebiscite-type vote (for or against) was held on the candidate; the results of the vote were announced in the local press and sometimes in *Trybuna Ludu* as well. All the changes of first secretaries after Skrzypczak's removal used this general procedure:

- A June 5 Warsaw committee plenum by open vote, with 3 abstentions, approved the resignation of First Secretary Kociolek. Jaruzelski himself nominated CC Secretary Wozniak for Warsaw first secretary, announcing that he had consulted with the Warsaw city Secretariat and other local secretaries on this. Wozniak was elected in a secret vote, with 10 voting against.[51]
- A June 23 Lublin plenum accepted First Secretary Kruk's resignation by open vote, with 3 abstaining, and elected Wieslaw Skrzydlo, a longtime local party figure, by 85 of 90 votes in a secret ballot. Kruk said that he simply felt it was time to retire after five years, including "a very difficult period," as first secretary. He explained that his old friend Skrzydlo had won support

during local consultations and that he had proposed him to the Politburo as his successor and the Politburo had approved.[52]

- A September 23 Torun plenum accepted the resignation of First Secretary Heza by a "significant majority" and also his resignation from the local Executive Committee by a majority, with 3 against and 14 abstentions. Local cadre chief Zenon Draminski, who met with "general approval" in widespread preplenum "consultations," was elected in a secret vote with 7 of the 99 votes cast against him.[53]

- An October 26 Krakow plenum accepted the resignation of First Secretary Dabrowa by open vote with 7 abstentions. Dabrowa nominated for his successor Krakow city mayor Jozef Gajewicz, who, he said, had won "full acceptance" by the province committee in preplenum consultations. No one else was nominated and Gajewicz was elected in a secret ballot with 89 out of 100 votes.[54]

- A November 30 Chelm plenum heard CC Secretary Swirgon announce that the Politburo had accepted the resignation of First Secretary Kropnicki, who was ill and needed a prolonged cure. The resignation was accepted in open balloting, and Swirgon then declared that after consultations with Chelm party units over "various candidates" the Politburo had decided to recommend Jerzy Szukala, deputy director of the CC's Bureau for Sejm Affairs, for first secretary. No one else was nominated, and Szukala was elected in secret voting with 70 of the 75 votes cast. Szukala's biography, as published in the local paper, contained no ties with Chelm, suggesting he was exclusively an outsider pushed on the province by the Politburo.[55]

- A December 9 Zamosc plenum accepted the resignation of First Secretary Mieczyslaw Kaminski, who pleaded that he lived too far from Zamosc and did not want to commute any longer. The local paper's account did not mention how his resignation was accepted, but did report that his successor—Lublin vice *wojewoda* Wladyslaw Kowal—was elected in a secret vote of 72 for, 1 against. He was nominated by the province Executive Committee after widespread consultations. No other candidates were nominated.[56]

In the changes of first secretaries during 1982 it was clear that the Politburo simply removed those of Gdansk, Katowice, Legnica, and Poznan—most of whom were too liberal—and had pushed or eased out those of Warsaw, Torun, and Krakow. In Kalisz,[57] Lublin, Chelm and Zamosc the leaders may have simply left on their own. Officials from Warsaw were sent in to Legnica, Warsaw, Poznan, and Chelm, while the new leaders of Katowice and Gdansk—though having local ties—were strictly selections from Warsaw. Kalisz,[58] Lublin, Torun, and Krakow appear to have been allowed to choose their own new leader.

The province plenums—with the exception of Poznan—appeared submissive; few votes were cast against the Politburo recommendations and there was no opposition candidate. At lower levels there were still occasional signs of resistance. For example, in the rebellious Torun city organization, almost a third of the city committee members voted against changing their first secretary. A June Torun city plenum accepted the city first secretary's resignation by secret vote of 32 to 14, while the new first secretary was elected in a secret vote of 37 in favor, 15 against.[59] However, even here there was no indication of any opposing candidate having been put forward.

In addition to suspending normal rules, the leadership reestablished control over province committees and other party and government organs by appointing special "plenipotentiaries," mostly military men. The establishment and role of the military plenipotentiaries were announced and explained by deputy chief of the National Defense Committee Secretariat Colonel Zdzislaw Malina in the December 23 *Trybuna Ludu*. He explained that the National Defense Committee (Komitet Obrony Kraju, or KOK) had established the post of "plenipotentiary-military commissar" (*pelnomocnik-komisarz wojskowy*) in ministries, provinces, towns, and even some plants to "supervise the tasks of eliminating the internal threat," "satisfying essential daily needs of the public," and "normalizing social and economic life." The plenipotentiaries were military officers—in most if not all cases, he said, the leaders of the "regional operational groups" created some months earlier to assist local authorities[60]—and were appointed by and subordinate to General Jaruzelski, as chairman of the National Defense Committee (KOK) and new Military Council for National Salvation (Wojskowa Rada Ocalenia Narodowego, or WRON). Their job, according to Malina, is to "ensure the execution of the orders" of the WRON and KOK, "strictly in accord with the rules of martial law." They had the right to remove *wojewodas*, plant directors, and other officials, and they were to supervise the work of province defense committees.[61]

These plenipotentiaries had apparently been designated ahead of time and were Jaruzelski's agents in implementing martial law on December 13. For example, General Wladyslaw Mroz, who was KOK commissar-plenipotentiary for Warsaw, later told a *Sztandar Mlodych* interviewer that on the night of December 12–13 he received a phone call ordering him to carry out the prearranged martial law operation. At 5:00 A.M. he presented Warsaw's mayor with documents authorizing him to act as plenipotentiary for the city. He insisted that he never gave orders to the mayor but just "suggested or proposed certain things," and "in no case" did the mayor "reject any of my proposals." Of course, if the mayor had refused to carry out his suggestions, he added, "he would have received an order."[62] Mroz convoked a meeting of the province defense committee (WKO) at 8:00 A.M. that morning and did most of the talking, since the other WKO members were, he said, in "deep shock" over martial law.[63]

"Plenipotentiaries" of the KOK soon began appearing for individual provinces around the country[64] and also for the Agriculture Ministry, Academy of Sciences, and other organizations. Virtually all of these were generals or colonels. In addition, the post of "plenipotentiary of the Politburo" (in some cases, "of the CC") began appearing in local papers toward the end of December. By late January, such plenipotentiaries had been identified for ten provinces—including Lodz, Krakow, Bydgoszcz, and Wroclaw. These plenipotentiaries appeared to be civilians and were not CC members or otherwise well-known figures. Some provinces—Piotrkow Trybunalski, Torun, Lomza, Legnica, Bydgoszcz, Krakow—had both military and party plenipotentiaries. *Glos Robotniczy* on January 13 also identified a "CC plenipotentiary for information and propaganda." While the creation of the military plenipotentiaries had been announced and explained, the establishment of these Politburo plenipotentiaries was not and their duties were not explained. The Politburo plenipotentiaries soon disappeared, but the KOK plenipotentiaries were still being mentioned in the press in early 1983.

While the powers of military plenipotentiaries over local government officials and economic leaders were spelled out publicly, their powers vis-à-vis party officials were not. Nevertheless, they appeared to be able to override party leaders also. A factory party committee secretary complained at the February 1982 CC plenum that even after two months of martial law, many local party organizations did not know what their own role should be. "In reality," he said, "it looks as if the military commissar and [factory] director decide all matters today. The party organizations are nowhere to be seen."[65]

At the next level down, to strengthen the province committee's control over subordinate local party organs, many provinces created "regional party work centers" (*rejonowe osrodki pracy partyjnej*) to coordinate and assist the work of lower party organizations, youth groups, women's organizations, etc. These appeared to be province analogues to the Politburo plenipotentiaries for controlling provinces. Thus, one article termed the "directors" of these units "actually plenipotentiaries" of the province committee Executive Committee and explained that each of Bydgoszcz's nine "ROPPs" would supervise geographic areas embracing from 130 to 300 primary party organizations.[66] Local papers made it clear that these organs were being created in response to a decision of the CC Secretariat.

These new organizations, which appeared to supersede local elected party committees of cities, towns, parishes, and factories, were apparently seen as a threat to party democracy by some party members. The establishment of these units reportedly engendered "doubts" among party members, who questioned "whether this is not an attempt to return to old structures."[67] Szczecin ROPP leaders told of being greeted "coldly" by local elected party leaders who feared they were coming to take over.[68] In response to fears that his unit would "limit the freedom of action of leaders of primary units," an ROPP leader in Kamienna Gora insisted that he was coming to help and persuade.[69] A January 20 *Sztandar Ludu* article about the ROPPs stressed that they would have no executive power and "are not replacing elected bodies." The article said that the director of an ROPP would have powers similar to those of a head of a province committee department.

After several months of their operation, Barcikowski told a *Zycie Partii* interviewer that the ROPPs were successfully filling a need for better coordination of local party organizations and that the leadership was planning to propose changes in the party statute to make ROPPs "normal bodies" in the party structure.[70] As of early 1983, however, this had not happened, and the late 1982–early 1983 party conferences produced occasional complaints against the ROPPs by officials of regular party organizations. At the Bielski-Biala province party conference, the party secretary of a local town complained that "too often instead of helping," ROPPs "simply take the place of the primary organization and try to lead them, thereby limiting their independence and initiative."[71] At the Opole province conference, the Opole city party first secretary called for redefinition of the role of ROPPs because "their work in present form can limit the initiative" of local committees.[72] And at the Poznan province conference a speaker stated that the "very concept" of ROPPs was "not thought through completely" because as links between province organs and local organs they "prolong unnecessarily the resolution of many matters." Instead, he said, they should focus on ideological and educational work, aiding small party organizations which lack lecturers and libraries.[73] The ROPPs appeared to play little role in the late 1982–early 1983 party conferences, but eventually their status was written into the party statute (at the 1986 congress).[74]

LIMITED PURGE OF THE PARTY

With the institution of martial law in December 1981, party organizations began a purge of party members who were too closely linked to Solidarity or who were too reformist. However, while harming a large number of people and receiving considerable publicity, this purge was not really very impressive, especially at the higher levels. A large number of party members were expelled, but nowhere near as many as had voluntarily quit the party before martial law. Many low-level party secretaries and Executive Committee members were removed, but only a small proportion of those elected in 1981. At the province level, changes were rare—even if sometimes significant. And at the top level—Politburo, Secretariat, and CC—there were hardly any ousters, especially in the first few months. Moreover, the regime tended to balance moves against liberals with moves against conservatives, to signify Jaruzelski's intent of steering a middle course. Thus, Gdansk First Secretary Fiszbach's ouster in January was coupled with the removal of conservative Katowice First Secretary Zabinski, and a crackdown on party factional lobbying approved by the February 1982 plenum ordered the closing down of both reformist horizontal units and conservative forums.

Disappointed conservatives soon began complaining that martial law was leaving the same old (liberal) people in positions of power, while ever-faithful "true communists" were still being excluded. Infighting between liberals and conservatives continued despite the restrictions of martial law, with moderates—especially Deputy Premier Rakowski and CC Secretary Barcikowski—holding the key positions, even as the regime pursued repressive policies.

Immediately after the introduction of martial law, a purge of rank and file party members associated with Solidarity began. Deputy chairman of the Central Party Control Commission Tadeusz Nowicki stated that during the first month since martial law was imposed, party control commissions at all levels had been working "more energetically than ever" to purge party ranks of persons who "displayed an antiparty position, a capitulationist attitude toward the political foe and antisocialist forces," and those "incapable of handling leading positions." He revealed that during the first three weeks of martial law, control commissions "at all levels" had expelled 1,100 persons from the party and "struck from the rolls" another 1,300.[75] By comparison, only 894 party members (including 65 former leaders) had been expelled by control commissions during the whole period from October 1980 to December 31, 1981.[76]

Party membership dropped rapidly in the first three months of martial law: 68,000 in January, 60,000 in February, and 48,000 in March.[77] Thereafter, the departures dropped back close to the "normal" departure rate of about 20,000 a month.[78] For all of 1982, there was a decline of 352,000, about 13 percent.[79] But a large number of these were voluntary resignations by those who quit the party in disgust or simply dropped out in disillusionment. Detailed figures published for March, April, and May showed 99,124 leaving during these three months, and of these, only 7,324 were formally expelled (by control commissions and other bodies and for both political and "ethical-moral" reasons), while the rest were simply "crossed off" membership rolls, half for specifically political reasons ("passivity," "neglecting basic duties of a party member," or violating party discipline).[80] No figures were given for voluntary resignations, but clearly a large percentage of those "crossed off" had quit or stopped paying party dues. A March 8, 1982 *Glos Wybrzeza* article analyzing why party membership was dropping explained that some members were removed from the rolls simply for failure to attend meetings or to pay dues, while others had angrily quit the party—liberals because they considered the party too conservative and conservatives because they considered the party too liberal. At Wroclaw's Pafawag plant (a Solidarity stronghold) 360 members were crossed off after August 1981 and of these, 333 had quit.[81] In Koszalin province, 58 percent of those crossed off in the first half of 1982 had resigned.[82] Those actually forced out of the party apparently amounted to less than half of the 13 percent of party members dropped during 1982.[83] This is much less than the massive resignations between June 30, 1980 and December 13, 1981, when 457,000 members—over 14 percent—left.[84] Virtually all of those leaving in 1980–81 were resignations. For example, in the second half of 1980, 97.6 percent of those leaving the party quit voluntarily.[85]

The loss of members—both through expulsions and resignations—hit some organizations very hard. The Zamech plant party organization in Elblag lost over one-quarter of its members during January and February: 390 members were "expelled or crossed off," reducing the party organization to 1,100.[86] The strongly reformist party organization at the Glogow mine in Legnica province lost almost half its members after martial law was introduced.[87]

In addition to the early surge of expulsions from the party, there was a considerable number of low-level party officials removed from the offices to which they had been elected in 1981. Jaruzelski himself at the late February 1982 plenum said that since December 13, as a result of both resignations and removals, 311 secretaries of province and local committees, 249 secretaries of plant committees, and 1,856 first secretaries of primary party organizations had been replaced.[88] Although this is a substantial number of individuals, it is a rather small percent of the total. For example, there were 2,359 plant committee *first* secretaries alone (Jaruzelski's 249 included both first secretaries and other secretaries) and about 100,000 primary party organization first secretaries in mid-1981.[89]

At the higher levels, ousters were few in number and clearly did not change the balance in favor of conservatives, especially in the first few months. Three province first secretaries were removed during January–February, and three CC members resigned or were removed. Moreover, the first two province first secretaries were removed with an obvious attempt to convey balance: The "resignations" of liberal Gdansk First Secretary Fiszbach and conservative Katowice First Secretary Zabinski were announced on the same day, and their removals were supervised by a mixture of moderate and conservative central leaders:[90]

- The removal of Fiszbach was carried out under the supervision of moderate CC Secretary Barcikowski and reformist Politburo member Jan Labecki, as well as by CC Cadres Department chief General Dziekan. His replacement, Maritime Minister Stanislaw Bejger, had long ties with Gdansk, but has proved to be considerably more conservative than Fiszbach.
- The removal of Zabinski was announced by conservative CC Secretary Olszowski, with moderate CC Organizational Department chief Kazimierz Cypryniak as well as Katowice *wojewoda* General Paszkowski also in attendance. The new first secretary was Politburo member Zbigniew Messner, longtime rector of the Economics Academy in Katowice and also province people's council chairman. Messner has appeared to be more centrist than Zabinski.

The third change—of Legnica First Secretary Jasinski, a Solidarity member—was carried out with CC Ideology Secretary Orzechowski and Cadres Department chief General Dziekan present. He was succeeded by CC Ideology Department deputy chief Jerzy Wilk, whose leanings were unclear.

The removal of two of the three dropped CC members was openly admitted to be punishment for opposing martial law. At the February 25 CC plenum Barcikowski proposed that the CC remove Torun factory party first secretary Marian Arendt and Warsaw University teacher Jan Malanowski from the CC. He stated that Arendt had "undermined CC resolutions at a nonparty forum, had used so-called horizontal structures for splitting activity, and had displayed an incorrect attitude toward the introduction of martial law," and that Malanowski "despite the resolution of the 4th CC plenum had not quit Solidarity, had questioned the leading role of the party, and had undermined the essence of relations with our allies."[91] CC member Zygmunt Bobrowski, a Skierniewice factory worker, resigned—for "personal reasons," according to Barcikowski.

Lodz worker Jadwiga Nowakowska elaborated on the three at a post-plenum aktiv meeting: "One of them, from Skierniewice, violated moral norms and submitted his resignation himself. Comrade Arendt from To-run spoke out against the introduction of martial law. Similarly with Professor Malanowski from Warsaw."[92] Siwak told Prague television on March 5 that "three members of the CC were expelled" and that "this constitutes the first stage of replacing cadres within the party which cannot, naturally, take place only at lower levels but which must also proceed within the leadership of the party and within its CC."[93] The removal of these CC members was the most direct evidence of opposition to martial law in the CC, although there were reports that three CC members had issued an unsigned attack on the regime,[94] and one reference to criticism of martial law at the plenum itself.[95]

Although hard-liners were pleased by the purge at the lower levels, they soon recognized the lack of change higher up and began protesting. When the February plenum opened, a number of speakers complained that while lower levels were being purged of those soft on Solidarity, higher levels were not being touched. Katowice miner and CC member Kazimierz Skwara stated that "in the party base a detailed verification of membership of our party has been carried out, but rank and file members are directing attention to the fact that a thorough verification also is needed in the composition of the CC." So he called for a purge of CC members "who have not carried out the resolution of the 4th [October] plenum."[96] First secretary of the Warsaw steel mill party committee and CC member Jerzy Trzesniewski declared that party ranks were being purged of "ideologically alien people and those who entered the party accidentally during the period of mass recruitment, but comrades are asking us: we are purging [our ranks] but what about up higher? There should be no place in the renewal process for constant innovators."[97] Bielsko-Biala pensioner and CC member Wiktor Koziolek assailed those who valued their membership in Solidarity more than membership in the party and called for a purge of those who "at the moment of trial stood aside."[98] Torun factory party committee first secretary Andrzej Wietrzykowski stated that at local meetings "older comrades were saying: 'Why do I have to be at a meeting along with those who organized strikes and who gathered signatures for or signed "acts of false accusation" against party leaders. How can I be in the same party as those who wanted to sell out the party?' " He called for examination of party members "starting from the top, with the CC and its apparat, from ministers down to foremen."[99] Finally, Albin Siwak, in a speech not delivered but added to the protocol, stated that "one of the most burning and urgent problems is the question of purging and decisive verification of party ranks and party organizations at every level. We are very late with purging, and it is high time to honestly and conscientiously finish this matter." He assailed those who opposed verification on grounds that it was just "revenge."[100]

Much to the conservatives' dismay, moderates continued to play an active role under Jaruzelski. Shortly after martial law was imposed, controversial reform advocate Rakowski became chairman of a new "Sociopolitical Committee" of the Council of Ministers set up to supervise a wide range of domestic matters—education, science, culture, information, and the media—for the new regime.[101] Starting with the early days of martial law, Rakowski was highly visible and acted as Jaruzelski's most frequent and prominent spokesman. Moderate Politburo members Kubiak, Barcikowski, and Labecki also continued to be active and were frequently cited in the press. The prominence of these moderates was deeply frustrating for hard-liners, who openly agitated against them.[102] Moderates also remained at the head of important regional party organizations: Dabrowa in Krakow,[103] Zawodzinski in Bialystok, Prusiecki in Elblag, Skrzypczak in Poznan, Miskiewicz in Szczecin. Fiszbach, though replaced as party leader, remained chairman of the Gdansk people's council for several months.[104]

Why did the moderates and reformers largely stay with Jaruzelski instead of dissociating themselves from a repressive regime which had halted their reform efforts? In addition to their commitment to the party and their inclination to bow to party discipline, they were clearly concerned about hanging on to the control they had won in the party and preventing the party from slipping back into undemocratic ways in the long run. Knowing Jaruzelski's sympathy for renewal, they apparently felt that if they remained in the establishment they could both influence application of martial law and resume party reform when martial law was lifted. This view in fact was openly stated by the reform-minded Gdansk leadership in the immediate wake of the announcement of martial law. In a statement (*oswiadczenie*) signed by the Gdansk province committee's Executive Committee and published in the December 18, 1981 *Glos Wybrzeza–Dziennik Baltycki*, the liberals appealed to those who wanted reform to stay in the party so that as soon as martial law was lifted they could resume the struggle to liberalize the party:

> What is most important in these days of culmination of tension is for PZPR members and party organizations today, now, to appeal to everyone, to our friends and to ourselves for common sense, reflection, wisdom, for consideration of the results of current events, so that in the midst of the drama we do not lose sight of tomorrow. This thought of tomorrow is the basis for a difficult hope, but the only hope—hope for solving our complicated problems under conditions which will be different from today's. Because Poland's tomorrow must be a tomorrow of accord, a tomorrow of carrying out the August 1980 social contract, a tomorrow of basic reforms.
>
> The process of improving the republic today is suspended, but is unavoidable. Any deviation from it threatens consequences in the distant future which no honorable person in the country and no honorable person in the party either wishes or would be able to take responsibility for. . . . And today, more than ever before, one must remember that a PZPR of honorable persons is and will be needed by the nation. . . . Let thinking guide our actions.[105]

The statement nowhere endorsed martial law—or even mentioned it— even though it presumably had to pass military censorship. The transparently expedient character of the statement apparently angered conservatives and the military as well. As Gdansk First Secretary Bejger recalled a year later, at the February 1983 Gdansk province party conference, the December 18, 1981 statement had reflected lack of understanding of the "nature of the threat and the reasons for introducing martial law" and had met with "disapproval" on the part of many party members. He asserted that only "a part" of the leadership acting "in the name of the Executive Committeee" had formulated the statement. He explained that the Executive Committee had quickly adopted a new "resolution" which "took a critical attitude" toward the first statement and gave a "correct evaluation to the need for introducing martial law."[106] The second statement, dated December 20 and published in the December 21, 1981 *Glos Wybrzeza–Dziennik Baltycki*, wholeheartedly endorsed martial law, praised the army and Jaruzelski for saving the country from "national tragedy," and declared it the obligation for every party member to support the WRON.

The continued strength and confidence of moderates were demonstrated at the first CC plenum under martial law—February 24–25, 1982—where several well-established moderates spoke and defended the line of accord.[107] Krakow factory committee first secretary Kazimierz Miniur made a strong argument for moderation: "We must not depart from the path of socialist renewal. We have suffered a setback because our first approach failed. On the other hand, if we deviate from this we will make a historic mistake." He said that General Jaruzelski, the WRON, party, and government "have taken the only correct, although the most difficult, path to the goal—the path of accord, the path of dialogue, and the path of reason." He called for the CC to turn to "force of political argument" rather than to the "argument of force." Apparently hoping to avoid a tough anti-Solidarity stance by the CC, he proposed that the plenum "adopt no official position" on the question of what kind of trade unions will be allowed.[108] Rakowski gave a long speech also strongly defending the path of peaceful solutions and dialogue. He argued that dialogue with Solidarity had to be continued as long as there had been any chance of success and that in fact martial law might have been violently resisted if dialogue had not continued until Solidarity had shown the public its intransigence.[109]

Despite calls for a purge of waverers and those who had been soft on Solidarity, moderates did not hesitate to lash back at conservatives. When Konin worker Czeslaw Borowski criticized Miniur's speech, Krakow worker Stanislaw Knap immediately rose to rebuff the "insinuation" that Miniur was guilty of "some sort of rightist deviation."[110] Politburo member Kubiak challenged Warsaw worker and CC member Albert Kosowski, who had called for a further purge in the media and culture and had attacked the CC Culture Department's policy. Noting that he himself as CC secretary was responsible for the Culture Department, Kubiak defended its work and also defended himself against labels thrown at him.[111] Labecki, in a speech added to the protocol, urged expulsion both of those who wanted to return to pre–December 13 conditions (reformers) and those who wanted to return to pre–August 1980 conditions (conservatives), but added that "the latter are unusually dangerous because they hide behind phrases about true communism or true socialism."[112]

The middle of the road line was strongly reinforced at the February plenum. In his opening report, Jaruzelski reasserted his commitment to reform, stating that "there can be no departure from the line of socialist renewal," and "the process of democratization of party life is irreversible." Although many primary party organizations and other bodies had caved in to hostile pressure, he said, this "does not, however, undermine the correctness and value of the democratic election mechanisms confirmed and improved by the 9th Congress." Then he struck out at both wings of the party—at liberal horizontal units and conservative forums. He stated that "horizontal structures, apart from the subjective intentions of some participants, weakened the party from within and created the platform for opportunistic and capitulationist tendencies." He declared: "Further activity by these structures would lead sooner or later to liquidation of the party." But he added that "so-called forums and similar forms of extraparty activity also harm the cause of the party. Their participants try to correct the party, 'review' it from the left, acting outside its democratic structures. The party does not need such help. True Marxism-Leninism does not rely on verbal pyrotechnics." He then asserted that "it is time to cease dividing the party into wings. In our ranks there is room for sincere, bold debate and a variety of views before resolutions are adopted." But one must not "depart from unconditional discipline in carrying out resolutions," and "there is no place for factional activity. . . . The party is neither a sect nor a debate club. The party speaks with one voice. . . . There can also be no return to the situation in which many party members and even many organizations chose for themselves from among party resolutions only some to carry out."[113]

The resolution adopted at the end of the plenum ordered a "decisive fight against opportunist and sectarian views" and any actions "aimed against the unity of the party and inconsistent with the statute and the demands of democratic centralism." "The CC recommends the cessation of activity of any movements, structures, forms, and seminars which have an extrastatutory character" and "obliges executive committees of province committees to fully analyze the situation in this sphere and adopt the necessary decisions by the end of March."[114]

Conservatives were stung by the plenum's action and, according to one article, quickly complained that the February plenum had unfairly penalized them by ordering abolition of their forums even though they—

the conservatives—had stuck with the party in its toughest test, had supported martial law, and had been proved right by the imposition of martial law.[115] This article argued that the conservative forums, no less than the liberal horizontal units, had "directed their activities mainly and almost exclusively against the leadership" and had violated the party statute and undermined democratic centralism by continuing to contest issues even after party decisions had been adopted. Moreover, it contended that the imposition of martial law could not be considered a "success of the extreme left-wing prompters" who claimed "we have been proved right."

The plenum's resolution against factions was not obeyed, however, and there were few reports of steps against local forums and horizontal units. The Katowice Executive Committee adopted a decision to dissolve the "Marxist-Leninist Seminar under the Province Ideological Education Center,"[116] and the Torun Executive Committee ordered the dissolution of the Torun Consultative Commission of Party Organizations (Komisja Konsultacyjno-Porozumiewawcza Organizacji Partyjnych—apparently the original horizontal ties unit) as "contrary to the PZPR statute" and took note of the dissolution of the "Iskra" party forum and club.[117] But conservative groups proved to be especially stubborn, and the Rzeczywistosc clubs and the Grunwald association continued activity despite the plenum orders. In December 1982 the Politburo issued another order aimed at these groups (see below).

MOVES AGAINST HARD-LINERS

While the initial martial law actions mainly hurt reformers and moderates, after several months Jaruzelski began moving more and more clearly against conservatives. This coincided with increasing conservative criticism of Jaruzelski's regime for failing to roll back reforms and for keeping too many moderates in power. Of course, Jaruzelski's feud with the hard-liners also served to give the regime an image of moderation, and hence it was perhaps understandable that regime spokesmen sometimes quietly informed reporters about the hard-liners' attacks on the regime.

The regime's maneuverings against conservatives were reflected in the fate of Olszowski and Grabski—the two most prominent hard-liners under Kania. Although Olszowski and Grabski followed opposite strategies in regard to the martial law regime, both wound up isolated and removed from power by Jaruzelski. Olszowski sought to keep as close as possible to the Jaruzelski regime, defending the imposition of martial law and appearing to act as one of the regime's leading spokesmen—until he was finally undercut and shifted to the post of foreign minister, apparently to get him out of domestic politics. Grabski, who openly criticized the policies of Kania and Jaruzelski before martial law, periodically criticized the Jaruzelski regime from conservative standpoints during 1982 also and finally was shifted into a minor diplomatic post. In late 1982 Jaruzelski started an open campaign against Grabski and his Rzeczywistosc clubs.

Olszowski was one of those most willing to discuss adopting force before martial law was adopted[118] and was one of the most outspoken supporters of martial law after it was adopted. For example, in a March 26 speech he applauded the imposition of martial law for ending "the open propaganda of the counterrevolutionary foe" and restoring the "principle of party leadership of the mass media," and he supported the "necessary restrictions on the operations of the mass media" imposed by martial law.[119] In fact, he went beyond Jaruzelski by claiming that martial law had been adopted on the basis of Politburo and CC decisions.[120]

Nevertheless, Olszowski appeared to lose some of his power with the imposition of martial law. He was not included in the ruling military junta (WRON) set up by Jaruzelski, and, while he remained CC secretary in charge of the media, he probably lost some of his influence when military censors moved into the media. And while he surely applauded the ouster of the liberal editors of *Glos Wybrzeza* and *Gazeta Krakowska* and the suspension of Bratkowski's Journalists Union, the editor of the hard-line weekly *Rzeczywistosc*, whom Olszowski had protected, was also removed. Olszowski continued to be publicly active, delivering speech after speech around the country, speaking out for a hard line, and appearing to represent or interpret regime policy. But his high profile probably made Jaruzelski view him as a potential rival or as an unwelcome spokesman for conservatives trying to exert pressure on the regime. Eventually signs appeared that Jaruzelski was trying to undermine Olszowski, and finally, in July, Olszowski was divested of his post of CC secretary and media and ideology chief and shunted into the less political job of foreign minister.

Already in early spring Jaruzelski began maneuvers to weaken and discredit Olszowski. When the March 20 dissolution of the Polish Journalists Union (SDP) stirred negative reaction as an excessively hard-line action, Jaruzelski tried to saddle Olszowski with responsibility for the harshness of the action, if not the action itself. On April 7 official government spokesman Jerzy Urban received five signatories of a letter protesting the dissolution and said "he was 'authorized to say that the government is sorry that the SDP was dissolved in an unseemly way' " and that journalists had a right to "feel annoyed"[121]—as if Olszowski, not Jaruzelski, had taken this action.

A second repressive action was soon also rightly or wrongly laid at Olszowski's door, and this one appeared to weaken his support among his own conservative clientele. When the ultraconservative periodical *Rzeczywistosc* finally resumed publication in late May, it carried an editorial announcing a new editorial team, minus its hard-line editor Tycner. Letters from unhappy readers immediately began complaining about the purge of *Rzeczywistosc*'s editors and that the new *Rzeczywistosc* no longer was militantly conservative and now was afraid to attack liberals.[122] The Association of Rzeczywistosc Clubs, headed by Grabski, on June 16 issued a statement protesting the firing of Tycner and directly blaming Olszowski for his ouster, according to British reporter Christopher Bobinski.[123] Moreover, Bobinski reported that Jaruzelski had quietly claimed that the ouster of Tycner had occurred without his knowledge, implying that Olszowski was responsible. As implausible as this might seem—in view of Olszowski's protection of Tycner at the November 1981 plenum—conservatives appeared to blame him for this.

Then suggestions of official dissatisfaction with the effectiveness of the media under Olszowski's leadership began appearing. On June 18 the Politburo discussed the work of the media and called for improvements, noting that the number of people reading newspapers had dropped.[124] An unpublished Politburo report complained that *Trybuna Ludu*'s press run had dropped from 1,200,000 in December 1981 to 880,000 by mid-1982, and even 10–20 percent of this smaller run was not being sold.[125]

Olszowski's status as one of the top trio of party leaders (with Jaruzelski and Barcikowski) ended when the July 15–16, 1982 plenum accepted his resignation as CC secretary. Olszowski loyally undercut any possible demonstration of resistance to the change by signing a letter read just before the vote on his resignation in which he "expressed agreement with the proposal made to him to work in the government apparat" because of the need to change responsibilities within the Politburo.[126] His resignation was accepted with only 5 votes against and 5 abstentions. On July 21 the Sejm approved his appointment as foreign minister (with 9 votes against and 32 abstentions).[127]

Olszowski remained a Politburo member, but his practical power in the party quickly declined. As foreign minister he began spending considerable time abroad, and some of his protégés in the media soon were replaced. On July 30, at a meeting with media editors, Jaruzelski personally introduced new CC Secretary Jan Glowczyk, who, he said, "now directs the party's propaganda activity," and also "newly named" director of the CC Press, Radio, and Television Department Bogdan Jachacz,[128] who replaced Olszowski appointee Tokarski. On December 3 Glowczyk also succeeded Olszowski as chairman of the Press and Publishing Agency (RSW Prasa-Ksiazka-Ruch), and Jachacz became deputy chairman.[129] A few days later Wladyslaw Loranc was removed as chairman of the State Committee for Radio and Television,[130] and then Glowczyk announced at a meeting of the committee that two of Loranc's deputies were also being removed.[131] The *London Times* linked Loranc's removal with a new, more candid line for television laid down by new CC Ideology Secretary Glowczyk.[132]

Grabski followed a path different from Olszowski, a path of open challenge to Jaruzelski. After being defeated for reelection to the CC and hence also the Politburo and Secretariat at the July 1981 congress, Grabski continued to work to organize conservative pressure and soon became chairman of the ultraconservative Association of Rzeczywistosc Clubs.[133] The association initially applauded martial law. A February 5, 1982 meeting of its board, chaired by Grabski, praised the takeover by the WRON for "upsetting" the "hopes of counterrevolutionary forces" to seize power and lead Poland away from socialism.[134] Despite this stand, Jaruzelski apparently felt the need to remove Grabski from the political scene. He reportedly met with Grabski during February and again in mid-May and offered him appointment as an ambassador, but Grabski refused.[135] By late spring Grabski was openly criticizing the regime. In June his Rzeczywistosc clubs publicly objected to the ouster of Tycner as *Rzeczywistosc* chief editor,[136] and Grabski held a press conference for journalists from socialist countries at which he criticized the Jaruzelski regime.[137] Moreover, documents circulated by the Rzeczywistosc clubs assailed Jaruzelski's regime for attacking leftists (hard-liners) and allowing rightists to keep their positions in the leadership and also singled out top officials of Jaruzelski's team for personal attacks (Deputy Premier Rakowski, Jaruzelski's personal assistant Wieslaw Gornicki, and government spokesman Jerzy Urban).[138]

When Jaruzelski finally moved to get rid of Grabski by appointing him to a minor diplomatic job abroad (commercial counselor at the Polish embassy in East Berlin), Grabski escalated his attacks with an October 12 letter to his party organization in a Poznan plant.[139] The six-page letter harshly assailed the deteriorating conditions under Jaruzelski and called for use of more force against Solidarity's underground structure, a thorough purge of the party, a crackdown on the Church, and elimination of liberal parts of economic reform.[140] The Rzeczywistosc clubs widely circulated the letter, and when the 10th CC plenum opened on October 27, some CC members had the letter, and, according to *Le Monde* reporter Bernard Guetta, some speakers expressed support for the letter.[141] According to the *London Times*, the Politburo met that night to discuss the letter.[142] The circulation of the letter and the support it may have been picking up was given all the more weight by the plans of the Rzeczywistosc clubs to hold a national congress on December 4. Grabski and other Rzeczywistosc leaders held a press conference on November 6 to discuss plans for the congress and to publicize their activity.[143] The hard-liners' offensive threatened to complicate plans for some sort of easing of martial law in mid-December. According to *Le Figaro*, a November 23 Politburo meeting heard some hard-line Politburo members discuss the Grabski letter and argue against plans to lift martial law.[144]

The regime responded with a public relations campaign to discredit Grabski as an overly ambitious extremist and to make Jaruzelski appear moderate and middle of the road. On October 29 the regime itself gave foreign correspondents a copy of Grabski's letter.[145] On November 3

Barcikowski assailed Grabski and his letter at a meeting of his local party organization in the Szczecin shipyard, and his remarks were publicized not only in the province paper *Kurier Szczecinski* but also in Warsaw's *Trybuna Ludu* on November 4. According to the fuller version in *Kurier Szczecinski*, a party member asked Barcikowski, "What is this letter of Grabski about which so much is being said?" Barcikowski explained that after his defeat at the 9th congress, Grabski had gone into retirement, but eventually "we sent him to work in the Polish trade adviser's office in Berlin," and he "used" the occasion of leaving for Berlin to send a letter to his party organization. The letter is "now circulating," said Barcikowski, and in it Grabski "gives us to understand that precisely he would have been able to handle everything, that he would have acted correctly." "Perhaps he really believes that," continued Barcikowski, but the letter "indicates its author's overly grand ambitions" and did damage by providing material for "hostile propaganda."

A long editorial in the December 22 *Zycie Partii* ("The Only Righteous One in Sodom?") refuted the charges in Grabski's letter and ridiculed him as an extremist, quoting some of his more objectionable statements (for example, that the present situation was worse than the past "illness of opportunism," that it amounted to "a process of incapacitation of the party, of its self-liquidation, planned from above, programmed in detail, and carried out by us often unknowingly"). The editorial stated that while the "huge majority of the public expects the lifting of martial law," Grabski wanted to extend martial law and make it harsher. It accused him of wanting to radically reduce party ranks through a "revolutionary ideological purge" conducted by "true communists" like himself. The aim of this purge, the editorial suggested, would be to "simply alter the results of the elections to leading party organs at the 9th congress." Everything Grabski writes and does as chairman of the Rzeczywistosc clubs "has one purpose: to revise the line of the 9th congress which was for him too conciliatory."

Grabski's letter apparently alienated some other conservatives. Even hard-line Politburo member Siwak criticized the letter for "incorrect" evaluations at a December 18 Pulawy meeting.[146]

Grabski defended himself at the November 6 Rzeczywistosc press conference, complaining that the foreign ministry, not he himself, had distributed his letter to foreign journalists and declaring that he would ask the party control commission to investigate.[147]

Finally, the regime took direct steps against Grabski and the Rzeczywistosc clubs. The organization was not allowed to hold its planned congress,[148] and the Politburo ordered it to disband. One of the organization's leaders told a British correspondent that the clubs were being dissolved,[149] and Barcikowski confirmed this during a late December speech at the Stalowa Wola steel plant. Barcikowski declared that "we cannot allow any factional actions and internal skirmishing," and therefore the Politburo "recently" had adopted a resolution on unity, including "a concrete decision" to dissolve all "para-party groups" such as the Rzeczywistosc clubs, the Grunwald organization, Krakow's "Kuznica" club,[150] and others.[151] Barcikowski's statement revealed a secret part of the decision, since the Politburo resolution as reported in the December 18–19 *Trybuna Ludu* had criticized the continued existence of unnamed "organizations, associations, and clubs" which "dissipate party energy," but had contained nothing concrete about any specific organizations.

PARTIAL RESTORATION OF THE PARTY'S ROLE

As martial law wore on, the regime attempted to reestablish the appearance of normalcy and restore the role of the communist party. Regular meetings of party bodies—the Politburo, Secretariat, Central Committee—were resumed and they began adopting decisions. However, examination of the activities of the leadership bodies in 1982 indicated that they still played little role in the key actions of the regime. At best, they had an advisory role—giving approval to key decisions worked out by Jaruzelski and his informal inner group of government, party, and military officials. (There is little evidence that the formal military junta— the WRON—really worked out decisions as a body any more than the Politburo did, even at the start of martial law.) Potential opposition or unreliable elements still remained in the CC (and perhaps the Politburo), and apparently for this reason Jaruzelski hesitated to ask CC plenums to formally debate and approve the most sensitive decisions—such as his new trade union law dissolving Solidarity in October 1982 and his "suspension" of martial law in December 1982. On these decisions, he largely bypassed the party leadership and relied on getting approval from the Sejm and/or broader groupings outside the party (such as the Patriotic Movement of National Rebirth—PRON, Patriotyczny Ruch Odrodzenia Narodowego) and then presented the CC with completed actions. At the regional level, special martial law organs—plenipotentiaries of the KOK, province defense committees (WKOs), regional party work centers (ROPPs), local committees of national salvation (OKONs)—continued very much in evidence, but elective party committees began to play a bigger role. The activeness and effectiveness of the lowest level—primary party organizations—remained unclear, since party membership had shrunk so much and apathy obviously had become a serious factor.

Although neither the Politburo, Secretariat, nor CC approved the adoption of martial law beforehand, party leader Jaruzelski began calling these bodies into session not long after December 13 to give an appearance of party participation in the new regime. The Politburo met on December 22 and January 12, although it apparently adopted no decisions. The following day's *Trybuna Ludu* carried only two sentences on the work of these sessions, indicating vaguely that they had simply discussed the current situation. The first Secretariat meeting was reported in the February 17 *Trybuna Ludu*—also in just two sentences—and was described as a meeting with province first secretaries and CC department heads. No approval of martial law by either body was announced. The first CC plenum of the martial law era was held on February 24–25 and adopted a resolution "recognizing the Council of State's decision to introduce martial law on December 13, 1981, and the establishment of the Military Council of National Salvation as fully corresponding to the needs of the situation."[152] Soon the Politburo was meeting relatively regularly. An official document in early 1983 stated that the Politburo had met forty-one times during 1982.[153] The forty-one meetings indicate sessions about every week and a half, a pattern indicating less frequent meetings than during the last months of Gierek's regime, when it met weekly,[154] and much less activity than under Kania, when it met an average of almost twice a week.[155]

The Jaruzelski regime's eagerness to publicize Politburo activities in order to reflect normalcy was revealed in the fact that it more faithfully reported Politburo sessions than its predecessors. *Trybuna Ludu*, as of the end of December 1982, had announced twenty-eight Politburo meetings during the course of 1982—out of the total of forty-one held. Despite the policy of openness under Kania, only twenty-one of the seventy Politburo meetings were announced in *Trybuna Ludu*. It appears that Politburo sessions during CC plenums in particular are not announced.[156] The brief accounts of 1982 sessions did not suggest real debates and often mentioned no decisions as having been adopted. Admittedly, the publicly reported activities of the military junta—the WRON—did not look much more impressive. The WRON held only thirteen announced meetings during the year, and some of them were purely formal (for example, meetings with groups of factory workers on January 13, 1982, and with farmers on February 4). A later statement by Kiszczak, however, indicated that it met more often than this and discussed key questions.[157]

The Secretariat had only eight announced sessions during 1982, but it normally meets much less often as a body than the Politburo anyway. From February 1980 to September 1980 it met only ten times and from September 1980 to June 11, 1981, only eleven times.[158] Often its announced meetings have been expanded sessions, especially meetings with province secretaries and CC department heads.[159]

Meanwhile, Jaruzelski appeared to rely mostly on persons outside the Politburo and Secretariat, especially military men. Some CC secretaries (Barcikowski, Czyrek, perhaps Olszowski and Milewski) probably had some input, but Jaruzelski appeared to depend more on government officials: Deputy Premier Rakowski, First Deputy Minister of National Defense Siwicki, and Internal Affairs Minister Kiszczak. The repressive aspects of martial law apparently fell to several generals: General Kiszczak, as minister of internal affairs, supervised the police actions; General Dziekan, as head of the CC Cadres Department, executed the removals of undesirable party officials; General Michal Janiszewski, as chief of Premier Jaruzelski's personal cabinet, supervised the purge of personnel in central government organs; and General Tadeusz Hupalowski, as minister of administration, did likewise for local government bodies.[160] Jaruzelski's personal assistants were all military men, usually with long service under him: Major Wieslaw Gornicki (head of his personal advisers),[161] General Michal Janiszewski (chief of the premier's office), and Colonel Boguslaw Kolodziejczak (head of the CC Secretariat's chancery).[162]

For dealing with the public, Jaruzelski turned to some persons—military or nonmilitary—who appeared to enjoy his special trust as well as a favorable public reputation. Two persons with well-established reputations for liberal or unorthodox ideas, Deputy Premier Rakowski and government "press spokesman" (*rzecznik masowy rzadu*) Jerzy Urban, became Jaruzelski's public voices and held highly visible posts in his regime.[163] Two military men with liberal reputations and close ties to Jaruzelski also often spoke out for the regime: Jaruzelski's personal assistant Major Gornicki (actually a career journalist who had long worked in the United States)[164] and his former assistant in the Defense Ministry Colonel Stanislaw Kwiatkowski. Kwiatkowski, who had much experience in public opinion studies in the Defense Ministry, was put in charge of a new government unit to sound out public attitudes for Jaruzelski.[165] Colonel Marian Kot was installed by early 1983 as director of the CC's Bureau for Letters and Inspection, to monitor complaints to the CC.[166] Colonel Miroslaw Wojciechowski, chief of the Interpress News Agency for foreign journalists, was named chairman of the State Committee for Radio and Television in early 1983.[167]

The fact that the Politburo and Secretariat, as bodies, were largely excluded from decision making, even in late 1982, is clearly shown by the procedure followed in the two most significant decisions in the second half of the year—on the new trade union law and on suspending martial law. The new trade union law eliminating Solidarity and laying down restrictive rules for organizing new trade unions was apparently worked out in September mainly in the Council of Ministers' Committee for Cooperation with Trade Unions headed by Deputy Premier Rakowski and in meetings not including the Politburo. A September 27 meeting of the Central Joint Action Commission of the PZPR and the two other parties—the United Peasant Party and the Democratic Party (with CC Secretaries Jaruzelski, Barcikowski, Glowczyk, Mokrzyszczak, Gorywoda, and Orzechowski, and Deputy Premier Rakowski representing the PZPR)—apparently approved the draft law for submission to the Sejm,[168] and Sejm commissions went ahead on September 30 and approved the new draft law.[169] This was well before the October 5 Politburo meeting which adopted a PZPR position on the draft law. The Politburo just gave its approval at the last minute and the Sejm formally adopted the law on October 8.[170] The CC did not hold a full-fledged debate on the law—even subsequently—but considered it only along with several other subjects at an October 27–28 plenum and adopted a decree urging support for the new trade union law.[171]

The Politburo and CC likewise played little role in Jaruzelski's suspension of martial law in December. A November 13 WRON meeting asked the Sejm to meet on December 13 for unspecified purposes, and on November 24 the PRON formally petitioned the Sejm to "end" martial law as soon as possible.[172] Western reports indicated that the possibility of lifting martial law was debated informally at the October 27–28 CC plenum,[173] at an unannounced Politburo meeting during the plenum,[174] and at a November 23 Politburo meeting,[175] but neither the Politburo nor the CC took any formal position on the subject—then or later.

At the same time, the party leadership bodies did take some less important actions—for example, to crack down on conservative opposition to Jaruzelski. The mid-December Politburo resolution on unity published in the December 18–19 *Trybuna Ludu* ordered an end to various clubs and associations in the party and, according to Barcikowski,[176] ordered dissolution of the Rzeczywistosc clubs, Grunwald association, and other conservative groups. Moreover, the party leadership bodies surely influenced Jaruzelski by the views expressed openly or discreetly by their members. Conservatives' objections to lifting martial law at the late October Politburo meeting and CC plenum may have helped influence Jaruzelski to take the more cautious course of only suspending martial law instead of lifting it.[177]

Although the Politburo and CC have appeared submissive, they apparently still included enough independent-minded members to make Jaruzelski regard them as unreliable. Examination of 1982 CC plenums indicates that overwhelming CC approval of Jaruzelski's proposals was something less than certain and that this may well account for his failure to raise controversial subjects for CC consideration. Two CC members were removed at the February plenum for opposing martial law, but the CC membership remained basically the same as in 1981 when it could not be manipulated by the leadership. Occasionally a CC member challenged regime actions even under martial law. For example, at the October 27–28, 1982 plenum Professor Zbigniew Kamecki of Warsaw's

Main Planning and Statistics School challenged the purge of journalists and scholars under martial law. According to an October 29 *Trybuna Ludu* account of the plenum discussion, he "questioned the basic correctness and objectiveness of the reviews and verification of cadres among journalists and academics and voiced concern whether the party's policy was sufficiently facilitating the attraction of people who could join the [social] accord."[178] Other speakers disputed Kamecki, especially on mistreatment of scholars. Finally, Olszowski himself defended the martial law regime's purge of journalists, saying that "associating verification of journalists with [acts of] revenge is slander."

Moreover, taking advantage of secret balloting, many CC members voted against personnel actions proposed by Jaruzelski. For example, at the July 15–16 plenum, the resignation of reformer Labecki from the Politburo was opposed by 56 of the 170 CC members who voted (31 no votes, 25 abstentions).[179] Manfred Gorywoda was elected a CC member and CC secretary and Stanislaw Bejger a CC member and Politburo candidate member, but with many no votes or abstentions. For CC membership, Gorywoda got only 113 of 170 votes and Bejger only 105; for CC secretary Gorywoda got only 119; for Politburo candidate member Bejger received only 110. In all these cases some 50 or 60 CC members felt bold enough to oppose the leadership. In Gorywoda's case a vote against him had a particularly anti-Jaruzelski implication, since he was a personal assistant to Jaruzelski.[180] In the case of those voting against Labecki's departure, the dissenters were apparently moderates. In other cases, conservatives apparently cast negative votes. When moderate Jerzy Jaskiernia was elected a CC candidate member at the October 28, 1982 plenum he received only 116 of the 180 votes—and presumably the opponents were not liberals.

Below the central leadership level, party organizations appeared active, but it is difficult to judge how big a role they actually played in decision making and how active party members were. During the so-called "midterm" report-back conferences held from October 1982 through February 1983, local party meetings appeared docile, with little criticism of higher authorities, judging by local press reports.[181] Military plenipotentiaries still played an important local role, and checks by the Armed Forces Inspectorate still occurred.

After a year of martial law, Jaruzelski remained cautious in restoring full power to party organizations and other institutions, and leaders in these organizations hesitated to publicly agitate against Jaruzelski and the military. The most outspoken reformers and Solidarity supporters either quit the party or were driven out after martial law was imposed. Hard-liners stayed and challenged Jaruzelski and were punished for their audacity. Most moderates continued to cooperate with Jaruzelski, hoping to maintain control after martial law and find ways of resolving the seemingly overwhelming socioeconomic problems with some cooperation by the public. Their attitude seemed reflected in a statement by former First Secretary Kania speaking at a December 1982 party conference in Gdansk's Paris Commune shipyard. The December 7, 1982 *Glos Wybrzeza* reported that Kania had declared the introduction of martial law an "undoubtedly necessary act to avert widening social anarchy and counter the real threat of civil war. . . . Today, when the prospect is close for suspending martial law and ending many restrictions onerous for citizens, the most important thing is, he stressed, to maintain the line of socialist renewal and create conditions for wide participation of workers in management and administration."

CHAPTER 7

AFTER MARTIAL LAW: "NORMALIZATION"

FOLLOWING SUSPENSION of martial law, the regime wavered between repression and support for reform but eventually moved further away from democratization. Jaruzelski appeared to increasingly prize order and discipline, and the influence of moderates waned. Democratic centralism was reestablished, and the atmosphere in the party and country became increasingly oppressive.

Under these conditions, elections inside and outside the party since 1982—while still more democratic in form than Soviet elections—have been tightly controlled. Choice within the party has been normally restricted to lower-level elections and to election of committees or delegates, rather than first secretaries. There were a few cases of challenges to first secretaries during the 1984 provincial elections—which at least illustrated that not everyone was submissive and that the democratic spirit had not been totally eradicated. Again during the early 1986 party elections and at the July 1986 congress choice was very limited—and Jaruzelski himself was reelected with no opposing candidate being presented. Moreover, the congress weakened the democratic provisions in the party statute and election rules.

Outside the party the regime established a new principle of two candidates for every seat in state elections, supposedly a major step in democratic forms. But the local people's council elections in mid-1984 and Sejm elections in October 1985 were so tightly controlled through various undemocratic devices that the officially favored candidate not only always won but won by a wide margin, nullifying the democratic impression that the two-candidate principle was supposed to produce.

Moderates were gradually squeezed out of party and government leadership—along with outspoken hard-liners—as the leadership became more monolithic and closed to diversity. Reformist hopes dimmed when the most prominent moderates, Rakowski and Barcikowski, were shifted out of their top jobs (deputy premier and CC secretary, respectively) in a big November 1985 reorganization. At the July 1986 party congress the last reformer—Kubiak—was dropped from the Politburo. Meanwhile, hard-liner Olszowski was excluded from the Politburo in November 1985, and Siwak, the last Politburo hard-liner, was dropped at the 1986 congress. Jaruzelski filled the top posts with more obedient, docile technocrats and, perhaps reflecting distrust of and disappointment in the effectiveness of politicians, increased the role of his military colleagues in the party, government, and police. At the 1986 congress Minister of Internal Affairs General Kiszczak, Defense Minister General Siwicki, and CC Secretary General Baryla all became full Politburo members.

Even with all this, Poland remained the most liberal communist state within the bloc (with the possible exception of Hungary) in terms of franker discussion of problems, more publicity for party and government decision making, and more sensitivity to public opinion. There still are democratic leftovers from 1981 which strikingly contrast with the Soviet system and indicate that a traditional Stalinist system has not been restored. Jaruzelski and the party remain publicly committed to renewal and even to the democratized election rules and are still using some of these rules in form if not in spirit.

CONTROL OVER ELECTIONS

Although suspending martial law at the end of 1982, the Jaruzelski regime remained largely the same as under open military rule and, leery of losing control again, did little to return to democratized procedures. The regime was unwilling to trust the party's CC or local party organizations and appeared to discourage wide choice of candidates in party elections. At the same time, it did not attempt to remove completely the provisions in the party rules and statute providing for choice in elections, and local party members occasionally used these rights to nominate alternate candidates from the floor at province conferences, sometimes resulting in real, close contests. In general, however, party organizations appeared under tight control and did not attempt to disobey central instructions.

The regime apparently had even less confidence in its popularity among citizens outside the party. Faced with the necessity of holding the overdue elections of local people's councils and the Sejm, the regime pushed through new election laws which for the first time mandated two candidates for every seat, and this was trumpeted as a major step toward democratization. However, other provisions in the election laws and various election practices nullified the opportunity for choice and resulted in very controlled elections despite the formal provisions for secret balloting and two candidates.

Martial law managed to reestablish effective control over lower party organizations, and a more submissive mood appeared reflected at party conferences in 1982, 1983, and 1984. Though in many cases these were the same bodies of delegates who rebelled against authority in 1981, after martial law they seemed tame and appeared to make little criticism of the leadership. Barcikowski, referring to the late 1982–early 1983 report meetings, said in a December 31, 1982 *Trybuna Ludu* interview that this time delegates were "more mature" and experienced, and so the "various fears and sometimes actual panic" that the approaching national series of report meetings had awakened among party officials had proved groundless.

Of course, the authorities encouraged this by stripping the most outspoken delegates of their delegate credentials ("mandates") before the local conferences (if they had not already quit in disgust themselves). A reporter in the December 16, 1982 *Glos Pomorza* called the new local (*gmina*) conferences less interesting than those of 1981, partly because "the people who clearly differed recently from the party line and also individuals linked with the demagogic political extreme and sometimes also discouraged people had disappeared from among the delegates to last year's 'stormy' conferences. Their absence understandably had to influence the tone, color, and scope of debate." In most province conferences between 5 and 15 percent of the 1981 delegates lost their mandates,[1] and in some cases this amounted to a large number of delegates. In Gdansk 65 of the 415 delegates elected in 1981 lost their mandates,

while another 38 were also absent from the 1983 conference.[2] Many of
the delegates to the Torun city conference—which had supported horizontal ties leader Iwanow against province First Secretary Najdowski in
1981—were missing: 134 of the 790 delegates were stripped of their
mandates or had renounced their mandates, and only 505 delegates showed
up for the December 1982 conference.[3]

By July 1983 Jaruzelski felt confident enough to formally lift martial
law and abolish the WRON, and when the time for the nationwide
regional party elections approached in late 1983, the leaders went ahead
with it—despite some expressed worries that they might get out of hand.
For example, at a September 19, 1983 conference of factory party first
secretaries, some local secretaries had urged that the elections be postponed. But Barcikowski told the secretaries that the elections must proceed as scheduled, since the resolutions of the 1981 congress "bind us"
to hold the elections by late 1983.[4]

Nevertheless, the leadership sought to ensure proper control by slightly
amending the election rules at the October 15, 1983 Central Committee
plenum and by issuing Politburo "directives" (*wytyczne*) on how to conduct the elections. Neither were published after the plenum, but subsequent press articles on the subject suggest that actual changes in the
election rules were few and that the main democratic features remained.
When the amended party election rules were finally confirmed by the
National Conference of Delegates on March 18, 1984, and published in
the March 28, 1984 *Zycie Partii*, they still provided for secret balloting
at all levels, "an unlimited number of candidates," and a two-term limit
to holding elective posts and still declared that "the number of candidates
must exceed the number elected."

The requirement that there must be two candidates for every post was
subverted, however, by reinterpretation of the statute provision granting
conferences the right to determine how to select candidates and by rewriting the election rules to give conferences the right to set the number
of candidates if they wished. This development was first revealed in a
December 7, 1983 *Zycie Partii* article which printed and answered a
question from a local party member: If only one person runs for first
secretary, is this not a violation of point 21 of the statute and point 6
of the election rules which state that the number of candidates must
exceed the number elected? The journal's answer was that while the

statute and rules provide for an unlimited number of candidates, they also provide that conferences can determine the number of candidates, and if a conference decides it wants to vote for only one candidate for first secretary, "it has the right to adopt that decision," and this "does not violate principles of democratic election process."[5] Moreover, the article argued, putting forward an opposition candidate for first secretary "when all delegates know that he has no chance of winning" is just a "formality" and would "demean" the election.

The results of the local party election conferences held throughout the country from October 1983 through January 1984 indicated that the party was back under control—even if not as orthodox as other communist parties. There were few attacks on the leadership (at least reported in the press) and candidates favored by the top leadership were in virtually all cases elected. At the province conferences the Politburo kept tight control over the process of electing first secretaries. They revived the practice of having a Politburo representative (usually a CC secretary) announce the Politburo's endorsement of a candidate for first secretary— who also was cleared with local party officials ahead of time. The official candidate was almost always the incumbent first secretary.

Many elements of the 1981 democratization remained, however—not only secret balloting, but more important, the right to nominate opposition candidates from the floor. In five province conferences opposition candidates for first secretary were nominated, and apparently in most, if not all, conferences extra candidates for province committees, province control commissions, and province auditing commissions were put forward from the floor, providing a choice of candidates for delegates to vote on.

Moreover, there was resentment expressed at the attempts to control the elections. In a February 11, 1984 Polish radio interview Organizational Secretary Mokrzyszczak acknowledged that in the case of province first secretaries the Politburo had resorted to recommendations and that "some of our comrades did not want recommendations of that kind . . . because they believed that it would be more democratic if it were the conference's initiative." During discussions at the National Conference of Delegates, March 16–18, 1984, some delegates criticized the process of electing first secretaries and questioned whether it was a "healthy situation" when the candidates recommended by the official electoral commissions always won and no one nominated from the floor was elected.[6]

The Politburo apparently was not too concerned about preventing choice in the election of committees. Election commissions at the province conferences nominated a slate of candidates for these bodies exactly equal to the number of seats to fill, but delegates then nominated others from the floor. Press reports rarely described the process, but in the few cases where they did, there were always candidates from the floor.[7] In most cases, the nominees from the floor were few in number: In Czestochowa 15 were nominated from the floor for the 97-member province committee; in Katowice only 4 for the 120-member committee; in Zielona Gora 15 for the 101-member committee. In all six cases where the exact number of candidates was reported, there were less than 20 percent more candidates than positions to fill—much less than the normal range in 1981.[8]

In one case, however, there were many candidates nominated from the floor, and most were elected to leadership bodies. At the Gorzow conference the electoral commission nominated only 58 candidates for the 79-member province committee, while 25 were nominated from the floor. Hence, at least 21 of those from the floor were elected. Similarly, there were 17 official candidates and 13 from the floor for the 25-member auditing commission, and 21 official candidates and 15 from the floor for the 31-member control commission. In the election 2 province committee secretaries and the chairman of the control commission were defeated for reelection to these bodies.[9]

In five province conferences there were also contests for first secretary, and in three of these the final vote was close. These provinces were not leading reform centers like Gdansk and Krakow or major party organizations such as Katowice and Poznan, and perhaps the Politburo did not feel threatened by challenges in such less sensitive areas:

- In Plock the challenger came close to defeating the candidate endorsed by the Politburo. With the incumbent retiring on grounds of ill health, the Politburo apparently lacked a well-established candidate, and its choice—the province agriculture secretary— won by only 53 percent of the vote (143 of 266 votes).[10]
- In Gorzow the incumbent first secretary was reelected with only

53 percent of the vote against three candidates nominated from the floor. The incumbent won 154 votes, the others 46, 42, and 39 votes.[11]

- In Olsztyn an opposition candidate challenged not only the official candidate but also government policy. Director of an experimental farm Edward Bauknecht was nominated from the floor as an opposition candidate and proceeded to act as such. Asking to deliver a speech before the vote, he described his career and then as a farmer vented his anger at the government. "Despite innumerable declarations, Polish agriculture continues to be treated improperly, and farmers . . . are treated as a lower category of citizens," he said. He also criticized various experiments in agriculture and urged loosening of the rules on economic reform. In the vote, of 336 votes cast, Bauknecht won 120 to the incumbent's 203.[12]

The other two province conferences with two candidates had only lopsided contests. In Radom the incumbent first secretary won 271 votes to his opponent's 34, and in Bialystok the incumbent was reelected with 265 of the 290 votes. Moreover, in the latter case the opposing candidate announced before the vote his intention of voting for the incumbent, indicating that the contest was pro forma.

Below the province level, press coverage of local conferences only rarely mentioned voting results or the number of candidates. But examples of spirited contests or ousters of incumbent leaders reminiscent of 1981 could still be occasionally found:

- A 819-member party organization in Krakow had a real contest when the incumbent first secretary surprised delegates by refusing to run for reelection. Four candidates ran to succeed him, but on the first ballot no one got over 50 percent. (The spread was 50, 35, 26, and 9, out of 120 votes.) Finally on the second ballot, with the field narrowed to two, plant party secretary Gurbiel won, 61 to 54.[13].
- The conference of a 562-member party organization at a Wloclawek plant was marked by extensive criticism of the incumbent first secretary and Executive Committee elected in 1981. "Very few" of the incumbent plant committee members, including the first secretary, were reelected to the plant committee, and the first

secretary voted out at the 1981 conference was brought back and elected this time by 90 of 109 votes.[14]

- The conference of an Olsztyn railroad party organization defeated the incumbent plant committee first secretary even for membership in the plant committee.[15]

The leadership's control appeared further confirmed when the delegates elected to the 1981 congress regathered on March 16–18, 1984, for the "National Conference of Delegates." The 1981 congress had decided that in order to establish more control over the leadership its delegates would have continuing mandates and would be able to reassemble to debate actions of their elected leaders and perhaps change the leadership. The congress also specified that midway between congresses a national conference of these delegates would be held. When the long-awaited conference was held, however, it turned out to be a tame affair— even though it was composed of most of the same delegates who voted most leaders out of office in 1981.

The conference was tame both because of the general intimidation and discouragement of reformers during two years of military rule and undemocratic control and because of more specific factors:

- A number of delegates were stripped of their mandates and excluded from the conference. Of the 1,960 delegates elected in 1981, 127 had lost their mandates.[16] This was only 6.5 percent, however, a much lower percentage than the number of province conference delegates stripped of mandates before the January-February 1983 report conferences (see above).
- The conference itself provided no opportunity for delegates to express opposition in secret balloting. There were no elections; the only votes were on approving the agenda and membership of the conference's directing bodies and on adopting resolutions. All these actions were adopted by open vote—apparently by show of hands. The only opposition registered was in adopting a resolution approving how the CC, Politburo, and Jaruzelski had carried out the congress resolutions (3 abstentions), a resolution on amending party election rules (2 abstentions), and a resolution on preparation of a party program (1 abstention).[17] *Trybuna Ludu* commentator Anna Pawlowska subsequently bragged that the res-

olution endorsing the leadership's carrying out of congress decisions was adopted "without one negative vote (with 3 abstentions)."[18]

- Delegates were given considerable opportunity to speak, but little of what they said was reported in *Trybuna Ludu*. Most speakers (341) spoke on the second day when the conference broke up into group meetings, and only brief summaries of these meetings were reported. Another 63 delivered speeches at sessions of the whole conference, and abridged versions of their speeches in *Trybuna Ludu* contained little criticism of leadership actions. There was some hint that statements in the group meetings may have been more critical. *Trybuna Ludu*, on March 19, 1984, reported criticism of the way province conferences had elected their first secretaries and the failure to elect any candidates nominated from the floor (see above).

In addition to party elections, the approach of election of government organs—local and provincial people's councils and the Sejm—presented the regime with a dilemma. It did not want to return to the discredited one-candidate elections of the past; it felt the need to demonstrate progress in democratization. But it also apparently had little confidence that the public would vote for regime-approved candidates if given a free choice. So the regime chose the tactic of making a notable step toward democratization by running two candidates for every seat. But it made sure that there could be no real choice by carefully controlling the nomination process and by including provisions in the law whereby the ballot would automatically go to the officially favored candidate unless the voters specifically crossed his name out.

A new law for the local people's council elections was pushed through the Sejm in January 1984, and elections were held on June 17, 1984. The law[19] had new provisions which, according to Barcikowski's speech to the January Sejm session,[20] were "innovative" and would be tested in local elections before the new law for election of the Sejm was prepared. The most notable feature of the new law was that it required twice as many candidates as there were seats. More than one candidate had sometimes run for seats in the past, but this time all seats were to be contested. Zdzislaw Tomal, deputy chairman of the Council of State, in explaining the draft law to the Sejm stated that the concept of two candidates per seat was a response to "many proposals" urging a choice of candidates. He hailed the new law as an "important step in democratizing the system of choosing candidates and then electing deputies from among them."[21]

The element of choice introduced by having two candidates on the ballot was nullified, however, by several other features, some in the election law itself and others applied in practice in conducting the balloting:

- Nominations were carefully controlled and manipulated. Electoral collegia presented candidates at public nomination meetings, and the public could reject these candidates and nominate others from the floor. However, the local election collegia made the final choice of 2 candidates for each seat.[22] Thus, for the Olsztyn city council, there were 346 nominated for the 85 seats, and the election collegium chose 170 candidates from the 346.[23]

- There was no choice between communist and non-communist candidates. Communist party members simply did not run against non–communist party candidates. An article in an internal PZPR journal[24] specified that electoral collegia were to pair one PZPR member against another PZPR member, one ZSL candidate against another ZSL candidate, and one independent against another independent—so as to avoid "organizational animosities." Moreover, it appeared that no party identification of candidates was put on the ballots: Lists of candidates published in local papers identified candidates in various ways but not by party affiliation.[25]

- The proportion of seats the PZPR would win was worked out before the election. Since there was agreement in advance on how many candidates each party would have and contests between parties were avoided, the end result could be easily calculated before the voting. Thus, in Nowy Sacz province there were 280 candidates for the 140 seats, and of these 124 were PZPR, 48 ZSL, 16 SD, and 92 independent—indicating that the PZPR would win about 44 percent (62 seats).[26] In addition, few prominent officials—such as PZPR province first secretaries—were on the ballot, depriving voters of any chance of crossing off their names as an anticommunist gesture.

- One candidate was chosen as the favorite and automatically received the vote unless the voter scratched off his name. Candidates were not listed alphabetically; electoral collegia decided which candidates to list first on the ballot—which in fact determined which candidate would win. The election law provided that unless a voter crossed off the first candidate's name, the ballot would automatically go to him.[27] Since most voters trooped in and in the long-established practice picked up their ballots and dropped them in the urn without marking them, this meant the no. 1 candidate would win. And in fact, results published in province papers showed the first candidate winning in virtually every case and by 90 percent or more.[28]

The failure of the overwhelming majority of voters to exercise any choice made the election such a farce that proposals for changing the system appeared even in the official press. In *Polityka* one article recognized that very few voters "exercised the right to vote for the second candidate,"[29] and others urged that secret balloting (going into a voting booth and marking the ballot) be made obligatory rather than optional, and that candidates be placed alphabetically on the ballot so that there would be no official preference for one candidate.[30] Legal scholar Barbara Zawadzka in the Institute of State and Law's journal acknowledged that there was a danger that antisocialist forces might "use the election as an occasion to attack socialist authorities," but she argued that the control over nominations "suffices to prevent candidates taking opposition political positions from getting on the ballot," and so the "system of preference for specified candidates" (for the candidates listed first) and encouragement of "passive voting" (allowing voters to cast unmarked ballots and counting these for candidate no. 1) should be eliminated as "excessive" precaution against opposition and as undermining the election's ability to mobilize public support.[31] She declared that "the system of preference should disappear from Poland's election law, just as it disappeared from Hungary's election law already fourteen years ago," and this had had "positive results" in Hungary and "has not threatened the socialist essence of state authority there." "Passive voting" can "reduce to zero" the value of having a choice of candidates, she wrote.[32] She was not alone. At a January 1985 Institute of State and Law conference on the 1985 draft law for elections to the Sejm, specialists on constitutional law and other participants uniformly urged an end to the preference system and that it be made obligatory for voters to mark their ballots in secrecy.[33]

In addition to the election of council members, the election of chairmen and deputy chairmen of the newly elected province people's councils in late June was rather tightly controlled. In fact, there was less choice offered than in the late 1980 people's council leadership elections. Most elections appear to have had only one candidate for chairman. In other provinces there was a contest but carefully controlled. Thus, in Koszalin two ZSL candidates were put up against each other.[34] But there were a few close contests and even some pitting PZPR candidates against noncommunists. In Kalisz the chairman was reelected by only 77 votes out of 132,[35] and in Slupsk a PZPR member won with 63 votes to 51 for a nonparty member, on the second ballot.[36]

The lack of free choice in the 1984 Polish elections was highlighted when the Hungarians held their election of a National Assembly and local councils in mid-1985. This election also was held under a new law (adopted in 1983) requiring two candidates for every seat (except for a "national list" of thirty-five top figures—including Kadar—who ran unopposed), but there were key differences from the 1984 Polish election:

- Nominations were less controlled and candidates could be nominated from the floor. In fact, dissident Laszlo Rajk won the required minimum of votes at one of the first nomination meetings and might have gotten on the ballot as a candidate if the authorities had not managed to pack subsequent nomination meetings with people who voted against him.[37] The Patriotic People's Front nominated two candidates for each seat, but third and fourth candidates were nominated in fifty-eight districts—providing some apparent alternatives to officially nominated candidates.[38] In all, there were seventy-one such "independent" candidates—i.e., those not nominated by the front.[39]
- Secrecy in voting was obligatory and there were no favored candidates. The Hungarian election law required voters to mark their ballots; failure to cross off one of the two names rendered the ballot invalid (except for the national list of thirty-five unopposed candidates, for which the old system still applied). Moreover, candidates were listed alphabetically on the ballot, with no one officially favored.

The result of the alphabetical listing and lack of automatic votes for the first candidate produced a dramatic contrast to the Polish election:

- For almost all 352 contested assembly seats the voting was close: 196 of the winners won by 60 percent or less, often by only a bare majority or even a plurality. Only a handful got over 75 percent of the vote.
- In forty-two cases no candidate won a majority and there had to be a runoff election. Some were eventually settled only by pluralities.
- Voters took advantage of the opportunity to make a choice to occasionally elect independently nominated candidates—reportedly twenty-five such candidates.[40]
- Voters also occasionally voted against some prominent figures (although these were leaders out of favor and the regime apparently did little to help them win). Former Premier Jeno Fock was defeated 44.8 percent to 54.3 percent,[41] and hard-line former Interior Minister and Politburo member Bela Biszku went down to defeat with only 26.6 percent of the vote in a runoff election.[42] The leadership had cautiously put most Politburo members on the unopposed national list where they would not be subject to possible voter wrath, and all received about 99 percent or more. Two Politburo members who for some reason ran in contested districts rather than on the national list did relatively well: Laszlo Marothy got 87.7 percent and Gyorgy Aczel got 70.3 percent. But some other current leaders did not do well: Foreign Minister Peter Varkonyi won with only 62.1 percent.[43]

The result of the Hungarian election appeared to be a striking success for the leadership: they had allowed a partially democratic election, and voters had given all current leaders a majority. There had been enough elements of voter independence—a few upsets and many close contests— to give grounds to argue that this was a real election and a step toward democratization. Imre Pozsgay, secretary general of the Patriotic People's Front National Council, stated that "for years there has been voting in Hungary; now there will be an election."[44] At the same time, nominations were tightly enough controlled or manipulated to prevent any hostile candidates from even getting on the ballot, let alone winning.

Despite the obvious lack of real choice and secrecy in the 1984 Polish elections and the recognition of this even in Polish press articles—and even the successful Hungarian experimentation with a more democratic system—Poland's leaders decided to use the same undemocratic methods for their late 1985 Sejm elections. The law for the Sejm elections adopted on May 29, 1985, retained basically the same features written into the 1984 law for council elections: Candidates were to be listed in the order set by election authorities (not alphabetically) and their age, occupation, workplace, and domicile (but not party affiliation) were to be indicated on election lists (article 61), and if the voter did not cross off the no. 1 candidate's name the vote automatically went to him (article 79).[45]

When the election was held on October 13, 1985, the results were as ridiculous as in the June 1984 local elections: The candidate listed first always won, and only 5 candidates out of the 460 winning candidates got less than 90 percent.[46] There were apparently no contests between candidates of differing parties, so the proportion of seats held by the PZPR, ZSL, SD, and nonparty members was determined beforehand.[47] Moreover, the desire for control was so strong that the regime even excluded nomination of independent-minded deputies such as Edmund Jan Osmanczyk, who had been tolerated throughout the Gomulka and Gierek eras.[48]

CONTRADICTIONS IN POLITICAL EVOLUTION

After ending martial law, the Jaruzelski regime continued to follow a political course combining elements of repression and tolerance, apparently reflecting the conservative and moderate elements in its leadership, as well as the impracticality of trying to reestablish complete control over the public. In hopes of coming to terms with the population, it tolerated exploration of ideas unthinkable in the Soviet Union. But it also repeatedly demonstrated its inflexibility in questions of political control and its willingness to use force to prove the futility of attempts to oppose it.

Initially during the 1983–1985 period the Jaruzelski regime coupled repressive measures with approaches aimed at eventually winning over substantial, if not majority, support among the public. It allowed discussion of unorthodox ideas about pluralism and a more democratized

Polish model of socialism—subjects which periodically drew fire from Soviet media. It—or at least some elements of the regime—gave the appearance of seeking a more relaxed, permissive model—in Hungarian style—where ultimate power remains in the hands of the leadership but many political and economic matters could be released from tight control. Moderates like Barcikowski and Rakowski (who appeared to become more conservative under Jaruzelski) remained key figures in the regime, and thoughtful innovators like Colonel Kwiatkowski pursued methods of overcoming the huge gap between the public and the leaders through compromise and concessions. When hard-liners in the security police murdered a prominent Catholic priest in October 1984 in an apparent attempt to force more repressive policies, the Jaruzelski regime sided against the police, put the killers on public trial and exposed secret police machinations, and ousted the top hard-liner in the regime, police supervisor Miroslaw Milewski.

After lifting martial law the Jaruzelski regime—along with many repressive measures—appeared to try to follow a middle-road course, and Poland remained more liberal than most other communist countries in allowing discussion of unorthodox ideas such as pluralism and a distinct Polish road to socialism. Moderates linked to the regime (Kwiatkowski, Urban, Rakowski) attacked conservatives (as well as anticommunist opposition) and advocated an unorthodox approach to Polish problems aimed at appealing to the Polish public—even though this irritated the Soviets. In particular, Jaruzelski's public opinion pollster, Colonel Kwiatkowski, assailed hard-liners in several articles starting in early 1983. For example, in a February 16, 1983 *Zycie Partii* article he ridiculed "leftist demagogues" who see "capitulationist, opportunistic tendencies" in the regime's policies and who "run down their own leaders." These people, he declared, think "only they know how to build socialism" and act "like priests guarding the sacred flame." In a March 7, 1983 *Tu i Teraz* article he assailed the hard-liners' habit of considering all foes as "enemies" to be suppressed instead of opponents to be debated with, and in an April 6 *Trybuna Ludu* article he struck back at conservatives who had attacked his earlier articles and declared that even "I, a military man," see "patient explanation" rather than "force" as the way to deal with society. In an

August 31 *Tu i Teraz* article he again ridiculed "conservative sectarians" and also ran down the present party apparat as office-bound officials who were unable to face opponents and who could work only with the protection of forces of public order.

Others put forward unorthodox ideas about a more liberalized Polish system, often in official journals. Jan Wawrzyniak in a September 1982 *Nowe Drogi* raised the concept of a form of "socialist pluralism," while Wojciech Sokolewicz in August 21, 1982 *Prawo i Zycie* and November 23, 1983 *Tu i Teraz* articles raised the idea of a unique Polish model of socialist democracy. Rakowski's old weekly *Polityka* (now edited by his longtime deputy Jan Bijak) floated a variety of unorthodox ideas, as did Rakowski himself in occasional interviews.[49]

Conservatives displayed alarm at the ideas floated by these people and journals. Jerzy Kraszewski, *Trybuna Ludu*'s correspondent in Moscow, argued in the February 1983 *Nowe Drogi* that the liberals were the "main danger" to Poland; Tadeusz Wrebiak in the March 17, 1983 and April 6, 1983 *Trybuna Ludu* assailed Kwiatkowski's articles for one-sidedly attacking conservatives while ignoring the dangers from the liberal side. Deputy editor of the conservative weekly *Rzeczywistosc* Boleslaw Porowski in the May 15, 1983 issue of his magazine assailed ideological laxity in the party and complained that anyone who tried to defend Leninist values was accused of being a "dogmatist, a conservative, and an opponent of renewal." He asserted that those who are arguing for a "Polish model of socialism" want to create "pluralism" where Marxism will be only "one of many" ideologies. *Rzeczywistosc*'s chief editor Jerzy Pardus in a May 22, 1983 *Rzeczywistosc* article denounced government press spokesman Jerzy Urban for ridiculing leftist "hurrah-revolutionaries" and accused him of not really being a Marxist.[50] In a June 5, 1983 article Pardus attacked Rakowski's former weekly *Polityka* and some other liberal publications for publishing articles by people who "long ago departed from Marxism." Attacks on the Kwiatkowski and Sokolewicz articles appeared in the October 9, 1983 and December 25, 1983 *Rzeczywistosc*, October 26, 1983, January 4 and 25, 1984 *Tu i Teraz*, November 29, 1983 *Trybuna Ludu*, and January 15, 1984 *Argumenty*, while many *Nowe Drogi* articles criticized Wawrzyniak's raising of pluralism.

Moscow lent support to the embattled conservatives, putting pressure on the Jaruzelski regime to rein in liberals and moderates. A May 6, 1983 article in Moscow's *Novoye Vremya* attacked *Polityka* for going overboard in its attempts to appeal to uncommitted Poles by publishing views "alien to proletarian, communist ideology" and by conceding the "bankruptcy" of Marxism. The author, Andrey Ryzhov, claimed some *Polityka* articles treated Poland's system as an "alien model imposed on the Poles from outside" and sought ideas from the West for a Polish path to socialism. He also assailed moderates Jerzy Wiatr (director of the Institute of Bases of Marxism-Leninism), former CC Secretary Andrzej Werblan (a prominent defender of the horizontal ties movement), and *Nowe Drogi* deputy editor Ludwik Krasucki for statements undermining orthodox communist positions. Moscow also signaled its support for the conservatives by reprinting Kraszewski's February *Nowe Drogi* article in the CPSU's main journal, *Kommunist* (May 1983, no. 7).

Despite this, the Jaruzelski regime did not cave in to Soviet pressure. At a May 31, 1983 CC plenum CC Secretary Jozef Czyrek, in delivering the main report, argued for continued dialogue with the uncommitted, stating that "we do not wish to multiply the ranks of our opponents."[51] Jaruzelski spoke to the plenum and while promising not to tolerate pluralism or "abandon principles of socialism," declared that "we must carefully study views that differ from ours but that are characterized by a sense of responsibility for Poland. . . . We have enough real foes who are passionate and stubborn. This is why we do not want to regard as adversaries those who are not adversaries in fact. Let us learn from Lenin, how he won for revolutionary Russia alienated people and those who were strangers to the idea of revolution."[52] He called for a "battle on two fronts," against both "opportunistic" and "hurrah-leftist" ideas.

Jaruzelski's friction with hard-liners continued and erupted dramatically when secret policemen murdered outspoken priest Father Jerzy Popieluszko on October 19, 1984, in an apparent attempt to aggravate tensions between the regime and the Church and force Jaruzelski into a more hard-line policy. Instead, Jaruzelski used the crime to strike at the police and remove the last of the hard-liners, Miroslaw Milewski, from the Secretariat. The weakening of the political police—one of the sacrosanct pillars of any communist regime—was an encouraging step toward reconciliation with the public.

Jaruzelski had had trouble with hard-liners in the Ministry of Internal

Affairs ever since becoming premier in February 1981. The ministry was the last bastion of hard-liners, and its loyalty to Kania and Jaruzelski was questionable. Shortly after Jaruzelski became premier, police beat up rural Solidarity organizers in Bydgoszcz in March 1981, provoking a monumental crisis between the government and Solidarity. The ministry at that time was led by Milewski, a lifelong security man who had risen through the ranks and become minister in October 1980. At the March 1981 CC plenum Milewski defended the actions of the police in Bydgoszcz and complained of public hostility toward the police and obstruction of police work. He also complained that foes were portraying his ministry as "a base of conservatism opposing the process of socialist renewal" and were setting it against the Ministry of Defense.[53]

When Milewski was moved up to the Politburo and Secretariat at the July 1981 party congress (as one of the hard-liners nominated on Kania's balanced conservative-liberal slate), Jaruzelski named his own longtime close deputy in the Defense Ministry, General Kiszczak, as minister of internal affairs. The replacement of professional policeman Milewski with an army general close to Jaruzelski opened the door for moves to remove police hard-liners and install people loyal to Jaruzelski.

Even though Milewski continued to supervise the police as CC secretary for administrative organs,[54] Jaruzelski and Kiszczak began quietly purging police organs in 1982 and 1983. Deputy Minister Adam Krzysztoporski was transferred to the Office of Maritime Economy in March 1982,[55] and First Deputy Minister Boguslaw Stachura was appointed ambassador to Romania in July 1983.[56] Kiszczak, in an October 27, 1984 television statement on the murder of Father Popieluszko, revealed that he had been purging the police of those who had been committing abuses and violating laws. He stated that during the preceding two years 2,464 MO (regular police) and SB (security police) had been fired for violating legality and discipline and abusing their posts, and 872 had been brought to "criminal responsibility."[57]

After Popieluszko's killers were caught and publicly exposed as SB officers, Jaruzelski and Kiszczak presented the murder as an act aimed against the Jaruzelski regime by hard-liners. They published the killers' statements that they were motivated by hostility to the Jaruzelski regime's allegedly soft line toward the Church, and they cited evidence that the SB men had deliberately left clues at the scene of the crime implicating the MO—apparently to turn public suspicions against Kiszczak and the Jaruzelski regime.[58] The regime put the killers on public trial during December and January and had them sent to prison.[59] This was unprecedented treatment of secret policemen by a communist regime; any secret police abuses are normally punished in secret, and the security police's image is carefully protected.

Although the sentences could have been heavier and most evidence implicating higher-ups was apparently suppressed, the case exposed SB abuses and led to the ouster of the top officials overseeing the police. Michal Atlas was replaced as head of the CC Administrative Department at the December 1984 CC plenum, and Milewski himself was displaced. On November 6 the Politburo authorized Jaruzelski to personally assume party supervision of the police, superseding Milewski,[60] and Rakowski soon confirmed to West German reporters that Milewski was "now on leave."[61] Milewski was finally formally dropped from the Politburo and Secretariat at the May 1985 plenum.

Kiszczak became the undisputed boss of the police, and two party officials with no police experience were put in direct charge. Skierniewice First Secretary Janusz Kubasiewicz was named head of the Administrative Department at the December 21–22, 1984 CC plenum, and a couple of days later Bielsko-Biala First Secretary Andrzej Gdula was named deputy minister of internal affairs.[62] Eventually, in December 1985, Milewski's slot—CC secretary for security—was filled by another general close to Jaruzelski, political administration chief Jozef Baryla.[63]

At the same time, however, the regime was also gradually enacting more and more controls into law, making permanent many of the restrictions of martial law. For example, at the October 1984 plenum Jaruzelski called for changes in the penal code and judicial system aimed at increasing the severity of punishment and tightening up the effectiveness of prosecution.[64] In another example, steps were gradually taken to reimpose controls on universities.[65] Meanwhile, the daring, unorthodox articles of 1982 and 1983—discussing subjects such as pluralism and a Polish path to socialism—gradually disappeared from the press. Symbolic of the damping down of polemics, the extremely outspoken Kazimierz Kozniewski was removed as editor of the lively magazine *Tu i Teraz* in February 1985, and the journal itself was closed down in May 1985.[66]

"NORMALIZATION"

As the next party congress approached in 1986, the Jaruzelski regime appeared to resolve its wavering between conservative and reformist tendencies by turning toward more conservative, more traditional positions. Proclaiming that "normalization" had arrived in the wake of the October 1985 Sejm election, Jaruzelski took steps which undermined the 1981 reforms more than anything since the original martial law itself:

- In a November 1985 reorganization—the biggest since 1981—he appeared to close the reform era by eliminating from top positions the leading moderates associated with the reforms of 1980–81 and by eliminating the diversity of views which had marked his regime even under martial law. Rakowski and Barcikowski were shifted to less powerful positions, and conservative leader Olszowski was dropped completely. This appeared to reflect Jaruzelski's increasing preference for a more monolithic leadership which would simply carry out his orders rather than debate them from diverse viewpoints. Reflecting apparent distrust of politicians and longing for order and discipline, he filled the top posts with technocrats with no independent power bases and no record of taking stands on controversial issues, and simultaneously he boosted the already strong position of his military colleagues. This trend—especially the increasingly open military domination—was reinforced when the new Politburo was elected at the July 1986 congress. Jaruzelski's three close military colleagues— Internal Affairs Minister Kiszczak, Defense Minister Siwicki, and new CC Secretary Baryla—were all added to the Politburo, reflecting their real power as the central core of the regime.
- The 1986 congress and preceding election conferences were tightly controlled, and few of the democratized 1981 features were followed this time. In some 1986 conferences leading up to the congress a minimal amount of choice was allowed in electing delegates to the congress, but various devices—including the highly unusual postponement of election of local leaders—were employed to guarantee control and prevent unforeseen occurrences. At the congress itself, delegates were allowed only very narrow choice in electing the new CC, Jaruzelski himself and the rest of the Politburo were elected without opposing candidates,

the last remaining reformers and hard-liners were dropped from the new Politburo, and the democratic provisions in the statute and election rules were considerably weakened.

The Jaruzelski regime, although still maintaining commitment to the 1981 reforms and the 9th congress, appeared to be moving in a retrogressive direction: less consideration of public opinion and less real attempt to encourage public participation, and less tolerance for diverging viewpoints and representation of differing wings of the party. The developments suggested the prospect of an increasingly isolated regime run by one man with less dissent by his colleagues and less input from the public. This had been the recipe for disaster in the past, leading to ill-considered policy decisions and subsequent public explosions under previous reformers Gomulka and Gierek.

The new swing to "normalization" was reflected most obviously in a big leadership reorganization in November 1985 which appeared to end an era by demonstrably reducing the influence of the moderates and virtually eliminating diversity in the regime. Figures such as Barcikowski, Rakowski, and Olszowski had risen independent of Jaruzelski, had their own political constituencies, had often taken clear public stands on issues, and had been involved in political controversies. Barcikowski and Olszowski had been Jaruzelski's equals in the Politburo for several years and would not be very hesitant about offering their own advice and even disagreeing with Jaruzelski.

The shake-up occurred at a November 11, 1985 CC plenum and November 6 and 12 Sejm sessions. In it, every top leader left over from the 1980–81 period except Jaruzelski himself retired or moved to less influential posts:

- Olszowski, 54, resigned from the Politburo for "personal reasons and his desire to devote himself to public and academic work."[67] On the following day he also left his post as foreign minister and was replaced with Marian Orzechowski, his onetime deputy and successor as ideology secretary, who also was not a Jaruzelski favorite and who was maneuvered out of the Secretariat in November 1983.

- Barcikowski, 58, gave up his post of CC secretary in charge of the economy and was elected deputy chairman of the Council of State. Barcikowski's replacement was the most important of the moves, since he was virtually second-ranking CC secretary after Jaruzelski and played a much bigger role than Olszowski or Rakowski. He had handled the key fields of party organizational work, relations with the Church, and general supervision of economic policy. His semiretirement appeared to be at least partially dictated by real health problems, rather than by disagreements with Jaruzelski. A *Zycie Gospodarcze* article (October 6, 1985) entitled "The Durable Politician" reported Barcikowski saying that because of his recent heart attack he "would not be active much longer." There was no sign of conflict with Jaruzelski, and, unlike Olszowski, Barcikowski remained a Politburo member. Moreover, as the only PZPR member among deputy chairmen of the Council of State he probably would serve as a stand-in for newly elected Council of State chairman Jaruzelski.

- Rakowski, 59, was shifted from deputy premier to deputy speaker of the Sejm and chairman of the Sejm Economic and Social Council (an advisory body set up to discuss government policy), a surprising downgrading in view of his closeness to Jaruzelski since 1981. With the end of attempts to negotiate cooperation with Solidarity, Rakowski's main function as deputy premier had disappeared, but he had become a leading spokesman for Jaruzelski's regime, especially with Westerners and intellectuals. No one was named to fill Rakowski's function as deputy premier. Rakowski's demotion may have been a gesture to please the Soviets and compensate for the removal of their favorite, Olszowski.

- Jablonski, 75, finally retired from the post of chairman of the Council of State and was succeeded by Jaruzelski, who gave up the post of premier.

- Kania, 58, was dropped from his main prominent post, as member of the Council of State (a post given to him by Jaruzelski after Kania's resignation as party leader). Kania retained minor posts such as chairman of the Sejm Commission for Self-Management Affairs.[68]

The new team of top men around Jaruzelski—Premier Messner and senior CC Secretaries Czyrek, Wozniak, and Porebski—consisted of specialists with limited experience in politics and no political base of their own—quite the opposite of Barcikowski and Olszowski, who had held a wide variety of political leadership posts in both party and government:

- Zbigniew Messner, 56, moved up from Jaruzelski's top-ranking deputy in the Council of Ministers to succeed him as premier. Messner was a professional economist, rather than a politician, serving as rector of the Katowice Economics Academy from 1975 to 1981. He became chairman of the Katowice province people's council in November 1980, and in the first days of martial law he was chosen by Jaruzelski to become first secretary of Katowice, one of the provinces with the strongest resistance to martial law. Jaruzelski's confidence in Messner was demonstrated again in November 1983, when he asked the Sejm to create a new post of deputy premier to coordinate economic leadership and selected Messner to fill this post. In nominating Messner for premier at the November 6, 1985 Sejm session, Jaruzelski said that he had been acting as "de facto first deputy premier" and praised his qualifications as an economist and coordinator of the economy.[69] Messner himself in a September 15, 1985 *Przeglad Tygodniowy* interview described his role as "economic coordinator" in the Council of Ministers and indicated that he had run the government in Jaruzelski's absence.
- With Barcikowski's departure, Jozef Czyrek, 57, became virtually second secretary. Czyrek was a foreign affairs specialist, working in the foreign ministry since 1952 and as foreign minister from August 1980. Added to the Politburo and Secretariat at the 1981 party congress, he took over supervision of the CC's Foreign Affairs Department and General Department and in mid-1982 left his post of foreign minister (when Olszowski was shifted out of the Secretariat to foreign minister). Jaruzelski found Czyrek a reliable supporter and during 1982 made him secretary for ideology (as well as foreign affairs), replacing Orzechowski.[70]
- Marian Wozniak, 49, was transferred from Warsaw first secretary to CC secretary, taking over Barcikowski's responsibility for economic affairs. Wozniak had spent most of his career in local and central economic planning organs and was relatively new to politics. In mid-1981 he had been elected first secretary of a small province near Warsaw (Siedlce), and at the July 1981 party con-

gress was elected a CC secretary and assigned to economic affairs. When Jaruzelski dislodged Kociolek as Warsaw first secretary in July 1982, he chose Wozniak to run the party organization óf the capital city, and Jaruzelski's confidence in him was also demonstrated by the fact that Wozniak was promoted to Politburo candidate member at the February 1982 plenum and full member at the July 1982 plenum.

- Tadeusz Porebski, 54, received no new post in the November 1985 reorganization, but as one of only four secretaries with full Politburo membership (along with Jaruzelski, Czyrek, and Wozniak) he also became a senior leader. Like Messner, he was an academic (professor of technical sciences and longtime rector of the Wroclaw Polytechnic), rather than a politician. He was elected first secretary of Wroclaw province in November 1980 and a Politburo member at the 1981 congress. In November 1983 Jaruzelski called him to Warsaw to become CC secretary, initially for schools and the intelligentsia. But when Barcikowski gave up supervision of party organizational work in mid-1985, Porebski apparently replaced him, becoming chairman of the CC's Intraparty Affairs Commission.[71] He supervised the October 1985 Sejm election, delivering the report on the election at the November 1985 CC plenum.

In addition to getting rid of the most prominent "politicians" and establishing a team of technocrats, the November 1985 reorganization appeared to increase Jaruzelski's reliance on his old military colleagues. His generals continued to control the key levers of power—the army, police, and party apparat—suggesting his trust of those outside the military remained limited. General Siwicki remained minister of defense, and General Kiszczak minister of internal affairs. Party cadres were supervised by General Wladyslaw Honkisz, who succeeded General Dziekan as director of the CC's Cadres Department after Dziekan's November 1984 death.[72] Moreover, even as Jaruzelski left the post of premier, he raised one of his trusted military protégés to a key post in the Council of Ministers leadership. General Michal Janiszewski, his longtime aide-de-camp in the Ministry of Defense and later in the Council of Ministers (as chief of the premier's office), was promoted to rank of minister and made a member of the Presidium of the Council of Ministers (a body normally including mainly deputy premiers).[73]

The increasingly conservative tendencies of the regime were also evident in its approach to the 1986 party election campaign. Despite the four and a half years of "normalizing" the party since late 1981, the leadership was apparently not totally confident of controlling party election meetings. This was suggested by several cautionary steps taken by the Politburo before the campaign began. At the December 1985 plenum which called the next congress for June 1986 it was announced that party officials would have individual talks with all party members prior to the election meetings and that the pre-congress conferences would only elect delegates to the congress and discuss the new party program, leaving election of local party leadership (for example, province party committees and first secretaries) until after the congress when a second round of conferences would be held to conduct these elections.[74]

The two steps were apparently aimed at sounding out and perhaps pressuring members before the conferences and at isolating election of delegates from election of local leaders and perhaps thereby minimizing any damage if party organizations became unruly. CC Organizational Secretary Mokrzyszczak explained in a January 8, 1986 *Trybuna Ludu* interview that the individual talks were aimed at eliciting party members' views before the conferences and that postponing election of local leaders was to help conferences focus on discussion of the program and avoid politicking. "Potential candidates often try to 'look good' rather than clarify their real views," he said, and "personal emotions eat up a huge amount of energy and attention." Moreover, he recalled that in the 1981 precongress elections those elected to local leadership were also elected congress delegates and monopolized too many functions.

During the local-level conferences the leadership did obey the election rules' requirement for choice, although only minimal choice was provided. At the province party conferences held during May 1986, all conferences had more candidates for delegate to the congress than there were seats. However, the range of choice was narrow. Of the forty-nine provinces, twenty-one had only 5 or fewer extra candidates, and most of the rest had only 6 to 10 extras. The greatest choice (36 percent more candidates than seats) was in Pila (36 candidates for 23 seats) and Lomza (19 for 12). Election commissions at each conference would nominate exactly as many candidates as there were seats, and the choice depended on how many were nominated from the floor. *Trybuna Ludu*'s accounts carefully reported the number of candidates nominated and the number elected at each conference, as if to demonstrate adherence to the rules. The local and central press reports of these conferences provided no indications of controversy over candidates, of upsets, or of election of unorthodox candidates.

During the lower-level party elections in March and April there were, however, occasional reports of extensive choice in electing delegates and of controversy or upsets. In particular, at conferences of large plants which elected a single delegate there sometimes were several candidates for the seat:[75]

- A delegate from among 3 candidates was elected at a Szczecin fishing enterprise party conference, at a Myslowice mine, and at a Sosnowiec mine; a delegate from among 4 candidates was elected at an Opole plant; and a delegate from among 6 candidates was chosen at a Gliwice combine.[76]
- A four-way contest for delegate to the congress developed even in the Szczecin police party organization, with the province police chief eventually winning the seat.[77]
- A close contest developed at the Stilon plant in Gorzow province when none of the 3 candidates (all factory workers or party cell secretaries) for delegate to the congress got enough votes on the first ballot and a second ballot was needed.[78]
- At a Zyrarda plant one candidate won by 68 votes to his rival's 36.[79]

Some contests ended in upsets. A nominee from the floor beat two other candidates in a Poznan plant party conference.[80] A local (*gmina*) conference voted down its first secretary's candidate for delegate to the province conference and elected someone else.[81] At a plant party conference in Zielona Gora the candidate for congress delegate nominated by the election commission was defeated by one of two candidates nominated from the floor.[82]

During the conferences the Politburo avoided going back to the old system of forcing party organizations to elect many Warsaw officials, a frequent source of special irritation. Almost all province conferences elected only 1 or 2 Warsaw officials (often ones with local ties) to their delegations to the congress. (Katowice had the most—6—on its giant

208-member delegation). Those officials included all Politburo and Sec-retariat members, almost all CC department heads, and a number of ministers. In contrast to the open protests against any outsiders during the 1981 elections, in 1986 the press gave no indication of any contro-versy over electing outsiders.

When the 10th Congress opened on June 29 it had a controlled at-mosphere sharply contrasting with the 1981 congress, and delegates were provided with much less choice even than in the 1986 province conference elections.[83] Most 1981 practices were altered: The congress chose a CC with very little room for choice; the new CC included many more officials and relatively fewer workers than the 1981 CC; Jaruzelski was elected by the CC (rather than by congress delegates) and with no opposing candidate; diversity was virtually eliminated from the Politburo, which was packed with Jaruzelski's military colleagues and personally picked protégés; and the key democratized provisions in the statute and election rules were weakened. Delegations apparently did not act independently, and there was no mention of a Central Group of Delegates being set up this time to negotiate with delegations. Unlike 1981, the press appeared under censorship, and local press reporting stuck to innocuous subjects and revealed little of the inner workings of the congress. Some elements remained: There still was some choice for the CC and secret balloting was used; workers still comprised the biggest element of the CC and many officials were not included; much of the congress was broadcast live; and the statute still included the two-term limit on office holding and some other reform provisions.

In the election of a new CC, congress delegates were presented with only a small choice—263 candidates for 230 seats (14 percent extra candidates) versus 279 for 200 CC full members (39 percent extra can-didates) in 1981. There was almost no information on who the defeated 33 were, even in the local press, and no vote totals were announced either. But the few available clues indicate that few officials were voted down this time. All province first secretaries were elected to either the CC or the newly combined Central Control-Auditing Commission, so it was clear that no province first secretaries had run and been defeated. From rare comments in local papers it appears that 24 of the 33 defeated candidates were rank and file workers.[84]

The worker-farmer rank and file element of the CC dropped to a minority, from 108 of 200 in 1981 to 111 of 230 in 1986.[85] The new CC did not become the traditional "who's who" of power holders, however. It included only a little over half the province first secretaries (27 of 49), only 5 of the 17 CC department heads, and only a handful of government leaders, army and police officials: 7 army officers, not counting Baryla, Kiszczak, and Siwicki, 4 police, including Kiszczak, 2 deputy premiers, and 2 other ministers. By comparison, in 1981 only 8 province first secretaries, no CC department chiefs, 8 army officers (including Kiszczak and Siwicki), 2 police, 1 deputy premier, and 2 other ministers were elected full CC members.

Dropped from the new CC were liberal local party secretaries Jan Labecki (who had retired from politics) and Kazimierz Miniur (still first secretary of the huge Huta imieni Lenina works in Krakow and elected a delegate to the congress), outspoken worker Jadwiga Nowakowska (who chaired one of the congress sessions), and CC candidate member Zbigniew Kamecki (who had criticized the purge under martial law), as well as conservative leader Olszowski.[86] Some reformers such as Kubiak, Rakowski, and Roman Ney remained.

Democracy was eliminated most thoroughly for the Politburo and First Secretary Jaruzelski himself. In striking contrast to Kania, Jaruzelski was elected by a plenum of the new CC elected by the congress, and he was the only candidate nominated and received 228 of the 229 votes. There is no evidence of any opposition to him or discussion of his candidacy at the congress.

Nor was there any sign that opposing candidates were presented against Jaruzelski's list of Politburo and Secretariat members at the CC plenum, nor was there any announcement of whether any votes were cast against them. Despite this, the CC plenum electing the new Politburo and Secretariat dragged on for one and a half hours longer than scheduled because of the need to "consult" CC members and "groups of delegates" (part of the new procedure written into the statute). The congress on July 3 was supposed to resume at 6 P.M. but had to be delayed to 7:20 because of the plenum, according to Zygmunt Szeliga in the July 12 *Polityka*. When Jaruzelski appeared before the congress to announce the election results, he apologized for the delay and explained that "democratic procedure is very time-consuming."[87]

The new Politburo and Secretariat eliminated the remaining liberals

(Kubiak) and conservatives (Siwak) and established a more homogeneous group of Jaruzelski military cronies and faceless new technocrats who simply owed their positions to Jaruzelski and were completely dependent on him. Dropped as full Politburo members were former province First Secretaries Czechowicz[88] and Opalko,[89] former CC Secretary Kubiak, and workers Grzyb, Romanik, Siwak, and Kalkus—7 of the 13 members. Added were three generals close to Jaruzelski (Internal Affairs Minister Kiszczak, Defense Minister Siwicki, and former Political Administration chief Baryla—who had been elected a CC secretary in November 1985), Secretary for the media Glowczyk, former Organizational Secretary Mokrzyszczak (moved to chairman of the new Central Control-Auditing Commission), Foreign Minister Orzechowski, Trade Union chief Alfred Miodowicz, and workers Zygmunt Muranski and Zofia Stepien. Dropped from the Secretariat were Mokrzyszczak and Swirgon (who was demoted to chairman of the Sports Association); added were Stanislaw Ciosek (head of the CC Sociolegal Department), Kazimierz Cypryniak (head of the CC Organizational Department), and Andrzej Wasilewski (director of the State Publishing House).

Changes in the statute and election rules approved by the congress weakened the 1981 reforms. The proposed changes presented to the congress were outlined in detail, along with reasons, in a weekly for primary party organizations (*Fakty i Komentarze*, June 18, 1986).[90] The revised statute and election rules were published in pamphlet form after the congress:[91]

- The statute provision that there is to be an "unlimited number of candidates" was cut out, and, while the provision that "the number of candidates must exceed the number elected" was retained, it was balanced by a provision adopted by the 1984 National Conference of Delegates that conferences have the right to determine the number of candidates (limiting it to one, if so desired).[92]
- The 1981 statute provision that first secretaries should be elected by the congress or by conferences rather than by the CC or province committees—"the first time in the history of our party" the statute contained such a provision, according to *Fakty i Komentarze*—was replaced by a provision that the CC and province committees will elect their first secretaries in secret balloting and determine the number of candidates "in open balloting" (article

21). The election of Kania by the congress itself and of most province first secretaries by their conference delegates in 1981 had played a big role in enabling rank and file delegates to influence the outcome—by nominating candidates from the floor, debating candidates' merits, and sometimes using secret balloting to elect an opposition candidate.

- The position of CC candidate members was abolished, and it was provided that gaps among CC voting members (because of deaths, expulsions, resignations) would be filled from among congress delegates or the party aktiv in general (article 51). Gaps among CC full members were supposed to be filled from among CC candidate members elected by a congress, but Jaruzelski clearly had found this too limiting because of the preponderance of workers and farmers elected to the CC in 1981. He had occasionally gone entirely outside the CC in choosing top officials. For example, he selected Gorywoda (July 1982) and Bednarski (November 1983) to become CC secretaries even though they were not even CC candidate members and had to be illegally added to the CC at the same plenums which elected them CC secretaries.[93]

Some 1981 statute changes were retained, such as the continuing mandate for delegates and the two-term limit for holding offices. The latter, *Fakty i Komentarze* said, "evokes emotion and controversy in the party, especially among its aktiv," with some considering it a "guarantee of democratization of intraparty life" while others called it just a "mechanical rotation of party cadres regardless of their real abilities."

ASSESSMENT AND PROSPECTS

Did democratization in the PZPR fail? It did in the same sense that democratic systems in the West faced by severe political or economic crises have sometimes been abandoned in favor of dictatorships or military regimes. The democratized system fell victim to the escalating conflict with Solidarity and increasingly severe economic crises, which placed heavy demands on it for decisive, bold leadership, leadership that the system—based on consensus and persuasion—could hardly provide.

Moreover, forces from within (hard-liners and others hostile to democratization) and from without (the Soviet Union and other neighboring countries) put extra strain on it in hopes it would fail.

Although it could be faulted for not providing decisive leadership, the democratized party system did function surprisingly well for several months in the very difficult matter of transferring power from Gierek-era leaders to new leaders charting an untried course. This orderly transfer of power was a major achievement.

The system stood up well under pressure by Soviet forces and Polish secret police and hard-liners. Provocations (probably including the Bydgoszcz beating of Solidarity organizers) and Soviet pressure (such as the June CPSU letter and repeated military exercises) appear to have had little effect or to have actually backfired. As chapter 5 indicates, Soviet or hard-line plotting appears to have played little role even in Kania's resignation. Soviet or hard-line manipulations may have been successful in aggravating the conflict during October and November 1981 and increasing the need for adoption of martial law. Yet Jaruzelski appears to have had substantial reasons of his own—the challenge by Solidarity and spreading strikes and economic decline—for the decision without which he probably would not have moved, despite Soviet pressure to do so.

Probably the most important failing of democratization was the failure to win the confidence of the alienated Polish public and even much of the party's own rank and file. The extreme skepticism of the public would have been very difficult to overcome in any case, but the party's foot-dragging on change and harassment of Solidarity and reformers provided plenty of ammunition to those who argued that the party was still unwilling to reform and was not acting in good faith. Of course, the party leaders faced the difficulty of presenting an image of enthusiasm for reforms even while simultaneously trying to persuade the Soviet Union and hard-liners that it was remaining a true Marxist-Leninist party and was fighting off reform.

A more difficult question is whether such a democratized system could have lasted had the crisis over Solidarity and the economic decline not precipitated its end. The population in 1980–81 put up with the communist party because it knew its powerful Soviet neighbors would not countenance anything but a communist regime of some sort. But the basic contradiction of a clearly unpopular communist party trying to rule the country may have ended the system sooner or later anyway. This leads back to the question long debated by communist reformers themselves (in Poland, the Soviet Union, and elsewhere): Can a communist party really be reformed? Some reformers, feeling that it can, stay within the establishment and work from within for change; others, more pessimistic, consider this hopeless and pass over into dissidence and opposition.

The prospects for reviving democratic procedures, both inside and outside the party, are uncertain, especially in the short term. Jaruzelski's actions in imposing military rule have probably destroyed most of whatever public confidence was so painfully built up by the party since 1980. To gain even the limited credibility it had by late 1981, the party had had to allow party members almost unlimited rights to elect whomever they wished—with no political bosses dictating the choices as they always had in the past. The angry rank and file used these rights to the hilt, throwing out most of the leadership. By reimposing—through military force—limits on democratization, both for the public and for the party rank and file, Jaruzelski negated this gain, making the public more disaffected than ever and perhaps ending the option of winning voluntary cooperation by much of the public. The handling of the party and state elections since 1982 showed that the regime has little faith in winning widespread support at present.

In addition, imposition of repressive measures in society outside the communist party surely makes it more difficult to restore some sort of democracy within the party. Relaxation of controls within the party would eventually prompt some party members to speak out against repressive measures against those outside the party, thereby undermining the effectiveness of such measures and making communist control over the country shaky. Moreover, without Solidarity as a powerful outside competitor, the main motive force to prompt party reform and to overcome inertia and resistance is lacking.

The pressure for reform within the party has been weakened by the great shrinkage of party membership—not only from expulsions but also from desertion of the party. This has caused a basic shift in makeup of the party, a shift which fosters obedience and apathy. One of the prime factors in the rebelliousness of the rank and file in 1980 was the fact that under Gierek huge numbers of new members were admitted to the party and without much attempt to indoctrinate them. Prodded by Gierek's slogan of "a party of 3,000,000 by the 8th Congress" (1980), party organizations had pushed party membership from 2,359,324 in mid-1975 to 3,080,000 at the January 1980 congress.[94] Party membership reached its peak in July 1980, when it stood at 3,149,768.[95] But the August 1980 events set off a mass exodus. Between June 30, 1980, and December 13, 1981, membership dropped by 457,000[96]—over 14 percent. After a year of martial law, it was down to 2,370,000[97]—almost back to the 1975 level before Gierek's campaign to expand the party. Official commentaries have frequently stressed that most of those who left the party since 1980 have been those who joined during Gierek's expansion. Most were younger members and factory workers who were the least disciplined. For example, of 197,300 members who quit between July 1, 1980, and May 15, 1981, 72 percent were workers.[98] Gierek's expansion had raised the percentage of workers in the party from 40.3 percent in December 1970 to 46.1 percent in January 1980; by January 1983 it had fallen back to 40 percent.[99] Although white-collar workers and professionals also played key roles in demanding reforms (it was they, rather than manual workers, who had dominated the 1981 congress), the loss of so many young workers will seriously weaken reform pressure in the party.

Yet prospects are not totally bleak. Jaruzelski's intention in imposing martial law was not to stop democratization in the party as such but to get control over the crippling strikes and over the increasingly aggressive Solidarity movement before it wound up stripping power from the weakened government and party. Jaruzelski repeatedly has reasserted his commitment to intraparty democracy—including democratic election rules. He did not put hard-liners in power and allow them to purge liberals and reformers and roll back reform—although in the quest for order and discipline he himself has gradually destroyed most reform. Reimposition of control advocated by Olszowski and especially Grabski apparently would have gone further and faster in rolling back party democratization and reestablishing a more traditional system.

Meanwhile, elements of democratization remain embedded in PZPR rules, and, more importantly, in its way of thinking. Following previous Polish reform periods, conservatives were unable to eradicate all the reforms adopted, leaving Poland more liberalized and pluralistic than before the reforms. The same appears true now. With the rules still somewhat democratized, the question is whether or to what extent the democratic spirit and activism of 1980–81 will revive at some point, whether party members will again be able or have the will to exercise a real veto power over the choice of leaders and policies. The main outside impetus of 1980—Solidarity—is now missing, but the Church remains a powerful counterforce and Polish society remains pluralistic in fact, forcing the party to adjust to other elements in society, rather than just dictating to them.

Moreover, there appears to be a certain recognition among many party leaders that some sort of democratization is needed to make the system work. For example, both Poland and Hungary have recently changed over to requiring two candidates per seat in their parliamentary elections, and they proudly trumpet this as evidence of significant progress toward democratization. Why progress toward such democratization is needed now when this kind of democratization was not considered necessary in the past is not explained. As the initial stage of "dictatorship of the proletariat"—rule by force over anticommunist opposition—gradually fades into the past, at least some party leaders appear to recognize the need to base their rule on popular acceptance and cooperation and that for this some form of public participation in policymaking and implementation is required. Of course, the basic dilemma is how to allow the public to really play a role—through free speech and free choice among candidates for leadership—without letting the voters (in the party or outside) "misuse" this right to defeat the leadership or even overturn the communist system.

POLAND AS A MODEL

Do COMMUNIST PARTIES have to follow the pattern of the Soviet communist party—i.e., adhere to traditional democratic centralism with its dictatorship by the leaders over the members? Are there any elements of democracy in communist parties or natural tendencies in a democratic direction? Was the PZPR of 1981 just an aberration—a communist party sliding from communist into social democratic in fact if not in name?

Judging by Poland in 1980–81 and the pluralism-factionalism long rampant in the PZPR, as well as the Yugoslav example over decades, communist parties do not necessarily have to exactly follow the Soviet model. Democratic centralism and discipline can be much weaker, decision making and politics can be much more open, and there can even be some room for choice in elections. But how far communist parties can deviate from the Soviet model—driven by national characteristics (pluralism in Poland and regionalism in Yugoslavia)—and remain an effective ruling body is not so clear.

There are factors within communist parties which can stimulate tendencies toward democratization, factors much less obvious than the oft-noted features basically excluding democratic possibilities. Although communist parties are organized to be undemocratic in structure, there are inherent bases for pressure for democratization in them—most notably, dissatisfaction with the constant abuses by leaders who are self-appointed, entrusted with great power, and not subject to rigid rule of law. With no control over them from below, such leaders are highly susceptible to making high-handed and disastrous decisions, to abusing their positions, and even to committing crimes. Despite periodic cleanups, corruption and abuses appear to have become chronic and to discredit the system, spurring reformers to insist on some form of "democratization" to rescue it.

DIFFERENCE FROM SOVIET MODEL

The essence of the 1980–81 Polish model lay in uncontrolled elections with real choice, a basic deviation from current Soviet-style elections. The reformed Polish party election rules substantially differed from Soviet party election rules in allowing and even mandating a choice of candidates and secret balloting. Soviet election rules also provide for some secret balloting and allow party members the right to cast votes against their leaders, but they are silent about whether there can be a choice of candidates and about procedure for electing the top leaders.[1] In practice, no choice of candidates is permitted and the voting results are kept strictly secret.

Such practice had not always been the case even in the Soviet Union. For example, early Soviet party congresses had allowed a handful of opposition candidates for the CC and had announced voting results.[2] But since the early 1920s apparently only as many candidates have been nominated as there were positions, and stenographic records of the congresses have only listed names of those elected, with no vote totals. On one occasion—the April 1923 congress—the announcement of voting results was proposed but shouted down.[3]

Khrushchev, in retirement, once described the procedure used at congresses and acknowledged that the list system with no extra candidates provided little choice for delegates despite the right to cast their ballot in secret. In his taped recollections, he stated:

> It's true . . . there were few opportunities presented to the delegates for making a choice, so to speak, for a choice in absolute terms. . . . Because the candidates were already on the list. And there were only as many of them as was determined necessary to elect to the CC, as CC members and candidates and members of the Auditing Commission, and no more. . . . And here each delegate was only given the opportunity to express his attitude to a particular candidate. . . . That is, to leave him on the list or strike him off.

He recalled that some delegates "sat and studied the lists" and thought about "who to leave on it and who not to leave." Stalin, he noted, tried to discourage this by "demonstratively, for all to see" picking up his ballot and dropping it in the urn "without even looking at it." Khrushchev relates how the results of the voting were announced. It was announced that Stalin had received such and such number of votes—6 less than the total cast, so that anyone could calculate that "6 votes had been cast against him." Khrushchev notes that 6 votes also had been cast against his own candidacy at that congress—which made him happy because "others had several dozen votes and even, I think, about a hundred cast against them." Nevertheless, they were elected, he noted, since they had a majority anyway.[4]

OTHER MODELS

There have been some elements of democracy or pluralism in a few other communist parties—especially in recent years—but previously there had been no real alternative democratic model to the traditional Soviet model. Eurocommunists in Italy and Spain talked about respecting parliamentary democracy in their countries and have had somewhat pluralistic parties. For example, the Spanish party dropped its label of "Leninist" in 1978 and split into several factions. The competition between these factions was resolved by split vote at its stormy December 1983 congress. But the pluralism did not really last, since the factions broke up into separate parties.[5] The Italian party dropped traditional democratic centralism in 1983 and, while still eschewing formal factionalism, allows a variety of opinions and informal groupings. It no longer imposes centrally chosen candidates on local party organizations, it allows internal leadership disagreements to be publicized in the press, and it allows "horizontal" communication between local party units.[6] However, while there are some parallels with the PZPR, the Spanish and Italian parties have not been in power.

Among communist parties in power, the only previous models of liberalized communism were in Czechoslovakia and Yugoslavia, but both provided relatively little in the way of a model. "Socialism with a human face" in Czechoslovakia in 1968 produced many proposals for democratization—some very similar to those raised in Poland in 1980—but it was quashed before widespread democratized elections could be held and before it could develop into a system. And it was replaced with a rather traditional ultraconservative system. Yet even its brief experience has been much discussed as a possible route for communist evolution. In contrast, the Polish renewal lasted over a year, producing not only a great amount of intraparty discussion on how to create and maintain a democratic system but also many months of practical experience at operating a communist party more or less democratically.

Yugoslavia has developed strong pluralism and some democratic forms (especially outside the party) during the past three decades of independence from Moscow, but while regional factions have engaged in open disputes, there has never been broad choice offered in party elections. The high point in terms of choice at national Yugoslav party congresses appears to have been in 1958, when there were nine more candidates for the CC than there were seats, and these were no real contests since the losers received only 1 to 5 votes apiece versus over 1,775 for almost all the victorious 135 candidates.[7] Opportunities for choice through the years have mainly occurred at republic congresses and local conferences, and even there choices were only offered on a limited scale and mainly during the period of liberalization in the 1960s. The 1964 party statute gave party organizations the right to present a choice of candidates, and there were subsequently occasional cases of limited choice and even of defeat of incumbent party secretaries.[8] The most recent party statute, that adopted at the June 1978 congress, permits more candidates than there are seats, but there has been little sign that this right has been exercised. At the congresses in 1982, there were no choices; delegates were presented with only as many candidates as there were seats.[9]

In the most recent party elections, however, it was decided that there should be more choice and that secret balloting should be used. A March 1985 CC plenum decision called for more candidates than positions to fill, even for high posts,[10] and a February 1986 plenum announced that the June 1986 party congress would elect the CC by secret ballot.[11] But at most only a narrow range of choice was offered for voting at republic congresses. Each republic drew up a large list (hundreds of possible candidates) for republic and national central committees, but these were cut down in back-room bargaining to only a few candidates more than the seats available. Thus, Croatia—perhaps the most "democratic" republic—started with 798 candidates for its republic CC but cut this to 110 for 97 seats and reduced an initial list of 289 for the Yugoslav CC to 20 candidates for the republic's allotted 15 seats.[12] Other republics presented less or no choice. For example, the Serbian congress was presented with a list of candidates for the Serbian CC and for Serbian representation on the Yugoslav CC which was exactly the same as the number of seats to fill.[13] At the June 1986 13th Yugoslav congress itself there was very little choice for CC members (only 14 write-ins), and the congress approved a statute provision that the number of candidates should be greater than the number of seats but that this was only optional.[14]

One thing which has obstructed free choice in Yugoslavia has been the need for carefully balanced ethnic and geographic representation for the sensitive nationalities and republics. The party statute allots each republic an equal number of members on the CC, and each republic (or region) picks its own representatives who are just ratified by the national party congress.[15] A free election among candidates at the national congress might degenerate into voting along ethnic or regional lines and result in one republic or nationality dominating.

Yugoslavia also provides a poor example because its democratization was part of its defection from the Soviet bloc, and any attempts to emulate Yugoslav experiments were clearly in the heretical category for other communist states. Poland, even while remaining within the bloc, produced a much more democratized party, allowing real choice in party elections. As with Hungary's economic innovations, Poland's political experiments are not clearly branded as antisocialist and completely outside the pale for consideration.

BASES FOR DEMOCRATIZATION

Is there any likelihood that other communist parties could evolve toward more democratically run parties? Many of the factors which changed the PZPR in 1980–81 are uniquely Polish, but some are found elsewhere—even in the Communist Party of the Soviet Union itself. One of the main factors is nascent hostility between rank and file party members and the party bosses with their privileges and power.

Democratic centralism, as usually applied, prevents change except from the top. Lack of opportunity to vote leaders out of office leads to leaders becoming entrenched and insensitive to the wishes of the public and even of the party rank and file. The insensitivity—even dictatorial approach— of leaders at various levels was a key factor fueling the drive for reform in the PZPR. It produced a rift between party leaders and the rank and file, so that the rank and file resented the privileges of the leadership and its "isolation" from the "party masses" and viewed the relationship as "them" versus "us." In the PZPR the terms *gora* (up there, or the bosses) and *doly* (down here, or the rank and file) became very widespread, and there was open talk about the gap between these. Lodz worker Jadwiga Nowakowska discussed the "informal division between activists and leaders" in an interview in *Trybuna Ludu*, February 2, 1981:

> An activist is one such as me. He acts at the lowest group level, is a secretary or member of an executive committee of a shop party organization (OOP) or a primary party organization (POP), and is elected to his post or in general does not even have a post. He is always among people and with people. He is within reach and in view. He must interpret, explain, persuade, sometimes suffer setbacks, undergo constant testing. But a leader? He most often is appointed to his post. He does not circulate among people "down here" [*na dole*] but from time to time stops by or drops in. Today here, tomorrow there. He answers questions which he himself selects, unless pressed to the wall. . . . We say that every leader of every level must belong to some workers' primary party organization. [But] workers say what good is such contact with a leader, as a primary party organization member, when he comes to a meeting [only] when he wants, citing lack of time. And if he does come, the meeting changes into a gala, with flowers and celebration.

The Polish rank and file appeared to turn with a vengeance on these leaders whom they could not identify with. As Nowakowska said: "The party does not applaud any more now, does not approve uncritically, as it used to, everything said or decided up there." The split was compounded by corruption, and party rank and file became convinced that anyone in a position of power was dishonest.

Similar problems, including signs that corruption could serve as a catalyst for reform, are evident even in the Soviet Union. Since Brezhnev's death, large-scale corruption has been revealed in many places high and low. The Gorbachev regime has attacked and removed many entrenched officials and initiated public exposures of abuses by officials as high as republic party first secretaries (for example, in Uzbekistan). Negative attitudes by workers and party rank and file toward the party elite have surfaced, apparently spurred by revelations of corruption and abuse of privilege. For example, *Pravda* on February 13, 1986, published a worker's letter which said that "I have the opinion that between the CC and the workers there is still an immovable, inert, and flabby 'party-administrative stratum' [*sloy*]" which "expects only privileges and is in no rush to use its energy or knowledge for the people." Another letter cited in the same article called for "social justice" and complained that "party, soviet, trade union, economic, and even Komsomol leaders sometimes deepen social inequality by using all kinds of special eating places, special stores, special hospitals, etc.," and it suggested that the bosses should have to go to normal stores and stand in line with the rest of the citizens. Newly appointed Moscow city First Secretary Boris Yeltsin used his speech to the 1986 CPSU congress to assail "social injustice" and an "inert stratum of time-servers with party cards." He declared that collectives of workers were "sharply" discussing questions of "social justice" and expressing "indignation" over "any manifestations of injustice" such as "special benefits for leaders." Warning of loss of respect for party members, he urged a sharp reduction in such special privileges.[16]

The hints of a gap between the leadership and the rank and file had appeared earlier and had prompted some less conservative Soviet leaders to express concern and seek ways to reduce the gap, even using the concept of "democratization." The concern first became evident in the 1970s in the republic of Georgia, where local republic First Secretary Eduard Shevardnadze (now Soviet foreign minister) experimented with various methods of bringing rank and file party members into decision making and sounding out public opinion before making decisions. In 1975 a Council on Public Opinion was created in the Georgian CC to carry out public opinion polling, and the results of these polls have sometimes been weighed in making decisions and in how decisions are announced.[17] New devices have been tried to give the party rank and file more sense of participating in decisions.[18] At the early 1981 republic party congress Shevardnadze boasted of a new "atmosphere of frankness" and better communication between leaders and led,[19] and Georgian Ideology Secretary Guram Yenukidze claimed that Georgia had restored "mutual trust between the party leadership and the broadest masses" and labeled this a big achievement.[20] Shevardnadze also used his speech at the early 1981 CPSU congress to criticize outdated ideas of the "relations between the leader and the led," and boasted of his "democratization" in the Georgian party, declaring: "Some of our communist leaders in places turned out to be unprepared to understand these complicated, profound processes and to follow them." "One such leader," he said, had complained to him that "this democratization of yours will end with me losing my job"—which was precisely what happened, he said.[21]

The gap between leaders and led—inside and outside the party—is currently accentuated by the widespread corruption plaguing the Soviet leadership class, and such corruption played a big role in alienating the party rank and file, as well as other citizens, in Poland. Of course, there is no evidence that relationships within the CPSU have deteriorated to anywhere near the extent that they had in the PZPR by mid-1980, and there is no powerful external factor—a Soviet "Solidarity" movement— to impel the CPSU to pay attention to its own rank and file and to allow more diversity of opinion and advocacy of alternative policies.

In addition to the corruption factor and sense of social inequality, Soviet leaders—like those in Poland—apparently see some sort of steps toward democratization as necessary to enliven the economic system. Soviet workers and farmers—like those in Poland—show little interest in hard productive work, and Gorbachev has repeatedly expressed the view that unless workers and farmers can be given a stake in the system and be persuaded to participate with initiative and interest it will be impossible to boost productivity and restore the necessary economic growth. Hence, at the 1986 CPSU congress he declared that "government cannot be the privilege of a narrow circle of professionals" and talked of deepening "democratization" of society, expansion of citizen participation, and expansion of the practice of electing leaders of brigades and some other categories of leaders at enterprises—foremen, leaders of shifts, workshops, and units, and managers of state farm subdivisions.[22] At a January 27, 1987 Central Committee plenum Gorbachev went further in calling for "democratization," stating that proposals were coming to the Central Committee to change party election procedures so that secretaries, "including first secretaries," could be elected by secret ballot and that party committee members have the right to nominate additional candidates from the floor. According to the January 28 *Pravda* version of his speech, he praised this idea and also proposals to alter state elections so that meetings held to nominate candidates for local and national soviets could discuss several candidates, instead of just one. He did add that such changes should not undermine democratic centralism, however, that "decisions of higher bodies, including those on personnel matters," should remain "compulsory for all lower party committees."

As this book goes to press in early 1987, experimentation with multi-candidate elections is beginning in the Soviet Union itself. A January 3, 1987 *Komsomolskaya Pravda* interview with Latvian party First Secretary Boris Pugo revealed that "for the first time" in the Soviet Union a local Komsomol organization had elected a secretary from among several candidates and that some other Komsomol organizations had recently copied this also. Pugo praised this for making election conferences more exciting and declared it wrong to have meetings all organized in advance, "even down to the length of the applause." TASS, on February 2, reported a three-way election contest for the first secretary of the Donetsk city Komsomol. This trend has even begun penetrating the party. *Pravda* and *Sovetskaya Rossiya*, on February 10, carried long accounts on the first multicandidate election in the party; two candidates ran for first secretary of a rayon (district) in Kemerovo province and the race was decided in a secret ballot by a vote of 29 to 20. Of course, such glimmers of "democratization" are just beginning in the Soviet Union, and it is far from clear how far Gorbachev might like to pursue this course.

While it is hard to imagine Soviet leaders embracing meaningful democratization, it appears that some—from Khrushchev in retirement to Gorbachev in his attempts to revitalize the Soviet system—recognize some of the defects in the traditional undemocratic practices. It was also surprising to see so many Polish leaders immediately recognize the need for democratic elections and checks on leadership as soon as Gierek's regime faltered in 1980. While undemocratic rule and reliance on force may be inherent features of communist parties, the need to reform the system to improve its effectiveness and even to ensure its continued existence may provide impetus in the opposite direction—toward some sort of democratization.

LEADERSHIP CHANGES, 1980–1986

February 1980 (elected at congress)	*August 24, 1980* (plenum)	*September 5–6, 1980* (plenum)	*October 5–6, 1980* (plenum)
	Politburo Members		
Babiuch[1]	Gierek[3]	[4]Barcikowski	Barcikowski
Gierek	Grudzien	Grudzien[5]	Jablonski
Grudzien	Jablonski	Jablonski	Jagielski
Jablonski	Jagielski	Jagielski	Jaruzelski
Jagielski	Jaruzelski	Jaruzelski	Kania
Jaruzelski	Kania	Kania	Karkoszka[7]
Kania	Karkoszka	Karkoszka	Kowalczyk[7]
Karkoszka	Kowalczyk	Kowalczyk	Kruczek[7]
Kowalczyk	Kruczek	Kruczek	Olszowski
Kruczek	[2]Olszowski	Olszowski	Pinkowski
Lukaszewicz[1]	[2]Pinkowski	Pinkowski	Werblan[7]
Szydlak[1]	Werblan	Werblan	Zabinski
Werblan		[4]Zabinski	
Wrzaszczyk[1]			
	Politburo Candidate Members		
Barcikowski	Barcikowski[3]	Waszczuk	[6]Kruk
Pinkowski[1]	[2]Waszczuk	Wojtaszek	[6]Ney
Pyka[1]	Wojtaszek		Waszczuk
Wojtaszek	[2]Zabinski[3]		Wojtaszek
Zandarowski[1]			
	Secretaries		
Gierek	Gierek[3]	[4]Grabski	[6]Barcikowski
Kania	Kania	Kania	Grabski
Lukaszewicz[1]	[2]Olszowski	[4]Kurowski	Kania
Pinkowski[1]	Waszczuk	Olszowski	Kurowski

Secretaries (Cont'd)

Waszczuk	Werblan	Waszczuk	Olszowski
Werblan	[2]Wojtaszek	Werblan	Waszczuk
Zabinski	Zabinski	Wojtaszek	Werblan[7]
Zandarowski[1]		[4]Wojtecki	Wojtaszek
		Zabinski[5]	Wojtecki

Members of the Secretariat

Kurowski	Kurowski[3]	Zielinski	[6]Gabrielski
Zielinski	Zielinski		Zielinski

[1]until August 24, 1980; [2]from August 24, 1980; [3]until Sept. 6, 1980; [4]from Sept. 6, 1980; [5]until Oct. 6, 1980; [6]from Oct. 6, 1980; [7]until Dec. 2, 1980.

December 2, 1980 (plenum)	*April 1981* (plenum)	*July 1981* (congress)	*October 1981* (two plenums)

Politburo Members

Barcikowski	Barcikowski	Barcikowski	Barcikowski
[1]Grabski	[3]Gabrys[4]	[5]Czechowicz	Czechowicz
Jablonski	Grabski[4]	[5]Czyrek	Czyrek
Jagielski	Jablonski[4]	[5]Grzyb	Grzyb
Jaruzelski	Jagielski[4]	Jaruzelski	Jaruzelski
Kania	Jaruzelski	Kania[6]	Kubiak
[1]Moczar	Kania	[5]Kubiak	Labecki
Olszowski	Moczar[4]	[5]Labecki	Messner
Pinkowski[2]	Olszowski	[5]Messner	Milewski
Zabinski	[3]Wronski[4]	[5]Milewski	Olszowski
	Zabinski[4]	Olszowski	Opalko
		[5]Opalko	Porebski
		[5]Porebski	Romanik
		[5]Romanik	Siwak
		[5]Siwak	

Politburo Candidate Members

[1]Fiszbach	Fiszbach[4]	[5]Glowczyk	Glowczyk
Kruk	Kruk[4]	[5]Mokrzyszczak	Mokrzyszczak
Ney	[3]Masny[4]		[8]Siwicki
Waszczuk	Ney[4]		
Wojtaszek[2]	Waszczuk[4]		

Secretaries

Barcikowski	Barcikowski	Barcikowski	Barcikowski
Grabski	[3]Cypryniak[4]	[5]Czyrek	Czyrek
Kania	Grabski[4]	Kania[6]	[7]Jaruzelski
Kurowski	Kania	[5]Kubiak	Kubiak
[1]Ney	Kurowski[4]	[5]Michalek	Michalek
Olszowski	Ney[4]	[5]Milewski	Milewski
Waszczuk	Olszowski	Olszowski	[8]Mokrzyszczak
Wojtaszek[2]	Waszczuk[4]	[5]Wozniak	Olszowski
Wojtecki[2]			[8]Orzechowski
			Wozniak

Members of the Secretariat

Gabrielski	Gabrielski[4]
Zielinski[2]	

[1]from Dec. 2, 1980; [2]until April 1981; [3]from April 1981; [4]until July 1981; [5]from July 1981; [6]until Oct. 18, 1981; [7]from Oct. 18, 1981; [8]from Oct. 28, 1981.

February 1982 (plenum)	*July 1982* (plenum)	*October 1982* (plenum)	*November 1983* (plenum)

Politburo Members

Barcikowski	Barcikowski	Barcikowski	Barcikowski
Czechowicz	Czechowicz	Czechowicz	Czechowicz
Czyrek	Czyrek	Czyrek	Czyrek
Grzyb	Grzyb	Grzyb	Grzyb
Jaruzelski	Jaruzelski	Jaruzelski	Jaruzelski
Kubiak	[3]Kalkus	Kalkus	Kalkus
Labecki[2]	Kubiak	Kubiak	Kubiak
Messner	Messner	Messner	Messner
Milewski	Milewski	Milewski	Milewski[8]
Olszowski	Olszowski	Olszowski	Olszowski
Opalko	Opalko	Opalko	Opalko
Porebski	Porebski	Porebski	Porebski
Romanik	Romanik	Romanik	Romanik
Siwak	Siwak	Siwak	Siwak
	[3]Wozniak	Wozniak	Wozniak

Politburo Candidate Members

Glowczyk	[3]Bejger	Bejger	Bejger
[1]Kiszczak	Glowczyk	Glowczyk	Glowczyk
Mokrzyszczak	Kiszczak	Kiszczak	Kiszczak
Siwicki	Mokrzyszczak	Mokrzyszczak	Mokrzyszczak
[1]Wozniak[2]	Siwicki	Siwicki	[6]Orzechowski
			Siwicki

Secretaries

Barcikowski	Barcikowski	Barcikowski	Barcikowski
Czyrek	Czyrek	Czyrek	[6]Bednarski
Jaruzelski	[3]Glowczyk	Glowczyk	Czyrek
Kubiak[2]	[3]Gorywoda	Gorywoda	Glowczyk
Michalek	Jaruzelski	Jaruzelski	Gorywoda[7]
Milewski	Michalek	Michalek	Jaruzelski
Mokrzyszczak	Milewski	Milewski	Michalek
Olszowski[2]	Mokrzyszczak	Mokrzyszczak	Milewski[8]
Orzechowski	Orzechowski	Orzechowski[5]	Mokrzyszczak
Wozniak[2]		[4]Swirgon	[6]Porebski
			Swirgon

[1]from Feb. 1982; [2]until July 1982; [3]from July 1982; [4]from Oct. 1982; [5]until Nov. 1983; [6]from Nov. 1983; [7]until Feb. 1984; [8]until May 1985.

May 1985 (plenum)	November 1985 (plenum)	June 1986 (congress)

Politburo Members

May 1985 (plenum)	November 1985 (plenum)	June 1986 (congress)
Barcikowski	Barcikowski	Barcikowski
Czechowicz	Czechowicz[3]	[4]Baryla
Czyrek	Czyrek	Czyrek
Grzyb	Grzyb[3]	[4]Glowczyk
Jaruzelski	Jaruzelski	Jaruzelski
Kalkus	Kalkus[3]	[4]Kiszczak
Kubiak	Kubiak[3]	Messner
Messner	Messner	[4]Miodowicz
Olszowski[1]	Opalko[3]	[4]Mokrzyszczak
Opalko	Porebski	[4]Muranski
Porebski	Romanik[3]	[4]Orzechowski
Romanik	Siwak[3]	Porebski
Siwak	Wozniak	[4]Siwicki
Wozniak		[4]Stepien
		Wozniak

Politburo Candidate Members

Bejger	Bejger	Bejger
Glowczyk	Glowczyk[3]	[4]Ferensztajn
Kiszczak	Kiszczak[3]	[4]Kubasiewicz
Mokrzyszczak	Mokrzyszczak[3]	[4]Michalek
Orzechowski	Orzechowski[3]	[4]Rembisz
Siwicki	Siwicki[3]	

Secretaries

Barcikowski[1]	[2]Baryla	Baryla
Bednarski	Bednarski	Bednarski
Czyrek	Czyrek	[4]Ciosek
Glowczyk	Glowczyk	Czyrek
Jaruzelski	Jaruzelski	[4]Cypryniak
Michalek	Michalek	Glowczyk
Mokrzyszczak	Mokrzyszczak[3]	Jaruzelski
Porebski	Porebski	Michalek
Swirgon	Swirgon[3]	Porebski
	[2]Wozniak	[4]Wasilewski
		Wozniak

[1]until Nov. 1985; [2]from Nov. 1985; [3]until June 1986; [4]from June 1986.

ROUGH GUIDE TO PRONUNCIATION

DIFFICULT LEADERS' NAMES

Barcikowski: Barchikovski
Czechowicz: Chekhovich
Czyrek: Chirek
Fiszbach: Fishbakh
Grzyb: Gzhib
Kiszczak: Kishchak
Labecki: Wabenski
Lukasiewicz: Wukashevich
Lukaszewicz: Wukashevich
Mokrzyszczak: Mok-shish-chak

Olszowski: Olshovski
Orzechowski: Ozhekhovski
Porebski: Porembski
Siwak: Shivak
Siwicki: Shivitski
Skrzypczak: Sk-zhip-chak
Walesa: Vawensa
Waszczuk: Vash-chuk
Wozniak: Vozhnyak
Wrzaszczyk: V-zhash-chik
Zabinski: Zhabinjski

DIFFICULT PROVINCE NAMES

Biala Podlaska: Byawa Podlaska
Bialystok: Byawistok
Bydgoszcz: Bidgosh-ch
Chelm: Helm
Ciechanow: Chehanuf
Czestochowa: Chengstohova
Elblag: Elblang
Gorzow: Gozhuf
Jelenia Gora: Yelenya Gura
Kalisz: Kalish
Katowice: Katovitse
Kielce: Kyeltse
Koszalin: Koshalin
Krakow: Krakuf
Leszno: Leshno
Lodz: Wudzh

Lomza: Womza
Nowy Sacz: Novi Sanch
Olsztyn: Olshtin
Ostroleka: Ostrowenka
Pila: Piwa
Piotrkow Trybunalski: Pyotr-kuf
  Tribunalski
Plock: Pwotsk
Przemysl: Pshemyshl
Rzeszow: Zheshuf
Siedlce: Shed-l-tse
Sieradz: Sheradz
Skierniewice: Skyer-nyevitse
Slupsk: Swupsk
Szczecin: Sh-chechin
Tarnobrzeg: Tarnobzheg

Walbrzych: Vaw-bzhih

Wloclawek: Vwo-tswa-vek

Wroclaw: Vruts-wav

Zamosc: Zamosh-ch

Zielona Gora: Zhelona Gura

DIFFICULT NEWSPAPER TITLES

Rzeczpospolita: Zhech-pos-polita

Rzeczywistosc: Zhech-i-vis-tosh-ch

Notes

1. THE DRIVE FOR REFORM

1. Detailed accounts of the beginning of the strikes, strikers' demands, and regime response can be found in Neal Ascherson's *The Polish August* and Kevin Ruane's *The Polish Challenge*.

2. *Trybuna Ludu*, August 19, 1980.

3. The CC's main paper, *Trybuna Ludu*, carried nothing of Kania's speech. But the September 1980 issue of the CC monthly *Nowe Drogi* did publish it, as well as the other speeches at the plenum. The only speech published immediately after the plenum was Gierek's concluding speech. Publication of Kania's report probably would have overshadowed Gierek and embarrassed him at the time. The *Nowe Drogi* issue, which printed the speeches, was signed to press on September 25, well after Kania had succeeded Gierek as party leader. The publication of the plenum speeches initiated a new policy of making public apparently complete versions of all speeches after each CC plenum—a practice which provided great insights into the key deliberations of the Polish party leadership.

4. In a June 14, 1981 speech Olszowski recalled how he had led a study of economic policy under Gierek but that his proposals to reverse the deepening indebtedness to the West had been opposed by Gierek, Premier Jaroszewicz, and Deputy Premier Szydlak. "This ended with me being excluded from the party leadership at the 8th congress" (February 1980), and "for some time I was without work. They proposed that I work in the West, but that did not interest me. I wanted to work in the USSR or another socialist country, but the leadership would not agree to this" (*Gazeta Robotnicza*, June 15, 1981).

5. *Trybuna Ludu*, August 25, 1980.

6. One account—by Stan Persky (*At the Lenin Shipyard*, pp. 112–14)—claims that the plenum turned critical and lasted six hours mainly because Defense Minister Jaruzelski insisted on a serious debate on the strikes and their causes. There is no public evidence of any role played by Jaruzelski, and the plenum account does not indicate that he even spoke.

7. Tadeusz Pyka had originally been chosen to deal with Gdansk strikers on August 17, but had been replaced with Jagielski on August 21 (*Trybuna Ludu*, August 22, 1980). Barcikowski, named head of the commission to negotiate with strikers in Szczecin, had been chosen precisely because he was somewhat at odds with Gierek, according to his own later version. When asked in a late 1984 interview why he had been selected, he explained that he had resigned as agri-

culture minister in 1977 because "I could not agree with certain agricultural policy decisions adopted by the government" and thereafter had "credentials of protesting against government activity during the second half of the 1970s," and it was felt that "it would be easier for someone like me to negotiate in Szczecin." Moreover, he added, there was no "lineup of persons eager" for this task, so the decision "fell on me." This was included in a collection of interviews with political figures published by Andrzej Kepinski and Zbigniew Kilar as *Kto Jest Kim w Polsce Inaczej* (Who Is Who in Poland, in Another Way), pp. 36–37.

8. Ascherson, *The Polish August*, p. 162.

9. *Ibid.*, p. 183.

10. The detailed "protocol" of the Gdansk agreement appeared in the September 6, 1980 issue of the weekly *Polityka*. *Trybuna Ludu*, on September 2, 1980, carried a long, but somewhat abbreviated description (*omowienie*) with all the essential details. English versions can be found in appendixes to Kevin Ruane's *The Polish Challenge*, Neal Ascherson's *The Polish August*, and Denis Mac-Shane's *Solidarity: Poland's Independent Trade Union*.

11. *Trybuna Ludu*, on September 2, 1980, carried a detailed description of the agreement. Ascherson's book also carries the apparent text of the Szczecin accord.

12. *Trybuna Ludu*, August 29, 1980.

13. *Trybuna Ludu*, September 9, 1980.

14. *Gazeta Krakowska*, April 24–26, 1981.

15. A book published later in the West by former *Gazeta Krakowska* workers described Regucki's liberal role as *Gazeta Krakowska*'s chief editor from 1970 to 1980, his fights with conservative CC Ideology Secretary Jerzy Lukaszewicz, his efforts to report on the 1980 strikes, and his appointment as Kania's aide in October 1980. They claim that Regucki's access to Kania was important for reformers, since he maintained confidential contacts with Solidarity leaders and oppositionists such as Jacek Kuron and Adam Michnik and also arranged for Kania to talk with liberals such as Stefan Bratkowski. *13 Miesiecy i 13 Dni "Gazety Krakowskiej" (1980–1981)* (*Gazeta Krakowska*'s 13 Months and 13 Days), pp. 17–19, 21, 51.

16. The group's conclusions were published in book form in the West in English as *Poland Today: The State of the Republic*. Also see Neal Ascherson's description in *The Polish August*, pp. 125–26.

17. Ascherson, *The Polish August*, pp. 125–26.

18. "Sprawozdanie KC PZPR za okres od VII do VIII zjazdu" (PZPR CC Report for the Period from the 7th to the 8th Congress), *Nowe Drogi*, 1980, no. 3, p. 40.

19. "Sprawozdanie KC PZPR za okres od VIII zjazdu do IX nadzwyczajnego zjazdu PZPR" (PZPR CC Report for the Period from the 8th Congress to the 9th Extraordinary Congress), *Nowe Drogi*, 1981, no. 8, pp. 57–58.

20. "Sprawozdanie CKKP PZPR za okres od VIII zjazdu do IX nadzwyczajnego

zjazdu PZPR" (PZPR Central Party Control Commission Report for the Period from the 8th Congress to the 9th Extraordinary PZPR Congress), *Nowe Drogi*, 1981, no. 8, p. 83.

21. Ascherson, *The Polish August*, pp. 126–27. The PZPR commission established to officially study the causes of the 1980 crisis also stated that there was unusual discontent at the late 1979–early 1980 election meetings and identified this as a warning to Gierek—which he ignored. According to the commission's report, these meetings produced "a unique and strong manifestation of growing criticism within the PZPR" as party members, especially at the lowest level, sharply criticized "declining living standards," economic injustice, a "basic lack of correspondence" between official propaganda and the truth, and violations of intraparty democracy and demanded changes in the system of government and administration. The commission's report (commonly labeled the "Kubiak Report," after commission chairman Hieronim Kubiak) was published in a late 1983 special edition of *Nowe Drogi*.

22. Ascherson, *The Polish August*, pp. 128–29.

23. *Ibid.*, p. 140.

24. Stan Persky, *At the Lenin Shipyard*, p. 71.

25. See Gierek's February 7, 1971 CC plenum speech, carried in Foreign Broadcast Information Service (FBIS), Daily Report, East Europe, February 8, 1971, pp. G28–31, or the description in George Blazynski, *Flashpoint Poland*, pp. 52 and 57. Blazynski describes the halfhearted attempts at democratization in the 1970s, using the label "consensus socialism" for this approach (pp. 38–39, 52–57, 64, 85).

26. See Olszowski's speech at the October 1980 plenum, *Nowe Drogi*, 1980, no. 10–11, p. 134. The longest versions of the speeches at the October plenum are to be found in the October-November issue of the CC journal *Nowe Drogi*. The CC's main newspaper, *Trybuna Ludu*, published shorter versions and on November 6 announced that the "full texts" of the speeches would appear in *Nowe Drogi*.

27. This and the following quotes from the October plenum speeches are from *Nowe Drogi*, 1980, no. 10–11.

28. Foreign Broadcast Information Service (FBIS), Daily Report, East Europe, October 10, 1980. (Hereafter, all references to FBIS will signify the East Europe Daily Report, unless otherwise indicated.)

29. This and the following quotes from Kania's report are from *Nowe Drogi*, 1980, no. 12.

30. The full versions of the speeches at the December plenum were published in *Nowe Drogi*, 1981, no. 1–2. Kania's report to the plenum was carried in the previous issue, however, *Nowe Drogi*, 1980, no. 12.

31. *Nowe Drogi*, 1981, no. 1–2, pp. 23–24.

32. *Ibid.*, pp. 24–25.

33. *Ibid.*, p. 72.

34. In an interview with Gabrys, *Trybuna Robotnicza* on May 4, 1981, stated that this was the first time a worker had become a member of the Politburo. Gabrys indicated that he expected to continue working in the mine between Politburo sessions.

35. The list of members is printed in *Trybuna Ludu*, December 3, 1980.

36. *Nowiny*, November 20, 1980.

37. *Trybuna Robotnicza*, November 18, 1980.

38. *Nowe Drogi*, 1980, no. 12, p. 18.

39. *Nowe Drogi*, 1981, no. 1–2, p. 54.

40. According to CC Organizational Department deputy head Ryszard Lukasiewicz in a discussion in the March 1981 *Zycie Partii*. At the February 1982 plenum Slupsk First Secretary Mieczyslaw Wojcik summed up the anti-apparat attitude: "I know no other party which so stubbornly fights its own apparat" (*Trybuna Ludu*, February 26, 1982).

41. Wlodzimierz Wodecki, "Cadres Policy—Proposals," *Zycie Partii*, February 1981, p. 20. The party unit was one of the working groups of the Gdansk Pre-Congress Commission—a local group working on proposals for the congress.

42. *Gazeta Wspolczesna*, April 28, 1981.

43. *Trybuna Ludu*, July 18–19, 1981.

44. A *Przeglad Tygodniowy* article, April 27, 1986, by Andrzej Malachowski, stated that in 1986 4,500 posts were on the nomenklatura of the Politburo and Secretariat—1,000 less than in the 1970s.

45. Witold Pawlowski in *Polityka*, November 8, 1980. Towimor stands for "Torunskie Zaklady Urzadzen Okretowych"—the Torun Marine Equipment Plant.

46. *Gazeta Krakowska*, April 29, 1981.

47. *Polityka*, November 8, 1980.

48. *Ibid.*; *Gazeta Krakowska*, April 29, 1981.

49. *Gazeta Krakowska*, May 19, 1981.

50. *Gazeta Robotnicza*, May 22–24, 1981.

51. *Gazeta Poludniowa* (Krakow), December 18, 1980.

52. *Gazeta Krakowska*, April 28, 1981.

53. *Trybuna Robotnicza* (Katowice), April 16, 1981.

54. *Trybuna Ludu*, June 4, 1981. *Le Figaro*'s correspondent Bernard Margueritte reported in *Le Figaro*, December 1, 1980, that Torun Consultative Commission chairman Iwanow had been expelled from the party but reinstated by his local party cell. On December 2, *Le Monde*'s Bernard Guetta reported that one of the Torun cell leaders had been expelled the previous week for "factionalism and clericalism."

55. *Trybuna Ludu*, June 4, 1981.

56. *Gazeta Pomorska* (Torun), June 2, 1981.

57. *Nowe Drogi*, 1981, no. 4, p. 88.

58. According to Organizational Department deputy chief Ryszard Lukasiewicz in his April 1981 plenum speech (*Nowe Drogi*, 1981, no. 5–6, pp. 192–93).

59. *Gazeta Wspolczesna* (Bialystok), April 6, 1981.

60. *Nowe Drogi*, 1980, no. 12, pp. 15–16.

61. *Nowe Drogi*, 1981, no. 4, p. 104, or *Trybuna Ludu*, March 30, 1981.

62. *Nowe Drogi*, 1981, no. 4, pp. 133–34.

63. *Gazeta Krakowska*, April 14, 1981.

64. According to reporters at a press conference given by Lukasiewicz (*Gazeta Pomorska*, April 17–20, 1981).

65. Lukasiewicz stated that Kurowski had expressed support at an April 9 conference held by the Organizational Department (*Gazeta Pomorska*, April 17–20, 1981).

66. *Polityka*, April 25, 1981.

67. In the local paper *Gazeta Pomorska*, March 16, 1981.

68. *Gazeta Pomorska*, April 17–20, 1981.

69. *Gazeta Pomorska*, May 18, 1981.

70. Accounts of speeches at the forum in the *New York Times* and *Washington Post* on April 16, 1981, reported demands for freedom of the press, democratization of the party and society, and changes in the leadership, including the resignation of Olszowski.

71. *Nowe Drogi*, 1981, no. 5–6, pp. 192–93. Lukasiewicz's speech was not actually delivered but was included in the protocol. Many of the above comments are omitted from *Trybuna Ludu*'s account, giving a rather different impression of Lukasiewicz's attitude.

72. *Trybuna Ludu*, April 28, 1981.

73. FBIS, April 30, 1981, p. G38.

74. *Trybuna Ludu*, April 30, 1981.

75. Werblan and Labecki had attended the Torun Forum and still defended the movement, while Lukasiewicz came away from it with a more negative attitude.

76. The comments of Zawodzinski, Rakowski, Labecki, Werblan, Maciejewska, Zielinska, and Putrament are from *Nowe Drogi*, 1981, no. 5–6.

77. *Nowe Drogi*, 1981, no. 5–6, p. 70.

78. *Ibid.*, p. 36.

79. *Trybuna Opolska*, May 18, 1981.

80. *Gazeta Krakowska*, May 22–24, 1981.

81. They were criticized by Gorzow First Secretary Ryszard Labus, former Radom First Secretary Janusz Prokopiak, *Trybuna Ludu* commentator Ryszard Wojna, workers Jozef Flaga and Albin Siwak, editor Mieczyslaw Rog-Swiostek, CC Cadres Department chief Kazimierz Rokoszewski, and Central Party Control Commission deputy chairman Jerzy Urbanski.

82. *Nowe Drogi*, 1981, no. 7.

83. *Ibid.*, p. 90. The plenum took a vote on expelling Werblan, but the proposal

was defeated with not one vote in favor (*Trybuna Ludu*, June 11, 1981). Werblan had, however, lost his job as director of the Institute of Basic Problems of Marxism-Leninism. The May 25 *Trybuna Ludu* announced a Politburo decision to appoint a new director after Werblan "asked to be released."

84. *Nowe Drogi*, 1981, no. 7.

85. *Trybuna Ludu*, June 12, 1981.

86. *Trybuna Ludu*, June 5, 1981.

87. *Polityka*, April 25, 1981.

88. *Nowe Drogi*, 1981, no. 5–6, p. 116.

89. *Glos Wybrzeza* (Gdansk), May 5, 1981.

90. *Dziennik Baltycki* (Gdansk), May 6, 1981.

91. *Trybuna Robotnicza* (Katowice), May 22–24, 1981.

92. See chapter 2. Some supporters continued agitating virtually until martial law was declared. *Gazeta Pomorska*, November 6–8, 1981, reported a local Torun meeting where party members were again calling for a second Torun forum of horizontal organizations.

93. CC Secretary Olszowski, questioned about Iwanow in *Sztandar Mlodych*, April 6, 1981, said that Iwanow had submitted an appeal of his expulsion to the coming party congress. Olszowski declared that he backed the control commission's decision and criticized Iwanow for rejecting Marxism-Leninism.

94. *Gazeta Pomorska*, May 29–31, and *Trybuna Ludu*, June 4, 1981.

95. *Gazeta Pomorska*, June 2, 1981.

96. According to *Trybuna Opolska*, June 3, 1981, and *Trybuna Ludu*, June 4, 1981.

97. *Gazeta Pomorska*, May 29–31, 1981, and *Trybuna Ludu*, June 4, 1981.

98. *Gazeta Pomorska*, June 5–7, 1981.

99. *Ibid.*

100. *Gazeta Pomorska*, June 8, 1981.

101. *Gazeta Pomorska*, June 19–21, 1981.

2. REFORM IN ELECTION PROCEDURES

1. *Nowe Drogi*, 1980, no. 10–11, p. 254.

2. Kurowski was head of the Organizational Department from March 1980 until his election as CC secretary in September. He was succeeded as head by his deputy, Andrzej Barzyk, but continued to supervise the department. He cooperated with reformers, even with the horizontal ties movement (see chapter 1).

3. The February 1981 *Zycie Partii*, in identifying the responsibilities of individual CC secretaries, stated that Kurowski supervised the Organizational Department but that Barcikowski also had "general supervision" over the department. It indicated that Kania himself supervised the Cadres Department.

4. *Nowe Drogi*, 1981, no. 1–2.

5. At the plenum Plock worker Antoni Wrobel stated that he had received the

draft of the new rules only two days before the plenum, Lodz worker Janina Zalewska said she had gotten them on November 28, and Lublin worker Jozef Janiszewski said his province committee had gotten a telex of the draft on Thursday, November 27. Wrobel said that he agreed that the draft rules make "real changes deepening democratization of intraparty life," but "when I return from the plenum my colleagues will ask me: With whom did you discuss this document in advance?" (*Nowe Drogi*, 1981, no. 1–2).

6. They were designated "provisional" (*tymczasowy*), the February 1981 *Zycie Partii* explained, because there was still "very lively" debate over changing the party statute (on which the election rules are supposed to be based), and this would only be resolved when the next congress was held. Moreover, the journal stated, the rules must remain provisional because many of the provisions in them are "mutually contradictory" and these problems still had to be worked out.

7. In an interview in *Gazeta Krakowska*, March 12, 1981.

8. *Zycie Partii*, April 1981, p. 9, and Organizational Department deputy chief Ryszard Lukasiewicz in *Trybuna Ludu*, April 2, 1981.

9. As explained by Ryszard Lukasiewicz in *Trybuna Ludu*, April 2, 1981, secret balloting now was to be obligatory for all elections with one exception: If the majority of a party committee wished, it could elect its secretaries by open vote. The rationale for this exception to secret balloting, he explained, is that these secretaries would have already been elected twice by secret ballot, to the party committee and to its Executive Committee. However, this exception was not applicable to the first secretary, who had to be elected by secret ballot.

10. *Trybuna Ludu*, July 21–22, 1981.

11. According to Kurowski's deputy in the Organizational Department, Ryszard Lukasiewicz, in *Trybuna Ludu*, April 2, 1981.

12. Olszowski mentioned this in his speech at the April plenum (*Nowe Drogi*, 1981, no. 5–6, p. 106).

13. *Trybuna Ludu*, February 3, 1981.

14. In a collection of interviews published by Andrzej Kepinski and Zbigniew Kilar as *Kto Jest Kim w Polsce Inaczej*, p. 361.

15. The statute did not appear in *Trybuna Ludu* or *Nowe Drogi* and seems to have been published only in pamphlet form—in a 1981 collection of documents entitled "The 9th Extraordinary Congress of the PZPR" (*IX Nadzwyczajny Zjazd Polskiej Zjednoczonej Partii Robotniczej*) and in a separate pamphlet entitled "The Statute of the Polish United Workers Party" (*Statut Polskiej Zjednoczonej Partii Robotniczej*).

16. According to deputy head of the CC Organizational Department Ryszard Lukasiewicz in *Trybuna Ludu*, April 2, 1981.

17. *Trybuna Robotnicza* (Katowice), November 3, 1980.

18. *Nowe Drogi*, 1981, no. 1–2, p. 127.

19. *Gazeta Poludniowa* (Krakow), December 22, 1980.

20. The Krakow conference was not the first case of such new practices. A

Lodz Polytechnic conference on November 27–28 had also used this pattern: electing its new party committee according to new rules specifying secret balloting and an "unlimited number of candidates" and electing its first secretary and Executive Committee directly at the conference, rather than allowing the school party committee to do this (*Glos Robotniczy* (Lodz), November 29–30, 1980).

21. In five cases, it was not specified in either the *Trybuna Ludu* or local accounts whether secret or open balloting was used. In some cases the local account specified while *Trybuna Ludu* did not. The first province council to elect its chairman by secret ballot was Wroclaw on November 14. At least one city council had already used secret balloting to elect its chairman (Torun on October 30).

22. In fourteen cases the accounts did not specify. The first province council election with two candidates for chairman was Wroclaw on November 14. The October 30 Torun city council election had two candidates, and the November 20 Szczecin city council election had three.

23. *Gazeta Robotnicza* (Wroclaw), November 15–16, 1980; *Slowo Ludu* (Radom), December 6, 1980; *Glos Robotniczy* (Lodz), December 9, 1980.

24. *Nowiny* (Rzeszow), December 19–21, 1980, and *Trybuna Ludu*, December 23, 1980.

25. "Sprawozdanie KC PZPR za okres od VIII Zjazdu do IX Nadzwyczajnego Zjazdu PZPR" (Report of the PZPR CC on the period from the 8th Congress to the 9th Extraordinary PZPR Congress), *Nowe Drogi*, 1981, no. 8, p. 67.

26. Bielsko-Biala, Chelm, Zamosc, Lodz, Siedlce, Legnica, Kielce, Slupsk, Krosno, Jelenia Gora, Warsaw, Nowy Sacz. Szczecin city also elected a non-PZPR chairman.

27. In fifteen cases the press accounts specifically indicated that there was only one candidate. Only occasionally did the press accounts specify the method of voting, and when they did it was open balloting. Occasionally—in at least four cases—the press reported some abstentions, rather than a "unanimous" vote.

28. A contest almost occurred at the December 10 Koszalin plenum. An opposing candidate for first secretary was nominated from the floor, but the candidate (the province *wojewoda* or governor) asked to have his name withdrawn, and so the contest ended before any voting or debate (*Glos Pomorza*, December 11, 1980).

29. The debate turned primarily on the fact that Bialecki was currently an official in another province and some preferred Olsztyn Secretary Mokrzyszczak. Some speakers urged departure "from the practice of entrusting party functions to outsiders," while others argued that Bialecki was not an outsider because he had been associated with Olsztyn since 1947. At the end of the debate, however, Mokrzyszczak spoke and asked to withdraw, saying he "did not yet feel up to leading the province party organization and that he was among those who were convinced that Comrade Bialecki should be first secretary." By a majority of 85 to 7, the plenum decided to hold an open vote, during which 84 voted for Bialecki,

3 against, and 5 abstained (*Gazeta Olsztynska*, January 26, 1981). Unlike the local paper, *Trybuna Ludu*'s January 24–25, 1981 account gave no hint of a contest.

30. *Trybuna Robotnicza* (Katowice and Bielsko-Biala), February 13–15, 1981. This time *Trybuna Ludu*, as well as the local paper, reported that there were two candidates and that secret balloting was used (*Trybuna Ludu*, February 13, 1981).

31. *Slowo Ludu* (Radom), March 17, 1981.

32. Unless secret balloting was used in some of the late 1980 elections for which local papers are not available or where accounts simply failed to report the fact.

33. The February 5 Suwalki and May 17 Szczecin plenums elected their sole candidates for first secretary "unanimously," according to local accounts (*Gazeta Wspolczesna*, February 6–8, 1981, and *Kurier Szczecinski*, May 13, 1981). Szczecin specifically used secret balloting, although reports on Suwalki did not specify. In Przemysl, critics called for a "vote of no confidence" in province First Secretary Zdzislaw Drewniowski and the rest of the Secretariat, all of whom then submitted their resignations. In "secret balloting" at a May 20 plenum, the majority voted to reject the resignations and keep Drewniowski and the other secretaries in their posts (*Trybuna Ludu* and *Nowiny*, May 21, 1981).

34. *Gazeta Olsztynska*, March 30, 1981.

35. For example, at a May 20, 1981 Przemysl plenum reported in *Trybuna Ludu*, May 21, 1981.

36. Charges of corruption or other abuses of position were circulated and played a role in province first secretaries' decisions to resign in Wroclaw (*Gazeta Robotnicza*, October 13, 1980), Tarnow (*Gazeta Poludniowa*, October 30, 1980), Koszalin (*Glos Pomorza*, December 11, 1980), and Radom (*Slowo Ludu*, March 17, 1981).

37. British correspondent Neal Ascherson wrote that strikers in the coal-mining area of Jastrzebie demanded the removal of Katowice First Secretary Zdzislaw Grudzien. Although the demand was not published in the important Jastrzebie accord (signed on September 3), Grudzien was soon replaced as province first secretary and later removed from the Politburo as well (Ascherson, *The Polish August*, p. 177). Later the local party organization voted to expel him from the party (*Trybuna Robotnicza*, February 11, 1981).

Stan Persky writes that workers in Rzeszow demanded the dismissal of province First Secretary Alojzy Kotarba after he had declared that that there was "no need for independent trade unions" and asked them to sign petitions promising not to organize unions free of party and government control (Persky, *At the Lenin Shipyard*, p. 146). Radom First Secretary Janusz Prokopiak, in submitting his resignation at a March 16 province plenum, insisted that he was not "running away in the face of attacks by Solidarity and I do this not because of the accusations against me" (*Slowo Ludu*, March 17, 1981). Bielsko-Biala First Secretary

Jozef Buzinski resigned at a February 12 province plenum in the face of charges by Solidarity that local leaders had mishandled a strike (*Trybuna Robotnicza*, February 13–15, 1981).

38. Kurowski at the October 16 Bydgoszcz plenum (*Gazeta Pomorska*, October 17, 1980).

39. Grabski at the October 29 Tarnow plenum (*Gazeta Poludniowa*, October 30, 1980), the November 7 Szczecin plenum (*Glos Szczecinski*, November 10, 1980), and December 10 Koszalin plenum (*Trybuna Ludu*, December 11, 1980), and Kania at the November 17 Warsaw plenum (*Trybuna Ludu*, November 18, 1980).

40. The *Trybuna Ludu* account, November 18, 1980, of the November 17 Lodz plenum reported CC Secretary Barcikowski presenting the plenum with "the proposal of the Lodz Executive Committee" to elect province Secretary Tadeusz Czechowicz as first secretary, and *Trybuna Ludu* in reporting the November 19 Rzeszow plenum, November 21 Walbrzych plenum, and November 26 Jelenia Gora plenum indicated that the candidate had been proposed by the province Executive Committee and "approved by the Politburo" (*Trybuna Ludu*, November 20, 22–23, and 27, 1980).

41. *Trybuna Ludu*, January 24–25, 1981, and *Trybuna Robotnicza*, February 13–15, 1981.

42. *Slowo Ludu* (Radom), March 17, 1981.

43. *Kurier Szczecinski* (Szczecin), May 13, 1981.

44. Although most had worked in the province in question at some earlier date and had a local tie which could be pointed out.

45. *Gazeta Olsztynska*, January 26, 1981.

46. *Nowe Drogi*, 1981, no. 5–6, p. 102.

47. *Glos Pomorza* (Koszalin), December 11, 1980.

48. *Trybuna Robotnicza* (Katowice-Bielsko-Biala), February 13–15, 1981. Solidarity in October and November had demanded the resignation of the province leadership (*Trybuna Robotnicza*, February 18, 1981), and CC Secretary Barcikowski at the February 9 CC plenum had blamed local leaders for mishandling local strikes and failing to "fully inform" Warsaw about workers' grievances (*Trybuna Ludu*, February 10, 1981). Although the province committee rejected central pressure at the February 12 plenum, it gave some ground a few days later, accepting the resignation of two of the criticized officials at a February 17 plenum (*Trybuna Robotnicza*, February 18, 1981).

49. The 1983 "Kubiak Report"—the report of the commission headed by Hieronim Kubiak to investigate the causes of the 1980 crisis—stated that the October 19–21, 1956 plenum had used secret balloting to elect a new Politburo and Secretariat and that this was the first time ever the CC had used secret balloting.

50. *Trybuna Ludu*, March 30, 1981. It was by no means rare for accounts of a plenum to not claim unanimity—for example, see the *Trybuna Ludu* accounts

of the December 1–2, 1980 and February 9, 1981 plenums—but the implications of these past omissions were unclear.

51. For Labecki's statement, see *Glos Wybrzeza*, April 9, 1981. Edward Pustelnik in his June 1981 plenum speech praised the lone dissenter for "raising his hand against everyone else" (*Nowe Drogi*, 1981, no. 7, p. 84).

52. *Dziennik Baltycki*, March 31, 1981.

53. *Gazeta Pomorska*, June 8, 1981.

54. *Gazeta Krakowska* and *Trybuna Ludu*, April 29, 1981. At the Torun province conference, some delegates led by Torun city First Secretary Waldemar Modrzynski even caucused outside the hall to decide whom to vote for—which caused a storm of protest since it smacked of factionalism (*Gazeta Pomorska*, June 23, 1981).

55. *Gazeta Robotnicza*, April 28, 1981.

56. *Gazeta Olsztynska*, May 8–10, 1981.

57. *Gazeta Pomorska*, June 8, 19–21, and 23, 1981; *Glos Robotniczy*, June 19–21 and 23, 1981; and *Trybuna Ludu*, June 27–29 and July 6, 1981.

58. "Sprawozdanie KC PZPR za okres od VIII Zjazdu do IX Nadzwyczajnego Zjazdu PZPR" (PZPR CC Report on the Period from the 8th Congress to the 9th Extraordinary PZPR Congress), *Nowe Drogi*, 1981, no. 8, p. 60.

59. By the same token, in places there was relatively little turnover. *Gazeta Robotnicza*, April 2, 1981, commented regarding Legnica province that despite the "impatient demands" for elections, when the elections were actually held, few leaders were ousted.

60. *Glos Robotniczy*, April 3–5, 1981.

61. *Glos Pomorza*, April 28, 1981.

62. *Gazeta Pomorska*, May 29–31, 1981.

63. *Glos Robotniczy*, June 4, 1981.

64. *Trybuna Ludu*, June 19, 1981.

65. *Gazeta Krakowska*, April 13 and 14, 1981.

66. *Trybuna Ludu*, June 10, 1981.

67. *Glos Robotniczy*, June 24, 1981.

68. *Trybuna Ludu*, May 23–24, 1981.

69. *Glos Wybrzeza*, May 25 and June 2, 1981.

70. *Gazeta Olsztynska*, April 29, 1981.

71. Even at some of the other twelve conferences (Lodz, Lublin, Tarnow) opposing candidates had been nominated but had refused to run. In Gdansk, the popularity of First Secretary Fiszbach apparently accounted for the lack of any opposition candidate. But while Fiszbach and province Secretary Andrzej Surowiec were reelected, no other members of the Gdansk province Executive Committee were reelected, according to *Dziennik Baltycki*, June 8, 1981.

72. Only the Pila conference, where First Secretary Michal Niedzwiedz was running unopposed, voted to use open balloting.

73. *Gazeta Krakowska*, May 13, 1981.

74. *Trybuna Opolska*, May 18, 1981.

75. *Gazeta Pomorska*, May 29–31 and June 12–14, 1981.

76. *Trybuna Ludu*, June 22, 1981, and *Nowiny*, July 6, 1981.

77. *Gazeta Poznanska*, June 25, 26–28, and 29, 1981.

78. *Gazeta Wspolczesna*, June 22, 1981. A few first secretaries who were not elected delegates were given special permission to run by their province conferences and then were reelected first secretary: Tadeusz Porebski (Wroclaw), Bogdan Gawronski (Kalisz), Wladyslaw Kruk (Lublin), Ludwik Maznicki (Zamosc), and Alfred Walek (Plock).

79. *Sztandar Ludu*, June 29, 1981.

80. *Trybuna Ludu* and *Gazeta Pomorska*, June 29, 1981.

81. *Glos Robotniczy*, June 23 and 24, 1981. For more on the Katowice Forum, see chapter 3.

82. *Gazeta Olsztynska*, June 2, 1981.

83. *Nowiny*, June 19–21, 1981.

84. *Gazeta Robotnicza*, June 24, 1981.

85. *Gazeta Krakowska* (Krakow), June 29, 1981.

86. Delegates questioned Kociolek's role in the bloody 1970 Gdansk put-down of strikers and Kania defended him, testifying that he had been there and seen how Kociolek had opposed the decision to use force. Kania reminded everyone that he had been the "initiator" of the decision to bring back Kociolek from relative obscurity and nominate him for Warsaw first secretary in late 1980. He assured his audience that Kociolek was a firm supporter of renewal and asked his audience to consider their vote on Kociolek "as an act of political confidence" in Kania himself. Skepticism was so strong, however, that Kania had to give yet another speech for Kociolek. Even with Kania staking his reputation on Kociolek, Kociolek only narrowly won reelection: by 247 out of 438 votes (*Zycie Warszawy* and *Trybuna Mazowiecka*, June 29 and 30, 1981).

87. Most of the twenty-four new first secretaries were province-level officials (thirteen) and five were lower-level party officials, but six were total outsiders.

88. Director of agricultural circles in Gizycko and chairman of the province agricultural union of peasant self-aid co-ops in Slupsk, respectively.

89. *Nowiny*, June 19–21, 1981.

90. *Sztandar Ludu*, July 10–12, 1981; *Glos Pomorza*, June 19–21, 1981; *Nowiny*, June 24 and July 6, 1981.

91. *Gazeta Robotnicza*, June 24, 1981. This article also identified him as a member of Solidarity.

92. *Gazeta Poznanska*, July 7, 1981. In 1983, after his removal as province first secretary, Skrzypczak reportedly wrote about his political rise and fall in an underground publication. According to a Radio Free Europe description, he told how as a rank and file party member and engineer at the Cegielski plant he campaigned as a representative of the horizontal ties movement and was elected as first secretary of the plant's party organization in the initial wave of reform

in October 1980. See J. B. de Weydenthal, "The Failure To Reform the Party in Poland," Radio Free Europe, RAD Background Report/18, February 13, 1984.

93. *Gazeta Poznanska*, June 25, 1981.

94. *Ibid.*

95. *Glos Wybrzeza* (Gdansk), September 14, 1981. In his 1983 underground memoirs, Skrzypczak said he was working to introduce pluralism into the system and that he had "good relations" with Solidarity. J. B. de Weydenthal, "The Failure To Reform the Party in Poland."

96. Tadeusz Kolodziejczyk, *Zycie Partii*, 1981, no. 9, pp. 5–6.

97. Some rules were a little flexible, allowing some outsiders to run.

98. The traditional branch trade unions, the rivals to Solidarity.

99. *Gazeta Olsztynska*, May 25, 1981.

100. According to a June 25 AFP (French Press Agency) English-language report, the vote was 214 to 202, with 70 abstentions (FBIS, June 26, 1981, p. G5). The following account of the conference is from *Gazeta Poznanska*, June 25, 26–28, and 29, 1981.

101. The June 25 AFP report quoted Grabski as calling the vote *amok wyborczy* (election run amok). See FBIS, June 26, 1981, p. G5. *Polityka*, July 4, 1981, also quoted Grabski complaining about "amok wyborczy," although apparently in reference to the whole election campaign, not just Poznan.

102. According to *Trybuna Ludu*, June 25, 1981, there was a second vote (this time, an open vote) after Grabski's appeal, but it reaffirmed the first vote, and, according to the paper, the conference reached an "impasse."

103. *Trybuna Robotnicza*, June 26–28, 1981.

104. *Gazeta Krakowska*, June 26–28, 1981.

105. *Trybuna Robotnicza*, June 26–28, 1981. Deputy Defense Minister Mieczyslaw Obiedzinski, though not included among those recommended by the Politburo, was elected a delegate from Katowice—the only outsider.

106. *Gazeta Krakowska*, June 29, 1981.

107. *Gazeta Krakowska*, June 26–28, 1981. Kakol had also taken a hard line in his April CC plenum speech.

108. *Glos Robotniczy*, June 19–21, 1981.

109. The following account is mainly from *Gazeta Pomorska*, June 29, 1981.

110. *Gazeta Robotnicza*, June 17–18, 1981.

111. *Gazeta Pomorska*, June 19–21, 1981.

112. *Gazeta Wspolczesna*, June 25, 1981.

113. *Trybuna Mazowiecka*, June 22, 1981.

114. *Gazeta Robotnicza*, June 17–18, 1981.

115. *Gazeta Lubuska*, June 15, 1981.

116. *Gazeta Lubuska*, June 22, 1981.

117. *Gazeta Olsztynska*, June 1, 1981.

118. Anna Sabbat in a July 29, 1981 Radio Free Europe report (RAD Background Report, 214, p. 7) characterized Jaskiernia as an "outspoken Jagellonian

University lecturer who ousted a colorless apparatchik" as chairman of the Socialist Polish Youth Union in April 1981.

119. Kania got 365 of about 389 votes, Rakowski 328, Klasa 222 (*Gazeta Krakowska*, June 15, 1981). *Gazeta Krakowska* reporters lobbied hard to persuade undecided delegates to vote for Kania, Klasa, Rakowski, and province First Secretary Dabrowa, according to their account in *13 Miesiecy i 13 Dni "Gazety Krakowskiej"* (*1980–1981*), p. 52.

120. *Trybuna Ludu*, June 12, 1981.

121. *Ibid.* The "passive right of election" (*bierne prawo wyborcze*) means the right to be nominated.

122. *Nowe Drogi*, 1981, no. 7, p. 119.

123. *Dziennik Baltycki*, May 18, 1981.

124. *Trybuna Ludu*, June 8, 1981.

125. *Trybuna Ludu* and *Gazeta Krakowska*, June 8, 1981. *Gazeta Krakowska* reported that Ney was elected in a secret vote by 98 votes out of 115 valid votes. Although most delegates to the congress were elected at province conferences, 365 were elected directly at conferences in big factory or school party conferences, such as this one. Ney told *Gazeta Krakowska*, May 21, 1981, that "only comrade Fiszbach and myself" among top leaders chose to run starting at the bottom.

126. *Gazeta Krakowska*, May 21, 1981.

127. *Gazeta Krakowska*, May 18, 1981.

128. *Gazeta Krakowska*, June 16, 1981.

129. *Trybuna Ludu*, May 30–31, 1981.

130. *Gazeta Krakowska*, April 29 and 30, 1981.

131. *Gazeta Krakowska*, April 30, 1981.

132. *Ibid.*

133. *Kurier Szczecinski*, June 1, 1981.

134. *Trybuna Ludu* and *Kurier Szczecinski*, May 25, 1981.

135. *Trybuna Ludu* and *Kurier Szczecinski*, June 1, 1981.

136. *Nowe Drogi*, 1981, no. 7, pp. 42–43.

137. *Ibid.*, p. 85.

138. *Trybuna Ludu*, June 15, 1981.

139. Warsaw television, April 10, FBIS, April 13, 1981, p. G47.

140. *Trybuna Ludu*, May 7, 1981.

141. *Trybuna Ludu*, June 15, 1981.

142. *Gazeta Krakowska*, June 15, 1981.

143. *Ibid.*

144. Including Deputy Premier Rakowski, CC Secretary Ney, CC Press Department head Klasa, province First Secretary Dabrowa, *Gazeta Krakowska* editor Szumowski, Jagiellonian University sociology professor Hieronim Kubiak, steel plant first secretary Kazimierz Miniur, and youth leader Jerzy Jaskiernia.

145. *Trybuna Ludu*, June 13–14, 1981; *Glos Wybrzeza* and *Dziennik Baltycki*, June 15, 1981.

146. *Gazeta Olsztynska*, June 1, 1981.

147. *Gazeta Krakowska*, June 22, 1981.

148. *Gazeta Poznanska*, June 29, 1981.

149. *Slowo Ludu*, June 19–21, 1981.

150. *Trybuna Ludu*, June 16, 1981.

151. *Trybuna Ludu*, June 17–18, 1981.

152. *Trybuna Robotnicza*, June 26–28, 1981.

153. *Trybuna Ludu*, June 26, 1981, and *Trybuna Robotnicza*, June 26–28, 1981. Zabinski did not start at the province level. *Trybuna Robotnicza*, on June 15 reported that he was elected a delegate to the province conference at the Wodzislaw local conference. It is not clear whether he was elected in his home primary party organization, however.

154. *Trybuna Ludu*, *Trybuna Mazowiecka*, and *Zycie Warszawy*, June 29 and 30, 1981.

155. *Glos Robotniczy*, June 23, 1981.

156. An early July Katowice Forum statement, reported by East Germany's ADN International Service on July 4 (FBIS, July 6, 1981, p. G36), mentioned Bratkowski's unsuccessful bid for election at the Warsaw conference.

157. According to a June 29 PAP broadcast (FBIS, June 30, 1981, pp. G8–9). While this broadcast said that Gabrys had been defeated in his home party organization, another broadcast, on June 12 (FBIS, June 16, 1981, p. G9), reported that he had been elected a delegate to the Katowice province conference from the city conference in his hometown of Chorzow. *Gazeta Krakowska*, on June 29, 1981, reported that Gabrys had been defeated for delegate to the congress at the June 28 Katowice province conference.

158. The conference voted (with 4 abstentions) to let Waszczuk run (*Sztandar Ludu*, June 17–18, 1981), but then did not elect him (*Trybuna Ludu*, June 19, 1981).

159. *Trybuna Ludu* and *Trybuna Opolska*, June 15, 1981.

160. John Darnton wrote in the *New York Times*, July 2, 1981, that at his Ursus Tractor Plant Wronski "was called a party hack who had not been on the assembly line in years."

161. *Trybuna Opolska*, May 18, 1981.

162. The first secretaries of Wloclawek, Chelm, Biala Podlaska, Suwalki, Piotrkow Trybunalski, and Gorzow were not elected delegates.

163. No incumbent CC members were elected by 24 provinces, while 14 provinces elected neither any CC members nor even candidate members.

164. FBIS, July 1, 1981, p. G1.

165. At the February 1980 congress, 294 of the roughly 1,800 delegates were elected at factory party organization conferences (*Zycie Partii*, February 1980).

166. Many plant committee secretaries were also identified as workers and could be classified in that category also. A rough count of delegates identified in

Trybuna Ludu indicates about 460 workers, 184 farmers, 205 factory and school committee secretaries, and 151 city and village committee secretaries.

167. The report of Mandate Commission Chairman General Wojciech Baranski at the congress. Warsaw radio, July 14, FBIS, July 15, 1981, p. G33.

168. *Gazeta Zachodnia*, May 22–24 and May 25, 1981. A "Poznan Forum of Communists" also arose, but it was clearly conservative. *Polityka*, July 4, 1981, said that this forum had set itself the goal "of opposing the nihilistic current in evaluating the past ten years and the total negation of the achievements of people's Poland." At a July 9 meeting, speakers called for ideological aggressiveness and a "resolute struggle against antisocialist elements" (*Gazeta Poznanska*, July 10–12, 1981). The conservative Katowice Forum, recognizing a sympathetic group, sent a message of "warm greetings" and support to the Poznan Forum of Communists; *Trybuna Ludu*, July 8, 1981. Representatives of the Poznan Forum attended a Katowice Forum meeting on July 10. Warsaw radio, July 10, PAP, July 11, FBIS, July 13, 1981, pp. G32–33.

169. In Lodz's *Glos Robotniczy*, May 21, 1981.

170. *Glos Robotniczy*, May 13, 1981.

171. *Glos Robotniczy*, May 25, 1981.

172. *Sztandar Ludu*, May 21, 1981.

173. The Glogow organization was regarded as radical. *Gazeta Robotnicza* on June 24, 1981, reported that hard-liner Siwak had accused the non-communist opposition group KOR of buying off the Glogow steel mill party organization.

174. *Gazeta Robotnicza*, May 18, 1981.

3. FACTIONS' STRUGGLE FOR CONTROL

1. *Nowe Drogi*, 1981, no. 3, pp. 78–83, or the abridged version in *Trybuna Ludu*, February 11, 1981.

2. *Trybuna Opolska*, May 18, 1981.

3. *Nowe Drogi*, 1981, no. 3, pp. 83–86, or *Trybuna Ludu*, February 11, 1981.

4. *Nowe Drogi*, 1981, no. 3, pp. 68–71, or *Trybuna Ludu*, February 11, 1981.

5. *Gazeta Wspolczesna*, April 3–5, 1981. In this interview he also indicated his reform sympathies by urging further liberalization of the party election rules, for example, by dropping the 50 percent limit on having more candidates than positions to fill.

6. The Bydgoszcz police apparently resented being misused or cast as the villains in this incident. At the early June 1981 Bydgoszcz city party conference Bydgoszcz city police chief Maciej Zegarowski read a letter from fifty Bydgoszcz policemen protesting central political leaders' misuse of the police for "harmful purposes," and the letter was published in *Gazeta Pomorska*, June 8, 1981. Zegarowski was subsequently fired by his police superiors. *Fakty*, July 4, 1981, as cited in a July 29, 1981 Radio Free Europe report: Anna Sabbat, "Poland's Extraordinary Ninth Party Congress, Part I," RAD Background Report 214, pp. 9–10.

7. Warsaw radio broadcasts on March 22 reported Jaruzelski arriving that

day in Silesia and reviewing Warsaw pact military exercises (FBIS, March 23, 1981, pp. AA1, AA3). He was back in Warsaw on March 23, delivering a speech at a meeting with an agricultural group, according to March 23 Warsaw broadcasts (FBIS, March 23, 1981, pp. G16–17). *Le Figaro* on March 25 reported that Moczar was in the hospital with a heart attack (FBIS, March 31, 1981, p. G24).

8. *Nowiny*, April 6, 1981.

9. *Gazeta Krakowska*, April 9, 1981.

10. *Gazeta Krakowska*, April 6, 1981.

11. The Bratkowski letter was never published in the central press, but the Wroclaw paper *Gazeta Robotnicza* on March 25, 1981, and the Polish Press Agency Maritime Press Service on March 29 (FBIS, March 31, 1981, pp. G39–40) reported the letter's contents in full, and excerpts from it were reported in the West. *Le Monde*, March 25, 1981, FBIS, March 26, 1981, pp. G10–11, and Hong Kong AFP in English, March 25, FBIS, March 25, 1981, pp. G11–12.

12. Olszowski headed the Congress Commission's Secretariat, as he himself noted at the April plenum (*Nowe Drogi*, 1981, no. 5–6, p. 106). Warsaw radio on April 16 mentioned that he was "directing the work of the Secretariat of the Congress Commission" (FBIS, April 17, 1981, p. G13).

13. Warsaw radio, April 3, FBIS, April 6, 1981, pp. G22–24. A shorter version of these remarks also appeared in the youth paper *Sztandar Mlodych*, April 6, 1981.

14. According to conservative writer and editor Jerzy Putrament's speech at the March CC plenum (*Nowe Drogi*, 1981, no. 4, pp. 72–73).

15. *Trybuna Ludu* on February 17, 1981, reported a meeting of Grabski's team (*zespol*) for social policy.

16. *Trybuna Ludu*, April 13, 1981.

17. *Nowe Drogi*, 1981, no. 4, pp. 102, 104.

18. *Ibid.*, p. 111.

19. *Ibid.*, pp. 137–38.

20. Warsaw radio, March 29, FBIS, March 30, 1981, p. G13.

21. *Gazeta Krakowska*, April 30, 1981.

22. *Gazeta Wspolczesna*, April 6, 1981.

23. *Nowe Drogi*, 1981, no. 4, p. 128.

24. *Trybuna Ludu*, March 30, 1981. According to *Dziennik Baltycki* (Gdansk), March 31, 1981, one CC member abstained in the vote on this action.

25. *Gazeta Krakowska*, April 6, 1981.

26. *Gazeta Krakowska*, April 24–26, 1981.

27. *Gazeta Pomorska*, March 31, 1981.

28. *Glos Wybrzeza*, March 31, 1981.

29. *Zycie Warszawy*, April 3, 1981.

30. *Gazeta Krakowska*, April 6, 1981.

31. *Trybuna Ludu*, April 9, 1981.

32. *Trybuna Ludu*, March 30, 1981.

33. Warsaw television, April 3, FBIS, April 6, 1981, p. G7.

34. *Glos Wybrzeza*, March 30, 1981.

35. For the Kostrzewska, Blajet, Nowakowska, Bryk, and Dabrowa speeches, see *Nowe Drogi*, 1981, no. 4, pp. 86, 91–92, 42, 85, 89. For other criticisms of the official position, see the *Nowe Drogi* versions of the speeches of Kalisz worker Wojciech Jarecki, Slupsk worker Stefania Paruzel, Gdansk shipyard worker Henryk Lewandowski, director of a Wroclaw scientific laboratory Wlodzimierz Trzebiatowski, Warsaw factory director Jerzy Bielecki, Warsaw worker Zygmunt Gajewski, Gorzow worker Antoni Pierz, and *Chlopska Droga* editor Mieczyslaw Rog-Swiostek. The quotations from plenum speeches in the following paragraphs are also from *Nowe Drogi*, no. 4.

36. *Glos Robotniczy*, April 10–12, 1981.

37. Rakowski chided Bednarski for just "limiting himself" to generalizations about the events instead of talking about the "unpleasant truth."

38. *Sztandar Mlodych*, March 31, 1981.

39. *Nowiny*, April 6, 1981.

40. *Trybuna Ludu*, March 30, 1981.

41. *Trybuna Ludu*, April 13, 1981.

42. *Sztandar Mlodych*, April 6, 1981.

43. *Gazeta Krakowska*, April 6, 1981.

44. The text was published in *Nowe Drogi*, 1981, no. 4, along with the other plenum speeches, both delivered and not delivered. See p. 155.

45. Tarnow First Secretary Stanislaw Opalko told *Gazeta Krakowska*, April 9, 1981, that after three Politburo members had resigned, the plenum had recessed and the Politburo met. Afterward, he said, Kania announced that there was no discord in the Politburo and therefore no need for resignations.

46. *Trybuna Ludu*, on March 30, in briefly describing Szymanski's resolution, added that First Secretary Kania "shared the view" expressed in the resolution.

47. *Trybuna Ludu*, March 31, 1981.

48. *Gazeta Krakowska*, March 31, 1981.

49. See his interview in the Gdansk paper *Glos Wybrzeza*, April 9, 1981.

50. Kania in an April 2 factory speech claimed that only one had abstained or voted against the resolution (Warsaw television, April 3, FBIS, April 6, 1981, p. G7), and Szymanski told *Trybuna Robotnicza*, April 6, 1981, that only one had voted against the resolution, and "all others voted for it" despite "various kinds of fabrications and rumors." The vote apparently was open, by show of hands. Edward Pustelnik in his June plenum speech praised the lone dissenter's courage in "raising his hand against everyone else" (*Nowe Drogi*, 1981, no. 7, p. 84).

51. *Dziennik Baltycki* (Gdansk), March 31, 1981.

52. PAP Maritime Service, April 5, FBIS, April 6, 1981, pp. G20–21.

53. *Glos Wybrzeza*, March 31, 1981.

54. Warsaw radio, April 9, FBIS, April 10, 1981, p. G10.

55. From portions of his speech published in the Krakow paper *Gazeta Krakowska*, April 15, 1981. A version of his remarks also was carried on Warsaw radio on April 9. See FBIS, April 10, 1981, p. G3.

56. Warsaw radio, April 9, FBIS, April 10, 1981, p. G12.

57. *Sztandar Mlodych*, April 6, 1981.

58. *Trybuna Ludu*, April 13, 1981.

59. At a Wloclawek party aktiv meeting (*Trybuna Ludu*, April 2, 1981, and *Gazeta Pomorska*, April 3–5, 1981), at an April 3 journalists' meeting in neighboring Bydgoszcz (*Gazeta Pomorska*, April 3–5, 1981), and in interviews in the April 6 Katowice paper *Trybuna Robotnicza* and April 7 Warsaw youth paper *Sztandar Mlodych*.

60. *Sztandar Mlodych*, April 7, 1981.

61. *Trybuna Robotnicza* on April 6, 1981, and *Sztandar Mlodych* on April 7, 1981.

62. *Trybuna Robotnicza*, April 6, 1981.

63. *Gazeta Pomorska*, April 3–5, 1981.

64. *Ibid.*

65. *Trybuna Ludu*, April 30, 1981.

66. The Politburo met on April 14 to discuss the new statute, and the Congress Commission met on April 16 to hear Kurowski give a detailed report on the statute (*Trybuna Ludu*, April 17, 1981).

67. For example, *Gazeta Krakowska* on April 15 published a local resolution, endorsed by Krakow's pre-congress commission, calling for extensive changes in the Politburo, including the immediate addition of ten workers representing party organizations at big industrial enterprises.

68. Radio broadcasters working in a studio in the CC building periodically broadcast reports on the contents of the speeches being delivered. An April 30 Warsaw broadcast stated that this was the "first time" there had been such reporting on a CC plenum—periodic live reports from the CC building covering the entire twenty hours that the plenum lasted (FBIS, April 30, 1981, p. G35).

69. *Nowe Drogi*, 1981, no. 5–6, p. 115.

70. See the speeches of Warsaw worker Zygmunt Wronski, Lodz worker Halina Zielinska, Zielona Gora worker Stanislaw Gierczyk, Torun worker Henryk Bieniaszewski, as well as Piotrkow First Secretary Stanislaw Skladowski, and Bielsko-Biala First Secretary Andrzej Gdula (*ibid.*).

71. Tarnobrzeg worker Boleslaw Drozdz and Legnica worker Genowefa Maciejewska (*ibid.*).

72. *Trybuna Ludu*, April 30, 1981.

73. *Trybuna Ludu*, on April 30, 1981, announced the results of votes on these resignations: Pinkowski's was accepted with 5 abstentions, Wojtaszek's with 1 against and 6 abstentions, Zielinski's with 1 abstention, and Wojtecki's was accepted unanimously.

74. According to CC Secretary Barcikowski (*Trybuna Ludu*, May 6, 1981).

75. In this speech he recalled bitterly how workers at his plant "made a hero" out of dissident Jan Narozniak when he visited: "The whole factory and my shop went out to greet him, but I stayed by myself" in my shop (*Nowe Drogi*, 1981, no. 3, p. 72). The Ursus plant was one of the strongholds of Solidarity, and Wronski clearly was out of step with sentiment at the plant.

76. Gabrys had been chosen for the honor of nominating Gierek for first secretary at the February 1980 congress, but in a *Trybuna Robotnicza* interview, May 4, 1981, he played this down as simply an "assignment" from the CC. In the interview he was noncommital on most subjects, even on the horizontal movement and strikes.

77. *Nowe Drogi*'s version of Rakowski's speech has him refuting conservative construction worker Albin Siwak's allegation that Rakowski had "made some sort of financial decision in favor of Solidarity and against the construction workers" and also assailing Kazimierz Kakol's attacks on past Rakowski press articles (*Nowe Drogi*, 1981, no. 5–6, p. 86). These statements were not included in *Trybuna Ludu*'s account.

78. According to CC Secretary Waszczuk at a Legnica meeting reported in *Trybuna Ludu*, April 25–26, 1981.

79. Soviet concern was demonstrated again by an April 23 visit by CPSU CC Secretary Suslov, who met Olszowski and Grabski as well as Kania.

80. *Sztandar Mlodych*, May 28, 1981. The forum's statements included a mid-May declaration and four resolutions, plus a later (May 28) attack on a Krakow party organization and a letter supporting conservative worker Siwak in his feud with Solidarity.

81. According to Michael Dobbs in the *Washington Post*, June 3, 1981.

82. *Trybuna Opolska* (Opole) and *Gazeta Krakowska*, June 1, 1981.

83. *Sztandar Mlodych*, May 29–31, 1981.

84. *Glos Robotniczy*, June 4, 1981.

85. According to *Glos Wybrzeza*, June 1, 1981.

86. The Soviet press agency TASS picked this up and reported that Gabrys was the forum's chairman (*Pravda*, June 2, 1981).

87. *Gazeta Krakowska*, June 1, 1981.

88. *Trybuna Ludu*, June 4, 1981.

89. While identifying himself with the Politburo stand, he also indicated some sympathy for the forum, complaining about vicious attacks on it and that liberal forums were not subordinating themselves to party orders as the Katowice Forum was (*Nowe Drogi*, 1981, no. 7, p. 51). Zabinski's Katowice paper *Trybuna Robotnicza* prominently reported that the Politburo had called the forum's activity "harmful" (June 3) and also that Katowice's delegates to the congress had met and condemned the forum and had called on the province committee to cut off any aid to the forum (June 3).

90. *Nowe Drogi*, 1981, no. 7, pp. 71–72.

91. *Ibid.*, p. 121.

92. According to the June 3 *Trybuna Ludu* announcement of the Politburo meeting.

93. *Nowe Drogi*, 1981, no. 7, p. 124.

94. He denied *Gazeta Krakowska* charges that he was linked to the forum but declared that the forum was right on many things and thanked it for support (*Nowe Drogi*, 1981, no. 7, pp. 89–90).

95. Reported in the local paper *Gazeta Pomorska* on June 1, 1981.

96. *Nowe Drogi*, 1981, no. 7, pp. 33–34.

97. *Ibid.*, pp. 35–37.

98. For example, at the April plenum he was called upon to explain a dispute between Solidarity and the old trade unions (*Nowe Drogi*, 1981, no. 5–6, pp. 133–34).

99. *Nowe Drogi*, 1981, no. 7, p. 40.

100. *Ibid.*, pp. 46–47.

101. *Ibid.*, pp. 96–97. Kusiak also attacked Rakowski and got into a personal exchange with Barcikowski (*ibid.*, pp. 97–98).

102. *Ibid.*, pp. 106, 108.

103. *Trybuna Ludu*, June 12, 1981.

104. Director of the Institute of Economic Sciences Jozef Pajestka and Lodz worker Jadwiga Nowakowska.

105. *Nowe Drogi*, 1981, no. 7, pp. 76–80.

106. *Ibid.*, p. 81.

107. *Ibid.*, pp. 84, 87.

108. *Ibid.*, p. 102.

109. *Ibid.*, pp. 123–24.

110. *Ibid.*, pp. 121–22.

111. *Ibid.*, p. 122.

112. *Trybuna Ludu*, June 11, 1981.

113. *Washington Post*, June 11, 1981.

114. FBIS, June 11, 1981, p. G13.

115. *Trybuna Ludu*, June 11, 1981.

116. FBIS, June 11, 1981, p. G13.

117. *Trybuna Ludu*, June 11, 1981. The *New York Times* on June 11 reported that the CC had voted twice on this, the first time 17 to 50 against and on the repeat vote 22 to 79 against.

118. *Nowe Drogi*, 1981, no. 7, pp. 49–51. He indicated his continuing conservative leanings by declaring that while "dogmatism is a flu or cold for the party, revisionism is a cancer."

119. *Gazeta Robotnicza*, June 15, 1981.

120. *Gazeta Krakowska*, April 22, 1981.

121. *Gazeta Krakowska*, April 24–26, 1981.

122. Szumowski was a reform leader in Krakow. A reporter on Krakow tel-

evision, he led a September 11 meeting of Krakow journalists which drafted a letter demanding that journalists no longer just act as agents for the party. Departing *Gazeta Krakowska* editor Regucki asked *Gazeta Krakowska* workers whom they wished as new chief editor, and the majority asked for Szumowski, who was given the job. According to his former coworkers, Szumowski introduced a whole new approach to reporting, insisting on objective truth and often ignoring information and instructions from central authorities: *13 Miesiecy i 13 Dni "Gazety Krakowskiej"* (1980–1981), pp. 20–22. *Gazeta Krakowska*, April 22, 1981, mentions Szumowski and Klasa being on the same side in a conflict in the 1970s. The paper had the name *Gazeta Poludniowa* (Southern Gazette) when Szumowski took over in the fall of 1980. He changed it back to its earlier, traditional name of *Gazeta Krakowska* at the end of December.

123. In an interview in the May 14 *Gazeta Robotnicza*, Szumowski flatly declared that the official version of Bydgoszcz events "turned out to be false." The paper also often presented political material in a manner objectionable to conservatives. For example, in reporting the June plenum it printed excerpts from the Grabski and Barcikowski speeches—including Barcikowski's attack on Grabski—side by side on page 1. At the Leszno party conference, Grabski assailed the press for manipulating reports of the June plenum speeches to set him and Barcikowski against one another (*Trybuna Ludu*, June 15, 1981).

124. *Gazeta Krakowska*, May 22–24, 1981. *Gazeta Krakowska* reporters later explained in a book published in the West that Olszowski's accusation that the paper was the curia's organ had not originally included the caveat "jokingly" but that he had insisted on adding that when he subsequently checked the *Gazeta Krakowska* report. *13 Miesiecy i 13 Dni "Gazety Krakowskiej"* (1980–1981), p. 47.

125. *Gazeta Krakowska* reporters later in a book published abroad argued that *Gazeta Krakowska* was not protected by Dabrowa and that Dabrowa frequently attacked the paper in private, even if not in public. *13 Miesiecy i 13 Dni "Gazety Krakowskiej"* (1980–1981), pp. 53, 70.

126. *Nowe Drogi*, 1981, no. 7, p. 47.

127. *Ibid.*, p. 97.

128. *Ibid.*, p. 121.

129. *Ibid.*, pp. 141–42.

130. *Trybuna Ludu*, June 11, 1981. Klasa's last act as head of the CC's Press Department, according to *Gazeta Krakowska* reporters in a book published in the West, was to block hard-liners' efforts to prevent PAP from circulating full information on the June plenum. *13 Miesiecy i 13 Dni "Gazety Krakowskiej"* (1980–1981), p. 51.

131. *Gazeta Robotnicza*, June 19–21, 1981. Tokarski had been chief editor of the pictorial magazine *Perspektywy* for the past nine years and was editor of papers in Poznan from the 1960s to the early 1970s. As editor in Poznan, he had worked under Olszowski, who was Poznan propaganda secretary until 1963, and Barcikowski, who was Poznan first secretary from 1968 to 1971.

Although Klasa's removal was not announced in *Trybuna Ludu*, Rakowski's magazine *Polityka* on June 20 and *Gazeta Krakowska* on June 25 ran special items calling attention to his removal. After his removal, Klasa thanked the Krakow party organization and *Gazeta Krakowska* for their support, saying that "without it I certainly would not have been able for ten months to hold the post of director of the CC Press, Radio, and Television Department" (*Gazeta Krakowska*, July 21–22, 1981). Klasa told *Zycie Warszawy* that he had resigned because of the "totally negative appraisal of the press, radio, and television voiced in the debate at the 11th plenum," specifically in the speeches of Grabski, Prokopiak, Kusiak, and Deputy Defense Minister Sawczuk. Warsaw PAP English, July 11, FBIS, July 13, 1981, p. G34.

132. *Gazeta Lubuska*, June 22, 1981.

133. *Kurier Polski* chief editor Cezar Lezenski was replaced on July 8; see the July 18 *Polityka* and also the July 13 *Kurier Polski* account of his July 10 farewell ceremony.

134. The February 1981 *Zycie Partii* had listed Olszowski in charge of the CC's Press, Radio, and Television Department and Ideological-Education Work Department, the Higher School of Social Sciences, and Center for Party Courses and of two lesser publications, *Zagadnienia i Materialy* and *Ideologia i Polityka*. It listed CC Secretary Waszczuk in charge of the CC Culture Department and the CC's main journal, *Nowe Drogi*. It did not mention *Trybuna Ludu*, but Waszczuk apparently supervised the party's main paper, since he had supervised the installation of *Trybuna Ludu*'s new chief editor in September 1980.

135. His list of Olszowski's responsibilities was exactly the same as the February *Zycie Partii* list except that it dropped the two minor publications and added *Trybuna Ludu* and *Nowe Drogi*. Thus, Olszowski took over the publications supervised by Waszczuk, who was defeated during the pre-congress elections.

136. *Trybuna Robotnicza*, June 26–28, 1981.

137. *Trybuna Mazowiecka*, June 29 and 30, 1981.

138. *Nowe Drogi*, 1981, no. 7, p. 79.

139. *Gazeta Krakowska*, May 22–24, 1981.

140. *Gazeta Robotnicza*, June 1, 1981.

141. *Trybuna Ludu*, May 22, 1981.

142. *Gazeta Robotnicza*, June 16, 1981.

143. As summarized in *Glos Robotniczy*, June 23, 1981.

144. *Slowo Ludu*, June 19–21, 1981.

145. *Trybuna Ludu*, June 15, 1981.

146. *Trybuna Ludu*, June 29, 1981.

4. THE UNCONTROLLED CONGRESS

1. Henryk Sroczynski in *Glos Robotniczy* (Lodz), July 15, 1981.

2. Sroczynski in *Glos Robotniczy*, July 24–26, 1981.

3. T. Kwasniewski in *Sztandar Ludu*, July 24–26, 1981.

4. Kwasniewski, *Sztandar Ludu*, July 24–26, 1981.

5. Henryk Galus in *Glos Wybrzeza* (Gdansk), July 15, 1981, and Sroczynski in *Glos Robotniczy*, July 15, 1981. Journalists had to go through two checks before they could get into the lobbies, according to Sroczynski, *Glos Robotniczy*, July 24–26, 1981. According to *Gazeta Krakowska*, July 15, 1981, a resolution by reporters asked to be allowed "to observe the congress from the highest balconies in the Congress Hall." It is not clear if this was allowed.

6. *Gazeta Robotnicza* (Wroclaw), July 16, 1981.

7. Ryszard Fedorowski in *Trybuna Robotnicza* (Katowice), July 20, 1981; Jerzy Glebocki in *Slowo Ludu* (Kielce-Radom), July 20, 1981; Maria Adamiecka in *Gazeta Robotnicza* (Wroclaw), July 20, 1981.

8. According to Jerzy Glebocki in *Slowo Ludu*, July 20, 1981.

9. Sroczynski in *Glos Robotniczy*, July 24–26, 1981.

10. Fedorowski in the July 20, 1981 *Trybuna Robotnicza* and Sroczynski in the July 24–26, 1981 *Glos Robotniczy*.

11. According to Sroczynski in the July 15, 1981 *Glos Robotniczy*. Television coverage of the congress was extensive. According to the July 16, 1981 *Glos Robotniczy* and *Kurier Szczecinski*, a spokesman for the State Commitee for Radio and Television said that the first television channel would broadcast seven hours, twenty-three minutes on the congress' first day, and channel 2 would broadcast three and a half hours. He said that the number of reports was limited "exclusively by technical considerations." He noted that there were 320 persons, including 50 journalists and 100 technical personnel, accredited at the congress from Polish television. One radio station would broadcast "nonstop," he said.

12. *Gazeta Robotnicza*, July 16, 1981.

13. *Glos Robotniczy*, July 15, 1981. Wroclaw's *Gazeta Robotnicza* on July 16 reported that 115 had voted in favor, and also that another 118 had abstained.

14. Fedorowski in *Trybuna Robotnicza*, July 20, 1981, and Sroczynski in *Glos Robotniczy*, July 24–26, 1981.

15. Fedorowski in *Trybuna Robotnicza*, July 18–19, 1981, described how his province's delegates came out after the announcement of the stunning results of the vote for CC members and told him the details.

16. *13 Miesiecy i 13 Dni "Gazety Krakowskiej" (1980–1981)*, pp. 55–57.

17. *Glos Robotniczy*, July 18–19, 1981.

18. *Sztandar Mlodych*, July 16, 1981.

19. *Gazeta Robotnicza*, July 17, 1981.

20. *Gazeta Robotnicza*, July 16, 1981.

21. *Gazeta Krakowska*, July 27, 1981.

22. *Gazeta Olsztynska* (Olsztyn), July 24–26, 1981.

23. *Trybuna Ludu*, July 18–19, 1981.

24. *Ibid.*

25. *Gazeta Olsztynska*, July 24–26, 1981.

26. *Gazeta Krakowska*, July 27, 1981.

27. Some exceptions: General Jan Pirog, rather than Lublin First Secretary and Politburo candidate member Kruk, was chairman of the Lublin delegation (*Sztandar Ludu*, July 6, 1981), and Walbrzych province Secretary Roman Norbert, rather than First Secretary Jozef Nowak, chaired the Walbrzych delegation (*Gazeta Robotnicza*, July 13, 1981).

28. *Trybuna Robotnicza*, July 2, 1981, reported the election of a secretariat for the Katowice province delegation. The Zielona Gora delegation elected a seven-member presidium (*Gazeta Lubuska*, June 26–28, 1981). The Kielce delegates elected a seven-member presidium and seven problem groups (*Slowo Ludu*, June 25, 1981). The province *zespoly* (working groups) of delegates in at least some cases continued operation after the congress. One of Gdansk First Secretary Fiszbach's duties, as outlined in a late October province committee reorganization, was to lead the province *zespol* of congress delegates (*Glos Wybrzeza*, November 2, 1981).

29. *Nowiny*, June 29, 1981, reported that Tarnobrzeg delegates had chosen First Secretary Janusz Basiak, former First Secretary Tadeusz Haladay, and plant director Jerzy Zaranski to maintain "permanent contacts" with the *zespol* organizing the congress. The presidium of the Krakow delegation met twice with the CZD, according to *Gazeta Krakowska*, July 13, 1981.

30. *Gazeta Robotnicza*, July 21–22, 1981.

31. *Gazeta Olsztynska*, July 23, 1981.

32. *Trybuna Ludu* and *Glos Wybrzeza*, July 7, 1981.

33. *Gazeta Krakowska*, July 1, 1981.

34. *Slowo Ludu*, June 25, 1981.

35. *Gazeta Robotnicza* July 13, 1981.

36. *Gazeta Krakowska*, July 1, 1981.

37. *Sztandar Ludu*, July 6, 1981.

38. *Dziennik Baltycki* and *Glos Wybrzeza*, July 10–12, 1981.

39. *Trybuna Ludu*, June 30, 1981.

40. *Trybuna Robotnicza*, July 1, 1981.

41. *Gazeta Krakowska*, July 1, 1981.

42. *Trybuna Robotnicza*, July 1, 1981, *Gazeta Wspolczesna*, July 6, 1981.

43. *Trybuna Robotnicza*, July 1, 1981, *Nowiny* and *Glos Pomorza*, July 9, 1981, and *Gazeta Krakowska*, July 13, 1981.

44. *Nowiny* and *Glos Pomorza*, July 9, 1981.

45. *Ibid.*

46. *Gazeta Wspolczesna*, July 6, 1981.

47. *Trybuna Ludu*, June 30, 1981. On the last point, local papers also filled in more details. Krakow delegates told *Gazeta Krakowska* (as reported on July 13, 1981) that in accord with the size of delegations, forty-five minutes would be allotted to Katowice delegates, thirty to Warsaw delegates, twenty-five each to Poznan and Lodz, twenty to Krakow and some others, and fifteen minutes each to the rest.

48. Tomasz Figaszewski in *Trybuna Robotnicza*, July 1, 1981.

49. *Gazeta Krakowska*, July 13, 1981.

50. *Sztandar Mlodych*, July 16, 1981.

51. *Glos Robotniczy*, July 16 and 17, 1981.

52. *Gazeta Pomorska*, July 17, 1981.

53. *Glos Wybrzeza*, July 18–19, 1981.

54. *Gazeta Robotnicza*, July 7, 1981.

55. *Gazeta Pomorska*, July 17, 1981.

56. For example, in *Gazeta Pomorska* and *Glos Wybrzeza*, July 3–5, 1981, and *Trybuna Robotnicza*, July 2, 1981. According to the Bialystok delegates, the Politburo had proposed "designating a 10 percent reserve in the number of candidates for leadership bodies for veterans of the workers' movement and six province committee first secretaries who are not delegates to the congress" (*Gazeta Wspolczesna*, July 6, 1981).

57. *Gazeta Pomorska*, July 3–5, 1981.

58. *Ibid.*

59. *Trybuna Robotnicza*, July 2, 1981.

60. *Sztandar Ludu*, July 6, 1981.

61. *Gazeta Wspolczesna*, July 6, 1981.

62. *Nowiny*, July 9, 1981.

63. *Glos Wybrzeza*, July 1 and July 3–5, 1981; *Gazeta Pomorska*, July 7, 1981.

64. *Gazeta Robotnicza*, July 13, 1981.

65. *Glos Robotniczy*, July 16, 1981.

66. *Gazeta Poznanska*, July 6 and 14, 1981.

67. *Gazeta Lubuska*, July 14, 1981.

68. *Trybuna Ludu*, July 16, 1981. *Gazeta Krakowska*, July 16, 1981, reported that 384 had voted against and 61 had abstained.

69. According to *Glos Robotniczy*, July 18–19, 1981, quoting congress spokesman Wieslaw Bek.

70. The variants were outlined by Elzbieta Borek in *Gazeta Krakowska*, July 1, 1981.

71. *Trybuna Robotnicza*, July 2, 1981; *Glos Wybrzeza*, July 3–5, 1981; *Gazeta Pomorska*, July 3–5, 1981; *Sztandar Ludu*, July 6, 1981; *Glos Robotniczy*, July 15, 1981; *Gazeta Robotnicza*, July 13, 1981; and *Gazeta Lubuska*, July 14, 1981.

72. *Gazeta Krakowska*, July 1, 1981.

73. *Gazeta Poznanska*, July 6 and 14, 1981.

74. *Gazeta Robotnicza*, July 13, 1981, and *Nowiny*, July 7, 1981.

75. *Sztandar Mlodych*, July 16, 1981.

76. *Gazeta Krakowska*, July 13, 1981; *Glos Wybrzeza*, July 14, 1981; *Gazeta Poznanska*, July 14, 1981; *Glos Robotniczy*, July 15, 1981; and Warsaw radio, July 11, FBIS, July 13, 1981, p. G16.

77. *Sztandar Ludu*, July 16, 1981.

78. The only indication the proposal came from Krakow is the statement by Krakow delegate Kazimierz Miniur that "our proposal on electing the first secretary did not pass" (*Gazeta Krakowska*, July 27, 1981).

79. According to Henryk Sroczynski in *Glos Robotniczy*, July 16, 1981.

80. According to *Glos Wybrzeza*, July 14, 1981.

81. *Glos Robotniczy*, July 15, 1981. This was not in *Trybuna Ludu*. The vote was not decisive, however, since some delegates were out of the hall and 925 was not a majority. The vote was taken at the closed session before the congress formally opened (in open session) at noon. There was not enough time to gather the other delegates and revote before the scheduled opening ceremonies, so the revote had to be postponed to the next day—but this itself removed the possibility of an immediate election.

82. Henryk Sroczynski in *Glos Robotniczy*, July 15, 1981.

83. Sroczynski in *Glos Robotniczy*, July 16, 1981.

84. *Gazeta Krakowska*, July 14, 1981, explained that the Presidium decides matters such as who will speak and the schedule for voting on motions, the Secretariat handles all the organization of the congress, the Resolutions Commission "proposes the texts of congress documents," the Mandate Commission confirms the "legality of the proceedings," and the Electoral Commission "makes up the lists of candidates." The Appeals Commission handles appeals against party punishments. For example, *Gazeta Pomorska*, July 16, 1981, reported that the appeal by horizontal ties leader Zbigniew Iwanow of his expulsion from the party had gone to the Appeals Commission. However, a member of the Appeals Commission later denied that it had received an appeal from Iwanow (*Gazeta Poznanska*, July 20, 1981). The congress Secretariat at previous congresses had conducted censorship of the speeches delivered at the congress, according to Henryk Galus in *Glos Wybrzeza*, July 24–26, 1981.

85. *Trybuna Ludu*, July 15, 1981.

86. *Gazeta Krakowska*, July 15, 1981. A July 14 radio broadcast specified that the Presidium had been elected unanimously (FBIS, July 15, 1981, p. G33).

87. According to *Glos Robotniczy*, July 17, 1981, delegates spoke of Rakowski's speech as "the beginning of real political debate" and as "controversial." *Dziennik Baltycki* on July 16, 1981, said that this was the first speech at the congress that won a real ovation.

88. According to the *New York Times*, July 16, 1981.

89. According to T. Kwasniewski in *Sztandar Ludu*, July 27, 1981.

90. Olsztyn First Secretary Mokrzyszczak later said: "I consider Grabski a conscientious person. Putting him at the head of this commission was a mistake. Being conscientious, Grabski did not want to be suspected of acting vengefully to those who clearly abused him in the spring of 1979. The congress declared the commission's proposal incomplete and disagreed with the proposal to turn

the matters over to the Central Party Control Commission. It decided to do the job itself and did it" (*Gazeta Olsztynska*, July 23, 1981).

91. According to *Glos Robotniczy*, July 17, 1981, the resolution to expel the first six was adopted with 5 against and 46 abstaining; a second resolution, to expel Grudzien, was adopted with 2 against and 4 abstaining.

92. Even according to the conservative *Trybuna Ludu* characterization on July 17, 1981.

93. *Trybuna Ludu, Glos Robotniczy,* and *Gazeta Robotnicza*, July 17, 1981.

94. *Trybuna Robotnicza*, July 17, 1981.

95. *Trybuna Ludu*, July 17, 1981.

96. *Glos Robotniczy*, July 17, 1981.

97. The congress broke up into sixteen working groups (*zespoly*) to discuss specific subjects: ideological and organizational unity, the role of the party statute, socialist democracy, the role of the media, youth, economic policy, market conditions, foreign policy, coal and other raw materials, agriculture, education, science, health, trade unions, social policy, and cadre policy.

98. The congress session apparently was to hear the CC announce the candidates, but when the session opened at 3 P.M. the plenum was still choosing the candidates, so the session listened to speeches (*Gazeta Olsztynska*, July 20, 1981).

99. Sroczynski in *Glos Robotniczy*, July 24–26, 1981, and Fedorowski in *Trybuna Robotnicza*, July 20, 1981.

100. The questioning ended at 7:20 P.M., and after a break, the vote began at 8, according to *Gazeta Olsztynska*, July 20, 1981.

101. The 10 P.M. session, at which the results were announced, was open and broadcast on television, according to *Gazeta Olsztynska*, July 20, 1981. After the vote, the session heard Rakowski report on the current situation. According to Kwasniewski in *Sztandar Ludu*, July 24–26, 1981, Rakowski spoke three times during the congress.

102. At 3 A.M. the debate stopped so that delegates could get several hours sleep, according to *Trybuna Ludu*, July 21–22, 1981. The session had started at 10 P.M., according to *Gazeta Robotnicza*, July 21–22, 1981.

103. Debate was encouraged by the use of a new right to reply. According to Jerzy Sadecki in *Gazeta Krakowska*, July 24–26, 1981, the congress introduced a "procedural innovation, namely the right to a two-minute reply," and this was particularly used during the discussion of the statute and resolutions. Delegates seeking recognition by the presiding officer would approach a microphone on the floor and call out their delegate mandate number and their name and ask to reply to a previous speaker, according to Sadecki.

104. *Gazeta Krakowska*, July 27, 1981.

105. Identified in *Gazeta Robotnicza*, July 13, 1981.

106. *Gazeta Robotnicza*, July 21–22, 1981.

107. The statute did in fact allow joint work by party committees, but without mentioning horizontal units.

108. According to reporter Maria Adamiecka in *Gazeta Robotnicza*, July 21–22, 1981.

109. *Trybuna Ludu*, July 21–22, 1981.

110. *Ibid.*

111. A July 16 PAP English broadcast reported the text of Bednarski's speech, which said that the commission was presenting a list of 200 candidates for CC members, plus "proposals" for candidates submitted additionally. He said the list of 618 for all bodies included 159 workers, 50 farmers, 4 state farmers, and 6 co-op members (FBIS, July 17, 1981, p. G1).

112. According to delegate Jerzy Majka in *Sztandar Mlodych*, July 16, 1981, by 6 P.M. on July 15, the list of candidates for the CC had risen to 275. *Gazeta Pomorska*, July 16, 1981, said that the Electoral Commission prepared the list in "close consultation with province delegations" which decided who would run from their areas. Nominations from individual delegates were passed through delegation heads, rather than being made directly from the floor. Gdansk delegate Romuald Szwengler later stated that "every delegate had the right and possibility of nominating candidates for party leadership bodies by means of his province *zespol* of delegates" (*Glos Wybrzeza*, July 27, 1981).

113. The lists of candidates for CC members and candidate members were separate, and unsuccessful candidates for members did not become candidate members. According to a July 16 radio account of spokesman Bek's July 16 explanation of the CC election, there were also 104 candidates for the Central Auditing Commission (70 seats), and 135 for the Central Party Control Commission (90 seats). See FBIS for July 17, 1981, p. G20.

114. The same system is used in the Soviet communist party except that delegates are given a list of names only equaling the number of seats and usually have little opportunity to exercise in secret their right to cross off names.

115. Four had already been defeated in contests for delegate and were not even on the list.

116. The list of candidates for the CC and other bodies was not published; only the list of those elected. Hence, a complete list of defeated candidates is not available. Nor was the number of votes received by individual elected CC members published. However, the list of candidates and the vote totals for many candidates, both successful and unsuccessful, can be reconstructed from reports in Western newspapers and in Polish provincial papers. Local articles had sometimes earlier provided a list of candidates from a particular province, which could then be compared with the list of newly elected CC members, while in other cases, local papers listed both successful and unsuccessful local candidates after the vote. As for the vote totals, they apparently were broadcast on the internal television monitors in the building where the congress was held, and some Polish reporters later mentioned them in articles in local papers. The totals for Jaruzelski (1,615), Kania (1,335), Olszowski (1,090), Rakowski (1,085), Barcikowski (1,262), and Albin Siwak (1,225) were cited by a reporter in *Gazeta Olsztynska* (Olsztyn),

July 18–19, 1981. Lodz's *Glos Robotniczy* on July 18–19, 1981, reported the number of votes received by that province's 10 candidates—both successful and unsuccessful—for CC membership. *Gazeta Robotnicza* (Wroclaw), July 27, 1981, quoted Jelenia Gora worker Edward Kazimierski as explaining that Nowy Sacz doctor Jozef Kurdzielewicz got more votes than anyone else (1,622), followed by Jaruzelski and Kazimierski himself, both with 1,615.

Western reporters managed to pick up the vote totals for some successful and unsuccessful Politburo members, enough to make up informative stories for the following day's papers. The *New York Times* and *Washington Post* on July 18 reported the figures for Jaruzelski (noting that he got more than all but two other candidates), Kania, Barcikowski, Olszowski, Rakowski, as well as for Fiszbach (951), Grabski (899), Dabrowa (790), Moczar (764), Jablonski (645), Kociolek (611), Jagielski (580), Zabinski (533), and Klasa (470).

According to the *New York Times* on July 18, 1981, 1,909 valid votes were cast and hence 955 were needed to achieve the necessary 50 percent for election. However, Polish commentator Jerzy Sadecki wrote in *Gazeta Krakowska*, July 18–19, 1981, that 1,070 was the minimum number of votes which had been necessary.

The failure of the regime to publish official tallies led to some complaints. According to *Glos Wybrzeza*, July 20, 1981, there were increasing questions in Elblag province about why the number of votes cast for individual CC members had not been published in the press.

There were also rumors that not all 200 had been elected on the first ballot—just as most province conferences had required more than one ballot to elect local bodies. However, spokesman Bek asserted that the full 200 had been elected on one ballot and no second ballot had been needed (*Trybuna Ludu*, July 18–19, 1981). A second ballot would have considerably lengthened the already lengthy process of tabulating the vote for the 618 candidates for various bodies. A member of the Vote Tallying Commission told an Olsztyn reporter that the vote counting had lasted from 5 P.M. Thursday to 5 P.M. Friday (*Gazeta Olsztynska*, July 18–19, 1981). Another member of the Vote Tallying Commission explained that the whole commission had moved to special quarters to count the vote, sitting four to a table. The votes for the CC were counted by fourteen of these tables. "We used no computers. We checked the ballots several times. Our work on this election lasted twenty-four hours. During this time we did not leave the hall" (*Gazeta Poznanska*, July 20, 1981).

117. Many Polish articles commented that both conservative and liberal "wings" were routed, and, as Dorota Terakowska wrote in *Gazeta Krakowska*, July 18–19, 1981, the delegates voted for "moderates" (*umiarkowani*) or "centrists" (*centrysci*).

118. There were, of course, relatively few officials on the list in the first place. According to *Glos Robotniczy*, July 17, 1981, there were only 13 from the central apparat running for CC members and only 6 for candidate members—whereas

the CC elected in 1980 had included 34 from the central government, 19 from the central party apparat, and 23 from the regional apparat among its 140 full members. The 13 included Jablonski, Jaruzelski, Jagielski, Rakowski, Deputy Defense Minister Florian Siwicki, Foreign Minister Jozef Czyrek, Agriculture Minister Jerzy Wojtecki, and Moczar, according to *Gazeta Robotnicza*, July 17, 1981. One delegate showed remarkable foresight when she told a reporter before the election that she feared a repeat of the process which occurred in some regional elections where "the active, well-known comrades were crossed off and only those whose views were not known were left" (*Gazeta Pomorska*, July 16, 1981).

119. The candidates were listed in *Gazeta Wspolczesna*, July 6, 1981. The veterinarian was only listed as a "reserve" candidate.

120. The candidates were listed in *Gazeta Krakowska*, July 13, 1981.

121. *Glos Wybrzeza*, July 18–19, 1981.

122. *Ibid.*

123. According to *Glos Robotniczy*, July 18-19, 1981.

124. *Gazeta Pomorska*, July 17, 1981.

125. *Gazeta Robotnicza*, July 27, 1981.

126. *Gazeta Pomorska*, July 17, 1981.

127. *Ibid.*

128. Despite the election upsets, few provinces would up grossly underrepresented or overrepresented on the new CC. Katowice and Warsaw got more than their proportional share (28 and 17 members, respectively, according to Helena Lazar in *Gazeta Krakowska*, July 24–26, 1981), and Lodz's paper boasted of its delegation's "big success" in winning nine seats (*Glos Robotniczy*, July 18–19, 1981). Krakow First Secretary Dabrowa boasted that his province had won more seats than other provinces of similar size and more than Krakow had ever had before (*Gazeta Krakowska*, July 23 and 27, 1981), although with the defeat of Dabrowa himself and the conservative attacks on Krakow delegates Rakowski, Klasa, and Szumowski (see below), some felt that Krakow itself was a target of resentment. *Gazeta Krakowska* editor Szumowski (who had not run for the CC) stated in *Gazeta Krakowska*, July 27, 1981, that "really, Krakow was strongly attacked." Gdansk, with only five CC members from its sixty-two-member delegation, was underrepresented, and its delegates expressed great regret over the defeat of their first secretary, Fiszbach (*Glos Wybrzeza*, July 20, 1981). The PAP Maritime Service on July 20 reported local "disappointment" at the underrepresentation of Gdansk (FBIS, July 21, 1981, p. G41). But they were partly mollified by the later election of local party secretary Labecki to the new Politburo. Only one province—Ostroleka, whose conservative First Secretary Szablak was defeated for reelection as CC member—wound up with no CC seat. Asked about his loss, Szablak said: "I do not feel that it is my personal defeat" (*Trybuna Mazowiecka*, July 23, 1981).

129. Maria Adamiecka in the July 17 *Gazeta Robotnicza* gave 27 for full member and 13 for candidate member. Helena Lazar in the July 24–26 *Gazeta*

Krakowska said 28 had run for CC member. Henryk Galus in the July 24–26 *Glos Wybrzeza* counted 42 first secretaries running for member and candidate member, while Kwasniewski in the July 20 *Sztandar Ludu* counted 43 for the CC and other central bodies. Dorota Terakowska in the July 18–19 *Gazeta Krakowska* stated that 22 province first secretaries had been defeated in the vote for CC and other central organs.

130. *Gazeta Olsztynska*, July 23, 1981.

131. *Gazeta Pomorska*, July 27, 1981.

132. *Gazeta Krakowska*, July 24–26, 1981.

133. *Gazeta Krakowska*, July 21–22, 1981.

134. According to Helena Lazar in *Gazeta Krakowska*, July 24–26, 1981.

135. According to reporter Maria Adamiecka in *Gazeta Robotnicza*, July 16, 1981.

136. *Trybuna Robotnicza*, July 17, 1981.

137. *Gazeta Robotnicza*, July 17, 1981.

138. *Gazeta Robotnicza*, July 17, 1981.

139. *Glos Wybrzeza*, July 24–26, 1981, and *Slowo Ludu*, July 21–22, 1981. *Sztandar Ludu*, July 20, 1981, listed 107 workers (not including foremen) and 38 private farmers in the new CC, Central Auditing Commission, and Central Party Control Commission, plus 36 military and 45 city and plant secretaries.

140. According to Helena Lazar in *Gazeta Krakowska*, July 24–26, 1981. Of the others, 19 belonged to no union and the rest belonged to the traditional branch unions.

141. Kania had been head of the CC Administrative Department—which supervises the police—during the December 1970 Gdansk demonstrations, and suspicious delegates questioned whether he was partly responsible for the bloodshed. Szczecin delegate Zdzislaw Pedzinski later said that during this questioning, Premier Jaruzelski defended Kania, asserting that Kania as Administrative Department head "had been a resolute advocate of avoiding the repressive decisions which were adopted at that time" (*Kurier Szczecinski*, July 30, 1981).

142. *Trybuna Robotnicza*, *Gazeta Pomorska*, *Gazeta Robotnicza*, and *Glos Robotniczy*, July 17, 1981.

143. *Gazeta Olsztynska*, July 23, 1981.

144. Henryk Sroczynski in *Glos Robotniczy*, July 24–26, 1981.

145. In the second statement, the delegate said only that Zabinski had decided who would go on Katowice's main list of candidates and who would be relegated to the reserve list. The rebellious delegate, Jozef Kopiasz, was punished by having his nomination for CC candidate member revoked by the delegation. *Trybuna Robotnicza*, July 17, 1981, and *Glos Robotniczy*, July 24–26, 1981.

146. *Trybuna Robotnicza*, July 27, 1981.

147. According to the Gdansk paper *Dziennik Baltycki*, July 16, 1981.

148. According to T. Kwasniewski in *Sztandar Ludu*, July 24–26, 1981.

149. *Gazeta Pomorska*, July 17, 1981.

150. Sroczynski in *Glos Robotniczy*, July 17, 1981.

151. *Kurier Szczecinski*, July 17, 1981, and *Gazeta Krakowska*, July 16, 1981. According to *Kurier Szczecinski*, July 30, 1981, the Szczecin delegate, I. G. Kaminski, was using the microphone located in the area where the Krakow delegation was seated, and when he began attacking Rakowski the Krakow delegates "tried to disrupt his speech."

152. Delegate Barbara Nawrocka-Kanska in *Gazeta Krakowska*, July 27, 1981.

153. Sroczynski in *Glos Robotniczy*, July 24–26, 1981. Former CC Secretary Andrzej Werblan, a onetime conservative, had become anathema to conservatives by taking up reform causes and playing a conspicuous role in the horizontal ties movement.

154. *Gazeta Krakowska*, July 21–22, and August 7–9, 1981. Klasa had been a delegate from Krakow and told *Gazeta Krakowska* that he felt "I made a mistake in agreeing to be put on the supplemental list" of Krakow's candidates for the CC (*Gazeta Krakowska*, July 21–22, 1981).

155. *Glos Wybrzeza*, July 24–26, 1981.

156. *Gazeta Olsztynska*, July 23, 1981.

157. Aldona Lukomska in *Gazeta Olsztynska*, July 24–26, 1981.

158. Jerzy Sadecki, *Gazeta Krakowska*, July 24–26, 1981.

159. Ryszard Fedorowski, *Trybuna Robotnicza*, July 20, 1981.

160. *Gazeta Krakowska*, July 21–22, 1981.

161. Interview in *Gazeta Krakowska*, August 7–9, 1981.

162. *Trybuna Robotnicza*, July 21–22, 1981, and *Gazeta Olsztynska*, July 24–26, 1981.

163. *Gazeta Krakowska*, July 24–26 and July 28, 1981. Hieronim Kubiak, who chaired the Motions Commission, later complained that Wolczew showed up at meetings of his commission to argue for orthodox positions. Interview in *Zdanie*, 1986, no. 5, p. 6.

164. *Gazeta Lubuska*, July 21–22, 1981, and *Gazeta Olsztynska*, July 23, 1981.

165. According to Helena Lazar in *Gazeta Krakowska*, July 24–26, 1981. This did not appear in *Trybuna Ludu*.

166. *Trybuna Robotnicza*, July 29, 1981.

167. The meeting was reported in *Trybuna Ludu*, July 30, 1981. Local papers, such as the July 30 *Gazeta Poznanska* and *Glos Robotniczy*, just reprinted the *Trybuna Ludu* report rather than carrying more detailed accounts.

168. *Gazeta Poznanska*, July 28, 1981.

169. *Kurier Szczecinski*, October 30–November 1, 1981.

170. As he boasted in *Glos Robotniczy*, July 24–26, 1981.

171. According to accounts in the July 20, 1981 *Trybuna Robotnicza*, *Kurier Szczecinski*, *Gazeta Krakowska*, *Dziennik Baltycki*, and July 24–26, 1981 *Glos Robotniczy*, Jaruzelski (who was presiding) was the one who nominated Kania; Jerzy Janicki, department chief at Warsaw's Ursus tractor plant, put forward

Olszowski; Krzysztof Dorosz, a Biala Podlaska farmer, proposed Barcikowski; and Hieronim Andrzejewski, a Poznan worker, nominated Rakowski. *Dziennik Baltycki* and *Gazeta Krakowska* printed somewhat more complete communiqués on the plenums than did *Trybuna Ludu*.

172. *Gazeta Krakowska*, July 27, 1981.

173. According to *Kurier Szczecinski* and *Trybuna Robotnicza*, July 20, 1981, and to Bek (cited by a July 18 PAP Russian broadcast, FBIS, July 20, 1981, p. G29). According to *Gazeta Olsztynska*, July 20, 1981, Barcikowski declared that he had agreed to run only under pressure from the CC. Jan Kwasowski in *Gazeta Wspolczesna*, July 20, 1981, wrote that everyone understood that Barcikowski "is not an opponent" of Kania and that "there are no differences in concepts and views between them."

174. *Trybuna Ludu*, July 20, 1981.

175. Sroczynski in *Glos Robotniczy*, July 24–26, 1981, and Fedorowski in *Trybuna Robotnicza*, July 20, 1981.

176. Henryk Galus in *Glos Wybrzeza*, July 20, 1981.

177. *Gazeta Olsztynska*, July 23, 1981.

178. AFP, July 15, FBIS, July 15, 1981, pp. G48–49.

179. AFP, July 16, FBIS, July 17, 1981, p. G26.

180. *Kurier Szczecinski*, July 20, 1981, and *Gazeta Pomorska*, July 23, 1981.

181. Henryk Galus in *Glos Wybrzeza*, July 20, 1981, said that the candidates had been "consulted on" in the delegations.

182. *Trybuna Ludu*, July 20, 1981.

183. *Ibid.* He explained that Foreign Minister Czyrek and Internal Affairs Minister Milewski would give up their government posts after becoming Politburo and Secretariat members. In fact, while Milewski quickly surrendered his police post, Czyrek did not leave his ministry post until a year later. Politburo member Opalko later explained that the principle of separation was the reason Deputy Premier Rakowski was not proposed for inclusion in the new Politburo (*Gazeta Krakowska*, July 27, 1981).

184. Interviewed in *Gazeta Krakowska*, July 23, 1981, the thirty-four-year-old Miniur said that he had been nominated by Krakow CC members, but that there had been little chance of winning, since the feeling in the CC was that as "an expression of confidence" in newly elected First Secretary Kania, CC members should endorse those he proposed for the Politburo and Secretariat.

185. Kubiak later stated that "even though it may sound absurd," he only found out that he would be a candidate for the Politburo and Secretariat one and a half hours before the CC plenum that elected him. Interview in *Zdanie*, 1986, no. 5, p. 6.

186. Messner became chairman of the Katowice province people's council in November 1980 but was rector of the Economics Academy from 1975 to 1981 (*Trybuna Ludu*, July 20, 1981 and November 7, 1985).

5. KANIA'S FALL; JARUZELSKI'S TAKEOVER

1. *Pravda*, September 11, 1981.
2. *Trybuna Ludu*, September 18, 1981.
3. *Trybuna Ludu*, September 17 and 18, 1981.
4. A summary account of the Solidarity congress and related events can be found in Kevin Ruane's *The Polish Challenge*, pp. 230–46.
5. *Glos Wybrzeza*, October 15, 1981.
6. *Trybuna Ludu*, October 19, 1981.
7. *Glos Robotniczy*, October 16–18, 1981.
8. *Trybuna Mazowiecka*, October 14, 1981, and *Zycie Warszawy*, October 15, 1981.
9. *Zycie Warszawy*, October 14, 1981.
10. *Trybuna Ludu*, October 14, 1981.
11. According to the October 14, 1981 *Zycie Warszawy*, there were also some speakers on the first day who disagreed with the criticism and challenged the critics to come up with "constructive proposals."
12. According to an October 13 radio broadcast (FBIS, October 15, 1981, p. G17). Kociolek's defense of the leadership was not even mentioned in the *Trybuna Ludu*, *Zycie Warszawy*, or *Trybuna Mazowiecka* accounts.
13. *Trybuna Ludu*, October 19, 1981.
14. According to the October 13 radio broadcast.
15. *Trybuna Ludu*, October 15, 1981.
16. See the text of the resolution in *Trybuna Ludu*, October 16, 1981.
17. Some of Kociolek's four deputies were engaged in some suspicious trips to Moscow, Prague, Berlin, and Budapest just before the plenum, suggesting that they may have conferred with Soviet, Czech, East German, and other foreign critics of Kania before launching their attacks. Secretary Stanislaw Galecki referred to recent Warsaw delegation visits to Prague, Berlin, Budapest, and Moscow in a speech at the city plenum (*Trybuna Ludu*, October 15, 1981). A Warsaw city delegation led by Galecki was reported visiting Moscow city officials in *Trybuna Ludu*, October 2, 1981; and a delegation led by city Secretary Jerzy Mazurek visited East Berlin, according to *Neues Deutschland*, September 25, 1981. (Moscow papers gave no additional details, and the Czech and Hungarian papers appear to have reported nothing about the visits to their capitals.)
18. *Trybuna Ludu*, November 18, 1980. Kania ally Barcikowski also extensively defended Kociolek's December 1970 role and presented him as a courageous advocate of peaceful solutions. In a late 1980 speech in Gdansk, reported in *Polityka*, December 20–27, 1980 (p. 2), Barcikowski noted that many Gdansk citizens and also party members held Kociolek personally responsible for the December 1970 shootings of workers. (Kociolek had gone on television to appeal to strikers to return to work, but when they returned to the shipyard the next day they were fired upon.) Barcikowski declared that Kociolek had not been informed of the regime decision to use force and in trying to arrange a peaceful

solution had been caught in the middle. Barcikowski even stated that "unfortunately . . . few people know" (because it was never made public) that it actually was Kociolek who delivered the critical report at the late 1970 CC plenum which replaced Gomulka—a report which, he said, presented "evaluations which later became the basis" for the reforms adopted under Gierek.

19. The accounts of the Warsaw conference in *Zycie Warszawy* and *Trybuna Mazowiecka*, June 29, 1981, clearly illustrated the depth of the opposition and the unusual efforts Kania expended to defend Kociolek. Kania took the floor in defense of Kociolek and delivered a long speech testifying on the basis of his personal observations at the time that Kociolek had opposed the use of force but had been overruled by others. He praised Kociolek as a man of principle who had resigned his leadership posts after the 1970 events because of his opposition to the decisions. Kania reminded his audience that he himself had been the "initiator" of Kociolek's rehabilitation and election as first secretary the previous November, declared him a reliable supporter of "renewal," and asked the conference to view the vote on Kociolek as an act of political confidence in Kania himself. Despite his remarkable testimonial, "some delegates demanded further explanations," and Kociolek himself spoke about his 1970 role and stressed that both in 1970 and now he considered political solutions, not force, the only road for resolving such conflicts. More debate prompted Kania to speak again and once more defend Kociolek. Finally, after "wide debate," a "majority" voted to allow Kociolek's name to be placed on the ballot as a candidate. In the end, Kociolek was reelected first secretary by only a small majority, 247 of 438 votes.

20. *New York Times*, July 15, 1981.

21. According to Siwak's CC plenum speech; *Nowe Drogi*, 1981, no. 11, p. 89.

22. Only faint echoes of the fight appeared in *Trybuna Ludu*, but the details can be gathered from the apparently verbatim accounts of the October 16–18 plenum published in the November issue of *Nowe Drogi*.

23. See Siwak's interjection during the plenum (*Nowe Drogi*, 1981, no. 11, p. 96), and the account in the Lodz paper *Glos Robotniczy*, October 28, 1981.

24. Kociolek's interjection during the plenum (*Nowe Drogi*, 1981, no. 11, p. 96).

25. *Nowe Drogi*, 1981, no. 11, p. 89. All of Siwak's references to Barcikowski were cut from the version of his speech appearing in *Trybuna Ludu*.

26. *Nowe Drogi*, 1981, no. 11, pp. 92–93. Kociolek's reference to Siwak and many other parts of his comments were excluded from the *Trybuna Ludu* version, although his disassociation from Barcikowski's generalization was included.

27. *Nowe Drogi*, 1981, no. 11, p. 96.

28. Kociolek said that "both yesterday and today, Comrade Siwak, I said that I didn't agree with the generalization which Comrade Barcikowski formulated at the Warsaw party committee plenum." The *Nowe Drogi* account records that

someone unidentified then spoke up, saying: "I was also at the Politburo meeting and can confirm that Comrade Kociolek said precisely what he asserted today."

29. This whole argument, starting from Siwak's reply to Kociolek's speech through Galecki's remarks, appears only in the *Nowe Drogi* account of the plenum (1981, no. 11, pp. 96–97). Rumors about the argument began circulating, and at a Lodz question-and-answer meeting reported in the October 28, 1981 *Glos Robotniczy*, CC candidate member Marek Bartosik was asked what the squabble between Siwak and Barcikowski was about. He explained that Siwak had criticized Barcikowski for his speech at the Warsaw plenum and his evaluation of that plenum; Barcikowski had refused to change his opinion and Kociolek had supported him; whereupon Siwak accused Kociolek of changing his mind, and then CC Secretary Michalek had asserted that Kociolek had not changed his mind. The episode was also alluded to in the speech of liberal Krakow CC member Kazimierz Miniur, when he attacked Galecki for calling Barcikowski "an adherent of dialogue with Solidarity." This is included in the version of Miniur's speech in *Nowe Drogi* and the October 22, 1981 *Gazeta Krakowska* but not in *Trybuna Ludu*'s version.

The bitter exchange at the plenum apparently convinced some CC members that there was indeed a split in the Politburo. Wloclawek farmer and CC member Artur Kwiatkowski, speaking at the plenum shortly after the exchange, said: "I didn't think that there is discord in the Politburo," but "just today, here, a little while ago I heard that there really is." In *Nowe Drogi*, 1981, no. 11, p. 104, but not in *Trybuna Ludu*'s version of his speech.

30. *Trybuna Ludu*, September 12–13, 1981.

31. This statement was reported only in the September 7, 1981 Wroclaw paper *Gazeta Robotnicza*'s version of his speech and not in *Trybuna Ludu*'s.

32. *Trybuna Robotnicza*, October 15, 1981.

33. According to Dan Fisher in the *Los Angeles Times*, October 15, 1981.

34. According to the October 28, 1981 *Glos Robotniczy* (for more on this, see below).

35. Rakowski later wrote that Kania "had not always acted as decisively as he should have." Moreover, Rakowski was closer to Jaruzelski by then and saw Jaruzelski as a stronger leader. He wrote later that as one of Jaruzelski's "closest coworkers" he had a very high opinion of him and had been pleased by his election (M. F. Rakowski, *Ein Schwieriger Dialog*, p. 107).

36. *Gazeta Poznanska*, October 20, 1981.

37. The statements by these speakers were in the March 30 and 31, 1981 *Trybuna Ludu*.

38. The following quotations from plenum speeches and description of proceedings are taken from *Trybuna Ludu*. Although *Trybuna Ludu*'s abridged versions leave out much material which appeared in the verbatim account printed in the November *Nowe Drogi* (signed to press November 27), they do include virtually everything related to criticism of Kania (except Miniur's defense—see

below). The full versions apparently were available to at least some provincial papers, since *Gazeta Krakowska* and *Glos Wybrzeza* published versions containing material excised by *Trybuna Ludu* (including some notable political sallies involving other leaders).

39. Kielce worker Czeslaw Stepien proposed this at the very beginning, during adoption of the agenda. It was added by general agreement (radio, October 16, FBIS, October 19, 1981, p. G1, and *Slowo Ludu*, October 23–25, 1981).

40. Grabski at the June plenum had stated that the Politburo under Kania's leadership was unable to overcome the present crisis.

41. Apparently the only defense of the Politburo (but not specifically of Kania) was made by a local Krakow plant secretary, Kazimierz Miniur, and his speech was not delivered but just added to the minutes of the plenum. Moreover, when *Trybuna Ludu* printed it, it cut out all his defense of the leadership. *Gazeta Krakowska*, however, on October 22, 1981 printed his complete speech, in which he said: "I want to protest against the brutality of the criticism of the Politburo and government" in the plenum speeches. He added: "Comrade Kociolek rightly spoke yesterday of the need to build up" the leadership's authority. This was also carried in *Nowe Drogi*'s version of the speeches (1981, no. 11, p. 207).

42. Katowice, with twenty-seven CC members the largest province organization and also site of much anti-Kania activity, also played no role. Only two of its representatives spoke—both miners—and neither criticized the leadership.

43. Poznan doctor Tadeusz Pisarski, *Gazeta Poznanska*, October 20, 1981.

44. Roman Golinski, *Gazeta Pomorska*, October 20, 1981.

45. Factory engineer Slawomir Krupa, *Trybuna Opolska*, October 20, 1981.

46. *Trybuna Ludu* covers the whole day's activity in only seven paragraphs. Even *Nowe Drogi*'s detailed account of the plenum adds nothing about this part of it. A reporter in *Trybuna Opolska*, October 20, 1981, characterized PAP's report on the third day as "enigmatic."

47. *Gazeta Robotnicza*, October 20, 1981. Orzechowski relates that the original draft prepared by the CC apparat had been rejected by the plenum on its opening day, and a new draft was worked out "from scratch" by a newly elected commission including only three Politburo members among the thirty-four members. He notes that the commission had settled on compromise language which could be accepted by all CC members, and as a result, even though the resolution was "controversial," the plenum adopted it unanimously. Engineer Slawomir Krupa stated in *Trybuna Opolska*, October 20, 1981, that many CC members had participated in writing the resolution and that the resolution finally adopted was the fifth draft.

48. Tadeusz Pisarski, *Gazeta Poznanska*, October 20, 1981.

49. *Trybuna Ludu*, October 22, 1981.

50. Roman Golinski, *Gazeta Pomorska*, October 20, 1981.

51. The role of Barcikowski and Jaruzelski was revealed by CC candidate member Marek Bartosik during a stormy question-and-answer session in Lodz,

reported in the Lodz paper *Glos Robotniczy* on October 28, 1981. Bartosik provided the most complete account of the Sunday session. Another participant, CC member Jan Bednarowicz, stated during the Lodz discussion that it was his impression that Kania had poorly handled the session, so that the voting occurred "right before the break for lunch."

52. This vote was reported in *Trybuna Ludu*, October 19, 1981.

53. District secretary Karol Stryjski, *Glos Robotniczy*, October 21, 1981.

54. Bartosik, *Glos Robotniczy*, October 28, 1981.

55. Stryjski, *Glos Robotniczy*, October 21, 1981.

56. Bartosik, *Glos Robotniczy*, October 28, 1981.

57. *Trybuna Ludu*, October 19, 1981.

58. *Glos Robotniczy*, October 28, 1981.

59. *Gazeta Pomorska*, October 20, 1981.

60. Karol Stryjski, *Glos Robotniczy*, October 21, 1981.

61. *Trybuna Ludu*, October 22, 1981.

62. *Gazeta Pomorska*, October 20, 1981.

63. *Trybuna Robotnicza*, October 20, 1981.

64. This question was asked in Lodz; see *Glos Robotniczy*, October 28, 1981.

65. See *Trybuna Ludu*, November 28–29, 1981.

66. *Trybuna Robotnicza*, October 19, 1981.

67. *Glos Wybrzeza*, October 23–25, 1981.

68. *Trybuna Ludu*, October 19, 1981.

69. *Kultura*, October 25, 1981.

70. *Nowe Drogi*, 1981, no. 11, pp. 87–88. Also in the October 19, 1981 *Gazeta Krakowska* version of his speech and the October 17 PAP version in FBIS, October 19, p. G34.

71. *Nowe Drogi*, 1981, no. 11, pp. 90–91. The October 16 decision was based on Bratkowski's failure to change his conduct after the commission's April warning (after his March letter attacking hard-liners), his "disorienting of public opinion" and "belittling of the danger of the activities of antisocialist forces" (*Trybuna Ludu*, October 17–18, 1981). The commission complained that it had summoned him three times to explain his activity but he had avoided appearing. The unit's action was confirmed on October 21 by the full Central Party Control Commission, which cited Bratkowski's invitation of representatives of horizontal units to the Journalists Union (SDP) on June 9 to organize pressure on the June CC plenum, his attempts to "turn the SDP into a political center," his support of Solidarity extremists, and most recently, his September 18 publication (in *Slowo Powszechne*) of an "open letter" blaming the regime for the existing sociopolitical tension (*Trybuna Ludu*, October 22, 1981). Olszowski praised the expulsion in a press conference with journalists from socialist countries; see the Czechoslovak paper *Pravda*, October 22, 1981.

72. PAP, October 16, FBIS, October 19, 1981, pp. G26–27.

73. *Sztandar Mlodych*, November 13–15, 1981.

74. Szumowski's letter was attacked as improper by a meeting of the Krakow Executive Committee (*Gazeta Krakowska*, October 20, 1981) and a plenum of the province committee in neighboring Nowy Sacz (*ibid.*, and *Glos Wybrzeza*, October 21, 1981). But various Krakow party organizations—including the big Lenin steel mill organization—sprang to Szumowski's defense (*Gazeta Krakowska*, October 27, 1981).

75. Warsaw Radio, October 31, FBIS, November 3, 1981, pp. G22–23.

76. *Dziennik Baltycki*, October 22, 1981.

77. See *Gazeta Pomorska, Trybuna Opolska*, and *Dziennik Baltycki*, October 22, 1981; *Glos Wybrzeza*, October 21 and 27, 1981; *Gazeta Krakowska*, October 27 and 29, 1981; and *Trybuna Ludu* (on a Lodz meeting), October 24–25, 1981.

78. *Gazeta Krakowska*, October 19 and November 9, 1981, and *Sztandar Mlodych*, November 13–15, 1981. Olszowski himself spent several hours talking with angry *Sztandar Mlodych* employees on October 21; see the *Sztandar Mlodych* account.

79. *Gazeta Krakowska*, October 27, 1981, and *Dziennik Baltycki*, October 22, 1981.

80. *Glos Wybrzeza*, October 15, 1981.

81. *Gazeta Robotnicza*, October 19, 1981.

82. Warsaw Radio, November 30, FBIS, December 1, 1981, pp. G5–6.

83. *Gazeta Krakowska*, October 26, 1981.

84. *Glos Robotniczy*, October 28, 1981.

85. Kubiak was also criticized for being too liberal at the October 16–18 plenum by Koszalin farmer Mieczyslaw Maksymowicz. The latter complained that during a television speech Kubiak had been too apologetic about party decisions and acted as a "relativistic scholar" instead of an "uncompromising communist" (*Nowe Drogi*, 1981, no. 11, p. 67).

86. *Nowe Drogi*, 1981, no. 12, p. 99.

87. *Ibid.*, p. 100.

88. *Glos Wybrzeza*, October 26, 1981.

89. *Gazeta Krakowska*, October 26, 1981.

90. *Gazeta Krakowska*, October 16–18, 1981.

91. *Gazeta Pomorska*, November 6–8, 1981.

92. After being elected first secretary at the October 18 plenum, Jaruzelski said that "I could have today tried to present proposals for eventual changes in the makeup of the Politburo and Secretariat," but "after considering this theme at a Politburo meeting," the Politburo decided that it "should approach the matter comprehensively," making changes in the Council of Ministers as well as the party leadership (*Trybuna Ludu*, October 19, 1981). Plenum participant Marek Bartosik stated to local questioners that "in my understanding," Politburo members gave their resignations to newly elected First Secretary Jaruzelski "because he should have the free right to choose the people closest to him" (*Glos Robotniczy*, October 28, 1981).

93. Siwicki was elected with 178 votes out of 187 cast, Mokrzyszczak received 173, and Orzechowski 163 (*Trybuna Ludu*, October 29, 1981).

94. Jaruzelski continued to retain the post of minister of defense.

95. The August 1981 plenum had established an Ideological Commission with Olszowski as chairman and Orzechowski as deputy chairman.

96. He explained in *Gazeta Robotnicza*, November 2, 1981, that his duties were to handle ideological matters. Elblag First Secretary Prusiecki told a local audience that Mokrzyszczak would handle organizational questions and Orzechowski ideological questions (*Glos Wybrzeza*, October 30–November 1, 1981).

97. Identified as such in the August 14, 1981 *Trybuna Ludu*.

98. The usually candid Politburo member Labecki actually denied this. At an early October meeting in Elblag province, he was asked about this and stated: "Information is circulating that at one of the Politburo meetings the matter of a state of emergency [*stan wyjatkowy*] was considered. These are false stories; the theme in general was not even raised" (*Glos Wybrzeza*, October 7, 1981).

99. *Nowe Drogi*, 1981, no. 11, p. 75.

100. *Ibid.*, pp. 74–75, 117–18.

101. Interview in *Gazeta Robotnicza*, October 20, 1981.

102. *Trybuna Ludu*, October 19, 1981.

103. *Nowe Drogi*, 1981, no. 11, p. 159.

104. *Ibid.*, p. 83.

105. *Ibid.*, pp. 155–56.

106. *Trybuna Ludu*, October 19, 1981. French Press Agency reports, apparently based on information from party members before the resolution was published, asserted that the resolution called for a "state of war." AFP, October 17, FBIS, October 19, 1981, p. G41.

107. In another indication of the extent of debate over the resolution, Lublin worker Zdzislaw Daniluk said on the first day of the plenum that "if the comrades who wrote the draft resolution had acquainted themselves with all the telexes which came from province committees to the CC they would not have written that content into the resolution" (*Nowe Drogi*, 1981, no. 11, p. 74).

108. The original commission proposed by Kania at the start of the plenum came under fire, judging by an exchange included in the November *Nowe Drogi* account of the plenum (pp. 70–72). Warsaw professor Zbigniew Kamecki complained that nine of the thirty-three members were not CC members or candidate members. After several minutes of debate, during which Kania defended the principle of including non-CC people on such commissions, Kania put it to a vote. The plenum voted against Kania's position, and the commission apparently was then reconstituted to include only CC members and candidate members.

109. Michael Dobbs in the *Washington Post*, October 18, 1981, reported that "reliable Polish sources" had told him that the October 17 plenum session was adjourned in order to allow overnight consultations with regional party organizations over the wording on a state of emergency.

110. *Trybuna Opolska*, October 20, 1981.
111. *Gazeta Krakowska*, October 29, 1981.
112. *Gazeta Krakowska*, October 27, 1981.
113. *Trybuna Opolska*, October 26, 1981.
114. *Trybuna Robotnicza*, October 20, 1981.
115. See the Czechoslovak paper *Pravda*, October 22, 1981.
116. Henryk Galus in *Glos Wybrzeza*, October 23–25, 1981.
117. *Trybuna Opolska*, October 26, 1981.
118. *Ibid.*
119. *Trybuna Opolska*, October 20, 1981.
120. *Trybuna Robotnicza*, October 26, 1981.
121. *Gazeta Krakowska*, October 26, 1981.
122. *Trybuna Ludu*, October 21, 1981.
123. *Nowe Drogi*, 1981, no. 12, p. 104.
124. *Trybuna Ludu*, October 19, 1981.
125. *Trybuna Ludu*, October 31–November 1, 1981.
126. *Trybuna Ludu*, November 30, 1981.
127. *Trybuna Ludu*, June 13, 1986.
128. Preparation of plans apparently had begun as early as September. President Reagan, in his December 23, 1981 speech on the imposition of martial law, presumably based on Kuklinski's information, stated that "martial law proclamations . . . were being printed in the Soviet Union in September" (*Washington Post*, June 4, 1986).
129. Warsaw PAP, June 5 and 17, FBIS, June 9, 1986, pp. G1–7, and June 18, 1986, pp. G1–4.
130. Rakowski, *Ein Schwieriger Dialog*, p. 117.
131. *Ibid.*, p. 133. The book stresses Rakowski's long commitment to compromise with Solidarity, his gradual disillusionment, and finally his recognition of failure after hearing the Radom tapes. Rakowski had been hired as deputy premier primarily to try to work out a compromise with Solidarity. He had written a January 17, 1981 *Polityka* article raising the idea of a partnership, and this had caught Premier Jaruzelski's attention. Rakowski later related that when he asked "my friend Kazimierz Barcikowski" why Jaruzelski chose him for deputy premier, Barcikowski replied: "If you hadn't written the article on 'Respect for One's Partner' no one would have thought of you" (*Ein Schwieriger Dialog*, p. 20). He had also written a book at the start of 1979 (*The Republic on the Threshold of the 1980's*) which noted the "gathering clouds" and called for reforms and included the idea of "partnership as the basis of our political system" but, as Rakowski explained, it could not be published under Gierek and appeared only later in 1981 (*ibid.*, pp. 23–24).

When asked in a late 1984 interview when he came to the conclusion that "partnership" was not possible, he said he developed that conviction in early fall when the Solidarity congress "dashed my hopes" (Andrzej Kepinski and Zbigniew

Kilar, *Kto Jest Kim w Polsce Inaczej*, p. 343). But when he went to Jaruzelski despairing over the Solidarity leaders' attitudes, he said Jaruzelski ordered him to continue trying to reach an agreement (*Ein Schwieriger Dialog*, p. 108).

Although the Radom meeting was closed to outsiders, it was easy to find out what was said, according to Rakowski, because Solidarity leaders recorded the speeches on cassettes and already the next day several regional chairmen played the tapes for their members, and thus "it was not particularly hard" to get the material. During an intermission in a Politburo meeting Rakowski looked over transcripts of the statements. On the same day excerpts from the tapes were broadcast on television and radio (*ibid.*, pp. 132–33). Rakowski describes his "bitterness and sadness" at the failure of the concept of partnership (*ibid.*, p. 137).

132. *Trybuna Ludu*, June 13, 1986. This interview is an excerpt from the second volume of interviews by Andrzej Kepinski and Zbigniew Kilar to be published as *Kto Jest Kim w Polsce Inaczej*, part two, in late 1986, according to *Trybuna Ludu*.

133. *Zdanie*, 1986, no. 5, p. 9.

134. Urban referred to this reason in his talk with the *Washington Post* reporters (*Washington Post*, June 4, 1986).

135. *Trybuna Ludu*, June 13, 1986.

136. Leader of the Catholic political faction PAX, Ryszard Reiff.

137. Olszowski, however, did claim that martial law was adopted with party approval. According to the East German paper *Neues Deutschland*, December 18, 1981, he said it had been adopted on the basis of the decisions of the fourth (mid-October) and sixth (late November) CC plenums and with Politburo authorization.

138. Including three generals whom he had earlier appointed ministers of internal affairs, mining, and local economy. A six-man "Committee of National Salvation" headed by Jaruzelski and Kiszczak had been set up a couple of months earlier, according to a statement by Siwak in Krosno, reported by a Solidarity source. See Timothy Garton Ash, *The Polish Revolution: Solidarity 1980–1982*, p. 234.

6. MARTIAL LAW AND THE PARTY

1. John Darnton in the *New York Times*, March 21, 1982, reported "reliable sources" stating that about sixty journalists had been interned after December 13 and that forty of these were still in detention.

2. The announcement on the press was made on radio on December 14 (FBIS, December 14, 1981, p. G38). It was later reprinted in *Prasa Polska*, January 1983, p. 57. The radio on December 13 also carried an announcement by the State Committee for Radio and Television explaining the new limited television and radio broadcasts and placing most radio and television personnel on leave (FBIS, December 14, p. G19).

3. Provincial papers issued three-day issues (as was normal practice on weekends) on December 11 covering December 11 through 13, and by December 14—a day after martial law was announced—most were able to put out the next regular issue.

4. The first separate issues of *Dziennik Baltycki* and *Glos Wybrzeza* appeared on February 2; according to *Prasa Polska*, January 1983, the first separate *Gazeta Krakowska* appeared on February 5.

5. *Washington Post*, March 13, 1982. According to a later book by *Gazeta Krakowska* workers, a guard was posted outside *Gazeta Krakowska* on December 13 with a list of people to be allowed in, and the list did not include Szumowski and most of the paper's workers. During February Szumowski and two of his best-known writers, Helena Lazar and Dorota Terakowska, were expelled from the party. *13 Miesiecy i 13 Dni "Gazety Krakowskiej"* (1980–1981), pp. 74–75.

6. *Prasa Polska*, January 1983, pp. 57–59.

7. *Prasa Polska*, January 1983, p. 57. *Glos Wybrzeza*'s circulation was 215,000, *Dziennik Baltycki*'s was 95,000 (*ibid.*).

8. *Le Figaro*, February 11, 1982.

9. PAP, February 4, FBIS, February 5, 1982, p. G43.

10. The January 16–17 issue was numbered no. 1 for 1982.

11. *Prasa Polska*, January 1983, p. 58.

12. The January 1983 *Prasa Polska* list of papers which resumed publication after martial law does not mention *Trybuna Mazowiecka*, and I have been unable to locate any issues.

13. *Prasa Polska*, January 1983, pp. 57–58. The new paper apparently ceased in mid-January.

14. On December 31 *Gazeta Robotnicza* resumed publication, and *Monitor Dolnoslaski* editor Zdzislaw Balicki became editor of *Gazeta Robotnicza* (*Prasa Polska*, pp. 57–58). I have seen no such "martial law" papers for other areas.

15. Adam Budzynski in the December 1982 issue of *Prasa Polska*. The verification process is described by former Polish journalist Leszek Lechowicz in "The Mass Media Under Martial Law," *Poland Watch* (Fall 1982), no. 1, pp. 41–49.

16. Warsaw radio, December 31, FBIS, December 31, 1981, p. G28. According to the *New York Times* and the *Washington Post*, January 2, 1982, thirty of the fifty staffers on *Kurier Polski* were dismissed. Cited by Anna Sabbat-Swidlicka in a February 1, 1982 Radio Free Europe Background Report, RAD BR 27, p. 17.

17. See Rakowski's article in this issue of *Polityka*. The February 19 *Washington Post* reported that one-third of *Polityka*'s staff had resigned rather than accept censorship.

18. *Prasa Polska*, January 1983, pp. 58–60.

19. *Trybuna Ludu*, February 15, 1982.

20. FBIS, February 4, 1982, pp. G9–10.

21. According to a January 13 PAP broadcast (FBIS, January 15, 1982, p. G13), and *Trybuna Ludu* on January 14, 1982.

22. According to a January 31 radio broadcast, FBIS, February 1, 1982, p. G23.

23. PAP on March 10 (FBIS, March 11, 1982, p. G17) had announced that *Rzeczywistosc* was resuming publication, but its first issue only appeared in late May (dated May 23). This issue listed Jerzy Pardus as chief editor, instead of Tycner.

24. *Le Figaro*, March 15, 1982.

25. *New York Times*, March 21, 1982.

26. *Los Angeles Times*, January 11, 1982, as quoted by Anna Sabbat-Swidlicka in a February 1, 1982 Radio Free Europe Background Report (RAD BR 27, p. 16).

27. See FBIS, March 17, 1982, p. G3; March 18, 1982, p. G8; March 19, 1982, p. G8; and March 24, 1982, pp. G2–4.

28. *Trybuna Ludu*, March 20–21, 1982.

29. *Trybuna Ludu*, March 22, 1982.

30. FBIS, March 24, 1982, p. G20.

31. When later asked why the instruction was not made public, CC Secretary Mokrzyszczak declared that "it was our internal matter," and "after all, people were sufficiently upset even without being informed that even the party had established 'martial law' for itself" (*Trybuna Ludu*, August 11, 1983).

32. For Barcikowski's speech, see Jozef Cegla in *Polityka*, March 6, 1982. For the Szczecin meetings, see *Trybuna Ludu*, February 2, 1982.

33. *Trybuna Ludu*, February 25, 1982.

34. *Trybuna Robotnicza*, January 25, 1982.

35. *Glos Wybrzeza–Dziennik Baltycki*, January 22–24, 1982.

36. *Glos Robotniczy*, December 23, 1981.

37. *Glos Wybrzeza–Dziennik Baltycki* and *Trybuna Robotnicza*, January 11, 1982.

38. *Trybuna Ludu*, February 6–7, 1982, and *Gazeta Robotnicza*, February 8, 1982. In a February 9, 1983 *Gazeta Robotnicza* interview, Wilk noted that he had come to the province as a "stranger . . . in a manner which recently was universally criticized," and there had initially been "a certain reserve" toward him.

39. Ignacy Wirski, *Zycie Partii*, November 24, 1982.

40. *Trybuna Ludu*, January 29, 1982.

41. *Rzeczywistosc*, May 23, 1982. *Trybuna Robotnicza* on March 26–28, 1982, reported that a Katowice plenum elected *Trybuna Robotnicza* chief editor Jan Zielinski as province ideology secretary. He won 88 of the 94 votes in a secret ballot.

42. According to Skrzypczak's later writings in an underground publication,

he had had conflicts with several powerful local officials: The regional military commander had objected to his taking public opinion polls after martial law was imposed, and Skrzypczak had unsuccessfully tried to get the local police chief ousted for corruption. According to his account, Barcikowski and CC Cadres Department chief Dziekan had told him he was being removed because his activity was "incompatible with the work of the state administration." J. B. de Weydenthal, "The Failure to Reform the Party in Poland," RFE Background Report/18, February 13, 1984.

43. *Trybuna Ludu*, May 29–30, 1982, and *Gazeta Poznanska*, May 31, 1982. Lukasik was an outsider whom the Politburo persuaded the 1981 Poznan party conference to elect as a delegate to the July 1981 congress.

44. *Trybuna Ludu* and *Gazeta Poznanska*, June 3, 1982.

45. *Le Figaro*, June 19–20, 1982.

46. *Trybuna Ludu*, May 29–30, 1982, and *Gazeta Poznanska*, May 31, 1982. According to Skrzypczak's underground account, he took a minor post in a Polish trading company in Nigeria. J. B. de Weydenthal, "The Failure to Reform the Party in Poland."

47. *Gazeta Pomorska*. August 30, 1982.

48. According to the *Trybuna Ludu* account, September 14, 1982.

49. *Trybuna Ludu*, September 24, 1982, and *Gazeta Pomorska*, September 24–26, 1982.

50. *Gazeta Krakowska*, October 27, 1982.

51. *Trybuna Ludu, Express Wieczorny*, and *Zycie Warszawy*, June 7, 1982.

52. *Sztandar Ludu*, June 24, 1982.

53. *Gazeta Pomorska*, September 24–26, 1982.

54. *Gazeta Krakowska*, October 27, 1982.

55. *Sztandar Ludu*, December 1, 1982.

56. *Sztandar Ludu*, December 10–12, 1982. *Trybuna Ludu*'s accounts of the above plenums specified the voting results in electing the new first secretaries in Warsaw, Lublin, and Krakow, but not in Torun, Chelm, and Zamosc.

57. Kalisz First Secretary Bogdan Gawronski resigned in February because of a "difficult family situation" (*Gazeta Poznanska*, February 18, 1982).

58. New Kalisz First Secretary Jan Janicki was a local man.

59. *Gazeta Pomorska*, June 23, 1982.

60. The government on October 23, 1981, sent "operational groups" of officers and enlisted men with "plenipotentiary powers" to various localities to ensure proper food supplies and transport and fight waste and mismanagement, according to Warsaw television on October 23 (FBIS, October 26, 1981, pp. G1–4). An article by Professor Mariusz Gulczynski in *Wojsko Ludowe*, July 1984, no. 7, pp. 40–44, on "The Military in the Political System of the Polish People's Republic (Experiences from the Years of the Crisis)" stated that there were 850 operational groups consisting of 3–4 soldiers in small towns and 191 groups of 10 to several dozen working in big cities.

61. These committees, according to Malina in a *Trybuna Ludu* interview, January 2–3, 1982, had been the bodies which had carried out the December 13 martial law orders. The committees, which had long existed, were chaired by the *wojewoda* and included his deputies, the province party committee secretaries, the province police commander, and the chief of the province military staff. They organized the work of leaders of local government and enterprises, whom they could remove if necessary, according to Malina.

62. Interviewing the plenipotentiary for Konin province, a *Sztandar Mlodych* reporter began by saying: "In the street one hears that you have unlimited powers. Is that true?" The plenipotentiary denied this and claimed only to assist and exert pressure. But he also mentioned that twenty-eight local enterprise directors and office chiefs had been dismissed and that he had made proposals to dismiss twenty-two others as well (*Sztandar Mlodych*, March 15, 1982).

63. *Sztandar Mlodych*, July 29–31, 1983. According to this article, Mroz's post was abolished on February 25, 1982, when General Mieczyslaw Debicki was named mayor of Warsaw and took over.

64. Local papers sometimes referred to "plenipotentiary of the Military Council for National Salvation" or a "commissar of the National Defense Committee," but most were listed as "plenipotentiary of the National Defense Committee." In addition, four provinces (Katowice, Elblag, Koszalin, and Radom) had military viceroys directly as *wojewodas* (governors), nonelective positions filled by the premier. These appointments—a general and three colonels—were announced in *Trybuna Ludu*, December 16, although a later reference (in *Zolnierz Polski*, July 1, 1984) stated that General Paszkowski's installation as Katowice *wojewoda* had occurred "just before the introduction of martial law." Paszkowski immediately became the boss in his province, overshadowing Katowice First Secretary Zabinski, judging by his activities and local press coverage.

65. Tadeusz Witoslawski, *Trybuna Ludu*, February 26, 1982.

66. *Gazeta Pomorska*, January 22–24, 1982.

67. *Nowiny*, January 25, 1982.

68. *Glos Szczecinski*, March 3, 1982.

69. *Gazeta Robotnicza*, March 3, 1982.

70. *Zycie Partii*, September 1, 1982, no. 14, p. 3.

71. *Trybuna Ludu*, January 31, 1983.

72. *Trybuna Opolska*, January 31, 1983.

73. *Gazeta Poznanska*, February 14, 1983.

74. *Statut Polskiej Zjednoczonej Partii Robotniczej, z uzupelnieniami i poprawkami uchwalonymi przez X Zjazd PZPR*, article 59.

75. *Trybuna Ludu*, January 18, 1982.

76. According to Central Party Control Commission chairman Jerzy Urbanski in *Trybuna Ludu*, January 30–31, 1982.

77. CC Organizational Secretary Mokrzyszczak in a June 12 television broadcast (FBIS, June 14, 1982, p. G6).

78. According to a *Zycie Partii* interview with Barcikowski, September 1982, no. 14, the "normal" departure rate was about 20,000 a month.

79. *Trybuna Ludu*, February 11, 1983. The December 1981 membership— 2,693,000—was indicated by Mokrzyszczak in *Zycie Partii*, 1982, no. 3, and in his television broadcast, June 12, 1982.

80. *Trybuna Ludu*, April 21, and July 12, 1982.

81. *Zycie Partii*, November 24, 1982, p. 9.

82. *Glos Pomorza*, July 28, 1982.

83. In a 1983 discussion, deputy head of the CC's Ideological Department Andrzej Czyz said that 48 percent of the 13 percent who left the party in 1982 were ousted for inactiveness or violating discipline. He said about 100,000 turned in their party cards during 1982 (*Gazeta Krakowska*, April 5, 1983). Judging by this, those removed for political reasons (either by formal expulsion or just by being crossed off the list) did not exceed 170,000.

84. Mokrzyszczak in *Zycie Partii*, 1982, no. 3. Membership had stood at 3,149,768 in July 1980, according to head of the CC's Organizational Department Cypryniak in *Trybuna Ludu*, July 16–17, 1983.

85. Cypryniak in *Trybuna Ludu*, July 16–17, 1983. A few members (6,100) were expelled between July 1980 and June 1981, mainly for nonpolitical reasons such as alcoholism and moral and financial abuses (*Nowe Drogi*, 1981, no. 8, p. 58).

86. *Glos Wybrzeza*, March 4, 1982.

87. According to Legnica First Secretary Jerzy Wilk in *Gazeta Robotnicza*, February 9, 1983.

88. *Trybuna Ludu*, February 25, 1982.

89. *Nowe Drogi*, 1981, no. 8, p. 60.

90. *Glos Wybrzeza–Dziennik Baltycki* and *Trybuna Robotnicza*, January 11, 1982.

91. *Trybuna Ludu*, February 26, 1982.

92. *Glos Robotniczy*, March 4, 1982.

93. FBIS, March 9, 1982, p. G7.

94. According to Konin worker Czeslaw Borowski in his plenum speech, *Trybuna Ludu*, February 27–28, 1982.

95. Although *Trybuna Ludu*'s accounts of plenum speeches include no criticisms of martial law by CC members, a remark in Gen. Edward Lukasik's plenum speech suggested that some speakers had in fact criticized martial law at the plenum. According to the longer version of his speech in the February 26, 1982 *Zolnierz Wolnosci*, he said: "Therefore I cannot share the view expressed here by some comrades that martial law has hampered the functioning of the party, limited its role and rights." *Trybuna Ludu* edited the speech to cut any reference to criticism by "comrades" at the plenum ("here") and to limiting the party's role: "I cannot consequently share the view expressed by some that martial law has hampered the functioning of the party" (*Trybuna Ludu*, February 26, 1982).

96. *Trybuna Ludu*, February 25, 1982.
97. *Ibid.*
98. *Trybuna Ludu*, February 27–28, 1982.
99. According to the "full text" printed in *Gazeta Pomorska*, March 4, 1982.
100. *Trybuna Ludu*, March 2, 1982.
101. *Trybuna Ludu*, January 2–3, 1982.
102. According to the *New York Times*, February 4, 1982, hard-liners were circulating a manifesto demanding the ouster of Barcikowski, Kubiak, and Rakowski. Bernard Margueritte in *Le Figaro*, February 15, 1982, reported that hard-liners, dissatisfied with the failure to change the party's course, had launched an offensive "against the moderates surrounding General Jaruzelski" (FBIS, February 18, 1982, p. G12).
103. Krakow remained relatively calm when martial law was imposed, which may have helped Dabrowa keep his post. On Krakow's calm after martial law, see Michael Dobbs in the *Washington Post*, March 7, 1982. It is probable that a key reason Fiszbach and Zabinski lost their posts was that Gdansk and Katowice were the main centers of reaction against martial law, and it was probably argued that new, firmer leadership was needed in those two provinces.
104. *Dziennik Baltycki*, on March 8, 1982, reported him chairing a session of the council's presidium. He eventually resigned in May. His resignation was reported by PAP on May 26 (FBIS, May 28, 1982, p. G18). According to Michael Dobbs in the *Washington Post*, February 27, 1983, Fiszbach became commercial attaché in Helsinki.
105. Despite the appeal, party members in Gdansk angrily quit the party in droves. Fiszbach on December 23 stated that 850 members had already turned in their party cards since the announcement of martial law, and he expressed his regret that many "honorable persons" had "mistakenly evaluated the situation" (*Glos Wybrzeza–Dziennik Baltycki*, December 24–27, 1981).
106. *Glos Wybrzeza*, February 7, 1983.
107. Rakowski, Kubiak, Labecki, Krakow factory secretary Miniur, Lodz worker Jadwiga Nowakowska, and youth leader Jerzy Jaskiernia. In contrast, virtually no well-known conservatives (except Central Party Control Commission chairman Urbanski) spoke. Siwak's speech was not delivered but just added to the record.
108. *Trybuna Ludu*, February 26, 1982.
109. *Trybuna Ludu*, February 27–28, 1982.
110. *Ibid.*
111. *Ibid.* The attacks on Kubiak, combined with lack of enthusiastic support from Jaruzelski, eventually forced him to leave the Secretariat in July 1982, although he stayed in the Politburo and remained chairman of the CC Culture Commission. In a later interview he complained that pamphlets attacking him were being spread even in the CC and at plenums: "I left in a situation of very sharp attacks on what I had done and on me personally" and because "I was

not able to find a common language with those with whom I had to in order to carry out my concepts." Indicating that he could not change his political views, he said he had acted in the spirit of the "new political culture" of people leaving posts but not going into oblivion: "A secretary criticized for ineffectiveness leaves his post but stays in the Politburo." Interview in the Krakow monthly *Zdanie,* 1986, no. 5, pp. 9–10.

112. *Trybuna Ludu,* March 2, 1982.

113. *Trybuna Ludu,* February 25, 1982.

114. *Trybuna Ludu,* February 27–28, 1982.

115. Ryszard Naleszkiewicz, *Sztandar Mlodych,* March 18, 1982.

116. *Trybuna Robotnicza,* March 26–28, 1982.

117. *Gazeta Pomorska,* March 30, 1982. The Torun committee also ordered a study of the "political line" of the conservative Rzeczywistosc Club.

118. In the Czechoslovak paper *Pravda,* October 22, 1981.

119. *Trybuna Ludu,* March 27–28, 1982.

120. *Neues Deutschland,* December 18, 1981.

121. Bernard Margueritte in *Le Figaro,* April 9, 1982. Former Polish journalist Leszek Lechowicz wrote that Olszowski had wanted to fire at least 6,000 or 7,000 journalists but had been "restrained by Jaruzelski." "The Mass Media Under Martial Law," *Poland Watch* (Fall 1982), no. 1, p. 46.

122. The letters were printed in *Rzeczywistosc,* July 11, 1982.

123. *The Financial Times,* June 18, 1982.

124. *Trybuna Ludu,* June 19–20, 1982.

125. Bernard Margueritte in *Le Figaro,* July 19, 1982.

126. *Trybuna Ludu,* July 17–18, 1982.

127. *Trybuna Ludu,* July 22, 1982.

128. *Trybuna Ludu,* July 31–August 1, 1982.

129. *Glos Wybrzeza,* December 6, 1982.

130. *Trybuna Ludu,* December 11–12, 1982.

131. *Trybuna Ludu,* December 13, 1982.

132. Roger Boyes in the *London Times,* December 10, 1982. It later developed, however, that Loranc was given another, probably higher post not as directly managing radio and television. In January 1983 he showed up as head of the CC's Ideological Department (first identification in *Gazeta Krakowska,* January 20, 1983).

133. The Rzeczywistosc clubs, according to an interview with Grabski in *Argumenty* (no. 1), March 14, 1982, began springing up in late September and early October 1981, and the association was formally established on December 6, 1981. The new clubs took the name Rzeczywistosc (Reality) because they agreed with the conservative line of the magazine *Rzeczywistosc,* and the magazine helped organize the clubs. Their expressed purpose was to propagate conservative views.

134. *Rzeczywistosc,* May 23, 1982, p. 3.

135. According to Christopher Bobinski in the *Financial Times*, June 18, 1982.

136. *Ibid.*

137. Bernard Margueritte in *Le Figaro*, June 22, 1982.

138. *Ibid.*

139. The date of the letter was given by Michael Dobbs in the *Washington Post*, October 31, 1982, and also in *Zycie Partii*, December 22, 1982, p. 14.

140. Roger Boyes in the *London Times*, October 29, 1982; Michael Dobbs in the *Washington Post*, October 31, 1982; Dan Fisher in the *Los Angeles Times*, October 30, 1982; Bernard Guetta in *Le Monde*, October 31–November 1, 1982; and Christopher Bobinski in the *Financial Times*, October 29, 1982.

141. *Le Monde*, November 10, 1982. The accounts of the speeches carried in *Trybuna Ludu* do not confirm this.

142. Roger Boyes, *London Times*, October 29, 1982.

143. PAP, November 7, FBIS, November 8, 1982, p. G30, and *Trybuna Ludu*, November 8, 1982. Bernard Margueritte in *Le Figaro*, January 11, 1983, reported that Grabski was given a "reprimand with warning" by party officials and a censure from his superiors for leaving his post in Berlin without permission in order to hold this press conference in Warsaw.

144. Bernard Margueritte in *Le Figaro*, November 29, 1982.

145. According to Dan Fisher in the *Los Angeles Times*, October 30, 1982.

146. *Sztandar Ludu*, December 20, 1982.

147. According to Bernard Guetta in *Le Monde*, November 10, 1982.

148. The December issues of *Rzeczywistosc* contain no mention of any such congress.

149. Roger Boyes in the *London Times*, December 10, 1982.

150. The "Kuznica" club was a longtime liberal Krakow group. According to *Trybuna Ludu*, December 23, 1981, Kubiak was one of the founders of this club. A Radio Free Europe article, February 21, 1983, indicated that it was founded in 1975 and that not only Kubiak but also Barcikowski, Rakowski, and former *Gazeta Krakowska* editor Szumowski had been associated with it. E.C.C., "Cracow's Party Intelligentsia Club Dissolved," SR/3, February 21, 1983.

151. According to "unauthorized fragments" of his speech published in the local paper *Nowiny* on December 23, 1982.

152. *Trybuna Ludu*, February 27–28, 1982.

153. "Information on the PZPR's Activity in 1982," *Trybuna Ludu*, February 11, 1983.

154. The official "Sprawozdanie" (report) on the intercongress period at the July 1981 congress stated that there had been thirty Politburo meetings between the February 1980 congress and September 5, 1980—a period of about thirty weeks (*Nowe Drogi*, 1981, no. 8, p. 56).

155. The "Sprawozdanie" at the congress reports seventy Politburo meetings from September 1980 to June 10, 1981—a period of forty weeks (*ibid.*).

156. For example, Bernard Guetta in *Le Monde*, November 10, 1982, mentioned an unannounced Politburo meeting during the October 27–28 CC plenum.

157. In an interview in *Trybuna Ludu*, June 13, 1986, he said that the WRON had "discussed the country's problems" fourteen times, focusing on security, the struggle against crime, economic questions, reorganizing the trade union movement, and cadre policy.

158. See the "Sprawozdanie" at the July 1981 congress; *Nowe Drogi*, 1981, no. 8, p. 57.

159. For example, in *Trybuna Ludu*, November 17, 1980, September 10, 1981, December 9, 1981, February 17, 1982, September 9, 1982, and October 15, 1982.

160. For the roles of Janiszewski and Hupalowski, see Jan de Weydenthal, Bruce Porter, and Kevin Devlin, *The Polish Drama: 1980–1982*, pp. 248–49. On December 17, 1981, Janiszewski sent out a letter ordering dismissal of employees who refused to sign loyalty pledges and renounce membership in Solidarity, according to *Le Monde*, January 25, 1982 (*ibid.*, p. 253).

161. In a December 1984 *Zolnierz Polski* (no. 52) interview, Gornicki specified that he had been working as Jaruzelski's assistant (in the office of the Council of Ministers) since October 1981 and when martial law was declared had been promoted to captain and then major and how headed a team of political advisers for the premier.

162. Kolodziejczak worked in Defense Minister Jaruzelski's cabinet from 1972 to 1981, then became chief of the first secretary's cabinet, and in May 1982 became director of the Chancery of the CC Secretariat (*Trybuna Ludu*, January 16, 1986).

163. Urban was one of the editors of Rakowski's weekly *Polityka* and at the same time served as adviser to Rakowski in the latter's function as deputy premier and in August 1981 was offered the post of government spokesman by Rakowski, according to Urban's account in Andrzej Kepinski and Zbigniew Kilar, *Kto Jest Kim w Polsce Inaczej*, p. 404.

164. According to biographic comments during an interview on Budapest television on May 19, 1983, he had worked five years in New York as a PAP correspondent (FBIS, May 20, 1983). Gornicki also was an informal adviser to Rakowski in late 1981, according to Rakowski's book (M. F. Rakowski, *Ein Schwieriger Dialog*, p. 77).

165. A Center for Study of Public Opinion was established in late 1982 specifically to "aid the government in adopting correct decisions and in improving the style and method of using power," according to Kwiatkowski in a *Trybuna Ludu* interview, December 15, 1982. Kwiatkowski explained that he had worked in Defense Minister Jaruzelski's office for the preceding ten years specializing in study of sociopolitical problems and that the armed forces under Jaruzelski had long used opinion surveys (by the Military Political Academy's Institute of Social Studies) as guides before "all important decisions" affecting army life. In a *Kie-*

runki article, May 6, 1984, Kwiatkowski indicated that his polling organization worked under the government's Sociopolitical Committee (headed by Rakowski) and the premier's office (General Janiszewski).

166. Identified in *Gazeta Pomorska*, January 31, 1983.

167. *Trybuna Ludu*, March 29, 1983.

168. The *Trybuna Ludu* account, September 28, 1982, of the joint meeting said that it had discussed the trade union situation and the coming Sejm session but contained no mention of any new trade union law. However, on October 5, 1982, *Trybuna Ludu* reported that an October 4 meeting of the United Peasant Party leadership had approved the position of its representatives at the joint party meeting and the draft trade union law which was to be put before the coming Sejm session—thus indicating that the September 27 meeting had in fact also approved the draft law for submission to the Sejm.

169. *Trybuna Ludu*, October 1, 1982.

170. There was open opposition to the bill in the Sejm. During the debate some Sejm members (such as independent writer Edmund Osmanczyk) spoke against the bill (PAP, October 8, FBIS, October 12, 1982, pp. G9–10), and according to the French Press Agency (AFP), 10 voted against and 9 abstained (FBIS, October 12, 1982, p. G10).

171. Published in *Trybuna Ludu*, October 30–31, 1982.

172. *Trybuna Ludu*, November 15 and November 25, 1982.

173. Guetta in *Le Monde*, November 10, 1982.

174. Roger Boyes in the *London Times*, October 29, 1982.

175. Bernard Margueritte in *Le Figaro*, November 29, 1982.

176. *Nowiny*, December 23, 1982.

177. This was suggested by Margueritte's report on the November 23 Politburo meeting in *Le Figaro*, November 29, 1982.

178. A longer version of Kamecki's speech on p. 5 of *Trybuna Ludu* quotes him as stating that the way the "verification" of cadres, especially of journalists, was conducted "aroused certain opposition among a significant part of society." He also questioned some of "our actions" regarding trade unions since the introduction of martial law and stated that Jaruzelski's "generally correct policy" on trade unions had produced "significantly less political effect because it was undermined by actions at various levels." Kamecki had displayed his moderate stance also at earlier plenums, for example at the October 18, 1981 plenum, where he assailed the "political extremists" in Solidarity "and likewise in our party" for seeking confrontation (*Nowe Drogi*, 1981, no. 11, p. 190).

179. *Trybuna Ludu*, July 17–18, 1982.

180. He had been director of the CC's Department for Planning and Economic Analysis from 1977 to 1980, when Gierek, unhappy with the department's unfavorable analyses, dissolved it. Gorywoda then was demoted to leader of a group of economic advisers to the premier and as such served as assistant to Jaruzelski until promoted to CC secretary for economic affairs at the July 15–16, 1982

plenum. See biographic background and statements by Gorywoda in an interview with him published in Andrzej Kepinski and Zbigniew Kilar, *Kto Jest Kim w Polsce Inaczej*, pp. 99, 103–4.

181. The delegates who assembled for these conferences were the same delegates elected at the pre-congress conferences in mid-1981—minus those who had been expelled from the party, who had quit, or who had moved away or died. The purge and local military control appear to have eliminated radicals and discouraged outspoken reformers from making the 1982–83 conferences as "stormy" as the 1981 conferences. About 10–20 percent of 1981 delegates failed to attend most 1982–83 province conferences, although in some cases absences were higher. Perhaps the most extreme case was the Torun city conference, where according to *Gazeta Pomorska*, December 13, 1982, only 505 of the 790 delegates elected in 1981 were present. Of the 285 missing, 134 had been stripped of their mandates. (The 1981 Torun city conference had been especially rebellious, voting in favor of expelled party reformer Zbigniew Iwanow against province First Secretary Najdowski.)

7. AFTER MARTIAL LAW: "NORMALIZATION"

1. Of twenty-one province conferences where the number of delegates removed was specified in the local press, in almost all between 5 and 15 percent had lost their mandates when the conferences opened in early 1983. This includes, however, not only those who were stripped of their mandates for political or moral reasons but also those who died or moved away.

2. *Glos Wybrzeza*, February 7, 1983.

3. *Gazeta Pomorska*, December 13, 1982.

4. *Trybuna Ludu*, September 20, 1983. The party statute set the term of office for party bodies up through the province level at two and a half years, meaning that new elections were due by the end of 1983.

5. Article 21 of the statute reads: "The number of candidates must exceed the number elected. Meetings, conferences, and the congress decide the method of choosing [*wylamianie*] candidates." Point 6 of the rules adopted in March 1984 and published in *Zycie Partii*, March 28, 1984, also states that the number of candidates "must exceed the number elected," but likewise gives conferences the right to determine the method of choosing candidates and specifically adds the right "to determine their number."

6. According to *Trybuna Ludu*, March 19, 1984.

7. In fourteen cases there was some indication of the number of candidates for province committee as well as the number elected, and in six cases the exact number of candidates was specified.

8. Of eighteen cases in 1981 where the number of candidates was reported, fourteen offered over 30 percent more candidates than seats. Among the areas with the greatest choice was Lodz, which had 196 candidates for 121 seats—62 percent more candidates than positions.

9. *Gazeta Lubuska*, January 23, 1984.

10. *Trybuna Ludu*, January 16, 1984.

11. *Gazeta Lubuska*, January 23, 1984.

12. *Gazeta Olsztynska*, January 16, 1984.

13. *Echo Krakowa*, December 14, 1983.

14. *Gazeta Pomorska*, November 29, 1983.

15. *Gazeta Olsztynska*, December 7, 1983.

16. The report of Zygmunt Galecki, chairman of the Mandate Commission at the conference, specified that 49 had been dropped from the party, 4 had resigned their mandates, 16 had died, and the rest had lost their mandates because of various party punishments. Of those with valid mandates, 1,776 attended (*Trybuna Ludu*, March 17–18, 1984). Galecki gave the figure of 1,960 delegates for 1981, but this does not conform to the 1,964 delegates cited at the 1981 congress itself. While overall changes were small, some delegations were considerably reduced. Only 193 of Katowice's 233 delegates attended (*Trybuna Robotnicza*, March 16, 1984), and over 20 percent of the delegates from Elblag, Legnica, Olsztyn, and Torun were absent.

17. *Trybuna Ludu*, March 19, 1984.

18. *Trybuna Ludu*, March 21, 1984.

19. The text of the law was published in *Odrodzenie*, February 28, 1984, the organ of PRON (the Patriotic Movement of National Salvation). PRON had been set up by the martial law regime in July 1982 as a device to widen the regime's support by organizing a front of all nonopposition political parties and groups. It was entrusted with carrying out the 1984 people's council elections.

20. *Trybuna Ludu*, January 27, 1984.

21. *Trybuna Ludu*, January 27, 1984.

22. See the description of the process in *Trybuna Ludu*, April 26, 1984, pp. 1–2.

23. *Gazeta Olsztynska*, May 19–20, 1984.

24. *Zagadnienia i Materialy*, April 26, 1984, no. 17. This journal is labeled for "internal party use."

25. See, for example, the lists in *Gazeta Poznanska*, May 23, 1984; *Trybuna Ludu*, June 11, 1984 (for Warsaw); or *Slowo Ludu*, June 8, 1984.

26. *Gazeta Krakowska*, May 19–20, 1984.

27. This was written right in the election law, articles 67 and 68. This provision was retained from the 1976 law (article 57). See the *Dziennik Ustaw Polskiej Rzeczypospolitej Ludowej*, January 17, 1976.

28. This was true of key provinces such as Warsaw, Katowice, Poznan, Krakow, and Lublin. In some provinces—such as Gdansk—papers published just the list of victorious candidates with no voting results. Some provinces' results did not appear in province papers at all. In only one contest in the eleven provinces where I found complete tabulations was there an upset (or even a close contest). *Nowiny*,

June 22, 1984, reported that in Tarnobrzeg province one no. 2 candidate won 6,510 votes to 5,378 for the no. 1 candidate.

29. Stanislaw Gebethner, *Polityka*, January 19, 1985.

30. Stanislaw Podemski, *Polityka*, January 19, 1985 and February 16, 1985. Vice President of the Council of State Kazimierz Secomski in a PAP interview, February 20, 1985, also brought up these proposals (FBIS, February 21, 1985, p. G12).

31. *Panstwo i Prawo*, February 1985, pp. 13, 20.

32. *Ibid.*, pp. 21, 25.

33. *Panstwo i Prawo*, March 1985, pp. 124–25.

34. *Glos Pomorza*, June 29, 1984. There was no PZPR candidate. In fact, the PZPR province first secretary nominated one of the ZSL candidates, who won 72 to 33. The four posts of deputy chairmen were split up: two for the PZPR, one for SD, and one for PAX.

35. *Gazeta Poznanska*, June 28, 1984. No party affiliations were given.

36. *Glos Pomorza*, June 26, 1984.

37. For a description, see Steven Koppany, "Nomination of Candidates for Hungarian Elections Completed," Radio Free Europe RAD Background Report/ 51, June 5, 1985, p. 8.

38. A full list of candidates with identifications appeared in *Magyar Nemzet*, May 25, 1985. Candidates were not identified by party, however.

39. *Magyarorszag*, June 16, 1985, p. 21, said that 156 candidates were nominated from the floor at nomination meetings, and 71 of these won enough votes to get on the ballot.

40. See Steven Koppany, Radio Free Europe, Hungary, Situation Report: "Election Results and Assessment," June 21, 1985, p. 10, and also Austrian television on June 10 (FBIS, June 10, 1985, p. F2).

41. Figures for the June 8 election were given in *Magyar Közlöny*, June 9, 1985 (the most complete list) and *Nepszabadsag*, June 10, 1985.

42. Runoff election figures were given in *Nepszabadsag*, June 24, 1985.

43. See the description in Steven Koppany's Radio Free Europe Situation Report, June 21, 1985; "Election Results and Assessment."

44. Radio Budapest, May 20, 1985, as quoted by Koppany, Radio Free Europe, Hungary, Situation Report: "On the Eve of the 1985 National Elections," June 21, 1985, p. 6.

45. The election law appeared in *Rzeczpospolita*, June 15–16, 1985.

46. One of the five was Stanislaw Kania running in Gdansk. He got 88 percent. The results for all candidates around the country were given in *Trybuna Ludu*, October 16, 1985.

47. Party identifications usually were not given in local or national papers' listings of candidates, but whenever they were given it was indicated that both candidates for a given seat belonged to the PZPR, or to the ZSL, or to the SD, or to no party.

48. Osmanczyk, a nonparty member, had represented Opole in the Sejm since 1957 and in recent years had spoken out against and voted against several government bills, especially under martial law. For some examples of his independence, see Jolanta Strzelecka's article in *Poland Watch*, "The Functioning of the Sejm Since December 13, 1981" (March 1985), no. 7, pp. 59, 61, 73. The regime managed to quietly block his renomination, but this did not go unnoticed or even unprotested. His exclusion was criticized by an article in the local Opole paper, *Trybuna Opolska*, August 31–September 1, 1985, and Osmanczyk himself argued in *Trybuna Opolska*, September 21–22, that his exclusion would end pluralism in the Sejm.

49. One of his frankest interviews was with Italian journalist Oriana Fallaci shortly after the imposition of martial law. In it he talked about Soviet pressure on Kania to crack down, about Suslov's criticisms during his April 1981 visit to Poland, about his own discussions with Jaruzelski over dealing with Solidarity and adopting martial law, and about the disintegration of the party ("It went bankrupt intellectually and politically"). He frankly asserted the argument that Poland's opportunity to exercise freedom is limited by its domination by the USSR. Ridiculing Solidarity leaders' "unrealistic ideas about freedom," he asked, "didn't they know where Poland is placed" and he asserted that Warsaw Pact forces would have invaded if martial law had not been imposed (*Washington Post*, February 21, 1982).

50. Labeling Urban a "moderate" seems awkward in view of his intemperate criticisms of Solidarity, the Church, and some reformers, but may be justified because of his equally vehement attacks on hard-liners. The outspoken Urban has been giving regular press conferences for the regime where he frankly (and aggressively) responds to reporters' questions, even on sensitive subjects such as the number of political prisoners. These press conferences—unique to Poland among communist states—reflect a refreshingly open information policy and at least one successful approach to improving the regime's image.

51. *Trybuna Ludu*, June 1, 1983.

52. *Trybuna Ludu*, June 3, 1983.

53. *Nowe Drogi*, April 1981, pp. 124–25.

54. His duties were specified by Politburo member Czechowicz in *Glos Robotniczy*, August 5, 1981.

55. *Trybuna Ludu*, March 2, 1982.

56. *Trybuna Ludu*, July 29, 1983.

57. FBIS, October 29, 1984, pp. G2–5.

58. On the killers' efforts to implicate the ministry, see Kiszczak's October 27, 1984 radio speech (FBIS, October 29, 1984, p. G3), a statement by Jerzy Urban in *Rzeczpospolita*, November 5, 1984, and Rakowski's interview in *Der Spiegel*, December 17, 1984, pp. 120–22. On statements by Capt. Grzegorz Piotrowski, leader of the killers, that the Jaruzelski regime was too soft on the opposition, see the *Washington Post* and *New York Times*, January 10, 1985. Piotrowski

specifically complained at the trial that the ministry blocked effective action against Popieluszko. Warsaw radio, January 8, 1985, FBIS, January 9, 1985, p. G3.

59. Piotrowski was given twenty-five years, his two subordinates fifteen and fourteen years, Col. Adam Pietruszka, deputy director of the department where Piotrowski worked, twenty-five years (Warsaw PAP, February 7, 1985, FBIS, February 7, 1985, p. G1). The director of Piotrowski's department, Gen. Zenon Platek, was suspended, according to Warsaw television on November 2, 1984 (FBIS, November 5, 1984, p. G1), and Kiszczak's November 6, 1984 speech to a Sejm commission (FBIS, November 7, 1984, p. G4).

60. *Trybuna Ludu*, November 7, 1984.

61. *Stern*, March 21, 1985, pp. 26–30.

62. *Trybuna Ludu*, December 24–26, 1984.

63. *Trybuna Ludu*, December 23, 1985.

64. See CC Secretary Czyrek's report to the plenum (*Trybuna Ludu*, October 27–28, 1984) and the Politburo theses published in *Trybuna Ludu*, October 24, 1984.

65. See the article on "The Normalization of Higher Education" by J. C. in *Poland Watch* (March 1985), no. 7, pp. 38–46.

66. Kozniewski's removal was announced in *Trybuna Ludu*, February 19, 1985, and *Tu i Teraz*'s last issue appeared on May 29. An article on Kozniewski's departure signed by the weekly's staff appeared in the February 27 issue, defending him against attacks "from right and left" and "from below and above."

67. *Trybuna Ludu*, November 12, 1985.

68. Identified on television on January 20, 1986 (FBIS, January 28, 1986, p. G3).

69. Warsaw radio, November 6, 1985 (FBIS, November 12, 1985, p. G7).

70. Indicative of his new responsibilities, Czyrek became chairman of the CC Ideological Commission at the May 31, 1983 plenum (*Trybuna Ludu*, June 1, 1983).

71. Porebski became head of the CC's Science and Education Commission in late 1983; for example, he was reported leading meetings of the commission in *Zycie Partii*, 1983, no. 22; and 1984, nos. 1 and 4. However, he was elected chairman of the Intraparty Affairs Commission on June 18, 1985 (*Zycie Partii*, 1985, no. 14).

72. Honkisz, like Dziekan, came from the military's political administration. He was deputy commander for political affairs for the air defense forces in the late 1970s under Jaruzelski, and by June 1981 (identified in *Trybuna Ludu*, June 25, 1981), he was deputy head of the armed forces' main political administration (as was Dziekan until he became party cadres chief).

73. His promotion to the Presidium was announced on television on November 15, 1985 (FBIS, November 19, 1985, p. G9).

74. See the CC resolution in *Trybuna Ludu*, December 23, 1985.

75. Large plant party organizations with over 650 party members had the right to elect a delegate directly to the congress, rather than via province conferences. In all, 265 delegates (of a total of 1,776) were elected in this fashion to the 1986 congress (*Trybuna Ludu*, June 30, 1986), as compared with 365 (of 1,964) in 1981.

76. *Kurier Szczecinski*, April 4–6, 1986; *Gazeta Poznanska*, March 24, 1986; *Trybuna Ludu*, March 27, 1986; *Trybuna Opolska*, April 5–6, 1986; and *Zycie Czestochowy*, April 14, 1986.

77. *Kurier Szczecinski*, April 10, 1986.

78. *Gazeta Lubuska*, April 5–6, 1986.

79. *Trybuna Ludu*, March 26, 1986.

80. *Gazeta Poznanska*, April 5–6, 1986.

81. *Gazeta Poznanska*, March 25, 1986.

82. *Gazeta Lubuska*, March 17, 1986. The winner was CC member Walerian Solinski, who had been a delegate to the 1981 congress.

83. Based on radio and television reports in FBIS June 30–July 3 and reports in *Trybuna Ludu*, June 30–July 5, one can reconstruct the schedule of the congress as follows. The congress opened on June 29 at 9 A.M. in open session. (The open sessions were broadcast live on the radio.) With Czyrek presiding, the congress unanimously elected its leading bodies (the Presidium, Secretariat, and various commissions), then heard Jaruzelski's report, and later in the afternoon other speeches. The members of the bodies elected on the first day had been "consulted on" with delegations, according to Czyrek's speech, as carried on radio on June 29 (FBIS, June 30, 1986).

The congress reopened on June 30 at nine in open session to hear speeches by Soviet leader Gorbachev and several Polish leaders. It went into closed session in the evening to hear a report by Mokrzyszczak (chairman of the commission for changes in the statute) and to vote on changes in the statute and election rules. (These changes had been discussed by province delegations in local caucuses in mid-June.)

On July 1 the congress broke up into problem groups for discussion, and then returned to open session in the late afternoon to hear speeches.

On July 2 it convened in open session at 9 A.M., went into closed session at 12 noon, and discussed candidates for the CC until late in the evening (8 P.M.), and then voted on the CC.

On July 3 it began with a closed session at 9 A.M. to hear Czechowicz announce the results of the CC election. Then the new CC met and elected Jaruzelski (nominated by Jablonski). No one else was nominated, and Jaruzelski was elected in a secret vote with 228 of 229 votes. Czyrek announced the results to the congress. Then Jaruzelski prepared a list of the new Politburo and Secretariat, which, after "consultation" with congress delegates, was elected by a second meeting of the CC late in the day. During the late morning and afternoon the congress in open session heard more speeches and discussed and voted on resolutions. Late in the evening Jaruzelski announced the results of the CC election of Politburo and Secretariat members and closed the congress.

84. Central and province papers ran almost no comments on the CC election, and even *Polityka*'s July 12 analysis of the election included nothing about losers or vote totals. A July 3 *Dziennik Baltycki* commentary mentioned that 112 workers had run for the CC. Comparison with *Trybuna Ludu's* July 8 calculation that 88 workers were elected suggests 24 workers were defeated. *Gazeta Lubuska* was the only paper that listed local (Gorzow and Zielona Gora) candidates for the CC, and from its list it is clear that the only 2 defeated candidates from those two provinces were workers. The *Gazeta Lubuska* list, published on July 2 (before the election), had Zielona Gora running 4 candidates (2 workers, 1 farmer, and the province first secretary) and Gorzow running 3 (2 workers and the province first secretary). All were subsequently on the list of elected CC members except 1 worker from Zielona Gora and 1 from Gorzow. Local party members after the congress sometimes asked their delegates about the opportunity for choice at the congress. For example, *Trybuna Opolska* on July 11 reported party members asking: "Were there more candidates for the Politburo than positions? Were resolutions or proposals adopted by split vote [*niejednoglosnie*]? Did anyone nominated from the floor get on the CC?" Local papers did not report the answers to these questions.

85. *Trybuna Ludu* on July 8, 1986, declared that the new CC included 88 workers and 23 farmers.

86. For more on Kamecki, see chapter 6. According to a July 12 *Polityka* analysis, nine CC members and two candidate members left between the 9th and 10th congresses. Only some of these were clearly reformers (Marian Arendt, Jan Malanowski, Zbigniew Ciechan).

87. *Trybuna Ludu*, July 4, 1986.

88. Czechowicz resigned as Lodz first secretary on June 26, 1986, to take up a job in the "diplomatic service" (*Glos Robotniczy*, June 27, 1986). He became ambassador to Hungary.

89. Opalko retired as Tarnow first secretary in January 1986 (*Gazeta Krakowska*, January 13, 1986).

90. Proposed changes were sent to province delegations which held meetings during June to discuss these proposals and also the party program, draft congress resolution, agenda and operating rules, and which candidates to put forward for election to the Presidium and other congress bodies. Local accounts were not informative, at best just mentioning topics discussed but no positions taken other than approval. In only one case—a June 26 *Gazeta Krakowska* account of Krakow's delegation—was there mention of discussion of candidates for the CC.

91. *Statut Polskiej Zjednoczonej Partii Robotniczej, z uzupelnieniami i poprawkami uchwalonymi przez X Zjazd PZPR* (Statute of the Polish United Workers Party, with additions and amendments approved by the 10th PZPR Congress). This pamphlet also includes an amended version of the party election rules, with

provisions in line with the statute. For example, as in the statute, the clause on "unlimited number of candidates" was dropped, but there are the clauses that there must be more candidates than the number elected and that conferences determine the number of candidates (article 6).

92. Article 21. *Fakty i Komentarze* noted that until 1961 the election rules had stipulated that the number of candidates must equal the number of positions, but that since 1961 they had required more candidates than positions.

93. An analysis of the new CC by Zygmunt Szeliga in *Polityka*, July 12, 1986, specified that four had been "co-opted" to full membership between the 9th and 10th congresses (Baryla, Bednarski, Bejger, Gorywoda) and seven to CC candidate membership.

94. The 1975 figure is from *Rocznik Statystyczny*, 1978, p. 22; the 1980 figure from *Nowe Drogi*, 1980, no. 3, p. 40.

95. Head of the CC Organizational Department Cypryniak in *Trybuna Ludu*, July 16–17, 1983.

96. CC Secretary Mokrzyszczak in *Zycie Partii*, 1982, no. 3.

97. Cypryniak in *Rzeczpospolita*, January 14, 1983.

98. *Nowe Drogi*, 1981, no. 8, p. 58. There were rumors of "whole truckloads" of party cards which had been turned in by workers and were being sent from factories, reported and disputed by a *Sztandar Ludu* [Lublin] article, September 2, 1982.

99. *Rocznik Statystyczny*, 1982, p. 28 (1970 figure); *Nowe Drogi*, 1980, no. 3, p. 40 (1980 figure); *Trybuna Ludu*, February 11, 1983 (1983 figure).

APPENDIX 1. POLAND AS A MODEL

1. CPSU election procedures are spelled out in "Instructions on Conducting Elections of Leading Party Organs," confirmed by the CC on March 29, 1962, and published in the *Spravochnik Partiynogo Rabotnika* (Party Worker's Handbook), 4th ed., 1963. These instructions provide for secret balloting to elect delegates to conferences and congresses and to elect members of party committees at conferences and congresses (but only up through the republic level; nothing is said about national congresses or CC plenums). A list of nominees for delegates or committees is worked out by a "conference of representatives of delegations," but delegates have the right to nominate others from the floor and also to criticize nominees and propose removing some nominees from the list. Delegates are presented with a list of candidates and in secret balloting have "the right to cross off individual candidates on the ballot or add new ones." There is no mention of whether the list of candidates can or cannot exceed the number of positions available. The vote totals for each candidate are to be announced to the conference or congress. While secret balloting is stipulated for electing delegates and committee members, procedure for electing the Politburo and Secretariat at CC plenums (and their local equivalents at republic or province plenums) appears to rely on open balloting—as the Polish rules did before renewal. Soviet rules say almost

nothing about the election of leaders except that open balloting is to be used for electing all secretaries and bureau members from the rayon level up through republic central committees. There is no elaboration on how this open balloting is to be conducted.

2. At the 7th Congress in March 1918, 15 members were elected to the CC with vote totals ranging from 23 to 34, while 7 others, who received only 2 or 3 votes apiece, were defeated. *Protokoly Syezdov i Konferentsiy Vsesoyuznoy Kommunisticheskoy Partii (b), 7. Syezd*, p. 177.

3. The stenographic record of the 12th congress contained this exchange when an official began to announce the results of the vote for CC members: "Comrades, of 408 who have the right to vote, 386 participated in the voting. Only Comrade Lenin was elected unanimously. Then the following comrades were elected." (Voices: "Announce the number of votes received." Voices: "Don't!" [*Ne nado!*]) Presiding officer: "Who votes for not announcing the votes? The majority." *Dvenadtsatyy Syezd RKP (b), stenograficheskiy otchet*, p. 661.

4. See the Russian-language transcripts of Khrushchev's tapes at Columbia University, part I, pp. 996—97. This passage is also included in the Russian-language selections from the transcripts published by Valeriy Chalidze in 1981 (as Nikita Khrushchev, *Vospominaniya*, kniga vtoraya), pp. 5—7. Khrushchev does not specify what congress he was describing.

5. At the end of the congress Gerardo Iglesias, who called for "renewal," was elected general secretary by 69 votes to 31 for former leader Santiago Carrillo. For more, see Eusebio Mujal-Leon's "Decline and Fall of Spanish Communism" in the March—April 1986 *Problems of Communism* (pp. 1—27) and Kevin Devlin's Radio Free Europe reports "Divided Spanish CP Faces Congress of Crisis" (RAD Background Report/285, December 29, 1983) and "Carrillo's Challenge Defeated at Stormy PCE Congress" (RAD Background Report/291, December 30, 1983). Also see Heinz Timmermann, *Kommunistischen Parteien in Westeuropa: Programme, Strukturen, Perspektiven*, part I: Italien, Frankreich, Spanien, pp. 42—43.

6. See Ronald Tiersky, *Ordinary Stalinism; Democratic Centralism and the Question of Communist Political Development*, pp. 112—13, 122—29, and Timmermann, *Kommunistischen Parteien in Westeuropa*, p. 16. Election contests and pressure to weaken democratic centralism and legitimize minorities within the Italian communist party prior to and at the 1983 congress are described in an article by Heinz Timmermann, "Die Genetischen Mutationen der KPI," in the West German SPD monthly, *Die Neue Gesellschaft*, no. 5, 1983.

7. See the stenographic report of the congress, *VII Kongres Saveza Komunista Jugoslaviye*, pp. 1145—47. The lowest vote for any winning candidate was 1,695.

8. April Carter, *Democratic Reform in Yugoslavia*, pp. 84—87, 95, and Steven L. Burg, *Conflict and Cohesion in Socialist Yugoslavia*, pp. 40—41. During 1965 party congresses in the republics, local committees proposed numerous candidates for republic central committees, but the republic nominating commissions reduced

these initial lists down to the number of seats available, and in only one republic—Macedonia—did the delegates at the congress actually have a choice in voting: 94 candidates for 87 CC seats (Carter, *Democratic Reform*, pp. 85–86, and *Borba*, April 1, 1965). During the 1968 republic congresses some other republics also presented delegates with a choice in electing CC members. For example, Croatia presented 78 candidates for 65 CC seats, and Slovenia 51 candidates for 45 seats (Carter, *Democratic Reform*, pp. 84–87, 95). In the case of Slovenia, there appeared to be some real contests. *Borba* said that the winning 45 averaged 453 votes apiece, while the losing 6 averaged 389—not far behind (*Borba*, December 16, 1968).

9. *Danas*, March 18, 1982.

10. Tanjug, March 9, 1985, FBIS, March 13, 1985, p. 130.

11. Tanjug, March 12 and 14, 1986. Choice was severely restricted by the fact that each republic had a set quota of seats on the CC and control over choosing its representatives on the CC (Tanjug, March 31, 1986).

12. *Vjesnik*, March 11, 1986; *Komunist*, March 14, 1986; *Nin*, March 16, 1986.

13. According to a May Serbian CC plenum decision (*Borba*, May 15, 1986) and a May 27 Tanjug account of the congress (FBIS, May 30, 1986, p. 14).

14. The congress approved a provision stating that "as a rule" the number of candidates should be greater than the seats to fill and voted down a proposal by one delegate to drop "as a rule" and make it mandatory to have more candidates than seats. Belgrade radio, June 28, 1986, FBIS, June 30, 1986, pp. 146–50.

15. Thus, in 1982 each republic elected nineteen of the CC members at its own congress, and their choices were simply endorsed ("verified," as the June 30, 1982 *Borba* said) at the national congress. Hence, there was no opportunity for a contest at the national congress.

16. *Pravda*, February 27, 1986. Some other speakers objected to such assertions that there is a class of officials who are only interested in privileges. Volgograd First Secretary V. I. Kalashnikov in his CPSU congress speech assailed the assertions in *Pravda* that there is "some kind of 'immovable, inert, and flabby party-administrative stratum' " as just "seeking sensation" and "running down cadres" (*Pravda*, March 2, 1986).

17. The republic paper *Zarya Vostoka* on July 6, 1979, for example, announced the results of a poll on attitudes toward cracking down on abuse of private ownership and, reporting a favorable public response, announced that the Georgian leadership was adopting tougher measures.

18. Starting in the late 1970s, various commissions were created in which rank and file members could work on problems alongside party leaders, and at the early 1981 republic party congress a worker was added to the republic party bureau and the congress broke up into discussion groups (just as the Polish party congress did later in 1981).

19. *Zarya Vostoka*, January 23, 1981.
20. *Zarya Vostoka*, January 28, 1981.
21. *Pravda*, February 26, 1981.
22. *Pravda*, February 26, 1986.

Bibliography

BOOKS

Ascherson, Neal. *The Polish August*. New York: Viking Press, 1981.

Ash, Timothy Garton. *The Polish Revolution: Solidarity 1980–1982*. London: Jonathan Cape, 1983.

Blazynski, George. *Flashpoint Poland*. New York: Pergamon Press, 1979.

Burg, Steven L. *Conflict and Cohesion in Socialist Yugoslavia*. Princeton: Princeton University Press, 1983.

Carter, April. *Democratic Reform in Yugoslavia*. Princeton: Princeton University Press, 1982.

de Weydenthal, Jan, Bruce Porter, and Kevin Devlin. *The Polish Drama: 1980–1982*. Lexington, Mass.: Lexington Books, D.C. Heath, 1983.

Dvenadtsatyy Syezd RKP (b), stenograficheskiy otchet. Moscow: 1968.

IX Nadzwyczajny Zjazd Polskiej Zjednoczonej Partii Robotniczej, 14–20 lipca 1981 r.—podstawowe dokumenty i materialy. Warsaw: Ksiazka i Wiedza, September 1981.

Ito, Takayuki. *Nomenklatura in Polen*. Cologne: Bundesinstitut für Ostwissenschaftliche und Internationale Studien, December 1983.

Kepinski, Andrzej and Zbigniew Kilar. *Kto Jest Kim w Polsce Inaczej*. Warsaw: Czytelnik, 1985.

Khrushchev, Nikita. *Vospominaniya*. Valeriy Chalidze, ed. 2 vols. New York: Chalidze Publications, 1981.

MacShane, Denis. *Solidarity: Poland's Independent Trade Union*. Nottingham: Spokesman, 1981.

Persky, Stan. *At the Lenin Shipyard*. Vancouver: New Star Books, 1981.

Ploss, Sidney I. *Moscow and the Polish Crisis*. Boulder: Westview Press, 1986.

Poland Today: The State of the Republic. Armonk, N.Y.: M.E. Sharpe, 1981.

Protokoly Syezdov i Konferentsiy Vsesoyuznoy Kommunisticheskoy Partii (b), 7. Syezd. Moscow: Gosudarstvennoye Izdatelstvo, 1928.

Rakowski, Mieczyslaw F. *Ein Schwieriger Dialog: Aufzeichnungen zu Ereignissen in Polen 1981–1984.* Düsseldorf-Vienna: Econ, 1985.

Rocznik Statystyczny. Warsaw: 1978, 1982.

Ruane, Kevin. *The Polish Challenge.* London: BBC, 1982.

Sanford, George. *Polish Communism in Crisis.* New York: St. Martin's Press, 1983.

VII Kongres Saveza Komunista Jugoslavije, 22–26 April 1958, stenografske beleske. Belgrade: Kultura, 1958.

Spravochnik Partiynogo Rabotnika. 4th ed. Moscow: Politizdat, 1963.

Staniszkis, Jadwiga. *Poland's Self-Limiting Revolution.* Princeton: Princeton University Press, 1984.

Statut Polskiej Zjednoczonej Partii Robotniczej. Warsaw: Ksiazka i Wiedza, 1982.

Statut Polskiej Zjednoczonej Partii Robotniczej, z uzupelnieniami i poprawkami uchwalonymi przez X Zjazd PZPR. Warsaw: Krajowa Agencja Wydawnicza, 1986.

Tiersky, Ronald. *Ordinary Stalinism: Democratic Centralism and the Question of Communist Political Development.* Boston: Allen and Unwin, 1985.

Timmermann, Heinz. *Kommunistischen Parteien in Westeuropa: Programme, Strukturen, Perspektiven.* Cologne: Bundesinstitut für Ostwissenschaftliche und Internationale Studien, no. 18, 1985.

13 Miesiecy i 13 Dni "Gazety Krakowskiej" (1980–1981). London: Polonia Book Fund (8 Queen Anne's Gardens, London, W41TU), 1985.

CENTRAL POLISH PUBLICATIONS

Argumenty. Weekly of the Society for Promotion of Lay Culture (TKKS).

Chlopska Droga. CC journal for agriculture.

Dziennik Ustaw Polskiej Rzeczypospolitej Ludowej. Council of Ministers bulletin for announcing laws.

Fakty i Komentarze. Weekly of the CC Ideological Department, for primary party organizations.

Itd. Student weekly.

Kierunki. Weekly newspaper of PAX.

Kultura. Cultural weekly.

Kurier Polski. Newspaper of the Democratic Party.

Nowe Drogi. Main monthly journal of the PZPR CC.

Odrodzenie. Weekly newspaper of PRON (Patriotic Movement of National Salvation).

Panstwo i Prawo. Monthly of the Institute of State and Law.

Perspektywy. Pictorial weekly magazine.

Polityka. Political-literary weekly edited by Rakowski until late 1982.

Prasa Polska. Monthly journal of the Journalists Union.

Prawo i Zycie. Weekly of the Association of Polish Lawyers.

Przeglad Tygodniowy. Warsaw weekly.

Rzeczpospolita. Government daily newspaper.

Rzeczywistosc. Ultraconservative weekly.

Slowo Powszechne. Daily of proregime Catholic organization PAX.

Sztandar Mlodych. Youth daily.

Trybuna Ludu. Main daily paper of the PZPR CC.

Tu i Teraz. Controversial Warsaw weekly led by Kazimierz Kozniewski (replaced by *Kultura*).

Wojsko Ludowe. Army monthly.

Zagadnienia i Materialy. Weekly of the CC Ideological Department for the party aktiv.

Zolnierz Polski. Weekly of the Ministry of Defense.

Zolnierz Wolnosci. Military daily.

Zycie Gospodarcze. Socioeconomic weekly.

Zycie Partii. Organizational journal of the PZPR CC.

POLISH PROVINCIAL PUBLICATIONS

Dziennik Baltycki (Gdansk).

Dziennik Polski (Krakow).

Dziennik Zachodni (Katowice).

Echo Krakowa (Krakow).

Express Wieczorny (Warsaw).

Gazeta Krakowska (Krakow, Nowy Sacz, Tarnow); before December 1980, called *Gazeta Poludniowa*.

Gazeta Lubuska (Gorzow, Zielona Gora).

Gazeta Olsztynska (Olsztyn).

Gazeta Poludniowa (Krakow, Nowy Sacz, Tarnow); after December 1980, *Gazeta Krakowska.*

Gazeta Pomorska (Bydgoszcz, Torun, Wloclawek).

Gazeta Poznanska (Poznan, Kalisz, Konin, Leszno, Pila); before mid-1981, called *Gazeta Zachodnia.*

Gazeta Robotnicza (Wroclaw, Jelenia Gora, Legnica, Walbrzych).

Gazeta Wspolczesna (Bialystok, Lomza, Suwalki).

Gazeta Zachodnia (Poznan, Kalisz, Konin, Leszno, Pila); after mid-1981, *Gazeta Poznanska.*

Glos Pomorza (Koszalin, Slupsk).

Glos Robotniczy (Lodz, Piotrkow, Sieradz, Skierniewice).

Glos Szczecinski (Szczecin).

Glos Wybrzeza (Gdansk, Elblag).

Kurier Szczecinski (Szczecin).

Nowiny (Rzeszow, Krosno, Przemysl, Tarnobrzeg).

Slowo Ludu (Kielce, Radom).

Sztandar Ludu (Lublin, Biala Podlaska, Chelm, Zamosc).

Trybuna Mazowiecka (Warsaw, Ciechanow, Ostroleka, Plock, Siedlce); before late 1980, called *Nasza Trybuna.*

Trybuna Opolska (Opole).

Trybuna Robotnicza (Katowice, Czestochowa, Bielsko-Biala).

Wieczor Wybrzeza (Gdansk).

Zdanie (Krakow monthly).

Zycie Czestochowy (Czestochowa).

Zycie Warszawy (Warsaw).

Index